COMPOSER AND NATION:

The Folk Heritage in Music

by SIDNEY FINKELSTEIN

Foreword and Afterword
by Carmelo Peter Comberiati

International Publishers *New York*

2nd edition, 1st printing, 1989
Manufactured in the United States of America

Library of Congress Cataloging-in-Publication Data

Finkelstein, Sidney Walter, 1909-1974.
Composer and nation.

Bibliography: p.
Includes index.
1. Nationalism in music. I. Title.
ML3545.F55 1988 780 88-23190
ISBN 0-7178-0671-5 (pbk.)

Proud Music of the Storm

I hear those odes, symphonies, operas
I hear in the William Tell *the music of an arous'd and angry*
people,
I hear Meyerbeer's Huguenots, *the* Prophet, *or* Robert,
Gounod's Faust, *or Mozart's* Don Juan.

I hear the dance-music of all nations,
The waltz, some delicious measure, lapsing, bathing me in bliss,
The bolero to tinkling guitars and clattering castanets.

I see religious dances old and new,
I hear the sound of the Hebrew lyre,
I see the crusaders marching bearing the cross on high, to the
martial clang of cymbals,
I hear dervishes monotonously chanting, interspers'd with frantic
shouts, as they spin around turning always towards
Mecca,
I see the rapt religious dances of the Persians and the Arabs,
Again, at Eleusis, home of Ceres, I see the modern Greeks
dancing,
I hear them clapping their hands as they bend their bodies,
I hear the metrical shuffling of their feet.

I see again the wild old Corybantian dance, the performers
wounding each other,
I see the Roman youth to the shrill sound of flageolets throwing
and catching their weapons,
As they fall on their knees and rise again.

I hear from the Musselman mosque the muezzin calling,
I see the worshippers within, nor form nor sermon, argument nor
word,
But silent, strange devout, rais'd glowing heads, ecstatic faces.

I hear the Egyptian harp of many strings,
The primitive chants of the Nile boatmen,

The sacred imperial hymns of China,
To the delicate sounds of the king, (the stricken wood and stone)
Or to Hindu flutes and the fretting twang of the vina,
A band of bayarderes.

Now Asia, Africa leave me, Europe seizing inflates me,
To organs huge and bands I hear as from vast concourses of voices,
Luther's strong hymn Eine feste Burg ist unser Gott,
Rossini's Stabat Mater Dolorosa,
Or floating in some high cathedral dim with gorgeous color'd windows,
The passionate Agnus Dei *or* Gloria in Excelsis.

Composers! mighty maestros!
And you, sweet singers of old lands, soprani, tenori, bassi!
To you a new bard caroling in the West,
Obeisant sends his love.

WALT WHITMAN, from *Proud Music of the Storm*

CONTENTS

FOREWORD TO THE 1989 EDITION

Sidney Finkelstein's contribution to the understanding of music with *Composer and Nation* is unusual in some respects, and well worth presenting again to a new audience. Only rarely have recent music writers looked at long spans of history. The age of the generalist and training for a long-range perspective have been on the wane for the three decades since this work first appeared. With the proliferation of scholars and the ever increasing historical detail available from their work, the task of compiling a one-volume history of music is formidable.

The recent activity of musical scholarship has discouraged a generalist approach. Much of the training at the university entails detailed work in narrow areas of concentration. Courses in music criticism, aesthetics, or musical historiography are rarely offered at the graduate level. A monographic history of music can not begin to account for the mass of detail churned out in the many dissertations and journal articles produced by the modern young scholars. For example, the recent international collaboration on the sixth edition of *The New Grove Dictionary of Music and Musicians* yielded twenty volumes, with further multi-volume spinoffs on musical instruments and American music.

Many contemporary writers on music have worried at the increasing specialization and accumulation of marginalia by the current generation of music historians. Donald Grout, author of the ubiquitous *A History of Western Music,* specifically mentioned this accumulation of detail and the primarily analytical approach by music scholars. In a festival essay written in honor of Oliver Strunk, Grout proposed that express philosophical analysis should underlie all historical writing, rather than the musical analysis usually found. He also urged that writing should be informed by value judgments and aesthetic judgments involving natures and choices.[1]

The English musicologist, Edward Dent, wrote similarly in a festival essay for Guido Adler. He attacked the style of the large encyclopedias of music, which to him assumed "if I may say so, that its readers are all well on their way to becoming professors at German universities. They are all preparing dissertations and *Habilitationsschriften.*"[2]

Compared to the musicological encyclopedias and dissertations, Finkelstein's *Composer and Nation* is humble indeed. Yet, it is in its modesty that the modern reader can approach this work. Well written, and intended for both the amateur as well as the musician, this volume approaches a time span of 300 years, from 1700 to the present. The presentation avoids detailed analysis of works and does not aim at complete coverage of historical detail.

Instead, Finkelstein surveys major details of what is usually called the modern era from an unpretentious sociological premise, namely that musical values and the relationship of the composer to society are reflected in the musical works. It follows then that the structure and texture of the work would reflect the composer's view of society and that important musical events offer insight into contemporary social and historical currents. Finkelstein presents an outline of the era from the viewpoint of the musical sociologist.

The sociology of music is a discipline that has mostly been pursued outside of the United States.[3] Aside from the more general nature of sociological inquiry, the sociology of music has not found a place in American university training. The tradition of American musicology is systematic, usually avoiding the political or social influences on music history.

Early in this century, Hermann Abert and Max Weber laid the groundwork for the discipline of musical sociology with studies that reflected the systematic nature of musicological study. Abert's *Die Musikanschauung des Mittelalters und ihre Grundlagen* (1905) and Weber's *Die rationalen und soziologischen Grundlagen der Musik* (1921) borrowed research techniques from the social sciences to establish a critical view of musical historiography. Both studies include detailed musical analysis; however, Weber's incomplete work is especially analytical, demonstrating the increasing rationalization of musical materials throughout the course of music history. Though grounded in solid musical analysis, the value of these studies lies in the light they shed on music from the perspectives of contemporary sociology and political economy.

In a similar manner, Theodor Adorno continued to place great emphasis on the immanent principles of musical composition, linking social awareness to his theory of the "material standard," in which the logic of musical laws superceded social function. Adorno's theories emphasize the aesthetic values of music and reduce the relevant importance of social class. Fundamental to Adorno's aesthetic judgment is the sophistication and complexity of musical structure, an emphasis for which Adorno is criticized by later authors.

A champion of the Second Viennese School, Adorno based much of his work on Hegelian historical idealism. Although a positivist examination of the musical market has a certain influence in his *Einleitung in die Musiksoziologie* (1962), Adorno was particularly engaged by the musical structure of the most complex works of the atonal and twelve-tone composers. Crystallized in these musical structures, and directly answerable to aesthetic judgment, the most advanced musical techniques represent to him the greatest advances in society. Adorno found critical reason and the ideals of freedom embedded in the music of Arnold Schönberg and his followers, a kind of *musica reservata* available only to the advanced appreciative skills of the educated class. The increasing isolation of the twelve-tone composers and their later academic followers was unwelcome to Adorno, for whom light popular music represented a negation of the best representative of ideology.[4]

Although strongly influential to the discipline, Adorno has been criticized for his bias and his work demonstrates the problematic value judgment implied in any selection of pieces for a history of musical culture. Recent scholars are divided on the criteria for identifying the classical music repertory.

Structural analysis alone does not provide sufficient context for that understanding. First investigated as part of the historical process by Max Weber, Carl Dahlhaus has convincingly proposed that the history of musical work's reception over time should not be the only indicator of that work's aesthetic value, either.[5] Furthermore, the problems associated with anachronism, misguided patriotism, and misunderstood intention have undermined both structural and reception analysis. Nationalist pride and the notion of structural complexity as musical progress have clouded the selection focus in past studies of both types.

Finkelstein emulates Adorno in his focus on musical masterpieces and how they embody social awareness; however, Hegelian overtones and the idea of progress are avoided in *Composer and Nation.* Also, Finkelstein reflected the positivist approach to the sociology of music, in that his study included popular and folk music. Rather than dismissing the music of lesser technical content, Finkelstein found great vitality in the music that most represented larger social classes.

The method of Finkelstein's approach finds the greatest resonance with the works of Marxist sociologists of music from 1930 to 1947, whose investigations have included systematic and historical facets, but are especially concerned with class structure. Methodologically influenced by Lenin's reflection theory, Boris Asaf'yev's theory of intonations identified specific social functions for music in feudal society. His

Musical Form as a Process (1930–47) laid down the principles of his theory and identified the specific intonations which transcended feudal society into the bourgeois era.

Turning away from Socialist Realism between 1947 and 1958, Soviet musicology recently has emphasized the national character of its musical production, with an implied value attached to Russian classics. The added value of national classicism is not unlike Adorno's value-added music of technological cultivation, but the popular appeal of music has never been totally depreciated in Soviet studies. The upheaval within the Soviet musicological world since 1947 has been described well by Boris Schwarz.[6] Several large scholarly works emerged from the severe nationalistic restrictions imposed on the writers, and the nationalistic determinations provoked much debate and the expansion of research on regional musics and popular topics.

It is at this very juncture of popular and serious, the relationship between music of classic value and that of nationalistic value, that we find Finkelstein's work. A work becomes representative of the folk with widespread acceptance. This acceptance influences the isolated serious composer, who then utilizes various aspects of the folk art. The product of the interaction, the affected work, is a direct result of social interaction. Genre and audience are powerfully transcended. Tied to economic conditions, the function of music within the various classes reflects the societal currents at different points in history. This formulation informs Finkelstein's analysis of the interaction of folk and serious and provides the independent focal point for his investigation. Finkelstein identifies works whose values are inherent in their representation of national ideals, but also works whose intrinsic structural value has been validated through reception.

Within this sociological framework comparing the relationship of folk music and the works of serious composers, Finkelstein discussed elements of musical melody and form, modern popular music, and the reception of great masterpieces by national societies, music critics and history. By concentrating on the various linkings since 1700, Finkelstein provides a coherent perspective for social patterns. Because of the power of the interaction, the commentary is compelling. Important historical trends are delineated, and the understanding of music within society and as a reflection of societal struggle is enhanced.

Music lovers should find Finkelstein's work a valuable resource for the added understanding and enjoyment of music. His sociological perspective provides a balm for what Adorno has described as a "neutralized consciousness,"[7] a condition from which many listeners suffer. His lively writing style, in the best tradition of the amateur, and his observation post—removed from the usual musicological context—make this new edition a welcome addition to musical and sociological literature.

An Afterword has been added to update this edition of *Composer and Nation.* Partially as a response to Finkelstein's prediction of the rise of jazz, the Afterword continues the investigation of popular music, with an eye towards its interaction with the isolated tradition of the contemporary academic composer, and the effects of increasingly sophisticated techniques of musical reproduction.

*****

The author wishes to thank Edward O'Hara at Manhattanville College for assistance in some matters of research and Dr. Chuck Henry and Nancy Todd for the use of their wonderfully cool cabin on Squam Lake in New Hampshire, where most of this work was accomplished.

August, 1988

Carmelo Comberiati
Purchase, New York

REFERENCE NOTES

[1]Donald Jay Grout, "Current Historiography and Music History" in *Studies in Music History: Essays for Oliver Strunk,* edited by Harold Powers, Princeton University Press, Princeton, N.J., 1968, pp. 23–40.

[2]Quoted by Denis Arnold, "The Profession of Musical Scholarship" in *Modern Musical Scholarship,* edited by Edward Olleson, Oriel Press, Boston, 1978, pp. 12–13.

[3]Konrad Boehmer provides a concise and informative history of the discipline in *The New Grove Dictionary,* 6th ed., s.v. "Sociology of Music."

[4]Boehmer cites Adorno's *Philosophie der neuen Musik* to illustrate the distinction between Schoenberg's advanced state of musical awareness, which resulted in social isolation, and Stravinsky's popular success with music of lesser integrity, *Ibid.,* p. 436.

[5]Carl Dahlhaus, *Foundations of Music History,* translated by J.B. Robinson, Cambridge University Press, Cambridge, 1983, pp. 150–165.

[6]Boris Schwarz, *Music and Musical Life in Soviet Russia 1917–1980,* Norton, N.Y.,

1972, pp. 249–258. Finkelstein also refers to this sad time in Soviet musical criticism, see below, pp. 292–300.

[7]Quoted by Christopher Ballantine, *Music and Its Social Meanings,* Gordon and Breach, N.Y., 1984, p. xvii.

INTRODUCTION: *MUSIC AS NATIONAL EXPRESSION*

I

Near the end of the eighteenth century, music was generally regarded as an international or cosmopolitan art of which Italians and Germans (including Austrians) were especially gifted creators. The Italians were especially the masters of vocal music, or "song," and the Germans of instrumental music, like the orchestral symphony. Thus the English music historian, Dr. Charles Burney, wrote in praise of the great Austrian composer, Joseph Haydn:

> *And though to Italy of right belong*
> *The indisputed sov'reignty of Song,*
> *Yet ev'ry nation of the earth must now*
> *To Germany pre-eminence allow*
> *For instrumental powers, unknown before*
> *Thy happy flight had taught her sons to soar.*

Burney indicated no widespread envy in England of these Italian and German accomplishments, nor any avid desire to emulate them. After all a country so preeminent in industry and trade as England could easily import such luxuries, and Haydn himself was quite willing to come to London and disclose the latest products of his symphonic genius.

Strikingly different was the attitude a century later in England. Scholars were studying the English heritage both of folk music and the popular music of Elizabethan times. Composers like the late Ralph Vaughan Williams were striving to use this heritage for the creation of a distinctively English symphonic music, and the symphonist whom Vaughan Williams most admired was not a German but the great Finnish national composer, Jean Sibelius.

Similarly in the United States, the composer Arthur Farwell wrote in 1903, "The first correction we must bring to our musical vision is to cease to see everything through German spectacles, however wonderful, however sublime, those spectacles may be in themselves. . . . France and Russia lead the world today in musical invention, in all that makes for greater plasticity of tone as an art medium."[1] Farwell was not suggesting that American composers replace German models with French and Russian ones. He was objecting to the academic acceptance of German music, however great, as a "universal" music and as such, the model of correctness. Russian composers had explored with exciting results the riches to be found in the soil of their folk music. French composers were striving for a distinctively "French" style, and many of them, like Debussy, were finding the most stimulating lessons for this purpose in the work of Russians like Mussorgsky. Similarly Farwell called for a distinctive music that the world could recognize as "American." And his was not a lone voice. A decade before, in the 1890's, a storm of this kind had been stirred up in American musical circles by Antonin Dvorak, who had been invited to teach at a New York conservatory. His own compositions were suffused with the spirit and substance of Czech and Slavonic folk song, and he advised American composers to study and use their own heritage of folk music, including the Negro spirituals that so entranced him.

There is no country today possessing a musical life, in which similar questions are not being hotly debated. Is the use of folk music in composition a superficial affectation, or does it infuse music with a national character down to its very roots? If so, is this desirable? Is "national" music of any kind a provincialism, opposed to a truly great "universal" music? Is the use of folk music simply a matter of quoting an actual folk song, or is there a deeper approach, more creative, involving the living core of folk music as a germ cell in musical growth? Can the folk music of a nation be married to traditional, existing forms, or should its use inspire new musical forms?

Out of the answers to such questions, favoring a consciously national art, has come a considerable amount of beautiful music in our century. Some of its composers, in addition to Vaughan Williams and Sibelius, are Leos Janacek of Czechoslovakia, Bela Bartok of Hungary, Roy Harris, Aaron Copland, George Gershwin and Virgil Thomson of the United States, Manuel de Falla of Spain, Sergei Prokofiev and Aram Khachaturian of the Soviet Union, Heitor Villa-Lobos of Brazil and Carlos Chavez of Mexico. Ernest Bloch, Swiss born, American by adoption, sought in many of his compositions to express a Jewish national feeling. Their works have won a solid place in the musical life of our time, and their national character seems to be no barrier to their universal acceptance.

These currents in turn have stimulated a fresh view of the musical past. Any textbook of music history will provide the information that "musical nationalism" raised its head in many countries during the nineteenth century. The writers view this in some cases with approval, in others with regret, and in still others with mixed feelings. Such national movements are described as offshoots of "romanticism." Thus the eminent scholar Alfred Einstein writes, "The attraction felt by the romantic composers of the nineteenth century for simple humanity, the movement back to the land, the impulse to get below surface politeness to the roots of things, led to the development of a side of the art ignored in the classical period; namely national music. And this brought into the swim those secondary musical people who had no part to play alongside of the representatives —Italian, French and German—of the universal music of the eighteenth century."[2]

Yet, one can ask, was the classical music that preceded the romantic, and the Baroque and Renaissance music that came before the classical, so exclusively "universal?" Vaughan Williams writes, "If we look at a collection of German *Volkslieder* we are apt to be disappointed because the tunes look exactly like the simpler Mozart, Beethoven and Schubert tunes. The truth is of course the other way out. The tunes of Mozart, Beethoven and Schubert are so very much like *Volkslieder*. . . . What we call the classical idiom is the Teutonic idiom, and it is absolutely as narrowly national as that of Grieg or Mussorgsky."[3] Going back to the Italian madrigal composers, of the late fifteenth century, Einstein finds in them "The beginnings of an Italian national music."[4] This Italian Renaissance music was avidly studied, along with Renaissance literature, in Elizabethan England. But the wealth of music that arose in England, much of it stimulated by the Italian, was no mere copy of Italian music. On the contrary, the anonymous songs like *Greensleeves,* the *Ballets* of Thomas Morley for voice with their strong folk-dance infusion, the pieces for virginals of Giles Farnaby, the solo songs of John Dowland, the madrigals of Frances Pilkington, were as English as the plays of Shakespeare. In Germany during the first half of the seventeenth century, Johann Sebastian Bach eagerly absorbed everything other musical lands had to teach him, transcribing Italian concertos and writing original concertos in "the Italian style," calling some of his works "French Overtures," and still others "English Suites." But at the same time his great religious works, the Cantatas and Passions, were suffused with the style and substance of the German Lutheran chorales. The truth seems to be that music took on a national character, and made use of folk and popular material, long before the rise of conscious national movements; in fact, with the rise of modern nations themselves.

It is this aspect of music that the present book proposes to study. It will examine key musical figures from various periods up to the present day, in historical order, attempting to show the various forms in which this question of national expression was raised and solved. The hope is to bring some perspective to bear upon problems of musical life today.

II

There is no contradiction between "national expression" and "universality," except when national expression takes the form of a rabid nationalism, with an accompanying chauvinism, racism and jingoism, such as belief in the eternal hostility of nations and in the superiority of one people over another. Democracy in society and politics, for example, is both national and universal. The American Declaration of Independence accompanying the revolutionary war, the French Declaration of the Rights of Man that followed the revolution of 1789, inspired a host of other nations to move towards their own national freedom and democratic life. What was universal was democracy, and antipathy to feudalism. What was national was the particular form this movement took in each country, in terms of its own institutions, traditions and culture.

Poetry teaches us the same lesson. In the great national poet of the United States, Walt Whitman, we can see clearly the close tie between a democratic love of country and a respect for the world's peoples. In the first preface to *Leaves of Grass* (1855) he wrote, "The Americans of all nations at any time upon the earth have probably the fullest poetical nature. The United States themselves are essentially the greatest poem." But it was the building of a democratic life and a community of immigrants from many nations that he was thus celebrating, not "blood" or "race." He added, "Here is not merely a nation, but a teeming nation of nations." This was the "poem" that he found in the United States, and it could only be discovered by one who also knew that the common people, including those who were coming from many lands to build a new life, were the heart of the nation. "The genius of the United States is not best or most in its executives or its legislatures . . . but always most in the common people." In his work, for the first time in the country's poetry, we recognize the presence of the working people building a new land. At a time when there were poisonous currents of racism, of jingoistic and chauvinistic nationalism, "Know-Nothingism" and attacks upon the Negro people and upon immigrants, he took up the fight against slavery, and also wrote in his poem *Mannhatta* of "Immigrants arriving, fifteen or twenty thousand in a week, The carts hauling goods, the manly race of drivers of horses, the brown-faced sailors. . . . The mechanics of the city, the masters, well-form'd, beautiful-faced, looking you straight in the eyes." And in *Salut au Monde!* he could say, "I salute all the inhabitants of the earth."

We can describe Whitman's Americanism in another way; that he was the most profoundly American of poets, precisely because his national feeling probed down to the common ties that linked all humanity. And it is for this reason that he became also the most "universal" of American poets; the one who most deeply inspired poets of other countries, and in fact even their musicians. But it was not simply "every" poet and musician that he influenced. Those who felt closest to Whitman were those who sought to give expression to their own love of country, in the same democratic terms. Thus Ralph Vaughan Williams, who raised the call for an English national music based on folklore, wrote his choral *Sea Symphony* to texts from Whitman's *Leaves of Grass*. And Vaughan Williams, in his love of nation, cut himself off sharply from both what he termed "truculent chauvinists" and the "lovers of every country but their own." His was a democratic view of both nation and national art . He wrote "Music is above all things the art of the common man," and these wise words: "If we have no musical soul of our own, how can we appreciate the manifestations of the musical souls of others?"[5]

III

Poetry of course is a different kind of art from music. But all arts have certain qualities in common. What is it that moves us about a work of literature and painting? It is not any factual information the words or picture may give us. It is that the words, or the lines and colors, add up to a unit from which a human being emerges before us. We can see this best in a story or painting which presents seemingly living people, whom we recognize as both different from us and yet also like ourselves. But it is true as well of a landscape painting or a lyric poem like Keats' *Ode to Autumn,* which evokes in us memories of nature. They present not a bundle of facts, but a peculiarly human response to nature; in other words, they present to us the poet or painter. They are human portraits. And so with music. A composer can put any tones together, and feel that he has "expressed himself." But only when the tones coalesce into an organic pattern, like a song, do we have a work of art. It is a unit, a human image, an aspect of the life of the composer taking objective form. Once created, it continues to live after the composer departs. It has become a social possession. The listeners take it to themselves, find it dear to them, and use it thereafter to express their own feelings of joy or sorrow.

All art creates primarily with human images. Words, the skilled handling of line and color, or musical tones, are only the technical means of giving them objective form. Art is a complicated way of working with the materials provided by nature, including the human body, in such a way that the finished product embodies not only the life of the creator but that of the onlookers or listeners. Thus in a drama, a playwright sets actual human beings in motion and speaking. When the onlookers recognize some part of themselves in these images, they are caught up in the life on the stage. And through this power that the human images of art have, namely of appearing to be not only something in the life of the artist taking objective form, but something in the lives of his onlookers, the playwright can play upon their mind and emotions. When they go back to their daily life, they are changed, because he has made his own discoveries of life their possession. What they have learned does not take the form of a set of facts that can be repeated. It shows itself in how they face life thereafter; in how much better they know their fellow human beings. And to the extent that people know their fellow human beings better, they know themselves better. To the extent that this knowledge is true, it enables them to live more freely. It is like a movement from darkness to light. There is another way of describing this form of "truth to life." It is that an artistic work of beauty seems at once fresh and new, and yet at the same time is something that the people who discover it feel they have always known. For it represents a step in their own growth.

The moving power of music, like all art, rests upon two truths underlying all human life. One is the basic kinship of people, underneath their differences. If this kinship, the awareness of common needs and mutual ways of growth, did not exist, then a work of art could not be both an individual creation and a social possession. The other is the ability of people, through cooperation, to learn from one another. Both are seen in the past history, as well as in the present life, of music. If a song from ancient times moves us today, it is because we discover a human kinship between the long dead singer and ourselves. If we are moved by a song from China or Africa, or if people in distant places are moved by an American folk song, it is again a discovery of human kinship.

Music speaks through a multitude of forms; simple human images, like a folk song, and complex human portraits, which present deep inner conflicts and resolutions, like a movement from a Brahms or Beethoven symphony. In this respect, it is again similar to the other arts, which can present a simple human image, like a character in a folk fable, or a complex human portrait, like Dreiser's *Sister Carrie.* But there is one crucial respect in which the human images and portraits of music differ from those of the other arts, such as literature and painting. The human images and portraits of literature and painting have both a general and a particular character. Those of music have only a general character.

Dreiser, for example, portrays Carrie as a specific individual in a specific social environment, that of Chicago in the 1890's. But we recognize a host of other people in her, including something of ourselves. For Dreiser reveals in Carrie a human being struggling to live, grow and stretch her wings. And he achieves this general character, or "typicality," not by taking her out of society, but by understanding the society about her so deeply, that he can show how it operates as an arena for this struggle, and how its basic forces shape the direction of her life, operating on her the more powerfully because she is not conscious of what these forces are. Thus we discover ourselves in Carrie, and are also different from Carrie, for we gain a consciousness that she lacked. The general or "universal" element in the portrait is not the disclosure of eternal and unchanging human qualities, but rather the revelation that human growth and freedom is always a social as well as individual problem. And so an understanding of the shape this struggle has taken in the past, opens up new possibilities for the present.

In music, the portraits or "psychologies" depicted are likewise shaped by a particular society. But music cannot give the specific social and individual documentation that literature can. For example, Beethoven's *Egmont Overture* embodies a profound human portrait. It starts with an evocation of oppressive sadness, moves through a turbulent and heroic conflict, breaks this off for a short, poignant funereal lament, and ends with a grand "victory" apotheosis. It is an inspiring psychological porttrait of a personality aware of deep miseries about him, who does battle, is faced by death, and yet never loses his faith in the victory of human liberty over tyranny. The music does not tell us that this is Count Egmont in sixteenth century Flanders, oppressed by Spain. It tells us the psychological shape this hope and conflict took in the early nineteenth-century Europe of Beethoven, which was inspired by the knowledge of Egmont's heroism, more than two centuries before. Today however, when we listen to the music simply as a work by Beethoven called "Egmont," we can miss even this social context.

But this difference between music and literature does not mean that they follow entirely different laws of art. In a work of literature, we must seek for precisely the qualities that music gives us so movingly; namely not merely the surface documentation and detail, but the human hopes, conflicts, frustrations and victories, which make the society it depicts and the people who both are shaped by it and shape it, significant to us. And often even in literature, we must add, so that we can fully understand the work, a social context of the writer's own time which the work itself does not give us. Only thus can we see art in its true greatness, as a revelation of a stage in human development.

Every human portrait in art, including music, has a social frame of reference. Can we appreciate fully the universality of a Hamlet without bringing into our thinking the morality of the competition for kingly power in Shakespeare's age, and so grasping the struggle between Hamlet's desire for a private life and the stern duty of taking up the public role of an avenger? Can we understand the appeal to us of the queer, cracked Don Quixote, with his mind in the past, if we do not know something of the seamy side of "progress" in Cervantes' Spain? And similarly with music, it is an aimless practise to seek some "story" in it. But to place a work of music into the context of its social setting, thus giving a particular clothing to its general portrait, is the only way to understand it completely, for it is this society, with its problems and conflicts, that has engendered the psychology revealed in the musical portrait. In Beethoven's time, when democratic and anti-feudal sentiments were moving all of Europe, it was no secret to his listeners that the stirring music he wrote for *Egmont* referred to the struggle against feudal absolutism in his own time. All his listeners were conscious of this conflict, for they were all in one way or another affected by it.

It is in such terms of human portraiture that music speaks. The composer's own psychology, as well as his understanding of others, is shaped by the role he plays in relation to the great social movements of his time, that affect him in company with all others. One of the most powerful social movements of the past five centuries profoundly related to individual freedom, has been the rise of nations, their struggle for independence, and the inner conflicts that accompany their growth. In this book the writer hopes to show that the forms which the composer constructs are guided by his relation to these movements, and that even the melodic material with which he creates his images or portraits comes from a social and national heritage which he takes up and reworks. It is with this process that folk and popular music are intimately connected.

1. SOCIAL ORIGINS OF MELODY

> *"In Wales the true remnant of the ancient Britons, as there are good authorities to show the long time they had poets, which they called bards, so through all the conquests of Romans, Saxons, Danes and Normans, some of whom did seek to ruin all memory of learning from among them, yet do their poets, even to this day, last."*
>
> —SIR PHILIP SIDNEY, *An Apologie for Poetrie* (1595)

I

The clerics of the late European Middle Ages who theorized about music regarded it as a refined and learned art of church and court. They sometimes noticed with disapproval the existence of a quite different music, used in their daily lives by the village peasantry, the former peasants who had become the working people of the towns, and the wandering popular entertainers, none of whom possessed the benefits of a learned musical education. With the rise of nations, marking the end of the medieval world, this common people's unlettered music, later to be called "folk music," came to be regarded as an important and inspiring part of the nation's cultural life.

The collection and classification of folk music has reached great heights in our time, bringing about a growing awareness of the complex problems involved in tracing its development and change. It is on the one hand an art of great antiquity. Sir Philip Sidney, in his *Apologie for Poetrie,* touched on the persistence among the folk of a tradition going back to the ancient tribal bards. In the early nineteenth century the Finnish epic, the *Kalevala,* dating from the first entrance of Christianity into Finland, was put together from thousands of fragments that existed as ballads and *runes* on the lips of the peasantry. And on the other hand, wherever folk music continues as a living tradition, it is a voice of its own times. It is distinguished by its combination of simplicity and artistic truth, or immediate relation to life; a product of the fact that it is a social and communal possession, constantly put to use like a well-handled tool.

In contrast to the complex psychological portrait embraced in a movement of a symphony, an opera aria or an art song, folk music presents a simple, uncomplicated human image. Thus Cecil Sharp writes, "The individual, then, invents; the community selects. . . . Folk music is the ungarbled and ingenuous expression of the human mind, and on that account it must reflect the essential and basic qualities of the human mind."[1] Bela Bartok writes, "Peasant music is the outcome of changes wrought by natural forces whose operation is unconscious; it is impulsively created by a community of men who have had no schooling. It is as much a natural product as are the various forms of animal and vegetable life. For this reason, the individuals of which it consists—the single tunes—are so many examples of high artistic perfection. In their small way, they are as perfect as the grandest masterpieces of musical art. They are, indeed, classical models of the way in which a musical idea can be expressed in all its freshness and shapeliness—in short, in the very best possible way, in the briefest possible form and with the simplest of means."[2]

The term "unconscious" does not mean that the folk singer is unconscious of what he is doing; only that because its changes and growth take place over generations, they represent no one person's conscious planning. Folk music represents in its simplest form, social consciousness; the experiences and thought held in common by people who labor, suffer and triumph together.

The realism, or immediate truth of life, of the imagery of folk song, is for example vividly apparent in the American Negro spirituals which were created in the second quarter of the nineteenth century. Many are a product of the absorption, by a stream of music originating in Africa, of the religious hymns found on American shores. That two such seemingly disparate bodies of music could combine to form a fresh, homogeneous and vital art hints at the fact that there are common, or similar roots, to all folk music, European, African and Asian. The appearance of these spirituals also indicates the conditions under which folk music, which sometimes goes on with little change for generations, suddenly puts forth new and powerful shoots. The conditions are those in which the people are themselves moving and striving for progress, using every means at their command. The spirituals flourished along with the struggle of the Negro people against slavery. They drew upon the Biblical images of yearning for freedom and defiance of tyranny. Some of them were used as signals on the Underground Railway or slave-escape routes. All of them served as an assertion by the enslaved people of their dignity, strength and humanity.

One scholar, George Pullem Jackson,[3] has argued that these Negro spirituals are merely crude or degenerate borrowings of "white" hymns. But the very evidence he offers argues the opposite. He cites the traditional hymn,

Saw ye my Savior, saw ye my Savior,
Saw ye my Savior and God?
O he died on Calvary, to atone for you and me
And to purchase our pardon with blood.

This to him is the Negro "borrowed" form.

Were you there when they crucified my Lord?
Were you there when they crucified my Lord?
O sometimes it causes me to tremble, tremble, tremble,
Were you there when they crucified my Lord?

What the comparison really indicates is that the Negro slaves took the old hymn, which with the passage of time had become rather dated, stiff and unreal, and gave it new life, transforming it into genuine, moving poetry by simplifying the images and bringing into them associations from their own lives. The Negro version has a feeling of the physical presence of the people, aghast at the torture and killing of a leader. And by the same process the melody has been transformed into something fresh, vital and deeply haunting, with a perfect marriage of word sound and musical phrase, as on the words "tremble, tremble," where the music also seems to tremble.

Jackson cites another example.

Ah poor sinner, you run from the rock
When the moon goes down in blood,
To hide yourself from the mountain top,
To hide yourself from God.

This to him is the Negro "borrowed" form.

There's no hiding place 'round here,
There's no hiding place 'round here,
O I went to the rock to hide my face,
The rock cried out; No hiding place!
There's no hiding place 'round here.

Again we have in the spiritual version a genuinely realistic poetic image, evoking actual memories of escape and search for hiding places. And the music has the lilting, syncopated rhythm characteristic of so much music with African roots, foreshadowing the cakewalk and ragtime. It is little wonder that when this body of song came to be widely known in America and Europe, in the 1870's and 1880's, it struck its hearers, many of whom knew the old hymnology, as a startlingly new, strange and stirring poetry and music.

II

In tribal society, music was connected with every side of life: planting, harvest, boating, hunting, the crafts, the rearing of children, the preparation for battle, the curing of illnesses, and the rituals associated with birth, death and the introduction of youth to adulthood. In what can be heard today of tribal music, like the music of the American Indians, we can find some of the simplest patterns in which music becomes a form of distinctly human expression, as a qualitative leap above nature sounds such as bird songs and animal cries.

As an example, there are two songs of the American Navajo Indians that have been recorded.[4] Each song has two short alternating phrases. One phrase is like a call or statement, often inflected differently upon each reappearance. The other is like a response or refrain. In both of these songs, the first phrase is made up of only three or four different notes, and the answering phrase or refrain is a monotone, a rhythmic pattern on a single note. If we call the first phrase "a," and the second "b," the song may be depicted as a b a b a b a, and so on, with the "a" often slightly varied.

This form, of a statement alternating with an answer or refrain, can often be found in speech itself, when it takes on the character of a public, social event, binding speaker and audience together in one common and exalted experience. Thus Franz Boas describes an African custom at which "the telling of a story is enlivened by affirmative exclamations of the audience. When the narrator says, 'the turtle killed the leopard,' the audience will repeat, clapping their hands, 'the leopard, the leopard.' "[5] A historic example of such speech taking on a repetitive, almost musical form is noted by the historian Herbert Aptheker:

"As the minute hand moved past midnight of December 31,

1862, marking the moment when Lincoln's Emancipation Proclamation was to take effect, an aged Negro woman said to 300 fellow fugitive slaves assembled half a mile north of Willard's Hotel in Washington:

> *Once the time was that I cried all night. What's the matter? What's the matter? Matter enough. The next morning my child was to be sold, and she was sold, and I never expect to see her no more till the day of judgment. Now, no more that! no more that! no more that! With my hands against my breast I was going to my work, when the overseer used to whip me along. Now, no more that! no more that! When I think what the Lord done for us, and brought us thro' the troubles, I feel that I ought to go into his service. We are free now, bless the Lord! (Amens everywhere). No more that! no more that! no more that, now! (Glory)!"*[6]

With the simplest pattern of two contrasting musical phrases, one answering or acting as a refrain to the repetitions of the other, we have a song coming to life. The two phrases are organically locked together, like the up and down swing of a paddle or axe, or the movement to the left of a dancer's body in opposition to the movement to the right of foot and hand. The unity of opposites, in the statement and answer of musical phrase, the variation and refrain, the voice of the individual and the response of the group, is the heart of melody. In fact, if we call these very short musical phrases of the Navajo song, embodying one direction of movement, "motifs," rather than melodies, we can say that when a pattern is created which has two opposing motifs in it, a melody is born, like a piece of living musical tissue, or a living cell. All melody has this opposition "built in." And to carry the analogy to a cell further, it is capable of infinite development.

The two ways in which tribal music develops are found as well in the entire art of music. One is that of being "strung out" in length, with a series of variations and repetitions. And basic to all musical construction is the fact that variations, evoking a feeling of sameness and difference at the same time, and the repetition at key moments of what has been heard before, have a cumulatively powerful psychological effect, as if the music had captured the mind and were imparting to the mind its own life.

The other form of development is for two or more lines of music to proceed simultaneously. Thus in African music one voice may spin out a line of melody, with variations and repetitions. Another may be heard with a series of different phrases, separated by silences. There may be a third line, consisting of a measured pattern of hand clapping or foot stamping. There may be still a fourth line, consisting of a complex rhythmic pattern from drums or plucked string instruments which being tuned, present their own melody clothed in percussive sounds. It is again basic to musical construction that two or more simultaneous musical lines can attach themselves to one another, each enriching the other. This many-voiced music is called "polyphony," although some scholars use the word "heterophony," in reference to many-voiced tribal music, reserving "polyphony" for the highly polished, controlled and organized many-voiced art developed in the European Middle Ages.

World folk music is a vast substratum of music over which the richly developed "Western" music of the past four hundred years, based on the system of major and minor scales, has been erected, drawing from this source in its origin and continually refreshing itself from the same source. In technical descriptions, this folk music displays a bewildering variety of note and rhythmic patterns. Yet this does not mean that the music of one people is a closed book to another. Asian folk melodies are easily appreciated by European ears, just as people accustomed to the music in major and minor scales of recent centuries can appreciate without great difficulty the melodies of medieval polyphonic music and of Gregorian chant, which itself is Asian in origin. Asian ears can appreciate European melodies. The difference in pitch or tuning of the music in one land from that in another is no great barrier, for the ear can make that adjustment. In fact, what makes Asian or African music sound so strange and "exotic" to Europeans is often not so much the melody, as the different traditions of sheer physical clothing in sound, like the instrumental colors and timbres, the unfamiliar percussive, string and wind-instrument sounds, the bells and gongs, the high-pitched voices. And ancient patterns recur in the music of different countries. Thus in American and European folk music we can find, along with rounded songs that sound like the simpler art songs, a music of continual repetition and alternation, continuing as long as the dance or poem continues, like that of tribal music. Examples are many of the American square dance fiddle tunes, like *Ida Red*: the Swedish and Finnish violin dancing songs; English Morris Dances; Irish and Scottish bagpipe reels; the dancing songs of Brittany which sound so much like African music; Basque ring dances; Yugoslav *Kolos*.

Basic to all folk melody is a harmonic principle; the presence of a "tonic" note, or "home" note, which is the tonal center or resting place of the melody, and a "dominant," an alternate or weaker resting place. About this axis of tonic-dominant all the other notes of the melody group themselves. Innumerable different melodies may be made out of a group of a few notes which, arranged in rising or falling order, is called a "scale" or "mode."

A vast amount of Asian, African, European and American folk music is built in terms of a pentatonic, or five-note, scale. Of course, in tribal and folk music, the musician does not think in terms of a basic scale or mode from which he selects the notes to make up his song. He works with the living material of a stock of melodic phrases. Thus Curt Sachs describes, in Asian music, "the strange procedure of 'putting together' one's melodies—in the truest sense of the word *com-ponere*—out of a limited stock of ready-made, characteristic 'melodicles' or turns. . . . This kind of composing has not been abandoned in the later West. It has left traces in the Gregorian chant, in the Lutheran chorale, the Calvin psalter, the art of the *Meistersinger,* and the folksong of all countries."[7] This is exactly the procedure of American jazz improvisation based on the Blues, as well as of folk Blues singers. In English and American folk music there are a great number of songs which conform not to the major-minor system but to some earlier pattern, either pentatonic, or one similar to the modes of medieval church music; for example *Greensleeves, Wayfaring Stranger, When Johnny Comes Marching Home, Henry Martin, He Never Said a Mumblin' Word.* There are folk singers, like the American Negro Mitchell's Christian Singers, who perform familiar hymns, such as *The Saints Are Marching,* or *Jesus Going to Make My Dying Bed,* in modal harmony. In many kinds of folk music there are "off-pitch" notes, like the "blue notes" in the Blues and American jazz, or the slides of Hungarian Gypsy music. There are "Calling" or "Crying" figures, with the voice sweeping through a group of notes, coloratura-like, similar to street and field cries. They are heard in American "Hollers" and Blues, and in Spanish *flamenco* music. The ear easily adjusts itself to them.

In other words, music is made up not of different languages that need translation, like world languages, but of a basic, immensely plastic material with elements common to all peoples.

III

Bartok, in his studies of Hungarian folk music, points out one aspect of this music which illuminates not only all folk music but also a vast amount of composed "art music." He divides folk music into two styles, one of which he calls *parlando-rubato*—translatable as "speech-accented"—and the other *tempo giusto,* or "rhythm-controlled." The first has melodic accents similar to the loose, irregular rhythms of speech or meditative thought, and its melodic turns frequently resemble speech inflections. It seems to have no fixed rhythmic beat, but the rhythm actually stretches and contracts, with little rhythmic patterns or note-groups appearing as "motifs." In the second, or *tempo-giusto,* the accented notes of the melody follow a regular rhythmic pattern, like that of controlled human movement.

There are many familiar examples of speech-accented, or *parlando-rubato* music, outside of Hungarian folk song, such as the Hebrew religious chants, the liturgical plainchant of the Catholic Church, and the wailing *cante hondo* music, generally known as *flamenco,* of Andalusia in the south of Spain. Dancing songs and marches are generally *tempo-giusto.* As Bartok points out, the distinction is not a hard and fast one. A vast amount of folk songs have both a *tempo-giusto* and a *parlando-rubato* character. And yet it is important to see that even here, there are some songs which can lean towards the speech-accented, while others lean towards the rhythm-controlled. In English music, for example, the *Coventry Carol, Brigg Fair, Lord Rendall, Barbara Ellen, Waly, Waly,* are speech-accented songs, while *The Wraggle Taggle Gipsies, John Peel, Who's Going To Shoe Your Pretty Little Foot,* are rhythm-controlled. In American song, *Shenandoah* tends towards the speech-accented type, while *'Tis the Gift to be Simple, Turkey in the Straw* and *Yankee Doodle* are rhythm-controlled. *Sometimes I Feel Like a Motherless Child, He Never Said a Mumberlin' Word, Go Down, Moses* tend towards the speech-accented, as do the Blues, despite their underlying rhythmic pulsation. *Plenty Good Room, Joshua Fought the Battle of Jericho, Down By the Riverside,* tend towards the rhythm-dominated.

The distinction is important first because it underlines the two origins of music; heightened speech, poetry chanting, story telling, on the one hand, and human movement, body rhythms, labor and dance, on the other. But as music progresses far beyond its primitive origins, the distinction takes on a qualitatively new character. It reflects the two sides of life, the *parlando-rubato* tending towards meditation, the subjective, the "inner world," and the *tempo-giusto* depicting the outer world of social activity. Both together make up the truth to life of music and all art. And so the distinction appears in new and complex ways in composed, or "art" music. It is seen in the contrast between the *recitative* and *aria* of eighteenth century opera, the one being *parlando-rubato* and the other *tempo-giusto*. And enriched by chord progressions and key changes, *parlando-rubato* music becomes no longer an imitation of speech, as it is in many opera recitatives, but a deep probing of the inner play of mood and thought in the mind, while *tempo-giusto* music becomes the basis for great structures full of the momentum, clash and clamor of outer life.

Johann Sebastian Bach offers such contrasts, as in the *Fantasta and Fugue in G minor* for organ or the *Chromatic Fantasy and Fugue* for clavier, the *fantasias* in each work being profound *parlando-rubato* music, while both *fugues* lean towards the *tempo-giusto*. Or Bach will create a "dance" music of inexpressible poignance and depth of feeling, by throwing a speech-accented melodic line over a rhythm-controlled basic form, as in the *sarabandes* of many of his *Partitas,* or the *Chaconne* for solo violin. With the symphonies and sonatas of Haydn, Mozart and Beethoven, we have the richest and most consciously controlled interplay of both *parlando-rubato* and *tempo-giusto* elements, the first comparable to a kind of connective tissue, the second to a bone structure, and both together adding up to a profound portrayal of a real world of inner and outer life, one organically tied to the other.

IV

Folk music grows and changes; generally slowly, but sometimes with great rapidity. Change may come about through the folk artist giving traditional material the impress of his own personality, in response to the life about him, or through the absorption of outside elements. What is important is not where the new material comes from, but that the people make it their own. Thus Bartok's definition of folk music includes this process of change. "The term 'peasant music' connotes, broadly speaking, all the tunes which endure among the peasant class of any nation, in a more or less wide area and for a more or less long period, and constitute a spontaneous expression of the musical feeling of that class. From the point of view of folklore, we may define the peasant class as follows: it is that part of the population engaged in producing prime requisites and materials, whose need for expression, physical and mental, is more or less satisfied either with forms of expression corresponding to its own tradition, or with forms which, although originating in a higher (urban) culture, have been instinctively altered so as to suit its own outlook and disposition."[8] Cecil Sharp says of folk music, "It is always in solution; its creation is never completed; while at every moment of its history, it exists not in one form but in many."[9]

Thus arises the fact that many folk songs of a people, while different from one another, seem to be part of one "family of melodies." A. L. Lloyd writes, "Many times we come across tunes which if you look into them have a deeper resemblance than merely being in the same mode; they are closely alike in shape, sometimes nearly note for note. So people say *When Johnny Comes Marching Home* is only a variant of *High Barbery,* and *High Barbery* is only a variant of *Henry Martin,* and before they know where they are they have linked together a hundred tunes all very similar."[10] Vaughan Williams describes folk song as "an individual flowering on a common stem."[11] Bartok traces this process. "Yet peasants—even individually—are not only capable of altering, but strongly inclined to alter, all the musical elements of which they take hold. . . . Repetitions of a tune will usually include slight rhythmic alterations; at times the pitch (or perhaps even the note itself) will be changed. . . . Then other performers may introduce other changes of similar kind; and the last link in the chain may turn out to be altogether different from the first."[12]

These family resemblances are easily noticeable; in Negro spirituals, for example, *Ezekiel Saw the Wheel* and *Joshua Fought the Battle of Jericho,* or between *Sometimes I Feel Like a Motherless Child* and *You Hear the Lambs A-Crying.* Or the Creole song, probably French in origin, *Pauve piti Lolotte,* sung by Negro slaves and used by the New Orleans composer Gottschalk in the 1840's for his piano piece, *La Savane,* can become, with a change from minor to major, and a faster tempo, the dancing song, *Skip to My Lou.* Of one family are a number of cowboy songs, like the slow and sentimental waltzes, *Night-Herding Song, I Ride an Old Paint,* and *Strawberry Roan;* or "hoe-downs" like *Turkey in the Straw* and *The Wild Wagoner.* In the Blues of the American Negro people, we can trace the process itself, richly documented on records and in live performances, through which a basic melodic shape can proliferate into a host of songs and instrumental improvisations, many of them distinctively different, and with a profile of their own, yet at the same time unmistakeably "Blues."

Carrying the thought further, we can observe families of melodies in the work of "art" composers. This is what Vaughan Williams pointed out when he said that the simpler tunes of Mozart, Beethoven and Schubert are so much like German *Volkslieder.* Obvious examples are Mozart's duet, *La ci darem la mano,* in the opera *Don Giovanni;* Zerlina's air, *Vedrai, carino,* in the same work; Beethoven's song, *Ich liebe dich; Schubert's* song *Die Forelle,* and the melody of the B flat *Entracte* from *Rosamunde,* which he also used as the slow movement of his *String Quartet in A minor, Op.* 29. All are of the same family. The thread can be carried further to Brahms. A German folk song he arranged, *Die Sonne scheint nicht mehr,* is of the same kin. And from this melodic root spring many of his riper and more profound melodies, such as the songs *Sapphische Ode* and *Die Mainacht,* and the slow movement of his *Violin Concerto.*

Turning to Russian music, if we compare the opening melody of the slow movement of Tchaikovsky's *Violin Concerto,* Lisa's aria *"It is Close to Midnight,"* in the third act of the opera *Pique Dame,* and the orchestral prelude of Mussorgsky's opera *Boris Godunov,* we discover that they are all of one family. It is possible to say that composed or "art" music only carries on, with a much richer heritage and far more complex tools, the process of development found in folk music; or in other words, that the great and distinctive melodies of "art" music are not unique in every phrase, but are made out of an inherited stock of living material, which exists as a social possession. And a composer who, like Haydn, Dvorak and Mussorgsky, is a master of the creative use of folk music is not one who simply takes over existing folk songs for his compositions. Rather, he has caught the secret of the malleable core of folk music, so that he too can create out of it a "family of melodies."

Even in its manner of change and growth, folk music offers a parallel to the relation between the individual creator and the social arena that we find in "art" music. For folk music is created not by people in groups, but by individuals. Folk songs can be sung by anyone, just as anyone can dance. But in every community there are individually gifted musicians, who become leaders of music life, just as there are gifted artisans, speakers and rebels. The existence of folk song, along with its growth, indicates the fact that throughout history, the number of talented people born far exceeded the few who were able to develop their talents in some cultivated field of fine art. Such among the Jewish people in Europe were the village musicians, who performed at weddings and festivities. Sokolov writes of Russia, "Many genres of folklore have indubitably been worked out and perfected by persons who had made a special study of their craft as poets and performers, and had developed their craft into a profession, that is, who had earned their bread by their skill in artistic creation and artistic performance."[13] An Egyptian tomb at Meir has among its carved reliefs, a blind singer; perhaps a prototype of the legendary Greek Homer, who was also blind, and of the blind singers and wandering beggar musicians of Europe and the United States. In the American Negro communities there were such outstanding and beloved leaders of song. James Weldon Johnson, in his *Autobiography of an Ex-Colored Man,* an autobiographical novel, speaks of "a wonderful leader of singing, who was known as 'Singing Johnson'." When in the 1920's and 1930's, in the United States, the phonograph record manufacturers discovered there was a market for Negro folk music (derisively termed by them "race" music), a number of these gifted individuals who otherwise would have been lost in anonymity came to be known much more widely; Blind Lemon Jefferson, Blind Willie Johnson, Leroy Carr, Big Bill Broonzy, Huddie Ledbetter, "Cripple" Clarence Lofton. It is true that many of them never thought of themselves as engaged in a process of creating music, despite their remarkable gift for melody, or for guitar and piano improvisation. To many of the Negro blues singers, as to the English folk singers described by Cecil Sharp, to write a "new song" really meant to create new words for an old song. They regarded themselves as poets, or balladeers. If in the process, they also changed and added to the musical stock they had taken over, this was simply a "natural" process, not to be made much of. And yet this is because the very music they have taken over seems to them to be not fixed but flexible and malleable.

V

A development in folk music of central importance to the entire history of music is its transformation from an "open," continuous, constantly repetitive or evolving form, to a "closed" or rounded song structure, with a beginning, middle and end apparent to the ear. Typical of such rounded songs is the early seventeenth century anonymous air, *Drink to Me Only With Thine Eyes.* The melody of the first line of verse is repeated for the second line of verse; there is a contrasting melody; then the first melody returns to end the song. Assigning letters to each melodic unit, we can picture the song as AABA. In *John Brown's Body,* there is an opening melody; then a variant of it (a different melody with the same rhythm); then the opening melody again, and finally a new, rounding out melodic phrase; A A' A B. In the beautiful old English song, *The Oak and the Ash,* we have an opening melodic statement that ends suspended, "up in the air;" then a response to it, which does not quite end the song, and a repetition of the response, with a change in the last few notes, or a "cadence," which definitely establishes the close of the song; A B B'.

For all the seeming simplicity with which this rounded and internally unified character is achieved, such songs represent a qualitative leap in musical power above the "open" or continuously flowing forms of tribal or earlier folk music. This does not mean that they make the older song forms archaic, outmoded or useless. The latter continue to serve their own social and expressive function. But the rounded song is made up of "opposites," of both melody and feeling, that are locked together as part of its internal organism. It proceeds through a first statement, a heightening of emotion, and a resolution. It has become a finished, objective human image, which is "freed" from its creator and can be taken up as a permanent social possession. The song is released from the exigencies of a particular occasion, and from the need to be continually reshaped by the performer. It is no longer an adjunct to the poetry being chanted and the story being told, or an accompaniment to dance which comes to an end only when the dancing stops.

Bartok describes this rounded character of song as "architectonic form," and in respect to Hungarian folk music, sees it as a later style, stimulated by "more modern and probably Western influences."[14] Yet whatever the influence or borrowing, the music becomes again "folk." Thus he says of such a borrowed tune or fragment, that if it is "so thoroughly assimilated that it finally becomes distinctively different from what it originally was, and perhaps by then has absorbed certain of the characteristic traits of the traditional style of the regional peasant music, and if the process results in a certain homogeneity, a new, homogeneous style of peasant music crops up: such is the style of recent Hungarian peasant music."[15]

This transformation in folk music to the rounded song begins to take place in Europe at about the same time as it does in composed or "art" music; namely with the waning of the Middle Ages. Medieval composed music had been largely devoted to church ritual, as an arm of Catholic theology and employed the melodic lines and modes of Gregorian chant. Even when this composed music, of masses and motets, attained its most refined and elaborate organization of polyphonic, flowing, intertwining melodic lines, it remained like Gregorian chant itself, an "open" music. Each melodic line was accented differently from those moving simultaneously with it, and the form as a whole was obedient to the words of the ritual. It could reach a high degree of inner subjective pathos and beauty of sheer sound, but it avoided any sense of earthy human imagery, or of human drama and conflict and the evocation of the "outer world." Curt Sachs points out that even the liturgical music by the consummate master of the sixteenth century, Giovanni Pierluigi da Palestrina (1525-1594) was meant to be performed with added "fluent graces and coloraturas."[16] Unity was achieved by the easy, continuous flow of one part into the next, not by a clash and contrast leading to an inevitable climax, and to a resolution of everything that had come before. Alfred Einstein writes of this vocal music, "In the language of exaggeration one might say that an *a capella* piece, provided it reached a satisfying length and preserved unity of tonality, could come to an end when it chose."[17]

The fine aristocrat art of secular poetry and song which flourished between the twelfth and fifteenth centuries, that of the troubadours of Spain, Portugal and South France, the trouvères of North France, and the knightly minnesingers of Germany, is also an "open," *parlando-rubato* music, with its flow dictated by the poetry. It was written down in a notation similar to that of Gregorian chant; that is, with no indication of rhythm and the time values of the notes. Such songs could have been sung, as Curt Sachs says, "in whatever rhythm the singer preferred; indeed, they may have had no definite rhythm at all. And since they were Mediterranean, they may have been dissolved in a good deal of free and improvised coloraturas anyway."[18] From at least the fourteenth century, composers who serve the church also write secular songs, largely for court and aristocracy, like Guillaume de Machault (c. 1300-c. 1370), Guillaume Dufay (c. 1400-1474) and Josquin des Pres (c. 1445-1521). But this kind of composition, reaching a beautiful interweaving of voices in the *chanson,* and culminating in the sixteenth century Italian madrigal, is also largely in "open" style, with the melodic accents following the accents of poetry.

In what area of musical life, then, did the rounded song arise, with its bold freedom from both church tradition and from the courtly musical forms? It could only have been in that area of which so little, comparatively, is factually known, because the church musical theorists ignored or despised it; namely that of the folk and the "popular." Its rise could only have represented folk music breaking out of its village and countryside isolation, absorbing "learned" elements, "learned" or "art" composers turning for some of their work to folk elements or "popular" style; and the interfusion or cross-seeding between the "folk" and "learned" provided by the host of wandering musicians. There were students with their lusty, irreverent songs, minstrels, jesters, actors, mountebanks and popular entertainers, often known for their iconoclastic criticism of clergy and aristocracy. The general style of this kind of song that emerges is that of a clear, simple and direct melody, sometimes *parlando-rubato* but also often highly rhythm-accented, or *tempo-giusto.* It often has an infusion of rhythms that we can recognize as "folk dance," because of the foot-stamping accents, so different from the gliding movements of court dance. It sometimes exhibits the "drone bass" typical of folk bagpipe music. Most important in this new style of song that appears is its rounded form, with its all-over feeling of outer life. And the poetry of these songs tends to have the realistic imagery and direct feeling for nature of folk poetry, as contrasted to the refined, fanciful imagery, with its formal rituals of love-making and chivalry, of court poetry.

Some of these rounded songs are definitely not folk songs, and are known to have been composed by men who were also masters of court and church music. But whatever their origin, they represent a popular vein. One of the earliest of such "architectonic" songs is the round, *Sumer is icumen in,* dating from the thirteenth or early fourteenth century. The "round," in which one voice after another takes up the same melody, is as Paul Henry Lang points out, one of the "ancient forms of popular music."[19] Manfred Bukofzer argues that this particular round is a composed song, not a folk song. But he says that the employment of cuckoo calls in the song is a "popular motif." Among Dufay's chansons, some contrast to the others in their lusty popular style and rounded form, like the drinking song, *He! compaignons.* In the *Locheimer Liederbuch,* a historic collection of anonymous German songs written down in about 1440, and which Hugo Leichtentritt describes as folk songs in a polyphonic arrangement[21] there are such simple rounded songs like *Mein Freud möcht such wohl mehren.*

The Burgundian composer Josquin des Près sometimes varied his open, refined polyphonic chansons with simpler, rounded songs, like *Bergerette Savoyard,* the poem of which, as much as the melody, indicates a popular or folk connection. It is in the Savoyard dialect, and tells of a shepherd girl who rejects the advances of an amorous nobleman. Heinrich Isaac (c. 1450-1517), born in Flanders, who wrote carnival songs for the Medici in Florence and also served the German Emperor in Vienna and Innsbruck, composed one such rounded song, *Innsbruck, Ich muss dich lassen,* that has become assimilated among the people as a folk song. Another great Flemish composer, Orlande de Lassus (c. 1530-1594), who served the courts of Sicily, Milan, Rome, Paris and Munich, composed along with elaborate polyphonic religious music, "open" in form, many earthy and rounded songs in the various national languages, like *Quand mon mary vient de dehors,* and the popular *Matona mi cara.* The latter, with its lilting refrain, is close kin to a host of anonymous folk songs.

In the sixteenth and early seventeenth century, when composers like Lassus, Palestrina, Victoria and Byrd in their religious work are providing the last beautiful and subjective examples of the elaborate polyphonic and modal Catholic ritual music, the creation of rounded songs in popular style becomes a swift-moving and irresistible current. Behind this lies the welling national consciousness, strengthened by the peasant revolts, by the increasing wealth and power of cities with their bourgeois mercantile and industrial life, by the church reform movements and the accompanying criticism of all medieval institutions. This spirit is alive in countries which are unable to coalesce into independent nations, like Italy and Germany, as well as in the first great independent nations that appear, heralds of a new age, like France, Spain and England. With the revolutionary rise of nations, the presence of the "nobodies" of medieval society, like the peasantry and the common people of the cities, forces its way into the consciousness of fine art. Creative artists turn to reflect with pride the national life, and this must inevitably include the common people.

Among the foremost arenas of this development is England. The composers of music, as well as Marlowe, Shakespeare and other great dramatists, serve not only the court but the great body of the city population. And now Sir Philip Sidney writes of folk song, in the *Apologie for Poetrie,* "Certainly I must confess my own barbarousness, I never heard the old song of Percy and Douglas that I found not my heart moved more than with a trumpet; and yet it is sung but by some blind crowder, with no rougher voice than rude style." Shakespeare in his histories, like *Henry V,* reminds his listeners of the presence of the common soldiers who do the fighting, as in the scene on the eve of the battle of Agincourt, when such soldiers speak to the disguised king. "But if the cause be not good, the king himself hath a heavy reckoning to make, when all those legs and arms and heads, chopped off in a battle, shall join together at the latter day and cry, 'We died at such a place;' some swearing, some crying for a surgeon, some upon their wives left poor behind them, some upon the debts they owe, some upon their children rawly left."

In drama and poetry the "learned" joins hands with the "popular" or folk-inspired and drama itself abounds in song. A host of beautiful, popular, anonymous rounded songs appear, like *Greensleeves, The Oak and the Ash, The Wraggle-Taggle Gypsies,* and the lusty soldier's song, *We Be Soldiers Three.* Gustave Reese writes, "Great quantities of ballad texts were printed as broadsides, usually with the direction to be sung to the tune of a current ballad air, such as Greensleeves."[22] The bustle of the city streets, with their tinkers, coopers, peddlers of brooms, criers of oysters and fruit, chimney-sweeps, is heard in the fantasies on street cries composed by Thomas Weelkes, Orlando Gibbons and Thomas Ravenscroft. Sets of variations are composed on popular or folk airs, like Thomas Morley's *Goe From My Window,* Giles Farnaby's *Wooddy-Cock* and Richard Farnaby's *Fayne Would I Wedd.* A madrigal art flowers, stimulated by the Italian madrigal composers but striking English roots. And among both the madrigals for groups of voices, and the songs for solo voice and lute, beautiful rounded songs are heard, like Morley's *Now Is the Month of Maying, My Bonny Lass She Smileth,* and *It Was A Lover and His Lass;* Weelkes' *To Shorten Winter's Sadness;* John Dowland's *Sleep, Wayward Thoughts* and Robert Jones' *Go to Bed, Sweet Muse.*

A rich body of rounded song rose as part of the Protestant Reformation, in the form of the hymns or chorales created or inspired by Martin Luther (1483-1546). Intended to provide the people with a popular religious music to texts in the German language, these chorales employed or adapted Catholic hymns and chants, popular German songs of the time, and newly composed songs in the popular vein. The marching hymn, *Ein' feste Burg,* became a battle song of the peasantry in their uprising of 1525. New, beautiful songs were added to the stock, like the Christmas song, *Es ist ein Ros' entsprungen,* widely known as *Lo a Rose Is Blooming* by Michael Praetorius (1571-1621) and *Mein G'mut ist mir verwirret* by Hans Leo Hassler (1565-1612). The latter song, originally written as a love song, was transmuted into one of the most beautiful chorales. It is used by Johann Sebastian Bach in his *Christmas Oratorio* and also as a recurrent chorus in his *St. Matthew Passion.*

Whatever the musical form of their origin, these chorales were reshaped in harmony, rhythm and structure by their new social use, becoming square-cut, architectonic, harmonized songs, adapted to the rising principle of composition according to the system of major and minor scales, and of modulation or key change. Even though, with the defeat of the peasant uprising and the triumph of the feudal princes, Germany failed to become a unified nation, these hymns remained in the popular consciousness as a national heritage, stemming from the historic effort to break out of medieval and feudal backwardness.

It is in song, and particularly in the creation of the rounded song, that the first great national musical expression takes place in Europe. Side by side appear the rounded songs known to be "composed," and the folk songs of this kind, the anonymous songs which have been preserved by and live among the folk. Whether these anonymous rounded songs are actually "folk" or should better be described as "popular" is not a question of central importance. If folk music is defined as the "spontaneous" creation of the peasantry and working people, then popular music may be defined as a composed music which attempts to serve the purpose of folk music, namely that of song, dance and entertainment for the great body of people. But as we have seen, folk music is also in a sense "composed;" it is the product of gifted individuals using traditional material, and serving the community. Thus the question of whether a song of this period is "folk" or "popular" becomes a matter of whether we happen to know who wrote it. The rounded folk song could not have appeared without some outside stimulus, just as the rounded popular song could not have appeared without drawing upon folk music. The rounded song, "folk," "popular" and "art," rises with the breakdown of the caste divisions and hierarchies that had characterized medieval and feudal life. It reflects the new fluidity of society, the consciousness of nation, and the recognition of the peasantry and working people as an organic part of the nation. Of the songs which have come to be known as "folk," Cecil Sharp's words in speaking of all folk music are apt: "The individual invents; the community selects." In other words, the important thing is that the people take back in changed form what had originally come from them. They put it to use and make it their own.

The great achievement of medieval folk music, other than serving as the creative expression of the great mass of "unlettered" working people, had been to provide a base for the development of national musical idioms. With the growth of nations, folk music continues to live on a new fluid level. Composers dip more or less freely into it, and also, in a "popular" or folk vein write melodies which are absorbed by the folk. In the late nineteenth and twentieth century, a new kind of "popular music" appears, however; an avalanche of song and dance manufactured as a business commodity, and reflecting the economic and social conditions making for an end of the isolation of countryside from city. On the one hand, this development raises the frightening apparition of the death of folk music as it had been previously known, supplanting it with a music of the most shoddy artistic values. But on the other hand, the very social conditions which raise this problem, bring the whole question of "people's music" to a new level. For the possibility also arises of the entire heritage of music, both "art" and "folk," becoming a widespread popular possession.

2. BAROQUE MUSIC AND POPULAR AUDIENCES

"Wisdom makes her followers bashful, sneaking, and timorous, and therefore you see that they are commonly reduced to hard shifts, must grapple with poverty, cold and hunger, must lie recluse, despised and unregarded, while fools roll in money, are advanced to dignities and offices, and in a word, have the whole world at their command. . . . In a word, to what side soever we turn ourselves, to popes, princes, judges, magistrates, friends, enemies, rich or poor, all their concerns are managed by money, which because it is undervalued by wise men, therefore, in revenge to be sure, it never comes at them."

DESIDERIUS ERASMUS, *In Praise of Folly* (1509)

I

Between the English revolution of 1642-49 and the French revolution of 1789, there is an ebb in the tide of national sentiments in Europe. Germany and Italy are divided into petty feudal principalities, with no movements stirring within them for national unity. In France and England, which are independent nations, the rich merchants make their peace with monarchic courts and the landed gentry. All join in exploiting the peasantry, both those that remain on the land and those that are driven off it to become the city proletariat. The arts display little interest in discovering the fact that the peasants and working people are human beings. There are dissenting exceptions, such as Rembrandt in seventeenth century Holland and Swift in early eighteenth century England. But in general the arts decline from the folk-suffusion and boisterous reflection of national life that had characterized the sixteenth and earlier seventeenth centuries, and had given a special quality to the art of a Shakespeare, Rabelais, Lope de Vega, Breughel and the inspired song composers. Yet folk and popular art have made an ineradicable impression upon musical composition.

The powerful new musical form to develop in this period is music drama, or opera. It is in part supported by the courts and aristocracy, and in part a business enterprise, since tickets of admission are sold to the city public. Its music has many popular ties. In Venice, where from 1637 on, the operatic theatres are opened to the general public, opera provides, as Bukofzer remarks, "song hits" for the city population.[1] Romain Rolland recounts this anecdote of Jean Baptiste Lully (1632-1687) who, born in Italy, had become the composer of ballet and opera for Louis XIV in France. Lully "was delighted to hear his songs sung on the Pont-Neuf and at street corners, with other words than those in the opera. And as he was of an odd turn of mind, he would sometimes have his coach stopped and call the singer and violinist to him, in order to give them the exact time of the air they were playing."[2] Henry Purcell (1659-95) writes many lovely rounded airs for London stage productions, and also dances, including rousing English "hornpipes" like that which the presumably Trojan sailors dance to in the opera *Dido and Aeneas.*

Folk music tends to be used when a composer wants to "turn to nature" or create a pastoral atmosphere, as if the peasantry were part of the natural scenery. It is also regarded as a light music, and does not find much place in the most profound and deeply subjective works, like the operas of Claudio Monteverdi (1567-1643). Monteverdi opens his opera *Orfeo* (1607) with the "bagpipe drone" and sprightly tunefulness of peasant music, but this is intended only to set the pastoral atmosphere of the first act, which represents the wedding ceremonial of Orpheus and Euridice, attended by nymphs and shepherds, and which has also some rounded airs. Monteverdi is bound by his profession to a court life which he despises, and of which he cannot express an open criticism. Only art offers integrity to him, and he reveals his aloofness from the life about him in the tragic inwardness of his music, such as so much of that in *Orfeo.* This opera, the text for which was written by Alessandro Striggio, expounds Monteverdi's concept of the creative artist, as symbolized in Orpheus. The lesson offered by Apollo in the opera to Orpheus is that the artist must uphold "reason," or the integrity of the mind, and not allow himself to be submerged in the irrationality of overwhelming passions.

Even more subjective, in its poignant flow of speech-inflected melodic lines, is the operatic masterpiece of Monteverdi's old age, *L'incoronazione di Poppea,* produced in Venice in 1642. The uncompromising portrayal of the depraved Roman Emperor Nero and his consort Poppea, who crush all who oppose them and ride roughshod over all human decencies in the triumphant progress of his lust and her ambition, is Monteverdi's commentary on the court life of his time. Monteverdi had no love for the courts. He had to spend much time and energy on shallow musical tasks, and was also poorly paid. He wrote in a letter of his experiences in Mantua, "I departed from that court so disgracefully that, by Jove, I took with me no more than twenty-five scudi after twenty-one years."[3]

The words of an earlier contemporary, the poet Giovanni Battista Guarini (1637-1612), whose poems Monteverdi often set to music, express perfectly the view of princes which the composer would later create in his musical portrait of Nero. "In appearance, the nobility speak politely; in reality, their acts of politeness are rare. In appearance, they seem gentle and affable; in reality, they are haughty and fierce. Things usually considered virtues—speaking the truth, acting righteously, loving sincerely, being truly pious, having inviolable faith, leading a blameless life—all these they hold to be signs of a base mind and a mean spirit. They cheat, lie, steal, and enrich themselves at the expense of others. They have no merit, no valor, and no reverence for age, rank or law; they have no restraint and no respect for love or for life. To them nothing is sacred or beyond the reach of their greed and lust."[4]

Yet folk music does begin to impart a special loveliness and strength to composed music. In the later seventeenth century and the early eighteenth, an Italian folk dance form attains an extraordinary currency in composition; the *Siciliana,* unmistakable in its slow, lilting 6/8 time and sweetly sad turn of melody. Arcangelo Corelli (1653-1713) uses it for example as the beautiful last movement of his *"Christmas" Concerto, Op. 6 No.* 8, a pastoral movement evoking the shepherds of the Nativity story. Johann Sebastian Bach uses it many times, as in the *Shepherd's Christmas Music* of his *Christmas Oratorio,* or the poignant alto aria, "Erbarme dich, mein Gott," in the *St. Matthew Passion.* Handel writes many touching *Sicilianas* for both voice and instruments, as in the *Concerto Grosso Op.* 6 *No.* 8. Antonio Vivaldi's concertos abound in *Siciliana* slow movements, like the notable one in the *Concerto Grosso Op.* 3 *No.* 11. And, to look ahead of our period, Mozart would use the *Siciliana* as the base for two of his most heart-rending movements: the slow one of his *A major Piano Concerto, K.* 488, and the last movement of his *D minor String Quartet, K.* 421.

Among the Italian composers who develop so inventively the instrumental forms of music, like the *sinfonia* (or instrumental prelude to a vocal work), the sonata for small groups of instruments, and the concerto for a group of soloists in interplay against an orchestra, Antonio Vivaldi (c. 1678-1741) shows an especially happy and prolific use of folk-style motifs. Thus his *Flute Concertos, Op.* 10 *Nos.* 5 *and* 6, may be called "dance poems," infused with the lilting sweetness of folk song. He likes to turn his concertos into "nature pictures," like the *Concerto Op.* 8 *No.* 5, *"The storm at sea," Op.* 8 *No.* 10, *"The Hunt,"* and the four concertos he calls *"The Four Seasons," Op.* 8 *Nos.* 1-4. Peasant dances are interspersed with other evocations of nature, like bird songs, hunting calls, tempestuous winds, the patter of rain. Yet it is not so much a pictorial as a truly human view of nature that Vivaldi creates. The "storm at sea" becomes a tempest in the heart; the bird songs become a song of delight in nature; the peasant dances are composed out of folk patterns with a deep enjoyment of their boisterous vitality. Vivaldi exhibits a principle that would be so marked in the nineteenth century; the special freshness and fertility in original melody, of composers who have a feeling for the malleable core of folk music, so that it flowers in their hands just as it does, more slowly in its folk existence.

In another composer of this time, Domenico Scarlatti (1685-1757), there is a fanciful use of folk material. The son of the eminent Neapolitan opera composer, Alessandro Scarlatti, Domenico spent twenty-five years in Spain as harpsichordist and music master to the Princess of the Asturias. In his harpsichord sonatas, as Ralph Kirkpatrick writes, he "imitated the melody of tunes sung by the carriers, muleteers, and common people."[5] Typical guitar figures, and rhythms of Spanish dances like the *jota,* are absorbed in his harpsichord style.

It is in Germany, however, that two composers appear, born in the same year, who create the most profound national expression of the era; George Frederick Handel and Johann Sebastian Bach.

II

George Frederick Handel (1685-1759) was the son of a surgeon-barber. His first musical training was in Germany, where a good part of what he learned was simply the Italian style at second hand. He then spent three years at the fountain-head of musical learning itself, Italy, becoming a masterful composer of opera in the Italian manner, and after 1712 settled in England. Here a partly mercantile-minded aristocracy, a flourishing and politically strong middle class, a constitutional monarchy, the presence of political battles fought openly on class lines, and an active journalism, made for much greater freedom of thought than existed in feudal-ridden Germany. Handel could furthermore feel at home because after 1714, England would choose a German-speaking king, namely George I, formerly Elector of Hanover, a gentleman both Protestant and properly respectful of the rights of men of property. And it was in the combined role of composer and business man producing and financing his own operas and musical entertainments, sometimes moderately successful, sometimes almost bankrupt, that Handel spent most of his years as an English citizen.

The dominant temper of intellectual life in England was middle class and rationalistic, seeing both nature and profit-making as beautifully ordered according to unchanging scientific laws, both being part of a God-created machine. There were dissenting voices, including Tory minded aristocrats, Jacobites who plotted for the return of the Stuart line of kings and for an absolute monarchy, and young gentry who formed gangs such as the Mohocks, showing their contempt for the existing order by acting like ruffians and cut-throats. With more than a touch of smugness, the middle-class political thinkers denounced the backwardness of the feudal minded aristocracy, while ignoring the great mass of bitterly impoverished and oppressed people on the land and in the cities. Catholics were discriminated against, representing both the extreme Tory-absolutist right and a great mass of the "disinherited," including the starving population of Ireland. It is a picture richly documented in the great critical and satiric literature of the time, by men like Defoe, Swift and Fielding.

It was the journalistic battles which helped Handel find his path. The rival opera companies were backed by different cliques, more or less Tory-minded. To the middle class, after their first period of gratification at being able to import so expensive an entertainment as Italian opera, with its high-priced virtuoso singers, opera in a foreign language seemed an affront to their national self-esteem. As Joseph Addison wrote in the *Spectator* (March 21, 1711), "Our great Grandchildren will be very curious to know the Reason why their Forefathers used to sit together like an Audience of Foreigners in their own Country, and to hear whole plays acted before them in a Tongue which they did not understand. . . . I have often been afraid when I have seen our Italian Performers chattering in the Vehemence of Action, that they have been calling us Names, and abusing us among themselves." Jingoistic sneers against the Italian people in general, ridicule of the silliness of the spectacles themselves ("Nicolini exposed to a Tempest in Robes of Ermine and sailing in an open boat upon a Sea of Paste-Board"), and a feeling that this was only a kind of aristocratic court entertainment, were combined with a genuine desire for a music drama with national roots. To quote Addison again, "the Recitative Musick, in every language, should be as different as the Tone or Accent of each Language; for otherwise, what may properly express a Passion in one Language, will not do it in another . . . an English Composer should not follow the Italian Recitative too servilely, but make use of many gentle Deviations from it, in Compliance with his own Native Language." (*Spectator,* April 3, 1711).

In 1728, John Gay's *The Beggar's Opera,* comic and satiric in plot, its music a medley of popular English airs and ballads, made a fantastic success, while Handel's Italian-style operas, far superior in beauty of music and artistry, were failures. Handel had no feeling for satire or popular English ballad melody, but four years later he wrote his first oratorio, *Esther,* a music drama in English on a Biblical subject. And it was oratorio that from about 1741 on became his major musical form, with a series of masterpieces that gave the English middle class a profound national musical expression.

The characters and events of these oratorios came largely from the Old Testament Bible and the Apocrypha; the stories of Esther, Deborah, the Maccabees, Saul, Samson, Joshua, Jeptha, Solomon, and the Israelites in Egypt. They were not fashioned for religious services, like the medieval Catholic Masses or the Lutheran Cantatas that Bach was composing in Leipzig. They were performed as splendid public concerts, with great choruses, brilliant instrumentation, and all the spectacular virtuosity of solo singing that had been developed in opera. Their religious spirit is devoid of mysticism. It is an obeisance to God for the gifts He has granted His Chosen People (the English). But they also embody the most democratic and progressive aspect of middle-class thought. Behind them is the tradition of militant morality that a century before had swept Charles I off the throne; the representation of Old Testament prophets and heroes as prototypes of the defiance of tyranny and of aristocratic privilege. Some are almost journalistic. *Judas Maccabeus* drew upon the heroic struggle of the Maccabees against the Greek tyrants to celebrate the victory in 1746 of the Duke of Cumberland over the followers of the Stuarts, on the field of Culloden. It happened that this victory was followed by a reign of terror in Scotland which earned the Duke the nickname of Billy the Butcher. Yet there is also in these oratorios something of the thinking that Milton had expressed a century before, in *Paradise Lost,* when, writing "to justify the ways of God to men," he said,

> *"but Man over men,*
> *He made not Lord; such title to himself*
> *Reserving, human left from human free."*

Handel's librettos, mostly written by mediocre verse-spinners, are far from Miltonic in grandeur of language and thought. They express with genuine conviction pride in progress over feudal backwardness, and contempt for aristocratic absolutism. Thus for example in *Belshazzar,* the dissolute king of Babylon, who is defied by the prophet Daniel and doomed by the "handwriting on the wall," is an obvious prototype of the absolute feudal monarch. His henchmen, the Assyrian nobles, are obvious Tory aristocrats and courtiers. Cyrus of Persia, who overthrows Belshazzar, is the just and reasonable monarch who proclaims, "to tyrants only I'm a foe." Similarly in *Saul,* the drama holds up to contempt Saul's snobbish daughter, Merab, who will not marry David because he is a lowly shepherd. And Jonathan, Saul's son, expresses the opposite view: "birth and fortune I despise; from virtue let my friendship rise."

The formal construction varies from one oratorio to the next. Thus *Messiah* is like a chain of tremendous choral and polyphonic hymns, with interspersed solos. *Israel in Egypt* is a great choral pageant, *Belshazzar* and *Saul* have on the other hand the dramatic actions, characterizations, and vivid color of music drama, being actual Biblical operas. There is no sharp demarcation in style between the lovely melodies of Handel's Italian operas and those of his English oratorios. There are long uninspired stretches in the oratorios, as in the operas, where it is Handel's superb technique and the momentum of the great moments that carry the music along. But the qualitative leap of the oratorios over the operas comes in the central place held in the oratorios by the choruses. They are the majestic pillars of the musical structure, with the recitatives and arias draped between them like garlands. In text, they represent the mighty collective and moral voice of the people, as if the chorus of Greek drama had taken on the spiritual message of the Hebrew prophets. And if, as in the operas, the melodic idiom still bears an Italian birthmark, this idiom is at the same time transformed in seriousness and grandeur.

The great choruses—for example, "By slow degrees the wrath of God" in *Belshazzar,* "Amen" in *Messiah, "Mourn Israel"* in *Saul,* "And the children of Israel sighed" in *Israel in Egypt,* "How dark, O Lord, are Thy decrees" in *Jeptha*—are like nothing that had been heard before on the English stage. Given depth and weight by their polyphonic piling up of voices, yet always clear and direct in expression, moving with unstoppable power to their climax, monumental in solidity and spaciousness, they become a thoroughly English music, their amplitude and structure the fit clothing for the social thinking behind them. For this reason, being a mirror of the dominant mind of the English people at a historic stage in their progress, the oratorios became a national heritage, not only revered by musicians but performed at festivals by the popular choral societies.

Missing from these oratorios, quite understandably, is the deepest sense of tragic anguish, the most penetrating searching of self. Also missing is the voice of the English folk. But the oratorios have a wide range of human imagery, and a touching meditativeness matching the joy in life, like the contrast in *Messiah* between the choruses "Behold the Lamb of God" and "His Yoke Is Easy." There is depth of feeling behind the overwhelming optimism. It is this breadth, combined with absolute clarity and sureness of effect, which so moved Haydn when he heard the oratorios in England, and which led Beethoven to consider Handel as the greatest of the "old masters."

III

Johann Sebastian Bach (1685-1750), born the same year as Handel, was in many ways Handel's opposite and counterpart. He was deeply attached to his own land, language and traditions, never being impelled to go abroad to search for a pot of gold. He was more international minded than Handel, in that he studied carefully the developed art of different countries, knowing for example the work of Handel while Handel paid no attention to that of Bach. At the same time Bach had deeper roots in German folk and popular music. His religious music differs from that of Handel, not only in that it was written for actual Protestant church service, but because it embodied his whole mind and thought, including the most heartrending outcries.

There is a far greater subjective turn in Bach, and a deeper sense of the tragic. But Bach is at the same time not bound to introspection, or other-worldly mysticism. Like Handel's oratorios, Bach's *Passions* and *Cantatas* contain a teeming world of human images drawn from real life, with a more earthy popular tone, and even more ecstatic joy, than can be found in Handel. Writing as Handel did for special occasions, or for current social use, he was at the same time more theoretical; more intent on raising and solving some fresh problem with each new work, and on exploring or expanding the powers of music itself.

Bach can be more folkish, and also more intricate, like a medieval craftsman who will add touches to a work that will never be seen, but are a necessary part of his preconceived design. Handel is almost wholly a direct reflection or voice of his times. Bach by comparison, in his music, seems to have lived a double life. He gives his times what it asks for—or at least that part of what it asks for that pleases him— and at the same time, often in the same work, will create another world of thought, completely detached, for the satisfaction of himself and for the few who ask the same penetrating questions that he does. The most obvious example of this double life in his music is the *Goldberg Variations,* composed for one of his former pupils who needed it to entertain a patron suffering from sleepless nights. It is mainly light and winsome music. Yet in its "secret" interlocking threads and unities, intellectual problems are set and solved that only a theory-minded musician like himself would ever discern. Handel's greatness was that he joined and gave apt expression to the genuine progress made by his age, for English mercantile capitalism was such a progressive force, beginning to create "more massive and more colossal productive forces than have all previous generations together." Bach, impelled perhaps by the social and economic backwardness of Germany, raised unanswered questions that applied even to so flourishing a country as England.

The difference between the two giants may be seen in the course of their music after their death. Handel's music remained current throughout the industrial revolution and the subsequent democratic revolutions, in which the bourgeois class sought for full political power. It helped inspire the great "classic" art of Haydn, Mozart and Beethoven. Bach's music was mostly forgotten after his death. Even his gifted sons made no effort to keep it alive. One of his sons, Johann Christian Bach, followed in Handel's tracks, becoming a famous "German" composer in England, making a liberal use of the Italian style. But in the second quarter of the nineteenth century, when searching questions were being raised of what kind of progress had been created by the victories of the bourgeois class—the seeming transformation of all artistic, intellectual, moral and spiritual values into cash and marketplace values, the outcry of the industrial proletariat, the first shocks felt of the cyclical crisis of capitalism—Bach's star began to rise. This is not to say that any answers to such questions, or even the questions themselves, may be found in Bach's art; only that a composer who planted his art firmly in his age and yet was not quite in accord with it, looking behind, above and beyond it, now became especially moving. Composers feeling the pull of romantic subjectivism discovered that long before them a mighty artist had foreshadowed their harrowing inner conflicts.

Seemingly a pious and loyal servant of his feudal princes, Bach was actually a man of sturdy independence. A musician in the Germany of his time not only was a hired craftsman, but was bound by innumerable petty rules and restrictions, which were hangovers from serfdom. Thus Bach's certificate of appointment as organist at Arnstadt read, among other things, "you are, above all, to be true, faithful and obedient to him, His above-mentioned Noble Grace, the Count, and especially to show yourself industrious and reliable in the office, vocation and practise of art and science that are assigned to you; not to mix into other affairs and functions . . . in your daily life to cultivate the fear of God, sobriety and the love of peace; altogether to avoid bad company and in general to conduct yourself in all things toward God, High Authority, and your superiors, as befits an honor-loving servant and organist."[6]

It was from Arnstadt, however, that he took four weeks leave to hear Buxtehude in Luebeck, and stayed away four months. The records of his interrogation upon his return show him to be most uncontrite. He was also reproved for his over-original music, and for such matters as "The organist Bach had previously played rather too long, but after his attention had been called to it by the Superintendent, he had at once fallen into the other extreme and had made it too short."[7] He obviously had no respect for the musical tastes of his employers. Once bound into service, a musician could not resign from a post without permission, no matter how attractive an offer could come from elsewhere. This problem was fought through by Bach at Weimar, where in 1717 he was arrested and thrown into jail for "too stubbornly" requesting his dismissal.[8] He won his point however.

There is no record of Bach's opinions on matters other than music. This is not surprising, since people in middle-Europe did not speak or write openly about controversial matters. Two generations later, Mozart would correspond with his father in code. And in the Germany of Bach's time there was no movement stirring for democratic advances, for economic progress, for an end to feudal hangovers and for the creation of a unified nation. His independence shows itself however in the very semi-obscurity of his life; his choice, for instance, of the post of Cantor at Leipzig, from 1723 to his death, serving the two churches of the city as teacher and as composer of music for church service. With his gifts merely as a virtuoso performer, on not only the organ but practically every other instrument, he could have gotten a spectacular position. As his son Carl Philipp Emanuel wrote, "in general he did not have the most brilliant good fortune, because he did not do what it requires, namely, roam the world over. Yet by connoisseurs and lovers of the art he was sufficiently honored."[9] Another pupil of Bach, Carl Friedrich Abel, wrote about both the old master and his son Carl Philipp Emanuel, that had they composed in "Naples, Paris, or London," and written in "a style more popular, and generally intelligible and pleasing," they would have "been indisputably the greatest musicians of the eighteenth century." [10] It never seemed to trouble Bach, however, that composers who he knew were shallow and inferior received more fame and money. What was important to him was that in Leipzig, he could preserve and exalt a tradition that, however it was scorned by "modernists" as old fashioned, had its roots in the national history and aspirations of the German people.

Countryside folk music meant little to Bach. His suites and

partitas, which he wrote for a variety of instruments, consist generally of strikingly powerful overtures followed by a chain of dances that are court rather than folk. Some of the dances are the gavotte, rondeau, allemande, courante, minuet, gigue, and sarabande. They are treated in a most original manner, the gigues often being masterpieces of fugal counterpoint and the sarabandes often being given a deeply expressive, *parlando* character. A remarkable example of an entire series of dance movements treated in a *parlando-rubato* style is the whole of the great sixth clavier *Partita.* It is probable that he shared the city-burgher patronizing attitude towards the peasantry. His *"Peasant Cantata,"* No. 212, is full of merry inventions on the countryside folk style, with an overture that is a medley of folk dances, ending in a *ländler* or rustic waltz. The text depicts the "happy peasantry" welcoming the new lord and lady of the manor. In the highly refined and serious *Goldberg Variations,* Bach composed, as a sort of comic relief a *Quodlibet* for the final variation. This is a form best described by the composer's first biographer, Forkel, when telling of the annual meetings of the Bach family.

"The first thing they did, when they were assembled, was to sing a chorale. From this pious commencement they proceeded to drolleries which often made a very great contrast with it. For now they sang popular songs, the contents of which were partly comic and partly naughty, all together and extempore, but in such a manner that the parts thus extemporized made a kind of harmony together, the words, however, in every part being different. They called this kind of extemporary harmony a *Quodlibet* and not only laughed heartily at it themselves, but excited an equally hearty and irresistible laughter in everybody that heard them."[11]

In the religious works there occasionally are tender and affectionate treatments of folk style, when the text evokes a pastoral or "shepherd" image. An example is the *Cantata No.* 104, *Du Hirte Israel*—"Thou Shepherd of Israel"—with its opening chorus like a German folk dance, in triple time with a drone bass, and its captivating bass aria which is an apotheosis of the slow folk *ländler* or dancing song. The most exalted example is the closing chorus of the *St. Matthew Passion,* with its sweet melody and gently rocking rhythm, like a lullaby.

However, what makes the Protestant religious works, the church cantatas and *Passions,* so profound a national expression is the central place held in them of the German language and the Lutheran chorales. These works were written to be performed before the communities which Bach served. The one important exception to this is the *B minor Mass,* which employs the traditional Latin text of the Mass and was not intended for local church performance. Much however of the music in this Mass is adapted directly from his German cantatas. These works are a tremendous flowering in the baroque era of seeds that had been sown by the folk and artisans of the Middle Ages.

There had been two main religious currents in medieval Europe; one which exalted Christ as a "King" in Heaven, a Great Lord surrounded by saints and angels as courtiers, and one which saw Christ as an outlaw, or leader of the poor, brought to trial and tortured by the "authorities." The latter was, to use G. G. Coulton's words, part of "the Bible of the Poor." And this approach, of translating the Biblical stories and lives of the saints into realistic terms, taken from ordinary life may be found in all forms of medieval popular art; the religious folk dramas, produced by the guilds, with their racy homespun speech, Christmas carols telling of Joseph and Mary as poor folk whose babe is born in a stable, carvings in cathedrals by anonymous artisans in which the saints and Biblical figures are portrayed as peasants, carpenters, blacksmiths and fisherfolk. Out of this rose the heretical demand that the Bible itself be translated into the vernacular languages, which Coulton describes as the "fight for the Bible."[13] A central aspect of the Lutheran revolt was the establishment of the German Bible, of religious services in German, and of the great tradition of popular hymns, or chorales.

It is this tradition that Bach seized upon and carried to its musical culmination, using for this purpose all the newly developed splendors of baroque major-minor harmony, architectural form and instrumentation. These *Cantatas* of which about 200 of the 300 Bach composed are extant, and the two *Passions,* represent a monument of music unique in history. Never before had a great composer taken over bodily an existing tradition of song, a social possession, kept it recognizable in its original form, and at the same time made it the warp and woof of his own musical invention. The chorales are musically and spiritually embedded in these works, and whether or not we call them a "folk music" is of little moment. Whatever their manifold musical roots, they had become a communal national possession. Latent in them was the national consciousness, the surge towards a German nation, that had inspired their origin, even though the national movement itself had been wrecked in the stalemated class struggles of the sixteenth century and the internecine wars of the seventeenth. To Bach's listeners they were familiar and recognizable even amidst the most complex polyphony which he wove about them.

Bach's audience would undoubtedly not have spoken of these chorales as embodying any hopes for a unified German nation. There was certainly no active movement of this kind then in Germany. And yet Bach's treatment of these chorales is always thoughtful and creative, revealing his own deep personal involvement with them and with the tradition, historical and cultural, that they embodied. He rekindled the fire that had once burned within them. Thus the chorale, *Ein' feste Burg ist unser Gott,* the "defiant battle hymn" with which Luther and his comrades had entered Worms, is transformed by Bach, in the first movement of the Cantata No. 80, *Ein' feste Burg,* into a fiery marching chorus, with the polyphonic piling up of one melodic line above another and the pealing trumpets adding to the unstoppable momentum and exhilarating pictorial splendor.

In the *St. Matthew Passion* Bach offers a combined sermon and music drama, which is not intended to be played on a stage, but the spiritual connection of which to classic Greek drama is not accidental. For Greek drama had sprung out of religious ritual, transformed by the genius of the dramatists who gave the old myths realistic and compelling human characterizations. The chorales are the collective voice of the people, commenting on the drama like a Greek chorus. And he recreates the medieval self-identification of the folk with the popular followers of Christ, as in the great lamenting duet which describes the capture of Christ, repeatedly broken into by the chorus crying "Let Him go!" Of course the Gospel of St. Matthew lends itself to such vivid social imagery. It is worth noting that the Gospel of St. John, which has much less popular feeling, and in which the social message of the Christ story is drowned in extreme anti-Semitic distortions, does not inspire Bach to similar heights of musical drama and characterization. Spitta writes that Bach in the *St. John Passion* "ranked as first in importance the musical form he required to give, rather than any striking dramatic rendering of a mass of people."[13] And this work, despite many beautiful passages, has not captured the imagination of later generations like the *St. Matthew Passion,* which has so many lessons in how the conflicts of real life and the presence of the common people as a force in history can be recreated in music.

As Rembrandt had done with his religious paintings in seventeenth century Holland, Bach in his music infuses the religious tradition with his own feeling for life and people, while apparently working within the accepted traditions of his time. He is no folk artist, but what he shares with the popular religious artists of the Middle Ages is the literal spirit with which they had approached the Biblical stories. It is so literal that the subject itself is brought down to earth. An "inverted reality" exalting the "other world" and negating the real world is turned back into a portrayal of real life. Thus in the *Cantatas* Bach is intent on finding the right musical illustration, emotional and at times even pictorial, for every stanza of the poem, and sometimes for even a word or phrase. And because of this very literalness, together with his own robust feeling for life, the cumulative feeling of the music in the end belies the spirit of the texts.

The *Cantata* texts, some of them written by contemporary religious poets, some of them taken from the Bible, some of them simply made up of the traditional verses of the chorale hymn, generally deal with the torment of real existence and the bliss of heaven. The world is hateful, they say; death is good, for the pious soul who resists the temptations of Satan will find happiness beyond the grave. Allusions to things in the real world are intended as symbol or allegory. But in Bach's settings it is the allusion to the real world of people's lives which sets off and inspires the music. Thus in the early *Cantata No. 21, Ich hatte viel Bekümmernis,* the duet between the "soul" and Christ becomes, in music, the most winsome and tender of real life duets, such as a young swain might sing to win over a hesitant maiden. In the *Cantata No. 78, Jesu, der du meine Seele,* the words, "we hasten with feeble, yet diligent footsteps, O Jesus, for help unto thee" inspire a blithe, popularly tuneful, rollicking duet for two female voices, evoking an image of two women hastening to the market. The words "Praise ye God in all creation," which open *Cantata No. 51* inspire a dazzling musical scene of festivity, with a blazing trumpet obbligato over the voice. While the words of the *Cantatas* themselves speak longingly of death, the music is bursting with life. It is the music of a devoutly religious thinker who cannot see religion, however, as a flight from reality. Religion must make sense in its application to every side of real life. In such a spirit the American Negro people, oppressed by slavery, would create a body of folk hymnology that, devoutly religious, also expressed their dignity as people and their struggle against slavery.

Especially apropos to the study of a national music is the manner in which Bach's original melodic inventions are inspired by the melodies of the chorales. This is most marked in the great series of "Chorale Cantatas," which Bach composed in his Leipzig years. The form was one of his own invention. German composers of previous generations had used the chorales as the basis for organ works, and had inserted them in church *Cantatas*. But in these "Chorale Cantatas" of Bach, the chorale is the foundation of the entire work, each separate movement being based on a successive stanza of the hymn text, and at the same time being a variation or elaboration of the chorale melody. They may be called sets of "variations in reverse," the first movement generally being an elaborate contrapuntal fantasia on the chorale, and the chorale in its simple, original and harmonized form appearing only at the end; a procedure psychologically advantageous only when the chorale itself, the basis for the variations, is familiar to the listeners.

In these works, no matter how disguised the chorale may be in melodic variants and counterpoint, Spitta writes, "(the listener) will feel that not a moment has passed during which he has not been hearing the chorale, either in its material form or in its inner spirit."[14] Again we see, on a new level, the birth-process of melody we have already observed in folk music, with its melodic families. Old melodies give rise to new ones. A striking example is the fourth movement of *Cantata No. 140, Wachet auf,* in which the soaring obbligato melody for strings is an inspired variant of the chorale tune, and at the same time creates a new human image, of joyous awakening. In the entrancing opening chorus of *Cantata No. 133, Ich freue mich in dir,* the orchestra develops happily a theme made of a phrase of the chorale. In the opening instrumental sinfonia of *Cantata No. 4, Christ lag in Todesbandem,* the first phrase of the chorale is transformed into an inexpressibly poignant melody. And of course in the chorale-preludes and chorale fantasias, which are elaborations of the chorales, composed for organ, we can see the same creative process at work. An example is the grand, sustained melody, one of the most wonderful ever written, and made out of the raw material of a chorale, in the late version of *Nun komm' der heiden Heiland* (BWV 659).

Bach is the first mighty example of a composer creating a host of grand and imperishable melodies by taking a social fund of popular song and reworking its living materials in response to new situations of life.

Bach's independence within a seeming conformity may be seen as well in his secular works. In the organ works such as the *Toccata in F,* and the great Leipzig *Preludes and Fugues* in E flat ("St. Anne"), E minor ("Wedge"), C major and B minor, he opens up a contrast and clash of mood within the framework of a single movement unlike anything else known in baroque instrumental art. It corresponds to the most impassioned and dramatic moments of his religious works, but is even more compact and intense. And the melodies of the secular works seem often to be of the same idiom as the chorale-inspired melodies of the religious works. There is a family kinship for example between the famous "Air" from the orchestral *Suite in D* (known to countless followers of violin recitals as the "Air for G string") and the melody of the Chorale-Prelude, *Nun komm der Heiden Heiland;* between the great melody of the *Prelude in E flat minor,* in Book I of the *Well-Tempered Clavier,* and the "Passion" chorale, *O Haupt voll Blut.*

Bach's mighty art rose in opposition to the trends most musicians of his time, including his own gifted sons, looked upon as "musical progress." For the prevailing trend was towards a music less contrapuntal, lighter in texture, more entertaining, sweeter and more tender in sentiment, and more capricious in form. Nor was the national-religious character of his music, with the great stature he gave to the chorales, especially welcomed. When Germany finally became united, something over a century after Bach's death, it was under the hegemony of the autocratic Prussian state. It had nothing of the militant, democratic morality upon which Bach drew, such as the spirit in which Luther had aroused peasants and plebians to study the Bible themselves for its moral precepts, and to do battle against what he called the "Roman Sodom." Bach was a giant voice of a nation which had no independent existence, except as a stifled movement in the past and a hope some few had for the future.

3. CLASSIC FORM AND CRITIQUE OF ARISTOCRACY

*He (Mozart) asked me whether I could easily make an opera from a comedy by Beaumarchais—*Le Mariage de Figaro. *I liked the suggestion very much, and promised to write one. . . . I set to work accordingly, and as fast as I wrote the words, Mozart set them to music. . . . I went, without saying a word to a living person, to offer* Figaro *to the Emperor.*

" 'What?' he said. 'Don't you know that Mozart, though a wonder at instrumental music, has written only one opera, and nothing remarkable at that?'

" 'Yes, Sire,' I replied quietly, 'but without Your Majesty's clemency I would have written but one drama in Vienna!'

" 'That may be true,' he answered, 'but this Mariage de Figaro*—I have just forbidden the German troupe to use it!'*

" 'Yes, Sire,' I rejoined, 'but I was writing an opera, and not a comedy. I had to omit many scenes, and to cut others quite considerably. I have omitted or cut anything that might offend good taste or public decency at a performance over which the Sovereign Majesty might preside. The music, I may add, as far as I may judge of it, seems to me marvelously beautiful'."

—Memoirs of Lorenzo da Ponte

I

Haydn and Mozart were the main architects of the "classic" style which flowered in the late eighteenth century. The seeds of this style were sown by the great baroque experimenters, from Monteverdi to Bach. But this "classic" style, for its own fruition, had to break through the shell of baroque practises and establish its own forms.

Three achievements of the baroque were crucial for the later development of music. One was the invention of large-scale forms, fit to embrace the variety and breadth of real life, like opera, and its offshoot, the dramatic oratorio. They were built of great blocks of sound, such as choruses, arias and recitatives, with each representing a different real-life image, as an outgrowth of the rounded song. Second was the creation of the first purely instrumental forms, different from dances or from the imitation on instruments of vocal polyphony. Typical was the three-movement concerto, with its built-in reflection of human psychology, starting with an impetuous, driving first movement, contrasting to this a meditative slow movement, and resolving the preceding contradiction in a lively, dancing finale. Third was the establishment of the system of musical construction based on two of the medieval modes, which became the major and minor scales, and which could move through a "circle of keys." Thus a work in its course could modulate, or move from one key to another, and in the harmonic world thereby opened up, there were limitless possibilities for emotional and dramatic expression. Established near the end of the seventeenth century by composers like Corelli and Alessandro Scarlatti, this harmonic-structural principle was searchingly explored in the great organ and clavier toccatas, preludes, fantasias and fugues of Bach.

The limitation of baroque music was that its eager embrace of real life took place within a formal lip-service to unreality. This paralleled the society which the composer served. Colossal changes were taking place, with colonial exploitation, trade and the development of industrial manufacture. But a monarchy and landed gentry held the reins of government as if their rule had been divinely affirmed for all time. A scientific, materialist view of life born out of the great discoveries in natural science made an uneasy truce with a theology taken over from the Middle Ages. In the same way composers, creating works bursting with life, like the Handel oratorios or the Bach cantatas and *Passions,* also paid homage in them to the authority of religious tradition. In opera, the dramaturgy tended to be restricted to an idealized portrayal of court life or the adventures of mythological heroes.

An important step was that the open forms and speech-inflected lines of medieval polyphony, with its dominating subjectivity, had been replaced by the rounded and rhythm-dominated forms of baroque counterpoint, in which a bass line or *continuo* set the underlying and controlling foundation above which melodic lines and arabesques were woven.

A wide door was thus opened to the reflection of "outer world" feelings in music. But the result was often a music too shallowly "outer," ornamental and decorative. There is an overabundance of dance forms in early eighteenth century music, heard not only in instrumental dance suites and ballets but also in sonatas and in the arias of opera and oratorio. Contrasting speech-inflected forms arose; the free recitative against the formal aria, and the instrumental *fantasies,* which moved like great interior monologues. And a deeply affecting side of Bach's art was his ability to give even the rhythmic baroque form a poignant meditative cast, like the dance movements in his *Partitas,* or his great speech-inflected fugues, such as that in C sharp minor from Book I of *The Well-Tempered Clavier.* But the individual "blocks" or separate movements that made up baroque form admitted only with great difficulty, if at all, an internal dramatic clash and conflict.

The new "classic" style, the essence of which was a dramatic clash from beginning to end within a single continuous musical structure, and an interplay of speech-inflected with rhythm-dominated music, was a product of many nations. Romain Rolland called it "a victory of humanity," adding, "This art became the property, the food of all; of all Europeans, because all races have collaborated in it, all have put something of themselves in it."[1] German, French, Italian and Polish musicians played a part. Notable was the contribution of Czech musicians. Unable to work in their homeland, Bohemia, which was part of the prison-house of nations ruled by the Hapsburg emperors, they served the various courts of Europe. Among them was Jan Stamic (1717-57)—his name Germanized in books as Johann Stamitz—who built at Mannheim an orchestra famous for its dynamic shadings and brilliant wind instrument color; George Benda (1722-95) who created the German language *sing-spiel,* or home-spun comic opera; Christoph Willibald Gluck (1714-87) who gave opera a deep seriousness and stateliness, and combined choruses, recitatives and arias in great musical arches spanning entire acts.

The classic style abandoned the "baroque bass" or *continuo,* and engendered its musical flow through a freely moving melodic line, no longer controlled by but supported by the bass and inspiring through its movement a rich and free play of harmony and inner voices. It employed dance rhythms but broke the manacles of dance forms, conceiving its musical movement through dramatic contrasts of rhythms, melodic themes, and dynamics. In its earlier stages, at about the middle of the eighteenth century, it seemed to be a simplification of the baroque style, doing away with the intellectual complexities of counterpoint and with the formalisms of dance structure, while bringing to music a sweetly agreeable sentiment.

With the last third of the eighteenth century, however, the classic style was enlarged in scope and deepened in emotional life, reflecting a world of turbulence and change. A devastating criticism was rising of aristocratic institutions and the remnants of feudalism, to be read in the works of Rousseau, Diderot and Beaumarchais in France, and of Lessing, Schiller and Goethe in Germany. Goethe's novel *Werther,* in 1774, set Europe weeping over its youth who killed himself because of unrequited love. But within the novel also lay a keen evaluation of the shallowness of upper-class social and intellectual life. The *Sturm und Drang* or pre-romantic current of the late 1760's was a protest against the stultifying conventionalities of society, although this protest and yearning for "freedom" also took such strange, subjective forms as a nostalgic medievalism and a fascination with morbidity, magic and witchcraft. But the best side of this criticism was its combination of rationality with humanity, its union of mind and heart, its deep appreciation of the preciousness of life and the rights of the individual, united to an awareness that such freedom had to be found in the development of society. It represented a search for an order and logic, not counterposed to reality but discovered in the very movement and conflict of social life. This, transmuted into music, was the essence of the classic style as developed by Haydn and Mozart, and raised to the loftiest heights by Beethoven. It combined a patriotic, anti-feudal sense of nation with an awareness of advanced views sweeping the world.

II

The composers Joseph Haydn (1732-1809) and Wolfgang Amadeus Mozart (1756-91) both faced the same contradiction; that of knowing they were artists with profound things to say, being aware of fresh winds blowing in the world about them, and yet compelled to work under servile conditions that had their origin in feudalism. Their lives were shaped differently. Haydn's story, to use a modern catch-phrase, was that of the poor boy who rose to success through hard work. Mozart was born the darling of fortune, but when he died was buried in a pauper's grave. Haydn was more cautious about the expression of his feelings toward the aristocracy; Mozart attacked the patronage system head-on.

Haydn was born of peasant folk in a small Austrian town near what is now the border of Hungary. After a hard struggle to develop his art and win a worthwhile post, he was fortunate, in 1761, in being hired by the Hungarian Esterhazy princes, who were among the wealthiest magnates in the Holy Roman Empire. Prince Nikolaus Esterhazy, who held the title from 1762 to 1790, and who put on the most lavish and splendid entertainments in Central Europe, was a music lover. As Haydn's genius expanded, the prince became genuinely proud of having so gifted a creator as his court composer. But however gilded the cage, Haydn was irked by it. The contract he signed on taking up employment with the Esterhazys was a typical example of feudal relations. It stipulated that he "shall be under obligation to compose such music as his Serene Highness shall command, and neither to communicate such compositions to any other person, nor to allow them to be copied, but he shall retain them for the absolute use of his Highness, and not compose for any other person without the knowledge and permission of his Highness."[2] Whether the Esterhazys actually expected Haydn to live up to this cannot be known. Mozart's *Requiem* was similarly commissioned by a Count who innocently believed that since he had paid for the work, he could publish it as his own composition. But such an attitude at the time was like holding back the tides. Haydn published many of his works. A great artist, he became a world possession, and the world spoke its praise. By the 1880's his music was being performed and his name celebrated (far more than that of his noble patrons) in Italy, France, Germany, England and Russia. Like a serf, however, not only was he bound to his employers for life, unless they were willing to release him. He could not even travel to hear music without his Serene Highness' permission, a permission most often politely denied.[3] Haydn wrote in 1790, "It is indeed sad to be always a slave."[4]

The death of Prince Nikolaus in 1790 left Haydn free to seek other employment, since the successor to the title, Prince Anton, had little interest in music. A munificent offer came from England to present some new works of his own at a series of concerts. Haydn, approaching sixty, made the arduous journey. His reception at these London concerts of 1791-92—they were public concerts, unlike those at the Esterhazy's private theatre—was stupendous. The more novel and daring the musical ideas he revealed, the more the press and public acclaimed him as the greatest living musical genius. He returned to England in 1794, staying until the next year, and composed six last symphonies—even more glowing in color, bold in conception, and stormy in drama than anything he had written previously. The King and Queen asked him to remain, offering him quarters in the palace. But he was too old to sink new roots and he was also deeply attached to his homeland. He went back to Vienna and the Esterhazy family, with, however, a new sense of independence. The French Revolution had broken out, and while this caused in Austria a tightening of censorship and general repression, certain feudal attitudes were abolished forever. Even the Vienna critics, who with the churlish snobbery of court flunkies had always heckled him, now recognized his genius. At the first public performance of his oratorio *The Creation,* in 1799, the police were called out to keep order among the people trying to enter to hear it. He was invited to conduct it in Paris, although France was at war with Austria. An award came from Sweden. It was amidst this general homage that he spent his last years.

Mozart enjoyed glowing admiration when he was barely six years old. A fantastic musical prodigy, the son of a violinist in the employ of the Archbishop of Salzburg, he was exhibited by his father in Germany, France, Belgium, Holland, Switzerland and England. The miserly Archbishop graciously gave his permission for this tour, although he suspended the father's salary. At the age of fifteen, Mozart conquered Italy, still recognized as the fountain-head of music, with his ability to compose vocal works in the Italian style. The career his father planned for him was that of a court musician. But early Wolfgang learned that the high and mighty could be stupid and penny-pinching. He wrote home when touring Italy with his father, "Have we played to the king of Naples? Nothing less, I assure you—and received for it the bows which the queen made to us in every place in which she saw us. The queen is unable to do anything of herself—and what sort of person the king is, it will be better to tell you than to write."[5]

He early became too independent to accept the manners of an aristocracy among whom music lovers were few and arrogance was a way of life. There was no obligatory pay for a performance. Sometimes it took the form of a useless gift, as an amusing letter illustrates. "I had to go yesterday with Cannabich to Count Savioli to fetch my present, which was, as I had imagined it would be, nothing in money, but a handsome gold watch. I would rather have had ten carolins than the watch, although with its chain and devices estimated at twenty carolins, for on a journey money is necessary. I have now, with your permission, five watches; and I have a great mind to have another watch-pocket made in all my clothes, in order that when I visit noblemen, I may wear two watches (as is now the fashion), and at least prevent any of them from presenting me with another watch."[6] The pay he received as a servant of the Archbishop of Salzburg was niggardly, and the Archbishop seems to have had an intense dislike of music itself, looking upon it merely as a necessary adjunct to his court ceremonies. An early biographer wrote of Mozart at Salzburg, "His talents were never undervalued until he sought to be remunerated for them. Then however he was told, in no measured terms, that his productions were worthless."[7] The letters Mozart exchanged with his father (which were written in code, since spies were everywhere about) indicate the low opinion both had of their patron, although the father begged him to be a little more circumspect. In 1781 however Mozart announced himself as no longer in the Archbishop's employ; a historic declaration of independence, not only on his own behalf, but on behalf of the composer and artist in general, from feudal treatment as a bonded servant.

Life after this was hard. There were certainly enough who recognized Mozart's genius. But there was also frightful jealousy. Even when he had been much younger, his father had angrily written, "The whole hell of musicians has arisen to prevent the display of a child's ability."[8] The court opera, for which he wrote a series of astonishing masterpieces, was particularly a nest of intrigue, favoritism, and cut-throat politics. The market-place was too weak to support him. Beethoven would later be able to make his way in Vienna as an independent composer, accepting gifts and commissions from any of the nobility who liked music, but insisting on composing exactly as he pleased. He would produce his symphonies before the general public in the theatres, and enjoy an income from publishers accepting practically everything he wrote. But that would be a decade after Mozart's death. The greatest homage that Haydn received in Vienna took place during the seventeen years after Mozart's death.

Anyone who believes however that Mozart's talents could not be appreciated by the public of his time, that he wrote "over their head" or strictly for "posterity," need only read of his reception, when, one night in 1789, he made an unexpected entrance in the Berlin opera house where his *The Abduction from the Seraglio* was being performed. " 'Mozart is in the house' ran like wildfire from the orchestra to the stage."[9] He was lionized in Prague, where airs from his *The Marriage of Figaro* (the anti-feudal satire of which Vienna found a little frightening) were turned into popular dances. For Prague he wrote his great masterpiece, *Don Giovanni*. He was invited to follow Haydn's footsteps in London, but he was on his deathbed while Haydn was in the midst of his first English journey.

Wonderful to read of, in that period of intrigue, jealousy and back-biting among musicians, is the self-effacing admiration that Mozart and Haydn had for one another. Mozart referred to the older man as his artistic "father." Both felt the stings of Viennese critics. Haydn's sin, as enunciated in 1772, was that he took folk music (which they described as "comic" music) too seriously. [10] Once, when some Viennese musicians and connoisseurs were engaged in tearing Mozart's *Don Giovanni* apart, they turned for confirmation to Haydn, who by then had an unassailable stature. He answered, "All I know is that Mozart is the greatest composer now living."[11] Mozart dedicated his set of six great string quartets (1782-85) to Haydn, an open acknowledgment of his musical debt. Both composers reflected the temper of the times. Thus in the midst of the *Sturm und Drang* outpouring of the late 1760's and early 1770's, Haydn wrote his poignant *Symphony No. 49 in F minor, "La Passione"* (1868), *the F Minor Quartet Op.* 20 *No.* 5 (1772), and the *"Trauer"* or *"Mourning" Symphony No.* 44 *in E minor* (1772). Mozart in 1773, aged seventeen, wrote the astonishingly stormy *Symphony No.* 20, *K.* 183, which is called the "little" G minor, to differentiate it from the "great" *G minor symphony, K.* 545, of his last years. Both Mozart and Haydn were members of the Masonic Brotherhood.

There is a basic Austrian folkish idiom which permeates the entire galaxy of Vienna composers. Thus Geiringer writes of Haydn's early work, that he "drew from the rich well of Viennese folk music which has been a source of rich inspiration to Mozart, Beethoven, Schubert, Brahms and many others."[12] We hear this idiom for example in Raphael's air, "Rollend in schäumenden Wellen"—"Rolling in foaming billows," in *The Creation.* It starts with an imitation of stormy waves, in the Handel oratorio tradition, and ends with a broad Schubertian melody that could fit perfectly *The Maid of the Mill.* The naive folk style tune that Papageno and Pamina sing near the end of the first act of Mozart's *The Magic Flute,* to the words, "Könnte jeder brave Mann solche Glockchen finden," is almost note for note the beginning of Schubert's song *Heidenroslein.* The melody of the slow movement of Haydn's *Symphony No. 93 in D* might have been lifted by Beethoven for the last movement of his "Pastoral" Symphony.

Haydn and Mozart differ however in their approach to folk music. With Haydn, the "country boy," the folkstrain is basic; part, so to speak, of his blood. This gives his music a lusty strength and directness of expression. Even when the music is humorous, its laughter is openhearted. Mozart was far more saturated in the polished, *galant* urban style of his time, which he turned to his own uses, sometimes sharpening it to the most refined and subtle wit, and sometimes "standing it on its head" to reveal the most anguished, heartbreaking feelings, going far beyond anything Haydn could write in this respect. Einstein, discussing their string quartets, expresses the difference in this way. "What divides them (Mozart's quartets) most sharply from Haydn's is that they are 'music made of music,' 'filtered' art. A quartet like Haydn's *Op. 33 No. 3,* the so-called *Bird Quartet,* remains quite alien to Mozart. It is composed, so to speak, if not in the open air, then at least at an open window."[13]

III

Not all of Haydn's melodies of course have a folk flavor. And even when we can call a melody "typical of folk music," it emerges from his hands with a polish and artistic concentration uniquely his own. But what is important is how intimately these melodies and motifs in folk style are connected to his great achievements in the realm of the symphony and string quartet. Haydn transformed the symphony into a form which Beethoven could take up and use to express the mighty conflicts, "inner" and "outer," engendered by the French Revolution. He made the string quartet into a vehicle for deep inward expression.

How he intensified the drama of these forms may be seen in his handling of the opening movements. The general pattern of a "first movement" was that of an exposition, presenting two "subjects," or groups of themes, of which the "second subject" was in a different key from the "first;" then a development section, carrying the opening material through many changes of key and other transformations; a recapitulation, in which the subjects returned in the opening key; and a coda, or "rounding out." Haydn expanded the development section to make it the dramatic heart of the movement. In his later works, he also transformed the recapitulation, with the psychological insight which told him that after the storms of the development, a simple return to the opening would sound unreal and naive. Likewise he made the coda into an intense review of the drama of the development. The basic character of the Haydn "first-movement form," (later known as "sonata form") is its organic tissue made of a combination and contrast of *parlando* and *tempo giusto* elements. By carrying his melodic *motifs* through changes of key, rhythm and dynamics, he could create a *parlando* or "speech-inflected" music which now entered the realm of impassioned declamation and a deep flow of inner mood. In contrast, the swinging, rhythm dominated melodies brought in a sense of the "outer world" of movement and life. He also intensified the emotional breadth of the other movements of the symphony, sonata and string quartet. He gave the songful slow movements a developmental and sometimes dramatic character; treated the *menuetto* third movements as musically rich rustic dances; gave the "happy ending" of the closing movement an added dramatic fire. And in work after work, we find that it is themes in folk style which Haydn will treat with such seriousness, making them the vehicle for his dramatic outbursts and deep meditations.

To give some examples of Haydn's deep and imaginative use of one such folk pattern, the triple time country dance, *ländler* or rustic waltz, there is the slow movement of the *Quartet in B flat, Op. 50 No. 1,* which becomes almost a "dance poem;" the slow movement of the *Symphony No. 102 in B flat,* where it takes on a dramatic intensity and poignant quality; the lovely soprano air, "With verdure clad," in *The Creation,* which is a wonderful example of how a composer can take popular motifs and transform them, giving them back to the people as a new song which is at the same time their own.

There are other popular patterns he uses; the march for example (originally a variant of the dance), as in the haunting slow movement of the *Quartet in F, Op. 77 No. 1,* and the boisterous slow movement of the *"Military" Symphony in G, No.* 100.

Nor does he employ only Austrian folk and popular material, but also Croatian and Hungarian, reflecting the presence of the many peoples of the Empire. Typical lighthearted examples of Hungarian gypsy music are the last movement of the *Trio for violin, 'cello and piano in G, No. 1,* (the "Gypsy Rondo," and the last movement of the *Harpsichord Concerto in D.* This sort of rollicking music might have pleased the Esterhazy princes, as a sort of jolly excursion among the folk. But Haydn also puts this material to deeper uses; the slow movement for example of the *Quartet in C, Op.* 54 *No.* 2, in which the first violin weaves poignant minor-key arabesques, in the *parlando* style of the Gypsy violinist.

It is typical of the great creative users of folk music, like Haydn, that far from this being a youthful style, a carryover from childhood, it deepens with maturity. Sometimes it takes half a lifetime for a composer to learn what he can really do with folk music, or to go through the experiences which make it loom up to him as profoundly important. The richest and most creative uses of folk material occur in Haydn's great works of the 1890's, in which the inner poetry and drama of his music also reach their height. Examples of the dramatic power are the great slow introductions to the last six symphonies. These introductions have their origin in the operatic recitative, but now become deep inner monologues or portentous declamations. In these last six symphonies the Haydn scholar H. C. Robbins Landon, notes six melodies, traceable to actual folk tunes, Croatian, Serb, Hungarian.[14] It is so with the quartets. In the last movement of a string quartet of this period, *Op. 71 No. 1, in B flat,* we have an exhilarating "Gypsy rhapsody," growing in the most subtle way out of typical folk turns of melody, syncopations, and drone-bass or "bapipe" effects. It is on a far higher level than the "Gypsy Rondo" movements. The oratorio *The Seasons* (1798-1801) is permeated with "pastoral" and folk music, such as the jolly dancing chorus, "Nun tönen die Pfeifen." An anecdote about this work illustrates Haydn's peasant sympathies. The libretto, which followed James Thomson's poem, *The Seasons,* was written by an aristocrat, *Baron* Gottfried van Swieten, with praises of "virtuous toil" and "industry" on the countryside that were as Geiringer remarks, "slightly nauseating.[15] Haydn said, "All my life I have been industrious, but it has never occurred to me to compose a 'Praise of Industry.' "[16]

One extraordinary composition of 1796-98 perhaps best sums up Haydn's feelings about folk music, the peasantry and nation; the *"Emperor" Quartet, in C, Op. 76 No. 3.* The work gets its name from the fact that the slow movement is a set of variations on the melody that Haydn had composed in 1797, as a patriotic national anthem. It is an extremely beautiful melody, about which arguments have raged as to whether it was or was not taken from a folk song. But there can be no question about the folk origin of the first movement. The main, opening theme is pure "country-side" folk, with its syncopation and the drone bass it develops. The folk quality is only subtly felt at first. And it is even less apparent in the development section, when the theme goes through one modulation after another, reaching a peak of dramatic excitement. But then at the very climax, to introduce the recapitulation, it emerges as a full-fledged, rousing and foot-stamping countryside dance. The quartet, because of the presence in the slow movement of the national anthem, must have had a special significance for Haydn, and it is as if he were saying through the first movement that the common folk were also the nation.

Haydn was not a "national" composer in the sense of the composers who consciously took this up as a slogan in the nineteenth century. But he is the start of the great line that leads to Smetana, Dvorak and Mussorgsky. In his creative and malleable use of folk material, demolishing the prevalent thought that this was exclusively comic or "buffoon" music, using it as a fit medium for his passionate expressions of feeling, deep meditations, tenderness, and dramatic proclamations, he says by implication that the people whom this music represents are not "nobodies," but human beings of deep feeling. They are important. Only by knowing them as kin can one know the nation.

IV

Considering the sophisticated circles in which Mozart was born and spent practically all of his life, it was hardly possible for him to have any other view of the peasantry and of "rustic music" than the patronizing one of the cities. Yet, he wrote many delightful folk-style waltzes, *ländler* and country dances, as a popular music for people to swing to in ballrooms and beer gardens. And touches of folk music, affectionately handled, enter his instrumental works. In the last movement of his *A major Violin Concerto, K. 219,* an early masterpiece, there is an episode in Hungarian Gypsy style. But this to Mozart, as to Vienna in general, fell into the category of "Turkish" or exotically "Eastern" music. In his scherzos he will sometimes insert sweet *ländler,* like that of the *E flat String Quintet, K. 614.* The last movement of his *G major Trio, K. 564* is a captivating set of variations on a folk-style waltz. Yet these speak for a lively interest in anything human in music; not for a special feeling of kinship like Haydn's for the peasant idiom.

Yet a popular music did lie at the heart of Mozart's style. It is the city popular music, of serenades, marches, entertainments, love songs, and "night music," a polished, airy music owing much to the Italian style but also turned into something indigenous to Vienna. His many *Serenades* and *Divertimenti,* as well as his early symphonies and concertos, exemplify his handling of this *galant* idiom, lovely in melody and refined in style. And his achievement was not to renounce this idiom but to transmute it. With a consummate mastery of the entire range of harmonic movement and modulation, he took this *galant* style, essentially lighthearted, *tempo-giusto,* a mixture of wit and tenderness, and turned it into a *parlando-rubato* music of inner monologue, disclosing the deepest unrest and tragic feelings; a side of reality not especially welcomed by his aristocratic public.

We can trace this transmutation in many works. The third movement, *Adagio,* of his *B flat Serenade for Thirteen Wind Instruments, K. 361,* is such a lovely piece of *galant* sentiment. In the slow movement of the later *C major Piano Concerto, K. 467,* he takes some of the exact material he had used in this serenade movement, simplifies it, and turns it into an expression of deep anguish, in the form of a dialogue between piano and orchestra. Another *galant* form is the *Romanze,* or genteel love song, usually starting slow, with one or two agitated middle sections. The air sung by the tenor in the first act of *The Magic Flute,* "Dies Bildnis ist bezaubernd schön," is such a *Romanze,* and a typical, beautiful, *galant* use of the form occurs as the slow movement of the *Serenade, "Eine kleine Nachtmusik," K. 425.* Then, turning to the slow movement of the great *D minor Piano Concerto, K. 466,* we again find a *Romanze,* but the *galant* atmosphere evaporates, replaced by the most poignant and personal musical speech. The slow movement of the equally great *E Flat Piano Concerto, K. 482,* starts with first orchestra, then piano, playing a touching, speech-inflected melody, like one of Mozart's more inward-probing operatic arias. Typical light "serenade" music enters, from the orchestral woodwinds. The piano further develops the opening melody. The "serenade" music appears again. The piano ignores it, to embark on a stormy, and then pathetic dialogue with the orchestra, based on the first melody. Then the "serenade" enters for the third time, and now the piano takes it up, turning it into utter heartbreak. Mozart rarely ends in so dismal a mood, and the last movement of this concerto is a combination of folk hilarity and radiant serenity.

The five masterpieces of comic opera that Mozart wrote in the last nine years of his life provide many clues to the content of his instrumental music, for the finely calculated musical imagery which he allots to his operatic characters recurs in the instrumental works, particularly the concertos. The comic operas are the finest flower of his combination of *galant* wit, representing the manners and conventions of society about him, and inner probings into the realities of life, with its unrest and yearning for freedom. Each opera differs from the others in both style, and the side of life it presents, or its content of thought. Together they make up a profound portrayal, sometimes realistic, sometimes symbolic, of his views of society and nation.

Mozart shared in the movement, patriotic and anti-feudal, for a German national theatre; for opera in a language the people understood. In a letter of 1783, he wrote, "I prefer German opera, even though it means more trouble for me. Every nation has its own opera and why not Germany?"[17] Two years later he wrote, "But then the German national theatre which is sprouting so vigorously would actually begin to flower; and of course that would be an everlasting blot on Germany, if we Germans were seriously to begin to think as Germans, to act as Germans, to speak German, and, Heaven help us, to sing in German! Completely convinced that I am talking to a true German, I have given rein to my tongue, a thing which unfortunately is so seldom possible these days." [18]Of course he had too agile a mind, and was too interested in every side of life and art, to limit himself to one vein. One of the remarkable aspects of his series of operas is their difference from one another, in subject, tone, emotional pattern, musical style, and in fact everything but genius. But two of the five great comedies are German operas, raising the popular *singspiel* tradition to a level of supreme art.

It is a mistake to think that Mozart would take any random libretto and set it to music. He knew what he wanted to say

Einstein writes of *The Abduction from the Seraglio* that it was "epoch-making" because in it Mozart "did full justice to the drama."[19] Mozart's father wrote when *The Marriage of Figaro* was in progress, "There will be a lot of running about and discussion, before he gets the libretto so adjusted as to suit his purpose exactly." [20]Of his mature operas, the one lifeless work, dramatically, is *Idomeneo* (1780-81), the subject of which had been handed to him by the Munich court. It is an essay in the outmoded "serious" Italian style, of pseudo-classical tragedy with a happy ending. Mozart solves the problem for the most part by writing "pure music." The opera is like a series of inspired *Divertimento* movements, beautifully elaborated for chorus and for the three high soprano voices that take the three leading roles. But it has never caught on as an opera. Except for some passages like the first scene of the third act, it lacks the dramatic life of the comedies, where some of the greatest music is inspired by the play of movement on the stage, the lightning changes of mood, the intriguing problems of realistic characterization, and the clash of the personalities.

The story of *The Abduction from the Seraglio* (1782), the first of the great comic series and the first of the two German language works, should not be taken as seriously as those of the later works. Yet it has some curious anticipations of the German masterpiece which came later, *The Magic Flute*. Both are set in the "mysterious East." In both the romantic hero is trying to rescue the heroine from a sumptuous palace, in which she is kept a prisoner. In both the hero has a servant who seeks his own mate. In both there is an evil, domineering henchman in the palace, who is later exposed. And in both there occurs the curious twist by which the awesome main "villain" who has seemingly captured the heroine (the Turkish Pasha in the *Seraglio,* the "magician" Sarastro in *The Magic Flute*) turns out to be the most moral figure in the play. Thus at the end, when the Pasha has foiled the rescue plot, he nobly releases the four prisoners, pointing out the injustices wreaked upon him by Europeans, with their "relentless greed," and yet abhorring revenge. "It seems to be a trait of your race to commit injustices. . . . I held your father too greatly in abhorrence ever to follow in his footsteps." But the morality of the Pasha does not dominate the opera as that of Sarastro dominates, musically and dramatically, *The Magic Flute*. In fact, the Pasha has no music at all. The censure of European "greed" is nevertheless an interesting thought for Mozart to have picked up. And some similarly interesting thoughts enter the play in regard to the independence of women. Thus Blondine, the servant of the heroine Constanze, repels the advances of Osmin, the clownish henchman of the Pasha, with such words as "Girls are not wares, to be made gifts of; I am an Englishwoman, born to freedom." Osmin is terrified. "She is capable of making all our women rebellious!" In another scene, the two men, the hero Belmonte and his servant Pedrillo, believe that they have rescued the two women, Constanze and Blondine. Suspicions suddenly come to the men, that the women might not have been entirely faithful, during their palace imprisonment. With fierce anger the wronged women turn on the men, forcing them to beg forgiveness. All this was of course primarily meant to evoke laughter. Yet it represents one of the more enlightened currents of thought of the time. And the rights of women, against the feudal "double standard," would blossom into a major theme of *The Marriage of Figaro.*

In the music, Mozart uses for his characterizations the rich variety of styles at his command. Constanze's great arias are an exalted version of the "grand manner" derived from Italian opera. Belmont's airs are in a lighter vein of the *Romanze,* or *galant* love song, with Mozart adding subtle comic touches, like the mock heart-beats in the orchestra during the first act air, *"O wie ängstlich."* There is an abundance, of course of the "Turkish" brand of Viennese popular music, featuring triangles and drums, and including one little masterpiece of exotic popular song, Pedrillo's serenade, "In Mohrenland gefangen war" with its melting "Moorish" chromaticisms. In the Austrian folk vein, but exalted into great art, is Osmin's first act air, "Wer ein Liebchen hat gefunden," and the duet between Blondine and Osmin in the second act, "O Englander!" is an enchanting folk *ländler.* Another rollicking example of popular song is the closing quintet. Mozart gave the people many fine songs to sing.

It was an act of courage for Mozart to use, for *The Marriage of Figaro* (1786), a play by Beaumarchais, who had been imprisoned in France. Although Mozart's librettist, Lorenzo da Ponte, assured the Emperor Joseph II that the "indecent" (meaning "subversive") lines had been taken out, the opera remains a two-front attack upon aristocratic privileges. One theme is the double standard in regard to women, portrayed in the

Count who is both a philanderer and insanely suspicious of his own wife. The other is the relation between servant and master, portrayed in the successful struggle of Figaro and Susanna for their right to love and marriage, against the interference of the same lascivious Count. As often in Mozart, the main characters are not "typed." They change, and they are rounded people. The Count is transformed into a loving husband (for how long, is anybody's guess). The cocky Figaro is given an aria of jealous rage, in the last act, almost reminiscent of the Count. The women are capable of both pathos and laughter. The music may be described as "urban popular" in style, but raised to a level of radiant beauty of melody, a sensitive responsiveness to every change of mood, a witty commentary upon its own sentiment, and a subtlety of interweaving threads—particularly in the great ensembles—unprecedented in opera. Figaro's air, "Non più andrai," which is also a satire upon the army, was one of Mozart's great popular "hits." It was orchestrated by Mozart and published as a popular dance (*Contredanses, K. 609*), and there is an amusing scene in the last act of *Don Giovanni* where it is heard from a stage orchestra as part of a "medley of popular tunes." There is deeper feeling, a touch of the "grand manner," in the two arias of the Countess. And there are many passages in which we can feel the breath of Austrian folk music; the choruses in the third act; the lovely "letter duet" between the Countess and Susanna, in which the folk style is justified by the Countess's explanation that this is a familiar *canzonetta;* the little air in the last act of Barberina, searching for a lost needle; and Susanna's great air, "Deh vieni non tardar," in which the music rises freely from its folk roots, a triple-time dancing melody, into a deep expression of love. This air illustrates the fine distinction Mozart draws between a genuine expression of heartfelt love, and a popular style song used for the game of love-making, as in the *galant* airs of the page, Cherubino.

In *Don Giovanni* (1787) Mozart creates one of his most inspired folk-music characterizations; the peasant girl, Zerlina. Like most of Mozart's women drawn from the common people—Blondine, Susanna, Despina—she is a remarkable person; far superior to her male counterpart, full of fire and wit, taught by hard life to be practical, with no high-flown illusions, willing to flirt and have fun, yet able to take care of herself. It is interesting to compare her captivating love aria, "Vedrai carino," to the equally moving love aria of the high-born Donna Anna,

"Non mi dir;" one in the folk vein, and the other in the "grand manner." High-born and low-born, to Mozart, have the same humanity.

The drama itself is based on one of those half-legendary stories that have a perpetual life, and continually take on a new significance. The story is of a rake, sensual and blasphemous, who invites to dinner the statue of a man he has killed, and finds that his invitation is accepted. It has a central place in Spanish drama, where the impious hero is Don Juan Tenorio. It is found in the folklore of other countries, and was a favorite of the Italian pantomime theatre. The fascination lies in the Don's combination of repellent cynicism, with the bravado of his defiance of not only society but the Devil himself. Mozart treats him musically like a chameleon, or an actor putting on one mask after another. His first act duet with Zerlina, the lovely "La ci darem la mano," is in folk style. He bubbles over with high spirits in his *galant* "champagne" area. He plays the lover in the second act with a Spanish serenade, in jota rhythm. The most striking change in musical characterization comes at the end, when the "stone guest" bursts into the Don's supper party, and drags him down to judgment. The music changes from rhythm-dominated *galanterie* to *parlando,* with the voices chanting over powerful, constantly modulating harmonies, chromatic upward and downward runs, and dissonant chords in the orchestra. It is like the nineteenth century breaking in upon the eighteenth, the heroic-flamboyant gestures of romanticism proclaiming their defiance of the tight little world of the *galant.* "No!" the Don cries, to demands that he repent. But in the end he cracks, with a despairing cry, intensified by a chromatic downward run in the orchestra. It is as if Mozart were showing both the emergence of a defiant individualism, and its collapse, because its defiance is of all society.

It is this critical detachment that keeps Mozart from ever being a romanticist. For all the heartbreak in his music, he never abandons himself to subjectivism. No one character in any of his work represents him; probably all have a part of him, which he can inspect ironically. For he can even laugh at himself. In such a context, Mozart's use of folk characters resembles that of Shakespeare. They are distant from him, they do not share his personal, poignant problems, but they are his ancestry, or the earth from which he grew.

It is the most remarkable testament to Mozart's breadth of

interests that he could have written two such works as *Cosi fan tutte* (1790) and *The Magic Flute* (1791), so completely different from one another, so close in time. But actually, the difference in style is due to the difference in milieu. *Così fan tutte* is wholly upper-class in subject; a satire, laughing but gentle, on love among young people who apparently have nothing else to do but play amorous games. *The Magic Flute* is Mozart's most folk-inspired work, not only a German language opera, in the *singspiel* tradition, but one not intended at all for court opera production. It was put on in a suburban theatre as a popular entertainment. The producer who commissioned it, Emanuel Schikaneder, was himself a comedian, singer, and impressario of a troupe of actors, who put on plays for popular audiences. He was one of the first Germans to act Hamlet. Like Mozart, he was a Mason, and the opera itself abounds in allusions to the Masonic liberal and humanitarian beliefs.

Così fan tutte is Mozart's most *galant* opera, spun of gossamer threads of music—gossamer gold, of course— and full of airy mockery. It proceeds on two levels, lovely to listen to as "pure music" and yet requiring the most careful matching of music against word to get the full play of his wit. And a third level emerges from the combination of the two, for the music will sometimes be mocking when the words seem to be serious, and serious when the words seem to be mocking. The story pretends to be in a real setting, unlike the fantasy of *The Magic Flute,* but it is utterly incredible. Two sisters have each a handsome adorer. The young men, on a wager, test the ladies' fidelity by pretending to go off to the wars, then returning in disguise, each making love to the other's sweetheart. Their assault breaks down the young girls' defenses. Then there is a general exposure, and consternation on the part of the women, but the four nevertheless go off to get married. There are profound moments in the music, as for example the great aria of one of the sisters, Fiordiligi, "Per pieta ben mio," music of deep inner conflict and aroused passion. And there is a very subtle psychology. It becomes apparent that of the sisters, Dorabella is a rather light-minded flirt, while Fiordiligi has a genuine conscience. Of the men, Guglielmo, who was originally betrothed to Fiordiligi, quickly learns to enjoy his new role, as a Don Juan, a breaker of hearts. (When Ferrando, who feels genuine anguish at the success of the stratagem, asks advice of Guglielmo in the second act, there is a witty allusion in the orchestra to the music of *Don*

Giovanni). Ferrando, originally betrothed to Dorabella, is a romantic, who puts women on a pedestal. And so, although the libretto never makes clear who at the end marries whom, the music makes it quite clear that at the outset the four were mismatched, and the new pairing, which started out as a pretense on the part of the men, is a much better arrangement. Folk music plays almost no role in the opera at all. The only character who might call for it is the pert, hard-headed ladies' maid, Despina. She is an attractive character but musically, however, no Zerlina.

The Magic Flute, on the other hand, is the first great contribution to a distinctly German national music since the *Cantatas* and *Passions* of Bach. It is distinguished as such not merely for its German language and use of popular traditions, but for the depth of its thinking, reflecting problems that faced the nation itself. The libretto was written by Schikaneder, with as always Mozart's careful attention and suggestions, and with perhaps the collaboration of another member of Schikaneder's troupe, Gieseke.[21] It is all fairy-tale fantasy and symbolism. It starts like a traditional fairy-tale romance. The handsome young prince Támino falls in love with the princess Pamina, simply on seeing her portrait. But she has been abducted by an evil magician, Sarastro. And Pamina's mother, the Queen of the Night, sends Tamino off to rescue her daughter. Sent along with him, as a squire or "Sancho Panza," is the bird-catcher, Papageno. But when the first act is about half over, the story is stood on its head. Tamino, arriving at the palace of Sarastro, discovers to his bewilderment that this is no evil place, but the temple of "Reason, Nature and Wisdom," (all of these being terms used at the time in the intellectual assault upon feudal institutions). As the plot develops, it discloses that the prince has been misled. Pamina, since the death of her father, had been subjected to the civil influences and "superstitions" of the Queen. For this reason, Sarastro had temporarily abducted her. And so, from the very standing of the plot on its head, a profound symbolism emerges. It is the conflict between "deceit" and "truth," between a tissue of lies and the disclosure of "reason."

The second act, which concludes the opera, takes up a more internal conflict of the heart and mind. It deals with Tamino's desire to be initiated into the temple, and with the series of ordeals which he must withstand, so that he can prove his right to marry Pamina. To a modern audience, not catching Mozart's allusions to the Masonic rites of his time, these ordeals seem childish, like a college fraternity hazing (which also is a residue of what were originally much more serious and significant secret society rituals). And yet these "ordeals" represent an enlightened thinking. They say that a person seeking to live as a "true man" and to be worthy of genuine love must conquer sensuality, impulsiveness, selfishness, grasping ambitions, feelings of hatred and revenge, and fear of death. Thus he wins "freedom" and lives as one who respects himself and loves his fellow men.

There are touches of anti-feudal satire amidst the buffoonery, and the likelihood is that in the orginal performance there were more, since Schikaneder, who acted the part of the "clown," Papageno, was known for his ad-libbing. (This was of course as far back as Shakespeare's day a common practise of those who played the clown). In the libretto, when Papageno first sees the prince Tamino, he asks, "Who are you?" Tamino answers, "I am of princely blood." And when Papageno asks, "What does that mean? I don't understand, explain it," merriment must have run through the theatre. When the Queen's ladies tell Papageno that he must go along with the prince on his dangerous mission, and that he can rely on the prince to protect him, Papageno replies, "Let the Prince go to the devil! I hold my life too dear. He'll run away." Again, in the opening of the second act, when the temple priests are discussing whether Tamino shall be accepted, one asks, "Does he love his fellow men?" Sarastro answers, "Yes." Another asks, "Will he have the strength to endure the ordeals that await him? Remember, he is a prince." Sarastro answers, "He is a man; that is enough." Princes were apparently not held in high esteem among the common people audiences.

The music is the least *galant* of Mozart's operas and the most folk-suffused. Along with the folk "tunefulness" it draws most richly upon what may be called his "learned" style, a style of long-breathed, sustained melody and of complex counterpoint (as in the *"Jupiter" Symphony,* with its wonderful fugal episodes in the *finale*). The first act abounds in folk style music, with "hit" melodies that show Mozart, in his "German" vein, to be a progenitor of Franz Schubert. Thus Papageno's entrance song, "Der Vogelfänger bin ich," is of the same family, although it differs in melody, as the song *"Das Wandern"* which opens Schubert's cycle *The Maid of the Mill.* And the music in folk vein extends beyond the folk characters. It is heard in the little 6/8 time passage sung by the Queen's three ladies near the opening; in the "padlock" quintet, which develops into one of Mozart's great ensembles; in the hauntingly beautiful air sung to Tamino by the three youths who guide him to Sarastro's castle, "Zum Ziele führt dich diese Bahn," which might have inspired the American folk song, "Goodnight, Irene;" in the duet, "Bei Männern" between Papageno and Pamina; in Tamino's sprightly air with flute obbligato, which is like a Mozart "Country dance," in the magic *glockenspiel* music, with which Papageno and Pamina cause their attackers to dance away.

The second act moves away from folk style. Papageno also fades more to the background. The dominant mood is inspired by the thoughts of human brotherhood, or the conquest of meanness, revenge and fear, and the music takes on both a "learned" and profoundly religious character. This is heard in the magnificent choruses at the opening of the act, and in Sarastro's great prayer for the welfare of Tamino, "O Isis und Osiris." The religious symbolism reaches its climax in the ordeal scene which frees Tamino from fear of death, "Der, welcher wandelt diese Strasse," which is based on a Lutheran chorale with a Bach-like counterpoint. It is a remarkable step for Mozart, the Catholic, to take, one perhaps inspired by his understanding of the national significance of the Lutheran chorales, or by the hope for an end to the religious differences that had torn the German people apart. There is also, in this act's music, a deeper probing of the mind. The Queen of the Night steals into the temple to destroy it, giving Pamina a knife with which to kill Sarastro. And Mozart provides a magnificent example of the power of music to express states of mind, in the contrast between the icy, coloratura brilliance of the Queen's aria, "Der hölle Rache," full of hardness and hate, and Sarastro's answering "In diesen heil'gen Hallen," with its peace and serenity.

There are some remarks in the libretto, part of Masonic thinking, about the inferiority of women, and their need for man's guidance, which Susanna of *The Marriage of Figaro* would have snickered at. But Mozart at the same time gives the most profound aria in the opera to a woman, Pamina, "Ach, ich fühls." It occurs when on the stage she is about to kill herself, believing that Tamino does not love her. Nobody in the audience of course took this melodrama seriously. But the music, abandoning "tunefulness" for a *parlando* style of deep psychological penetration, is the kind which Mozart uses in his instrumental works to portray his own deep anguish. With its chromatic phrases, and development to a climax of wide leaps of the voice, it expresses genuine heartbreak and tragedy, picturing a woman who has spiritually lost her own mother. Later, she and Tamino are given the most rapturous of love duets. There is still folk-style music in this act around Papageno, a pot-pourri of waltzes, ländler and country-dances. And he takes part in one delightful bit of satire. Shortly after Pamina's frustrated attempt at suicide, Papageno decides that he will never find a mate, and he too prepares to hang himself. But the tune to which he sadly sings, "Farewell, cruel world," is a rustic waltz. It is typical of Mozart that he should thus be able to burlesque one of his own earlier most tragic musical scenes, that of Pamina's heartbreak.

Mozart needed courage to write this "Masonic" opera, and its greatness as a music-drama is a sign of the fact that in writing directly for the common people, he gave them his best, most serious thinking. Between 1780 and 1786 the Freemasons had become somewhat respectable in Vienna, even boasting some public officials and members of the nobility among their members. But then the mood of the court changed. Many members were frightened into leaving the Order. With the outbreak of the French Revolution, in 1789, its origins were ascribed to the Freemasons. Yet *The Magic Flute* was performed twenty-four times in the month following its opening, and one hundred times, in Vienna, during the following year. But on December 5, 1791, Mozart was dead.

It was especially sad that Mozart should have died then. Not only was he but thirty-five years old, and accordingly the world has lost inestimable treasures. There was also a spirit of freedom beginning to rise in Vienna and Austria, despite the harsh repressive measures of the court. This spirit could be felt in the new, untouchable status of Haydn. Although technically still in the Esterhazy service, he was no longer the musician in livery, but the "great man" of the city. It could be felt musically, in the turbulence and passion of Haydn's symphonies and quartets of the 1790's, such as the very last symphony, *No. 104 in D.* It could be felt in the continued success of *The Magic Flute.* By 1794 the opera was the rage far beyond Vienna, although that was the year the frightened court banned the Freemasons. And in 1794 a gifted young pianist and composer, who had come to study with Haydn, wrote a letter from Vienna indicating not only the unrest in the city but his own boldness of mind. "Many persons of importance have been arrested; they say there was fear of a revolution breaking out—but it is my belief that so long as an Austrian can get his brown beer and sausages, there will be no revolution. The gates in the suburb are ordered to be closed at ten o'clock at night. The soldiers have loaded guns. One dare not speak too loud, for otherwise the police will accomodate you for the night."[22] The writer was Ludwig van Beethoven.

V

This boldness and directness of thought would be translated into a boldness and directness of musical expression. And helping make this possible was also the fact that within a few years, in Central Europe, the social status of the composer would change more radically than it had in the entire preceding century. Bringing freedom from exclusive dependence upon aristocratic patronage, replacing the livery of a servant with the plain dress of a citizen addressing all others as his equals, was the bourgeois marketplace. By 1800 Beethoven's works were being eagerly sought by publishers, widely purchased, and bringing him a considerable income. The bourgeois marketplace had of course its own contradictions. It demanded that a priceless work of art be bargained for, sold and consumed like a manufactured commodity. Later composers would bewail the brutal competition forced on them by the marketplace, and its contempt for artistic standards, some of them even lamenting the passing of the old court patronage. But the marketplace was a step to liberation. And Beethoven, conscious of its contradictions, realist and visionary in one, projected—half jokingly, and yet with deep insight—a still further liberation, sounding like the socialists's, "From each according to his abilities, to each according to his needs." Sometime in January, 1801 he wrote this letter to the publisher Hoffmeister, in Leipzig:

"You may perhaps be surprised that I make no difference of price between the sonata, septet and symphony. I do so because I find that a septet or symphony has not so great a sale as a sonata, though a symphony ought unquestionably to be of the most value. I only ask ten ducats for the concerto, for, as I already wrote to you, I do not consider it one of my best. I cannot think that, taken as a whole, you will consider these prices exorbitant; at least, I have endeavored to make them as moderate as possible for you. . . . The entire sum for the four works will amount to 70 ducats; I understand no currency but Vienna ducats, so how many dollars in gold they make in your money is no affair of mine, for really I am a very bad man of business and accountant. Now this troublesome business is concluded;—I call it so, heartily wishing that it could be otherwise here below! There ought to be one grand *depot* of art in the world, to which the artist might repair with his works, and on presenting them receive what he required; but as it now is, one must be half a tradesman besides—and how is this to be endured?"[23]

4. CLASSIC FORM AND SOCIAL REVOLUTION

"For the true originality of the artist no less than that of his work consists exclusively in their being vitally bound up with that which is only intelligible as part of the real subject-matter treated. When the artist has fully appropriated this objective reason, without mixing up with it, to the detriment of its clarity, details he may have borrowed from his personal experience or other sources which do not strictly belong to it; in that case alone will he stamp the material with the genuine mark of his own artistic mintage. . . . In this way the originality of art absorbs every accidental trait peculiar to a given personality; but it only absorbs it that the artist may follow without reserve the impulse and bent of his genius as inspired through every fibre of the material he moulds, and instead of reflecting a purely barren wilfulness and caprice of his own may give an objective form to his true artistic inviduality conjoined with consummate accomplishment. To have no 'manner' was ever the one great 'manner,' and in this sense alone can we describe originality to Homer, Sophocles, Rafael, and Shakespeare."

—GEORG WILHELM FRIEDRICH HEGEL, *The Philosophy of Fine Art.*

I

Ludwig van Beethoven (1770-1827) was of Flemish ancestry, and born at Bonn, in the Electorate of Cologne. It was one of the principalities of the Holy Roman Empire, and being on the Rhine, was particularly sensitive to the ideas emanating from revolutionary France. His father was a mediocre musician and his mother the daughter of a cook. In 1787 Ludwig, having made a local musical reputation, went to Vienna and played for Mozart, who is reported to have said, "Keep your eyes on him; some day he will give the world something to talk about." In 1792 he went again to Vienna, to study with Haydn. Thereafter the city became his home.

Beethoven's consciousness of "nation" went through different periods not because of any caprice on his part, but because of the hectic course of world events, to all of which he reacted like a thoughtful and enlightened mind. There were five such periods in his development, to which we can roughly give these dates: 1790-99; 1800-04; 1805-15; 1816-22; 1822-27.

The letter of 1794 quoted near the end of the last chapter makes it quite clear that in Vienna at the time, Beethoven did not think of himself as an Austrian, nor of the Austrians as his people. Vienna, which was honored by possessing not only the Imperial court, but also more aristocracy to the square mile than any other city in Central Europe, was the foremost musical center where a talented, ambitious pianist and composer could spread his wings. But it was not "homeland." In 1800 he wrote to a Freemason friend, Dr. Franz Wegeler, in Bonn: "My native land, the beautiful country in which I first saw the light of the world, is ever as beautiful and distinct before mine eyes as when I first left you. In short, I shall regard that time as one of the happiest of my life, when I see you again, and can greet our father Rhine. You will only see me again when I am really great; not only greater as an artist, but as a man you shall find me better, more perfect; and if in our native land there are any signs of returning prosperity, I will only use my art for the benefit of the poor."[1] He yearns for a "homeland," and sees it not in Austria but in the Rhineland. To have such national and patriotic ideas is a renunciation of the thinking in the feudal minded courts. And he adds to this the non-feudal concept of himself as an "artist," not a hired, talented craftsman. He also sees that growth as an artist must be accompanied by growth as a social human being.

Beethoven's first published works, of 1793-1800, have obvious ties to the heritage of which Haydn and Mozart were the foremost masters, but what is also important, from the very first, is the difference they show. Absent from his temperament are the peculiarly Mozartian qualities of a serious-comic spirit, a *galant* wit under the surface of which lie tragic undercurrents and heartbreaks. For example the last movement of Beethoven's *First Piano Concerto Op. 15* (1797) and that of Mozart's *A Major Violin Concerto K. 219* are both humorous, and have a light "Turkish music" episode. But Beethoven's humor is rough, boisterous and more than a little unsubtle. Mozart's movement (written when the composer was only nineteen), is at the outset more *galant,* and then goes through mercurial changes, with an airier wit and also a suddenly serious, passionate outburst.

For another example, the theme which opens the last movement of Mozart's great *G minor Symphony, K. 550,* was also used by Beethoven as the main theme of the first movement of his first published piano sonata, *Op. 2 No. 1 in F minor.* Mozart unfolds through this theme a series of surprises, interlacing wit with anguish. At the beginning of the development section of the movement, to prepare the listener for the onset of tragedy, he provides a sudden harmonic jolt, making the theme part of a twelve tone row, presenting all the twelve tones of the chromatic scale before any one of them is repeated. It anticipates, but only as a special touch for a limited purpose, a harmonic pattern that Schönberg in the twentieth century would make the basis for an entire style. Beethoven's development of the same theme is also dramatic, but in a straightforward and unsubtle manner. In both comparisons cited, Mozart's music happens to be deeper and greater than Beethoven's. But that is not as important as the new manner Beethoven shows, of a blunt directness of expression. He does not need Mozart's protective comic mask. There is more freedom in the air he breathes. And this is seen as well in actual life, as in his relations to the Viennese aristocracy. He will write works that they find entertaining, and he will accept their patronage. But he will not shape his main output to their tastes. They must go along with him on the path he has chosen.

From the outset, Beethoven is a bold experimenter, turning over the heritage to discover what can be done to extend its expressive powers. And this is marked as well in his differences from Haydn, who also has this emotional directness. Beethoven is less prolific than Haydn in sweetly singing and folk-inspired melodies. But he aims at deeper psychological matters, taking up short motifs, often far more bare melodically than Haydn's, and developing them harmonically into sustained interior monologues. Examples are the slow movements of all three piano sonatas of *Op. 2* (1795), the whole of the brooding, introspective *Piano Sonata Op. 7* (1797), and the *Second Piano Concerto, Op. 19* (1795-98).

II

The second period, beginning roughly about 1800, finds Beethoven seemingly on the top rungs of success. As Bekker writes, "In his thirtieth year he had won a position seldom attained by others in old age."[2] He has made a name not only with titled patrons but with the general audience, giving his first public Vienna concert on April 2, 1800. The next year brings the terrible awareness of his growing deafness. But he fights off his misery. And he makes himself a representative now not of "nation" but of the liberal, anti-feudal and democratic sentiments that had been touched off by the French Revolution, and which had started fires blazing in all Europe. He becomes a "patriot" of international humanitarian progress.

There is an especially interesting letter of 1802, to a Leipzig publisher, Hoffmeister. "Do you mean to go poste-haste to the devil, gentlemen, by proposing that I write *such* a *sonata?* During the revolutionary fever, a thing of the kind might have been appropriate, but now, when everything is falling again into the beaten track, and Buonaparte has concluded a Concordat with the Pope—such a sonata as this? If it were a *missa pro Sancta Maria a tre voci,* or a vesper &c., then I would at once take up my pen and write a *Credo in unum,* in gigantic semibreves. But good heavens! Such a sonata, in this fresh dawning Christian epoch. No! No! – it won't do, and I will have none of it. Now for my answer in quickest *tempo.* The lady can have a sonata from me, and I am willing to accept the general outlines of her plan in an *aesthetical* point of view, without adherence to the keys named."[3] It indicates many things. One is that Beethoven keeps abreast of European politics. He is an admirer of Napoleon, in spite of the hostilities that have occurred between France and Austria. Napoleon seems to him to have been carrying on the ideals of the French Revolution. Yet he now has some doubts, because of the treaty between Napoleon and the Pope. He fears a maneuver to stifle further progress, a "fresh dawning Christian epoch," meaning a renewed epoch of close ties between Church and State, with a clerical-police censorship over freedom of thought and intellectual life. Also, the letter makes clear that Beethoven's objections to writing what is apparently a sonata with a political viewpoint, even a kind of "program," is only based on immediate practicality. He has no objection to this in principle. He will of course choose his own keys, not those the lady apparently suggested. And he will work out the music "aesthetically."

What sonata Beethoven had in mind for the politically conscious lady, nobody knows, or even whether he wrote it and ended by dedicating it to somebody else. But it could well have been the germ of what blossomed in his mind as the great

Symphony No. 3, "Eroica," which he began in 1803 and produced in 1804. As everyone knows, he wrote on the title-page of the symphony, "Buonaparte." Then, when his pupil, Ferdinand Ries, brought the news that Napoleon had proclaimed himself Emperor, Beethoven changed the title-page, crying, "Now he too will trample on all the rights of man and indulge only his own ambition. He will exalt himself above all others, become a tyrant."[4] It is safe to say that the symphony, while not intended as a biography of Napoleon, was dedicated to the struggle of the "hero" for the rights of man, against aristocracy and tyranny.

In the works of 1801-04, his experimentation goes far beyond his former boundaries. This is especially seen in the piano sonatas; *Op. 27 No. 1,* with an unorthodox formal layout which curiously anticipates his great *A flat Sonata Op. 110* of many years later; its fellow "Fantasy" Sonata, equally unconventional, *Op. 27 No. 2,* to which the title "Moonlight" has stuck like a burr; the *"Pastoral" Sonata Op. 28,* which is a wonderful exercise in the structural use of rhythmic motifs. And in this period the attachment of a "poetic" idea to an instrumental work becomes an important aspect of his thinking as another step beyond Mozart and Haydn.

Of course, there was a base in the preceding classic tradition for such a relation between "pure music" and literary ideas. The symphony itself had grown out of the Italian opera overture, or *sinfonia.* Haydn had extended the dramatic aspect of the symphony, with its statements followed by answers, its outbursts of declamation and sharp dynamic contrasts. The great slow movements of Mozart's piano concertos were obviously carved out of the substance of his operatic recitatives and arias. And so when Anton Schindler, Beethoven's secretary and early biographer, says that Beethoven's sonatas were described as "operas in disguise,"[5] this meant that Vienna audiences were hearing in Beethoven's music, as they had heard in Haydn's and Mozart's, a kind of declamation, monologue and drama which had formerly been the province of opera. Beethoven, however, added both more intense drama and a more definite frame of reference.

Ries says, "Beethoven, in composing, frequently imagined for himself a definite subject."[6] Much later, in 1823, Schindler writes that he asked Beethoven, "Why he had not affixed to the different movements of his sonatas an explanation of the poetic ideas they had expressed. . . . His answer was that the age in which he composed his sonatas was more poetic than the present, and that at the former period such explanations would have been superfluous."[7] Beethoven himself attached to the third movement of his *Piano Sonata Op. 26* the title, "Funeral march on the death of a hero," thus making it one of the early steps towards the great funeral march of the *"Eroica" Symphony.* He said that the slow movement of the *Quartet in F, Op. 18 No. 1* was inspired by the tomb scene in *Romeo and Juliet,* and that the clue to the *Piano Sonata Op. 31 No. 2* lay in Shakespeare's *The Tempest.* It was he who said, of the opening theme of the *Fifth Symphony,* "Thus Fate knocks at the door."

Of course, the invention of literary programs for Beethoven's works by subsequent critics and commentators has been carried to the point of absurdity. Thus there have been discussions over the precise battles of Napoleon depicted in the *"Eroica Symphony,* and the *scherzo* has been described as portraying this absurd scene: "a crowd, full of excitement awaits the hero; he arrives and addresses them in the trio."[8] The clue to his method lies in Beethoven's own letter, about the "political sonata," when he says that he will proceed "aesthetically," or in other words, by recreating the "poetic" idea in terms of the principles of organization, consistency and unity proper to musical form. Thus, he does not present musical cryptograms, or guessing games. He presents human images and portraits, psychologically true, as music can do so well. Accordingly, in the slow movement of the *Quartet in F, Op. 18 No. 1,* the "tomb scene of Romeo and Juliet," it would be absurd to seek the moment that Romeo enters or Juliet awakes. What it presents to us is Beethoven's meditation on the needless death of two young lovers. And so the music revolves about his own philosophy of death, which is that one never accepts it without a struggle. Unmistakeable are the deep lament, the partly consoling answer, and the struggle, which starts with the development section and reaches its greatest intensity in the coda. We can accordingly recognize in this movement a great step towards the profound meditation on death in the Funeral March of the "Eroica." The point of such an approach, namely towards a "human portrait" rather than a narrative, is that it discloses for us not a story Beethoven is telling, or a musical "illustration," but his own views of life and human character; his own "self" as well as the subject of the work. And such an approach fits perfectly "sonata form" itself, the value of which is that it can capture, in so malleable a way, human psychology, with its storms, contrasting moods, questions and decisions.

The "Eroica" marked a turning point in Beethoven's approach to "nation," for world events were then taking a new turn. Napoleon, as Beethoven had recognized when he changed the dedication of the symphony, had become an absolute monarch. And from this point on, Napoleon showed himself openly as an enemy of the national independence and sovereignty of other peoples. He was exporting to other lands, not democracy, but kings of his own choosing. The movement that began to rise slowly against him was a Europe-wide popular war of national liberation. It is this that in the end caused his defeat. In the process, the freedom movement aroused deep conflicts and fears in the mind of the kings and princes whose lands were thus being "liberated," for it threatened their own absolutism.

It is in this third period that Beethoven thinks as an Austrian, and a German patriot. Thus in a letter of 1806, he speaks of himself as feeling "the patriotism of a German," which makes Vienna "precious to him."[9] But this does not mean that he abandons the fervent depiction of human victory against tyranny. He carries this banner even higher. The opera *Fidelio* and the *Egmont* music make this clear in their texts. But the same spirit characterizes all the big works of this period, with their storm and conflict, their jubilant feeling of humanity making great strides forward. The story is told of the French grenadier who, on hearing the opening of the finale of the *Fifth Symphony,* with its crescendo and then the brass entering in a tremendous processional, cried out, *"C'est l'empereur, vive l'empereur."* He caught the spirit of the music, although he attached to it his own illusions about Napoleon.

Beethoven also, at this time, develops a richer use of folk style in his works, as in the *Fourth Symphony,* where the ravishing dance melodies are much refined from their folk base, and the *Sixth Symphony, "Pastoral,"* where folk-style melodies adorn every movement, including the slow *ländler* in the scene "by the brook." His patriotism is not inspired by any homage to the Austrian aristocracy, but by the opposite. He expresses contempt for many of the nobility. In 1806, he wrote half-jokingly about the titled personages who controlled the Vienna Imperial Theatre, "I can't get on with this princely theatre rabble."[10] In 1810 he wrote, "There is nothing smaller than our great folk."[11] The same year he expressed pleasure at the fact that a song of his had been taken up by a Freemason lodge.[12] Two years later he would write of the "many rich folk who betray inward poverty."[13] There was no contemporary he admired more than Goethe, as the intellect and the many-sided national poet he was. Yet he roundly scolded Goethe for his obsequiousness to people of title. "Court air suits Goethe more than becomes a poet. One cannot laugh much at the ridiculous things *virtuosi* do, when poets, who ought to be looked on as the principal teachers of the nation, forget everything amidst this glitter."[14] This also underlines Beethoven's own exalted concept of the artist, so different from the role allotted by the aristocracy. The artist is the "teacher of the nation." And a later letter confirms this in respect to himself. "I have always tried from childhood onwards to grasp the *meaning of the better and the wise* of every age. It is a disgrace for any artist who does not think it his duty to do at least that much."[15]

Behind Beethoven's feelings about the court and aristocracy was his sensing of the fact that they were becoming the obstacle to the freedom of their nation; a fact that would be glaringly evident in Spain, where the king and nobility humbly accepted the rule of the French invaders, while it was the city population and peasantry who carried on insurrection and guerilla warfare. In 1806, the year that he described himself as feeling the "patriotism of a German," Beethoven furiously broke off friendship with Prince Lichnowsky, who had requested him to perform for the French officers in Austria. In 1809 Beethoven roundly cursed the French who were invading Vienna. The same year, he wrote to his friends, the publishers Breitkopf and Haertel in Leipzig, "What do you say to this dead peace,—I expect nothing solid any more in this age"[16] The "dead peace" was the obsequious surrender of the Austrian court to the French.

In fact, it was not until Napoleon's defeats mounted up, in 1813, that the Austrian government threw its weight into the war against Napoleon. But from 1809, the common people were taking an active part in the liberation movements. This was the year of the Spanish guerilla war, which continued until the French were evicted. There was insurrection in the Tyrols. In 1812, the common people of Russia rose in guerilla war to harry the French, retreating from Moscow. And Napoleon's retreat through Prussia touched off a national liberation movement in that country as well, to which the Prussian court had to give its approval, although terrified at the accompanying secret societies and inflammatory statements. Early in 1812, when Napoleon's star was beginning to wane, Beethoven finished his overwhelming outburst of joy, the *Seventh Symphony.* It was not meant of course as a celebration of victory, but it discloses his own exuberant joy in life, and sense of untrammeled freedom, as if a weight had been lifted. On its heels came the *Eighth Symphony,* which plays about with a *ländler* in its first movement, and is throughout, with its stops, starts and surprises, his most hilariously witty work.

III

The period that followed the conclusive defeat of Napoleon, in 1815, brought a sharp turn and set-back of democratic hopes. The Council of Vienna, of 1814-15, and the Holy Alliance formed by Austria, Prussia and Russia, engineered by Metternich, set about ruthlessly stamping out the democratic and national liberation fires that had been ignited in Europe. Absolute monarchs were put back on their thrones. Promises made of constitutions were revoked. The Alliance tried even to reach out to the Americas. The atmosphere in Vienna was particularly thick with clerical-police censorship, witch-hunts, arrests and persecution of dissenters and liberals.

In an atmosphere in which censorship extinguished the light of the mind, superstition replaced reason, a dreamy escape replaced the bold facing of social realities, and patriotism lost its democratic anti-feudal character to become a cloak for the return of the old aristocracy, Beethoven could no longer find a public role. Thus a new period begins for him. So far as big-scale symphonic-heroic works are concerned, there is a decade of silence. He turns to the more intimate form of the piano sonata, for works of harrowing inner conflict, and deep anguish, reaching its most heartrending expression in the slow movement of the Sonata Op. 106, "Hammerklavier," (1818-19).

The reasons frequently offered for Beethoven's "late period" anguish are personal matters. Cited are the isolation caused by his deafness, his financial difficulties caused in part by war inflation, the unpleasant court struggle he carried on to become the guardian of the son of his dead brother Carl, and love affairs with women whose social position made it impossible for them to marry him. It is true that these matters affected Beethoven deeply, but to make them the dominant element in his musical thought is to mistake his character as an artist. A man addressing society, thinking of his role as that of a "teacher of the nation," does not occupy his hearers with his private troubles. Thus Beethoven's deafness was a terrible blow. But it was as early as 1801 that he had to face the agonizing fact that this failure of his hearing was incurable. Yet he embarked from this on a decade of grandly optimistic, heroic works. There would again be great outbursts of joy in the works of his very last years.

Beethoven's art, like all art, is "self-expression." But the question remains, what kind of "self" is thus expressed? His was that of a social human being, whose deepest feelings derive from his awareness of the great social movements outside of himself, that affect both him and every other human being about him. In a letter of 1815, he lamented, "I may say that I live almost alone in this greatest city of Germany, and am forced to live apart from all those whom I love, whom I could love."[17] This is the outcry not of a man who has withdrawn from society—"Who can escape the storms from without?"[18] he says in another letter—but of one who finds obstacles blocking his deepest desire, to live socially.

The anguish is a social one. He has his country. In a letter of 1815 he writes of himself as "a poor German, or rather Austrian."[19] In Vienna he is an untouchable figure, for his great works have made him a world citizen. Schindler wrote in his biography, "If space permitted, I could relate interesting particulars of Germans, Russians, Swedes, Poles, Danes, French, and especially English, who approached Beethoven with all the deference they would pay to a sovereign."[20] In 1820, he could proudly tell a Berlin publisher, "You need only put this address, 'to Ludwig van Beethoven, Vienna.' " But if it was taken for granted that he was the musical genius of the age, this did not keep his material circumstances from being frequently miserable, nor did it mean that an active public was listening to him any more. The democratic hopes had been blighted. A pall of reaction hung heavy. His own democratic reputation was probably laughed off as one of his "eccentricities," as in the case of a venerable reformer still living in a period of reaction, who is too esteemed to be denounced, but must therefore be treated as a queer character, a representative of an outmoded generation. In 1815 he wrote to Breitkopf and Haertel a letter which curiously recalls the "brown beer and sausages" letter of two decades before: "Now farewell, your present political state does not please me, but-but-but-well, children who are not grown up want dolls—so there is nothing more to say."[21]

The great works from 1815 to his death in 1827 lay bare Beethoven's tremendous inner struggle. He was practical enough to be unable to hope for any immediate break in reaction and a leap forward by the people. And so the struggle became one to regain a general faith in humanity, with a hope for the future. The last great piano sonatas depict this slow, painful wrestling with despair. It is revealed down to its utter depths in the slow movement of the *"Hammerklavier"* but even here we see that Beethoven is always a fighter; there are the hammering blows on a single note in the closing section, and the colossal fugue that follows creates a mood of driving defiance. The slow movement of the *Sonata Op. 110,* is likewise tragic, but the closing fugue has a grand and hopeful mood. Then with the *Sonata Op. 111* (1822), heartbreak dissolves into serenity.

This may be said to mark another turning point, the regaining of a firm unshakeable faith in humanity. It is blazoned forth in the *Ninth Symphony,* with its setting of Schiller's "Ode to Joy," and its refrain, "All men are brothers." This symphony, which had been tentatively planned as early as 1817, was completed in 1823 or early in 1824. With it, and its companion work in time, the *Missa Solemnis* (1818-23), Beethoven has exorcised anguish and taken his place again as a citizen of the world.

There are still heartrending expressions in the five string quartets that follow, as in the *Cavatina* of the *Quartet Op. 130,* but for all the inner probing of the quartets, the moods are generally more serene and hopeful. Over the slow movement of the *Quartet Op. 132* Beethoven inscribed, "Song of thanksgiving to the Divinity from one who is healed of illness." He had been seriously ill in 1825, the year of this quartet. But illness had dogged him all of his life. And it is not extreme to suggest that the illness of which he felt healed was that of having almost lost faith in people. Also in this last period come some wonderful musical jokes like the *Rondo, Op. 129,* for piano which he entitled, "Rage over a lost penny," and in which he throws handfuls of purposefully jarring modulations, dissonances and rhythms, with a whimsical laughter foreshadowing Ravel and Prokofiev. There is the last movement of the *Quartet Op. 135,* over which he wrote, "Must it be? It must be! It must be!" and parodied in the music the inflections of speech. Indeed the last movement of the *Ninth Symphony* begins with one of these merry jokes.

Only a man who had been able to get out of his own skin, who had triumphed over every blow dealt him, who knew his worth and yet could laugh at himself, would have been able to write as he did in 1824, "Apollo and the Muses will not yet hand me over to the Scythe Man, for I still owe them much; and before my departure to the Elysian Fields, I must finish what the spirit suggests to me and commands me to finish. It is to me as if I had only written a few notes."[22]

IV

The classic style, of which Beethoven was so great a representative, is perhaps best characterized by Hegel's remark that "to have no 'manner' was ever the one great 'manner.'" A truly classic work, once created, seems like something that has always existed, or else is something created by the real world itself, with the artist only a self-effacing collaborator. It embodies the deepest personal feelings, and yet retains solidly its sense of real and outer life. It seems to be shaped with complete freedom, ignoring rules and set patterns, following wherever life calls, and yet is clear and defined in outline, firm, strong and rounded in architecture. Its elements, such as, in music, themes, motifs, expository and developmental sections, recapitulations, whole movements, are themselves clearly outlined and defined. It achieves all-over unity not through a homogeneous texture, the rubbing out of transitions, continuous flow, but through sharp contrasts, oppositions and conflicts which are resolved and then reappear on a new level. In this, it follows the dialectic of life, which also proceeds through conflicts and resolutions. A truly classic art can appear only from a social mind, whose deepest personal feeings are bound up with the issues that affect his fellow men along with himself; one who tries to shape the world as much as be buffeted by it. Thus the classic achievements of Beethoven are a tribute not only to his genius, but to the colossal world changes of his time, of which he made himself the spokesman, and of which the profound human portraits in his work are the fit embodiment.

Folk music as such does not loom high in Beethoven's big works. He uses it occasionally as in the *"Pastoral"* Symphony, where it becomes part of a "nature" piece, or in the "Rasoumovsky" String Quartets, where he inserted three Russian folk tunes to please his Russian admirer, Count Rasoumovsky (slow movement of *Op. 59 No. 3, scherzo of Op. 59 No. 2, Finale of Op.59 No. 1)*. There is an engaging Polonaise in the last movement of his *Triple Concerto, Op. 56*. In a letter of 1820 to the publisher Simrock, he transcribed two Austrian folk songs, with the comment, "I think a hunt after folk songs is better than a hunt after men of the so praised heroes."[23] He wrote a quantity of popular-style songs, choruses, marches and dances, which do not display the affectionate, creative attachment that his younger contemporary, Franz Schubert, would show to such forms.

Beethoven's search is for motifs that, however unimpressive when out of context, would provide the exact building or germinating elements for his great psychological portraits in music. Sometimes he finds them in popular imagery, as in the march motifs that suffuse the *Fifth Syphony*. In any case, to shape these motifs exactly as he wanted them is a long and laborious process, as his notebooks show. It is not the motif, theme or opening melody that suggests the course of the music. Rather, it is when he has established the general concept of the movement itself, that he fixes the motifs and themes in their final shape. But in two works of the greatest importance both to Beethoven and to the world, he deliberately and consciously adopts popular-style melodies, distinctly recognizeable as such. They are the *Third, "Eroica" Symphony* and the *Ninth*. In both the concluding movements are largely in "popular style"; a fact which throws great light upon his social thought.

The *"Eroica" Symphony* deals not with Napoleon, as Beethoven showed by his angry change of the dedication, but with the great democratic revolutionary movement of which Napoleon had seemed for a time the symbol. The four movements of the symphony give us four great human portraits which this event suggested to Beethoven, or four aspects of the event itself.

The first movement throws us in the midst of the conflict, and for this Beethoven found apt to his purpose the classic "sonata form" or "first movement form" as developed by Haydn. It consisted of four approximately equal divisions, "Exposition," "Development," "Recapitulation" and "Coda," with each section a dramatic transformation of the previous one. (Mozart favored a quite different plan, in which a comparatively short development section is a poignant commentary on the wit of the exposition). The exposition begins with two thundering chords, after which the 'cellos present the first theme. It was shaped by Beethoven from a melody that Mozart had written at the age of twelve, in the overture to a little opera, *Bastien and Bastienne.* But what had been a light rococo melody as Mozart wrote it, is now given a driving, proclamatory character. It is expanded upon, with its impact intensified. Then, about thirty-five bars past the opening, an answering, second motif, is heard, a chromatic and plaintive descending phrase, like the first theme "upside down." There are dissonant chords, which presage the conflict and unrest to come later; then the exposition is rounded out, coming to a definite end, with a transformed version of the first theme, in which what remains is its powerful rhythmic drive. The development section has two parts. First is the portrayal of struggle. The plaintive, reflective answering motif is heard and expanded, with then the first theme appearing in the bass, the two being pitted against each other. A searing depiction of conflict and unrest follows, reaching a climax in a succession of clamoring dissonant chords and "shock" changes of key. Then comes the second part of the development, with a new thought, an awareness of losses in the struggle. The first, or main theme, is transformed into a hauntingly sad, minor key melody, sung by the oboes. Feelings of struggle continue, but the sadness becomes dominant, the music almost coming to a halt. Then the recapitulation presents not merely a return to the opening themes, in the opening key, but at the same time, a qualitative leap. The French horn sings the main, or first theme, but it is now magically transformed. Its eighth note, instead of descending, as before, now remains high, becoming the same as the seventh note. And this little change has the psychological effect of a banner waving, or an announcement of victory. The coda is a succinct summary of what had passed before, evoking the tragic feelings of the development, and then proclaiming the main theme over and over again in its changed, exultant and "victorious" form. The portrait this movement presents is that of one who, living through these great storms and struggles, aware of the losses they bring, comes to the conclusion that they are a great triumph for humanity.

The second movement is in the popular form of a funeral march, but enlarged to embrace a tremendous grandeur and tragic sorrow. It is a social lament, placing the "hero's" death in the context of the life of which he was a part. As in the traditional march, the opening slow march strains are followed by a contrasting "trio" section, and Beethoven takes advantage of this to offer a new musical thought, on a colossal scale; a change to major, a quickening of pace, and an exalted mood, a move to the "outer world." The opening funeral march strains reappear, and then a struggle of fierce intensity rises, with a fugal piling up of voice upon voice, and a climax of harrowing dissonances. It expresses the Beethoven philosophy; one does not submit to anything, including death, without a fight. The funeral march strains then re-enter, and in the coda, even the exalted "trio" music is transformed to a lamenting minor key.

The *Scherzo* must have especially startled its first hearers, with its radical departure from the Mozart *menuetto* or the Haydn rustic dance. With its romantic quality of an indefinite melody being born out of harmony and rhythm, its bustling momentum, its middle section of horn calls, it is the most pictorially evocative of the four movements, arousing memories of stirring excitement, rushing movement, the sounds of the hunt, a feeling perhaps of storms blowing through the world.

The last movement brings in the popular note. It is as if Beethoven, surveying the great revolutionary movement of his time, knew that the common people also belonged in the picture. The movement is a set of variations on a country-dance theme. The dance melody was familiar to Vienna listeners, for Beethoven had introduced it to them three years before as the finale of a highly successful ballet, *The Creations of Prometheus,* and then had made it into one of a set of twelve *Country-Dances* which had been written for use in the city's ballrooms. The movement opens with a fanfare, or "curtain raiser." Then appears not the country-dance melody, but a motif that will later act as the bass of the melody. Giving away the show, however, is the three-note "snap," which would immediately have said to the listeners, "country dance." It is typical of the hand-clapping or foot stamping effect in country-dance melodies, and in fact this three-note "snap" can be heard today in not only Austrian but also English, Dutch, Norwegian, Swedish and Yugoslav folk dances. After two variations on the bass motif, the popular dance melody itself appears. The bass motif comes back, as the subject of a short, "learned" fugue, then the popular dance appears again, and it is transformed into a stirring, heroic march, a worthy companion to the "Marseillaise." Again it returns in its original dance form. And then it is made the subject for a stirring "development section," going through dramatic modulations and rhythmic changes, as if Beethoven were saying that this "popular theme," and the people themselves, were capable of deep and stormy feelings. From this point on, the popular-style or "country-dance" melody dominates the movement, but it is divested of its rhythmic dancing pattern. It is handled with increasing breadth and nobility. What might have appeared at the outset as a "comic" subject now takes on a majestic clothing. The movement ends with the kind of passage that Beethoven customarily called (as at the end of the *Egmont* music), *Siegessinfonie* or "Victory music."

V

Twenty years elapsed between the "Eroica" and the *Ninth Symphony,* including ten years in which no symphony, or any big orchestral work, had come from Beethoven's pen. The *Ninth Symphony* thus was Beethoven's re-entry as a "public speaker" on the Viennese and world scene. It was also the first of his symphonies to match the "Eroica" in length and breadth of scope. Many questions have been raised as to why Beethoven chose to end the *Ninth Symphony* with a choral movement, but no satisfactory answer can be found on a purely formal basis. The clue to a very simple and logical explanation lies in Beethoven's remark to Schindler in 1823. When asked why he did not explain the "poetic" ideas of his earlier works, he answered that the earlier age "was more poetic than the present, and that at the former period such explanations would have been superfluous." And the fact is that in the ten years of Beethoven's "silence," between the *Eighth* and *Ninth Symphonies,* there had been a change not only in political atmosphere but in musical taste.

The public for Beethoven's "middle period" works had been grounded in the classic style of Mozart and Haydn, as well as in Gluck and the Italian opera, so close to the classic style. But at about 1815, the waltz, which had slowly emerged out of the hob-nailed, foot-stamping *ländler* into a gliding ballroom dance, swept through Vienna. At the Council of Vienna, all the city went "waltz mad." Enormously popular in Vienna, in the early 1820's, were the operas of Gioacchino Rossini (1792-1868). Rossini of course was a composer of genius, who incidentally both admired and was much respected by Beethoven. His new style of Italian comic opera, of which *The Barber of Seville* is an especially imperishable example, brought lightness of texture, and sweet and sparkling melody to the Italian stage. Like Mozart, if far from Mozart's greatness, Rossini made comedy a fine art. And his "serious" masterpiece, *William Tell,* produced in Paris in 1829, two years after Beethoven's death, was the first great step towards an Italian music raising the cry for Italian liberation from Austria. It makes a considerable use of folk music, especially in its choruses.

To Vienna audiences Rossini's operas provided a perfect escape music. They offered no disturbing insights into world changes, human personality, psychology or views of life. Marvellously uniting word and melody, exploiting the florid possibilities of every register of the human voice, male and female, they provided wonderful material for the galaxy of virtuoso singers who in every capital became the favored entertainers of upper class society. We can get an inkling then of why, with this change of taste, Beethoven would find that perhaps he could no longer trust Vienna audiences to follow his musical thought; that he had better set his last movement to words. He chose Friedrich Schiller's "Ode to Joy" (and to liberty). This symphony was Beethoven's answer to the Holy Alliance; not as sharp as his English contemporary Byron was then writing,

> *Ship off the Holy Three to Senegal;*
> *Teach them that 'sauce for goose is sauce for gander,'*
> *And ask them how* they *like to be in thrall?*

but, considering his situation, a similar act of courage.

The first movement of the *Ninth* is a portrayal of struggle, but not like that of the "Eroica," which reflects an existing conflict affecting all European society. That of the *Ninth* is a struggle between an awareness of existing misery, and faith in the future. The germ of the entire conflict is presented in the very first theme, which slowly and mysteriously takes shape. It is in two parts; a sad, descending phrase, answered by a more abrupt, lively and dancing phrase, *parlando* answered by *tempo giusto.* We can refer to them crudely as the germs of "reflective sadness," and "joyous affirmation." The actual shades of feeling created by the music are much more subtle. As in the "Eroica," the beginning themes engender further thematic answers, and the entire exposition is a spacious opening act of the drama. Again as in the "Eroica," the development section is in two parts. The first part builds with only the first half of the opening theme, the sad, descending phrase, and creates a mood of deep, anguished questioning. Then the second half of the opening theme enters, the more joyous statement, and the remainder of the development expands on this affirmation. The start of the recapitulation is the most remarkable example in all Beethoven of the kind of "return to the opening" which is at the same time a psychological transformation, a leap forward, the very climax of the development itself. The first theme returns, in its complete form, but different harmonies, and the tremendous opening up of the entire orchestra, with trumpets and drums, change it completely. Sadness is wiped out. The coda, as in the "Eroica," recalls some of the sadness of the development section, but only to answer it with an even more ringing proclamation of joy.

The second movement *Scherzo* is a blithe combination of the "learned" and "gay." It is a fugue of considerable length and "paper" intricacy, which however moves like a spring zephyr. The middle section "trio" is a distillation of a peasant dance, a jolly excursion in folk-style music. Of the slow movement, all a short word-description can do is crudely to indicate its general character. It is one of those wonderful, serene late Beethoven slow movements (like the variations of the *Sonata Op. 111,* or the slow movement of the *Quartet Op. 132*) in which there is the deepest inner sensitivity, without heartrending cries or expressions of agony. All of that has been put behind, fought through and conquered. The movement consists of variations on two themes, which offer a subtle contrast; the first, heard at the outset, meditative, *parlando,* and the second *tempo giusto,* almost dance-like, alternating between duple and triple time. And as a further subtlety, the themes are really variations of one another.

Then comes the concluding choral movement which, like the last movement of the "Eroica," has a popular flavor.

It opens with a piece of hilarious foolery. There is first a portrayal of noisy, clamorous argument. It is a pictorial "comic opera" conflict, in contrast to the genuinely dramatic and emotional inner conflicts so familiar in Beethoven's music. Then comes a recitative from the 'cellos and double-basses, which likewise is a mock recitative, a parody of speech inflections, in contrast to the profound, *parlando* "inner monologues" so familiar in Beethoven. Following this, phrases appear in turn of the first, second and third movements, to all of which the 'cellos and basses, with their mock recitative, seem to expostulate.

At last appears the new theme of the movement, the melody

which will later be connected with the "Ode to Joy." To this the recitative expresses eager acceptance, for after their excited rejoinder, the 'cellos and basses take up the melody and repeat it. The melody itself owes something to early Mozart. It could have been shaped out of a motif in his *Offertorium, K. 222.* But whatever its origins, Beethoven has made it into a grand, rounded popular style song, the kind which once heard impresses itself on the memory. The melody is repeated over and over, with a gradually swelling orchestra, as if to fix it in the mind of the listeners, almost as if he intended the audience later to rise and sing it.

Then Beethoven goes through the opening comedy again, but this time, after the noisy orchestral squabble, it is a human voice, the baritone soloist, that says in the recitative, "O friends, no more of such sounds." The baritone takes up the grand and joyous song, with its refrain, "*Alle Menschen werden Bruder*"— "All mankind are brothers." The chorus repeats it. The movement then proceeds as a "Cantata" in popular style. The term "popular style" as used in this respect has a distinct connotation. It is the style of the great choral sections of the "comic opera" *Fidelio,* contrasting to the "learned" style of Beethoven's choral writing, like that heard in the *Missa Solemnis,* with its complex, interweaving polyphony. The quartet of soloists go through a series of variations on the "Ode to Joy" melody, using three stanzas of Schiller's poem, and ending with a tremendous climax, and modulation, on the words, "The angel standing before God." Just as there was a march in the variations movement of the "Eroica," so now there is a joyous march variation, introduced by the orchestra and taken up by the tenor solo and chorus.

There follows, as in the "Eroica" last movement, a departure from simplicity, the orchestra embarking on a "development section" opening up new and rich emotional dimensions. The chorus re-enters, returning to the original melody. Again we hear "All men are brothers." Then the music again becomes "learned." There is a slow, ecstatic and moving chorus, on words telling of God the Creator, dwelling in the starry skies. A clue to the thought inspiring this mystical passage may be found in a Beethoven letter of 1824. "We thank God for the expected steam cannon, and for the already existing steamships. What swimmers to far off regions will there not be to procure us air and freedom?"[24] The thread is taken up by an energetic, soaring double fugue. There are passages of awesome, *parlando* meditations for the chorus. Then gradually the popular style returns, and the final variations are unalloyed joy and welcome to life.

Thus Beethoven, harried and sick, feeling the weight of dismal times, won the battle with himself, inspired hope in other people as forthrightly and directly as possible, and gave them a grand, strong and joyous song to enshrine in their heart. His work was prophetic, for not long after, in July 1830, another revolution in France would give the Bourbon king Charles X his walking papers, crack the reactionary structure built by the Holy Alliance, and send a wave of excitement through Europe.

5. PATRIOTISM AND PEASANT MUSIC

"The literature of the poor, the feelings of the child, the philosophy of the street, the meaning of household life, are the topics of the times. It is a great stride. . . . This writing is blood-warm. Man is surprised to find that things near are not less beautiful and wondrous than things remote. The near explains the far. The drop is a small ocean. A man is related to all nature. This perception of the worth of the vulgar is fruitful in discoveries."

—RALPH WALDO EMERSON, *The American Scholar* (1837)

I

In his essay, *The Romantic School,* Heinrich Heine unburdens his heart about the narrow chauvinism in the Germany of his time.

"We would have submitted to Napoleon quietly enough, but our princes, while they hoped for deliverance through Heaven, were at the same time not unfriendly to the thought, that the united strength of their subjects might be very useful in effecting their purpose. Hence they sought to awaken in the German people a sense of homogeneity and even the most exalted personages now spoke of the Christian-Germanic races, of the unity of Germany. We were commanded to be patriotic, and straightway we became patriots,—for we always obey when our princes command.

"But it must not be supposed that the word 'patriotism' means the same in Germany as in France. The patriotism of the French consists in this: the heart warms; through this warmth it expands; it enlarges so as to encompass, with its all-embracing love, not only the nearest and dearest, but all France, all civilization. The patriotism of the Germans, on the contrary, consists in narrowing and contracting the heart, just as leather contracts in the cold; in hating foreigners; in ceasing to be European and cosmopolitan, and in adopting a narrow-minded and exclusive Germanism."[1]

Of course neither chauvinism nor humanitarianism are monopolies of any race or nation. Heine recognizes this when he speaks in the same essay of "the idea of humanitarianism; the idea of the universal brotherhood of mankind," and adds, "an idea to which our great minds, Lessing, Herder, Schiller, Goethe, Jean Paul, and all people of culture in German, have ever paid homage." But behind the backward mentality that Heine keenly observed was the fact that in the German states, feudal princes were strong, and democratic institutions were non-existent. Thus anti-Semitism, which Napoleon had partly relieved in Germany, returned after Napoleon's defeat with a virulence unmatched elsewhere in Europe. And just as the reference to narrow-minded "foreigner-hating" brings to mind the chauvinistic nationalism that Richard Wagner would express later in the century, so "we always obey when our princes command" comes uncomfortably close to the national feeling expressed in the works of Heine's contemporary, Carl Maria von Weber.

Weber (1786-1826) came to maturity at the time of the North German patriotic uprising against Napoleon, which he served with patriotic songs like *Captain Lutzow's Wild Ride.* He got into some difficulties in Dresden, where he was director of German opera and where the King of Saxony had sided with Napoleon. But Napoleon was in decline, and Weber's patriotism helped his popularity. Then his opera, *Der Freischütz* (1820) hailed as the first German national opera, made a tremendous sensation in Dresden, Berlin and Vienna, as well as outside of Germany.

Weber's patriotism was sincere, and clothed in an engaging loveliness of melody born out of a sensitive feeling for German folk music. But he paid little attention to the real life of the German people of his time, or to the most progressive thought and literature of his time, being dismally lacking in a penetrating critical mind. His instrumental music, mostly forgotten, is gifted but lacking in emotional intensity. He loved dance music, and his piano sonatas, like that in *A flat Op. 39,* have an elegance in this respect that foreshadows the waltzes of Chopin. His piano piece, *Invitation to the Waltz,* a chain of waltzes with an introduction and coda, was the prototype of the orchestral "waltz poems" that Joseph Lanner and the Strauss dynasty would raise almost to the level of an Austrian national art. Absent competely from *Der Freischütz* is anything resembling the sharp satire of aristocracy in Mozart's *Marriage of Figaro,* the social humanitarianism of *The Magic Flute* (the style of which however influenced Weber considerably), or the call to freedom from tyranny of Beethoven's *Fidelio.*

Der Freischütz purports to retell an old folk tale, but it is actually a bourgeois sentimental romantic comedy and melodrama. A young forester, Max, seeks the hand of the beautiful Agathe. Hoping to excel as a marksman, he is tricked into selling his soul to the devil, who offers to give him "magic bullets" that will hit any target. The devil's horrible plan is that one of these bullets will kill Agathe. But a saintly hermit mysteriously intervenes, Agathe remains among the living, and Max's soul is saved. All the superstitious elements, including the scene of the casting of the magic bullets, with its romantic evocation of weird horrors, are treated seriously, as if they were actual life. But in the course of accomplishing the happy ending, the realities of life are glossed over. Piety and faith solve everything and of course the people express their deep piety not only to the saintly hermit, but also to their feudal lord, the Duke Ottokar, who appears as a kindly but stern "father of his people." The music lacks Mozart's fine characterizations, but it exhibits Weber's wonderful, creative feeling for folk idioms, not only in the peasant choruses and dances, hunting choruses and bridal songs, but in the extended numbers. Thus Max's aria *"Durch die Walder"* begins in folk style and develops freely and rhapsodically, and the duet between Agathe and Annchen is like a chain of peasant waltzes.

Other ambitious operas by Weber, like *Euryanthe* and *Oberon,* have had far greater difficulty in holding the boards, for as dramas they are utterly silly, and lack even the folk mileu of *Der Freischütz.* Opera is an organic unity of text and music, and even when the drama part of it seems to a later generation superficial or silly, it must possess some qualities that reflect a real interest in life on the part of the composer. If the fairy-tale of *Oberon* seems no more a hodge-podge than *The Magic Flute,* Weber lacked the wit and intelligence of a Mozart who could discover possibilities in such a story and give it a new level of significance. Yet this is a pity, for these works have many musical beauties; the overtures, for example, and in *Oberon,* such passages as the great monologue-aria of Regia, addressed to the sea, or the mermaid's chorus, one of those enchanting folk-style melodies that become an undying popular possession.

II

Franz Schubert (1797-1827), was also one of the generation following Beethoven, although he outlived Beethoven by only one year. He came to maturity in Vienna in the dismal years of the Holy Alliance Inquisition. His national expression is much more profound than Weber's. But it was in a strictly "unofficial" capacity that he became the great bard and singer of the Austrian nation. It was a national feeling without jingoism, or sycophancy to the feudal lords; one in which the people could find their own hope and heartbreak reflected. At a time when a stultifying pall of sentimental piety and censorship hung over Austrian life, he showed an eagerness to know what was the best thought of his time. He read Goethe, Schiller and Scott, and recognized the genius of Heine (born the same year as Schubert) by seizing on Heine's poems almost as they came off the press, and using them as texts for some of his greatest songs. Shortly after he finished his schooling he became the guiding genius of a group of cultural minds—musicians, poets, painters, mostly young—whose "Schubertiads" or evenings of music and talk in home or tavern represented some of the best intellectual life of the city. As for their attitude towards the clerical-police state, there is no open expression of it, but a hint may be found in the fact that in 1820, one of the group, Johann Senn, who belonged as well to a suspect Freshmen Students' Association, was arrested. While his lodgings were being searched, his friends, including Schubert, used according to the police report "insulting and opprobrious language" towards the officers. Schubert and three others were reprimanded, while Senn, after a fourteen month trial, was deported.[2] At the age of seventeen, Schubert sold his school books in order to hear Beethoven's *Fidelio.*

It was a time when all the arts were engaged in exploring the sensitivities of inner life and psychology, and Schubert's history-making contribution was to conquer this realm in terms of the song for voice and piano. Haydn, Mozart and Beethoven had written many songs for solo voice, and so had minor composers like Zelter and Zumsteeg. The form was a popular one. There were no "art song specialists" giving recitals, as in our own day. Songs were written to be sung in the homes, and they followed as models the real or simulated folk songs, ballads and simpler operatic airs of the time. Schubert retained this popular character implicit in the form, and among his six hundred and three songs, a great number are close to the strophic form of folk song, with successive stanzas set to the same melody. Most were meant for "anyone" to sing, although a performance that does full justice to what is in them is another matter.

Schubert had a fine ear for the music of speech, and for melody as an expansion of speech, but what was more important, he shaped his melodies and their variants to the character, psychological life and human situation implicit in the poem. In some songs, he would vary but one stanza of what was otherwise a strophic repetition of melody. At the other extreme, he would compose a song continually developing, or evolving in emotional life, to its very end; sometimes using rounded melody, and sometimes an affecting declamation like an impassioned melodic speech. He enriched the piano accompaniments, often using a fine evocation of nature, or human action, like ripples of water, winds, the rustle of leaves, the post-horn call, a galloping horse, serving a purpose similar to the humanized nature-imagery of a great lyric poet.

All this was erected on a base of his unerring feeling for the lyric germs of the folk and popular music of his time, and its capacity for proliferation into ever new melody. Thus many of his songs, like *Heidenroslein, Die Forelle, Auf dem Wasser zu Singer, Der Lindenbaum,* the almost hackneyed *Serenade,* and *Das Wandern,* move into the popular consciousness like freshly beautiful and yet familiar music, some becoming "new folk songs." Unequalled in prolific melodic invention, Schubert never fell into the common musical practise of writing pseudo-melody, moving up and down the notes of a chord or the degrees of a scale to simulate a melodic line; the kind of melody Beethoven called a *Schusterfleck*—"cobbler's patch." And this is because to Schubert, every melody, tune or variant, whether *parlando-rubato* or *tempo-giusto,* was the clothing of a real human situation; a valid human image.

How a group of beautiful melodies can be different from one another and also kin to one another, or in other words the proliferation of melody from material given by society to the composer can be traced in both Schubert's instrumental works and his songs. Thus he wrote many examples for piano of the *ländler,* the dancing songs of the Austrian countryside, kin to the *ländler* which Beethoven and Mozart also composed, yet with a lilt or pathos that is at the same time "Schubert." He also composed many waltzes close in feeling to the Austrian peasant waltz, and far different from the lushly romantic and sentimental orchestral waltzes that would be composed by Johann Strauss, father and son. All this was a wonderful "popular music," that is, a music intended for home entertainment, not for public recitals. And waltzes and *ländler* infuse the scherzos of his chamber and symphonic works, like that of the great *Ninth Symphony in C Major.* But new in music (only Haydn had hinted at this before him) was his affecting use of such peasant-born melodies as material for his most moving and dramatic musical structures, like the first movement of the *Unfinished Symphony,* in which the inspired second theme is inspired by the *ländler,* or the entire first movement of the *Fantasy Sonata for Piano in G, Op. 78.*

Schubert also handled Hungarian folk and popular music affectionately, as in the second movement of his *C major Fantasy for Violin and Piano, Op. 159,* and the last movement of the great *C major String Quintet, Op. 163.* His *Divertissement a la hongroise* for piano four hands is a prototype, more musical and less spectacular, for the Liszt *Hungarian Rhapsodies.* And the most profound and beautiful tribute to Hungarian music is the slow movement of the great *Ninth, C Major Symphony,* an *Andante con moto "all 'ongarese."*

III

Schubert is commonly spoken of an an inspired and prolific inventor of melody, but not generally realized is what lay behind this. It was an ability to take up a social fund of melodic raw material and handle it with the greatest plasticity, shaping and reshaping it, exhibiting the same process of foliation of one melody into another that folk music exhibits over a long span of time. The simplest way to trace this astonishing process is in the many variation movements of his piano and chamber works, where we can trace step by step the process of a melody changing into another so different that we would not see the kinship had we not followed the stages. Or there is the melody which apparently haunted him so much that it appears in various works; in the *Entr'acte* music for the play *Rosamunde,* the slow movemoment of the *A minor Quartet, Op. 29,* and the *B flat Piano Impromptu, Op. 142,* where it becomes the subject for a set of variations. It seems as if Schubert could have gone on forever creating new melodies out of it.

Creating new melodies out of old is more than a matter of being able to manipulate musical notes and rhythms. For the new to be an unshakeable musical form in its own right, behind it must be a deep and revealing thought about life. A great and varied melodist is a person of social mind and broad human sympathies. And what makes Schubert so supreme a composer of song is not simply a gift for melody, but the breadth and penetration of his psychological insight. This may be seen in his two great song-cycles, *Die schöne Müllerin* (1823) and *Die Winterreise* (1827), which also exhibit in their differences from one another the two opposite poles between which his song-writing moves. The earlier cycle is close in form to folk style and the strophic song. The later is close to the declamatory, *parlando-rubato,* inner monologue style.

The theme of the twenty songs of *Die schöne Müllerin* is young love, and it tells us that there is no single kind of music that can be called "love music," for "love" can imply anything from the most blithe joy to the deepest frustration. The cycle opens with what could be a perfect folk song, *Das Wandern,* depicting the care-free miller boy wandering along a country road. The next three songs, *Wohin? Halt,* and *Dankgesang an den Bach* preserve the air of folk song, although there are beautiful departures from the strophic form, in key change and variation. The mood has developed to one of excited anticipation and yearning. The lad hires himself to the miller, whose mill wheels are turned by the brook, and who has a pretty daughter. The songs now develop step by step the rising ecstasy of love, with doubts appearing and then banished. Masterful musical psychology is the contrast between *Ungeduld,* in which the miller lad, alone, speaks of the rapture of love, and *Morgengrüss,* which is a "morning greeting," an address of love by the boy to the miller maid.

Peaceful contentment and joy follow, with the lad convinced that the maid is his. Then doubt arises. Does she really love him? A rival appears, a gaily dressed hunter, and from this point on we have frightful torment, rage, anger and despair. Finally the miller lad, alone, speaks of the rapture of love, and *Morgen*-cording to the words, he drowns himself in the brook, but this is hard to believe from the music. Rather what Schubert captures with such insight is the adolescent thought of "ending it all," so common in such a situation. The last two songs, the dialogue of the miller and the brook, and the lullaby of the brook, are masterpieces of tender sadness and serenity. They are Schubert's expression of love for the miller lad himself, whose innocent adolescence is of course left in the brook.

Just as the text of the songs are a development of one theme, so in the music it is possible to find threads of melodic variation from one song to another. This is not to say that the cycle can be even remotely described as a set of variations. Each song is a different human image, and a closed, rounded art work in its own right. But there are also family melodic ties. *Wohin?* is a free variation on *Das Wandern,* which itself is close kin to a blithe, carefree song Schubert had written a year before, *Der Musensohn.* Subtly connected in melody are *Der Neugerige, Morgengrüss, Die liebe Farbe,* in which the thought of death enters side by side with love, and the great *Trock'ne blumen,* which starts with despairing sadness and ends with an ecstatic vision of the coming of spring. Another closely connected group is *Danksagung an den Bach, Des Müller's Blumen, Der Müller und der Bach, and Des Baches Wiegenlied.*

In *Der Winterreise,* or "The Winter Journey," the spirit is entirely different, although for the texts Schubert turned again to the poet, Wilhelm Müller, whose lyrics he had used for the earlier cycle, and the theme on the surface seems to be that of disappointed love. But there are no love songs in the cycle, as there are in the earlier one. In the first song, *Gute Nacht,* the "stranger," the teller of the tale, says farewell to the home of his sweetheart, and in the second song, *Die Wetterfahne* or "The Weathervane," we learn of her fickleness, for she has given up love to marry for money. And from this point on we get a portrayal of the most frightful loneliness, of a man moving out of human society, sometimes attempting to buoy himself up with hope, sometimes trying to find inner courage and strength, but gradually succumbing to a frightful desolation, almost of a mind on the verge of cracking. Schubert must have discovered such feelings in himself, but of course the portrayal is not of himself. A short time later he could write the tremendous expression of openhearted joy in life, the *C major Symphony.*

A subtle tie between two songs connects *Die Winterreise* with the miller-maid song cycle, the fact that the tragic song *Der Wegweiser* or "The Signpost" is a free, minor-key variation of the light-hearted *Wohin?* or "Whither?" in the earlier work. This could have been planned on Schubert's part, for the ironic connection in the poem is clear. But the twenty-four songs of the later cycle are far more complex and far-reaching in their extension of the horizons of musical expression. Only one song can be described as in folk style, *Der Lindenbaum,* which indeed has attained the status of a German folk song, although it has in one stanza an impassioned "art song" variation. For most of the twenty-four, with all their beautiful melodies, the form tends towards the declamatory, or a combination of melody with recitative. Yet it is possible to trace a family melodic connection between *Wasserfluth, Auf dem Flüsse, Rast* and *Einsamkeit.* We can hear in *Gefror'ne Thranen* a deeply sad variation on *Der Lindenbaum,* which follows it, and then see *Der Lindenbaum* undergoing a grotesque distortion in *Letzte Hoffnung.* Here again a subtle irony also connects the texts of the two songs, one being "The Linden Tree," and the other, "Last Hope," in which the poet describes a single leaf left on a tree, and compares its falling to his own dying hopes.

This unique masterpiece, in its vocal lines and harmony, foreshadows developments in music as far as the twentieth century. The great lesson it teaches is that such developments of technique and form never rise out of experimentation with new devices for their own sake. They are called up by what the artist discovers in real life. The question is not that of whether a composer should use "traditional harmony" or "experimental" and "new" harmony. It is that of different sides of life and of human psychology calling for different styles of musical expression. Thus in the song *Rast* the notes of the melody are at first close together, and then expand into wide leaps, suggesting the vocal line of Wagner and Richard Strauss. But to Schubert, the wide leaps of the voice are a way of presenting deep unrest and agitation. When twentieth century composers point to these elements in Schubert as justifications for their own style, they are only tacitly admitting that unrest and hysteria are the main sides of life which they depict.

Similarly in the song *Letzte Hoffnung* the jagged piano figure, suggesting the fluttering of a single leaf on a bare branch, and the declamatory vocal line above it, move towards the extremes of classical tonality, suggesting the music of the end of the nineteenth century. But to Schubert it is a way of portraying this deep loneliness and inner desolation. In the extraordinary concluding song, *Der Leiermann,* the poet describes a half-frozen organ grinder in the village, turning the crank of his musical box with nobody dropping a coin in the cup or paying any heed to him. But he keeps on playing, and the poet says, "Wonderful old man, will you take me with you, and play my songs too?" The song ends musically with a cry of anguish. And throughout the song the music refuses to modulate. There is an insistent note, part of an *ostinato,* or phrase incessantly repeated in the same key, from which the melody cannot break away. In twentieth century music the hammeringly repeated *ostinato* phrase would become, especially in Stravinsky, a major formal device. But to Schubert, it is only one of many musical-psychological tools, and here he employs it because it is so perfect a depiction of a mind obsessed.

There have been some silly allegations of lack of poetic taste in Schubert, because, along with poems by great writers like Goethe, Schiller, Shakespeare and Heine, he also frequently set poems by lesser poets like Wilhelm Müller. This approach misses the basic relation between the poem and its musical setting. It is not necessary to find a great poem in order to write a great song. What distinguishes a poor poem from a good one is not the subject matter, but the inner life and depth of portraiture that the poor poem lacks. And it is perfectly reasonable for a composer to be attracted to a poem for its subject, and supply with the music the inner human life missing in the poem.

The situation becomes different with the later writers of art song, notably Hugo Wolf (1860-1903), who provides a musical "reading" of a poem, phrase by phrase, syllable by syllable, and accent by accent. The composer does not find a subject in the poem, but finds himself in it, the poem being a mirror of his own state of mind. Here the beauty of the poem is central to the song. But for all the refinement and inspired beauty of the songs, the approach is not an "improvement" on Schubert's but a sign of a deeply subjective turn which contrasts to Schubert's many-sided acceptance of life.

Schubert's handling of "sonata form" still falls within the classic style. It presents clearly defined themes, which come to a definite end, and a clear demarcation between exposition, development, recapitulation and coda. This arises not out of the use of a model, but out of the classical mode of thought, seeing each section as linked to its predecessor by being its "opposite." But not only does Schubert use themes that are more broadly songful than Beethoven's motifs. He expresses a different psychology. Unlike Beethoven, he will present in the lyrical exposition no hint of the drama to come. The development section will come as a sudden overturn of mood, an outburst of heartbreak and anguish. The *"Unfinished" Symphony* is of this pattern, and the first, second and last movements of the great posthumous *A major Piano Sonata.* The recapitulation is closer to the exposition than it is in Beethoven, and the coda has less dramatic importance. Translated psychologically, it means that if, like Beethoven, Schubert feels the drama and opposing forces of life, he can accept but not resolve the conflict. His art embodies, on a far higher artistic plane, the contrasting unresolved moods found in folk music; a deep sadness, and on the other hand an unshakeable, sunny joy in life.

In Schubert we find a mirror of the Austrian people themselves, shaken by the events of 1770-1815, knowing that an old world had passed away, yet not seeing a clear path, suffering a deep unrest, feeling new and mysterious chains being forged. Schubert himself felt the oppression of the market-place. He cried in a letter to his father, in 1825, "If only some decency might be expected of those—of art dealers! But the wise and benevolent dispensations of the State have well and truly seen to it that an artist shall ever remain the slave of every wretched huckster."[3]

Schubert had too unshakeable a love of life, too much of a sense of the open air, too openhearted an ability to get out of his own skin, to be a full-fledged romanticist. But paths lead directly from his work to romantic music. The "art song" as an "inward" expression became a major form with Schumann, Brahms and Hugo Wolf. Similarly his short piano pieces, with their poetic inwardness, attracted later composers. His *Impromptus,* except for that in B flat, with its variation form, may be called "songs for piano." Schumann developed the form further and more "inwardly" for such works as his *Novelletten,* or for the eight pieces which he bound together to make the heartrending masterpiece, *Kreisleriana.* And Brahms took up a similar form in his beautiful *Intermezzi* for piano. We can find clues to Wagner's vocal style in Schubert's great declamatory songs like *Der Doppelganger, Der Atlas,* and *Gruppe aus dem Tartarus.* In fact the latter song foreshadows the forging scene in *Siegfried.* And in the piano accompaniments of Schubert's songs, with their evocation of nature as a mirror of human feeling, we can find the germ of Wagner's nature pictures, which he suffuses with the emotion of his operatic characters and weaves about their meditations and monologues, like the Rhine music, storm music, fire music, forest sounds, bird calls and hunting horns.

Most romantic perhaps of all Schubert's work is the *Wanderer Fantasy* for piano (1822). The song itself, *Der Wan-*

derer, from which Schubert extracted the motif on which he built the *Fantasy,* presents a typical romantic myth-figure; the nameless wanderer, who can never find the refuge, home, native land or happiness he longs for. In the piano work, the first movement is not rounded out. After the development, instead of proceeding to a classical recapitulation, it "melts" into the slow movement. This is the procedure that Liszt would take up for his *E flat Piano Concerto.* In Schubert's *Fantasy,* again, all the four movements are built with transformations of the one "Wanderer" theme; a form of unity, giving the work a brooding "stream of consciousness" character, that Liszt, Berlioz and Wagner would lean heavily upon. Liszt chose the *Wanderer Fantasy* to orchestrate as a piano concerto, for his own use.

But what links Schubert to the Mozart of *The Magic Flute* and the Beethoven of the last movement of the *Ninth Symphony,* is his feeling for the ordinary people of his city and country. They are a major audience, which he willingly serves. His songs have a double life; they are "art songs," demanding the most self-effacing devotion on the part of the performer (in fact the Schubert songs created a new kind of concert artist, the singer of *lieder*), and at the same time they live on people's lips. He had a higher regard for the "public"—a loose and ambiguous word—than did romanticists such as Berlioz, Liszt and Wagner, who sought as heroes to impress and amaze their audiences. And their "public" was largely upper middle class and aristocracy, who had the best seats at opera and concert hall. Schubert's was a few rungs down in the social ladder and it seems to have loved his work. He got a pittance from publishers, but his songs were sung. Typical newspaper notices, of 1828, are "This characteristic composer's name already sounds honourably from all lips, just as his songs are sung wherever triplet frippery has not yet ousted all feeling for truth and beauty" (Dresden);[4] "These are the latest book of songs and more or less developed vocal pieces by the composer mentioned, who for some time has been not a little valued and liked everywhere" (Leipzig);[5] "These three developed songs by the generally lauded and favored composer. . . . All three are very well suited to sociable entertainments" (Leipzig).[6] And his national character was recognized. Thus a Dresden writer (perhaps Tieck) linked Schubert to Mozart, Haydn and Beethoven, and added, "The truly great Lablache, who understands and honours German music, and highly esteems Schubert's song compositions, for instance, repeatedly expressed his astonishment at the lack of all patriotism in Vienna."[7] (Lablache, born in Italy, was one of the most celebrated opera singers of the day). But it is not surprising that official Vienna did not recognize the great national voice in Schubert, for his love of country did not seem to include obsequiousness to Prince Metternich and his police censors.

IV

In the music of Frederic Chopin (1810-49) the use of folk musical sources is openly bound to a proclamation of patriotism and a call to national freedom. Even the sadness in so many of his works is not a private sadness alone; but an awareness of a nation suffering. There is a parallel in the combination of folk song with patriotic connotations to the *Hungarian Rhapsodies* of Franz Liszt (1811-86). But the differences are profound. Liszt handled Hungarian folk melodies with great enjoyment and taste. They were, as he knew, primarily Gypsy melodies. He wrongly assumed that they were the only Hungarian folk music, a gift of the Gypsies to the nation. [8]His rhapsodies echo in piano tones the timbres of folk instruments, and make the piano itself sound like the apotheosis of a Gypsy band. They have the vitality and full-bodied life which folk music lends so effectively to musical composition. But folk music, to Liszt, is not a medium through which he can express his own varied feelings of life. The *Rhapsodies* are like a hugely enjoyed vacation among the folk, and there is accordingly a lack of deep personal involvement in them, and a monotony of mood. This contrasts to the variety of emotional life that Chopin will create in even a modest set of *Mazurkas*.

The comparison holds true with other forms. Liszt's *Polonaises* are a bravura exercise in Polish national dance. Chopin's *Polonaises* portray each a different side of Polish national life. Liszt's *Etudes* are brilliant objective exercises in pianistic sound and technique. Chopin's *Etudes,* while they are constructed each about a different technical problem, are also varied human images suffused with a touching, often poignant, lyricism.

Liszt was a genius who, as Bartok once pointed out, almost inexplicably combined the inspired and tawdry in his work. Perhaps this was due to the fact that he had challenging ideas about everything and serious convictions about nothing. One of his best works, the *B minor Sonata* for piano, exhibits his remarkable formal inventiveness. The classic first-movement sonata form here is expanded to comprise the entire sonata. There is a first and second theme group, forming an exposition. Instead of a development section, however, a slow movement is inserted, which is at the same time made up of a plastic reshaping of the themes with which the sonata had opened. The recitative-like or declamatory nature of all the themes, and the constant plastic reshaping of the same themes into different meditative and declamatory statements, are typical of romantic form, abandoning the classic architecture made of oppositions and contrasting images of life for a rhapsodic flow of personal mood, which in Liszt has a fine sensitivity bounded by sentimentality on one side and bombast on the other. Many of his works, like the orchestral tone poems, have fallen into disuse, because their astonishing novelty—the most transitory of musical qualities—has worn off and the flashes of inspiration are not sufficient to carry them. Yet they gave other composers, notably Wagner, a host of useful ideas. And among the great ideas of the time he handled spectacularly and yet too lightly, was that of national self-identification and national expression.

With Chopin, music becomes for the first time an expression of an oppressed nation struggling for freedom. And with his art European musical life discovered the presence of fresh resources outside of the narrow musical scene as viewed by academicians. Of course the land which had produced Copernicus was no newcomer to European culture, just as the land which had produced a Jan Huss was no newcomer. But the repression of small nations by the Holy Roman Empire and the Hapsburg monarchs, in the seventeenth and eighteenth centuries, had tended to wipe out of general knowledge the truth of how richly many peoples, including those of Poland and Bohemia, had contributed to the advancement of science and culture.

Chopin rarely used actual folk songs in his compositions. But for a critic to reiterate, as Herbert Weinstock does in his book on Chopin,[9] that one mazurka after another is "not a folk song," becomes a little pointless. Of course it isn't a folk song. However, Chopin's rhythm, harmony and melody flowered out of patterns peculiar to those of Polish music, both that of the peasantry and that of the aristocracy. In the mazurkas there is hardly a section which those knowing the traditonal Polish dance music would not regard as familiar and typical. Thus his works became a precious addition to the national heritage, old and at the same time new, rooted in traditional soil and watered by the consciousness of the historic struggle for freedom taking place in Chopin's own time.

Chopin was keenly aware of the difference between a mechanical and creative use of folk strains. In a letter of 1831 he complained furiously of the practises of another Polish musician. "Most of all he enrages me with his collections of pothouse tunes; senseless, vilely accompanied, and put together without the slightest knowledge of harmony or prosody, with contredanse cadences; these he calls a collection of Polish folk songs. You know how I have longed to feel our national music, and to some extent have succeeded in feeling it;—sometimes he gets hold of something of mine, now here, now there; starts to play it in a tipsy, cackling pothouse or parish organ style; and there's nothing you can say, because he won't understand anything beyond what he has picked up."[10] Later, critics would be astonished by Chopin's harmony, so "daring" and yet exactly right, both in catching the exact shade of feeling he wanted and in its fitness to the scale patterns of Polish folk melody. The concept of folk music as involving, in its creative use, not merely or especially "tunes," but also harmonic and rhythmic patterns peculiar to its own idiom, is a gift of the nineteenth century national composers to music, which would be developed extensively in the twentieth century.

Part of the nineteenth century national picture is that in a country suffering from economic backwardness and repression there was little room for a composer to make his way. Only in the great centers, where there were publishers, a thriving concert life, and critics of prestige, could reputations be made. And so Chopin in his young manhood, not forseeing that he would never return, left Poland for Vienna and then Paris, where he spent the last eighteen years of his life. Whether his musical forms would have been different had there been an active, bustling musical life, a public arena, in his homeland, can only be a matter of speculation. But certainly some of the romantic character of his art is due to the fact that he raised the cry for his country's freedom as a lone voice in voluntary exile. Poland had been divided in the eighteenth century, between Austria, Prussia and Russia. The French revolution of 1789 had touched off the Polish revolution led by Kosciuszko, but the uprising was defeated, and in 1795 the final partition among the big powers took place. Napoleon brought reforms, wiping out many of the old feudal practices, but the Council of Vienna restored the grip of reaction. Again the revolutionary year of 1830 set Poland ablaze, but once more the insurrection was crushed. Unable to take part in the revolt of 1831, Chopin wrote in his journal, "Alone! Alone!—There are no words for my misery."[11] It was of the refugees, many of whom went back to join secret societies, that Chopin became a musical voice.

Chopin was sceptical of democracy. The Polish independence movement itself was divided between genuine forward looking democrats, and a nobility who sought to preserve their privileges over the serfs. The political marketplace in France could make anyone cynical of democratic forms lacking in content. Chopin, unlike Berlioz, was sensitive to the misery of the poor. He wrote upon his arrival in Paris, in 1831, "You know there is great distress here. The lower class is thoroughly exasperated, and would be glad at any moment to change the character of their misery; but unfortunately the government has taken too many precautions in this matter; so soon as the smallest street crowds collect, they are dispersed by mounted gendarmerie."[12] The words "change the character of their misery" indicate his cynical attitude towards the democratic slogans of bourgeois politicians.

His great musical gifts were soon recognized, and yet the musical life in which he found himself, becoming a hobby, amusement, or adjunct to the salons of the rich and titled, made him uncomfortable. He wrote in 1832, "I have got into the highest society; I sit with ambassadors, princes, ministers, and don't even know how it came about, because I did not try for it. It is a most necessary thing for me."[13] In 1848, a year before his death, he wrote, "For the bourgeois class, one must do something startling, mechanical, of which I am not capable. The upper world . . . is so surrounded by the boredom of conventionalities, that it is all one to them whether music is good or bad, since they have to hear it from morning to night.[14]

Thus for all the acclaim, he was lonely and an alien, and intensifying his subjectivism was the tuberculosis that ravaged him. He had felt the touch of death as early as 1831, when he was first entering his maturity as a composer. By 1842, disease was far advanced. He wrote, "And for me, the morning—by the time I finish choking, it is 10 o'clock."[15] This points up the double aspect of Chopin's art. On the one hand there is the deep sadness of the "outsider," who is not only an exile but is wasting away physically, and on the other hand, there are the ties to his land and people, and the bright flame of the independence dream, which take him out of himself. Patriotism is the antipode to his subjectivism. How firm was the national tie can be read in his letters. He wrote to his Polish teacher, Joseph Elsner, "It is useless for Malfatti to try to persuade me that every artist is a cosmopolitan. Even if that were so, as an artist I am still in the cradle, but as a Pole I have begun my third decade."[16] He wrote in 1848—in 1846 another abortive insurrection had been crushed—"We . . . are both left orphaned Poles. . . . God knows how all that will turn out, so that there may be Poland again."[17] An inexpressibly tragic letter of the same year, written from London, eleven months before he died, reveals this conflict between his national feelings and the torment of his bodily decay: "Meanwhile, what has become of my art? And my heart, where have I wasted it. I scarcely remember any more, how they sing at home. That world slips away from me somehow; I forget, I have no more strength."[10]

To remember "how they sing at home"; this gives the clue to Chopin's art. The most obviously national of his piano works are the *Mazurkas* and *Polonaises.* The charming early works in these forms tend to be rhythm-dominated national dances. But as his art develops, the dance form takes on an expanded, deeply personal and poetic character. He uses *parlando* melodies, and in the *Mazurkas,* for instance, two such reflective speech-inflected melodies will operate as "statement" and "answer," building up their dialogue to a climactic outburst. But Chopin never loses touch with the basic mazurka elements; the alternation of major and minor, the curve of the folk melody itself, the repeated beats on a single note or *ostinatos,* like the foot-stamping of the dance. The *rubato* or rhythmic elasticity built into his music is like the rhythmic elasticity of a dancing-song, reflecting movements now abrupt, now languorous. The spirit can be heroic, as in the great *C sharp minor Mazurka, Op. 41 No. 1;* sad yet powerfully protesting, as in that in *B minor, Op. 33 No. 4;* a cry of pain, as in that in *C sharp minor, Op. 30 No. 4.* With a similar creative handling, the *Polonaise,* the traditional march-like castle dance became a heroic call for freedom. There are times when the *Polonaise* form in his hands takes on a deeply brooding character, as if the "Polonaise" or "call to freedom" were struggling under an oppressive weight; examples are the *E flat minor Polonaise Op. 26 No. 2,* the *C minor Polonaise, Op. 40 No. 2,* and most of all the *Polonaise-Fantasie in A flat, Op. 61.* In a different vein is the *F sharp minor Polonaise, Op. 44.* Beginning and ending with the "castle" dance in its most fiery, heroic and revolutionary spirit, it has for its middle section a mazurka, the peasant dance, thus presenting a concentrated picture of the nation as a whole.

But while the *Mazurkas* and *Polonaises* make up a major part of Chopin's music, the national spirit moves outside of them as well. The *Waltzes,* generally more light and elegant, are Polish or Slavic waltzes, not Viennese. The national feeling is also found in his clanging, heroic declamation, like that of the *"Revolutionary" Etude, Op. 10 No. 12,* the *24th Prelude, in C minor,* and the closing movement of the *B minor Sonata.* The last movement of his *Piano Concerto No. 1 in E minor, Op. 11,* is like an exalted version of his earlier *Krakoviak Op. 14, or* "Dance of Cracow," for piano and orchestra, the second theme of the concerto movement being like a banner flying. Within Chopin's compositions lies a great body of national song. It is not song intended to be sung, although it lives as melody in the mind and on the lips of innumerable people. It is song conceived for the piano, which was Chopin's own most personal instrument, and not in the sense of a vocal line transcribed for piano but in the sense of the piano itself becoming a wordless singer in its own unique voice. To create this "voice" Chopin revolutionized the method of writing for piano. And through this he became the great Polish bard, offering this precious treasury of song which both gave the nation a consciousness of itself and the world a consciousness of the presence of Poland, despite its loss of independence.

Song is the clue to many aspects of Chopin's art. It has become a commonplace to say that in order to play Chopin well, a pianist must know how to "sing" with the keyboard and his fingers. And the form Chopin often uses is that of the three-part song or dance and coda, elaborated with expressive ornament and sensitive, imaginative harmonic color. We can find clues to the connotations of his piano melodies in the relatively small group of songs that he composed for human voice, and which he intended as songs in folk style or in the popular vein. No. 16 of the posthumously published set of songs, *Op. 74,* called *Lithuanian Song,* has a family tie for example to the melody of the *B major Nocturne, Op. 32 No. 1,* although the *Nocturne* is of course a bigger work, with a stirring declamatory coda, like a call out of dreamy sadness.

Many of the *Nocturnes* have a subtle dance lilt; that in *G minor, Op. 37 No. 1* has the touch of a mazurka. In the poignant *C sharp minor Nocturne, Op. 27 No. 1,* the stormy middle section has a hint of the *Polonaise,* like a sudden memory of the oppression and patriotic struggle of his country. He will work in forms that are basically even simpler, like a single speech-accented melody, rising to a climax and rounded out, as in some of the *Preludes.* Or, more ambitiously, he will create a compressed version of sonata form, with an exposition of two contrasting groups of themes, an impassioned development section, and a declamatory, heroic peroration that replaces the recapitulation and coda. Typical of this are his four great *Ballades,* the last of which, in F minor, also has the breath of a polonaise upon it. The name "ballade" is a reference to the *Ballads* of the great Polish national poet and revolutionist, Adam Mickeiwicz (1798-1855), and the music, while not applying to any particular poem, captures the mood of old epic folk tales, with their love, yearning and striving for happiness.

Chopin was too lonely and personal a voice for big-scale classic musical architecture. For this kind of public musical oratory, it is necessary to feel oneself in actual contact with a public, like Beethoven, or to take it up as a tradition and challenge, like Brahms. Chopin's most ambitious works for solo piano are the *Sonata in B flat Minor* and the *Sonata in B minor.* For the make-up of both he adapted forms typical of his shorter piano works. Thus each sonata opens with the kind of curtailed sonata-form movement of his *Ballades.* The *Scherzo* that follows in each is similar in style to his four great independent *Scherzi.* The slow movement of the *B flat minor Sonata* is the famous funeral march which Liszt described as "the funeral march of an entire nation weeping its own ruin and death."[19] That of the *B minor Sonata* is a tender nocturne. The closing movement in each is a declamation; that of the "funeral march" sonata being short, sombre and despairing, and that of the later sonata being a fiery patriotic exhortation. The quality they have is that of all Chopin's mature writing. The music is a complete self-revelation, and there is not a perfunctory bar, nothing which does not come from the heart.

V

Still another fresh current entered the stream of European music with the work of Mikhail Ivanovich Glinka (1804-1857).

His instrumental works, like *Kamarinskaya,* and his operas, *Ivan Soussanin* or *A Life for the Tsar* (1835-6) and *Russlan and Ludmilla* (1837-42) were filled with Russian folk material. A passage from an article by the great Russian critic, Vissarion G. Belinsky (1811-48), called *A View on Russian Literature in 1846,* throws a fine insight on the significance of these musical works. He starts with a reference to the age of Peter I, at the opening of the eighteenth century.

"Our salvation then lay not in nationality but in Europeanism; for the sake of our salvation it was essential not to stifle or annihilate our nationality (that is impossible, or suicidal if it is possible) but to suspend, as it were, its development and progress in order to engraft new elements onto its soil. So long as these elements were as incompatible as oil and water with the native element, everything with us was rhetoric, both habits and their expression—literature. But we had here a vital principle of organic concretion through a process of assimilation, and literature therefore moved steadily from the abstract principle of lifeless imitation towards the living principle of originality. And we have at last lived to see the day when a translation of several of Gogol's stories into French has drawn the astonished attention of all Europe to Russian literature—we say *astonished,* because Russian novels and stories have been translated into foreign languages before this, but instead of attention they had engendered in foreigners an anything but flattering inattention to our literature on account of the fact that they had considered these Russian novels and stories translated into their languages as retranslations from their own languages: so little did they have in them that was Russian, independent and original. . . . The time is irrevocably past when even any kind of foreign mediocrity seemed superior to any Russian talent. While knowing how to give credit to things foreign, Russian society is now able to set proper store on its own works, and to avoid boastful or humble extremes. . . . To be able at one and the same time to perceive the superiority of a foreign work over one's own and yet to take one's own more to heart is no sign of false patriotism or narrow bias: it is merely a noble and legitimate striving towards cognizance of self."[20]

This puts beautifully not only the connection, true of every national culture, between learning from others and "cognizance of self;" but also the truth that a nation makes a contribution to world culture only with this "cognizance of self," revealing the "universal" ties and significance, the "typicality" of its own traditions, history and way of life. Thus Glinka's work was in music the turningpoint from the absorption of outside influences to the creation of a Russian art that had at the same time depth of character, mastery of tools, and rich representation of life. Glinka himself was a reform-minded landowner who recognized that the peasantry had to be freed from serfdom, and that the only truly Russian music of his time was that heard from the lips of the peasantry. He knew it as an extraordinarily rich folk music, in the many sources it drew upon and the varied aspects of life reflected in it. He learned his way about opera from the Italians, such as Bellini. Yet the crucial lesson he drew was that just as the Italians had given their language a musical clothing, so he could create a melody infused with Russian folk strains and a declamation flowing out of the sounds and inflections of Russian speech. Before the rise of a scientific examination of folk music, he had a sensitive feeling for its characteristic shapes, modal melodies and antiphonal choruses.

In *Ivan Soussanin* Glinka took over a story that had already been handled in Russia by the the Italian composer, Cattarino Cavo. The opera presents a serious episode from Russian history, and in its course builds up a warm picture of Russian village life and marriage ceremonies. The drama was acceptable to the Tsar, since it told of how a peasant hero, at the cost of his own life, saved a young Tsar by leading astray a band of Polish invaders. Yet never before had a peasant taken the center of a tragic opera, and been invested with music of such strength and dignity. Ivan's great scene in the fourth act, beginning with the monologue in which he tells himself that the invaders' suspicions are being aroused, and ending with his defiance of them as they are about to kill him, typifies Glinka's achievement. Recitative moves towards aria, aria moves towards recitative, both becoming a recognized Russian melodic speech of the most stirring emotional impact. It foreshadows the special qualities that would make Russian music, near the end of the century, the most powerful stimulating force to enter European music.

Russlan and Ludmilla foreshadows this influence in a differway. The libretto, based on a poetic retelling of old folk tales by Alexander Pushkin, is a loosely written comedy of love, battle and magic. Certainly no masterpiece as a libretto, it nevertheless makes an interesting comparison to *Der Freischutz*. In Weber's opera, the audience is expected, at least temporarily, to take the magic and superstition seriously, and the virtues extolled among the folk are the medieval ones of piety and subservience to their superiors. *Russlan and Ludmilla* has more of the spirit of folkish "make believe," the adventures, marvels and magic apparitions are invested with a blithe humor, and the emphasis is on the most social qualities of people. Love, friendship, courage and kindliness conquer evil, malice and selfishness. And the special contribution of Glinka's art, with his feeling for the characteristic melodic curves of Tatar, Persian and Turkish music, is the marriage of European music with Asian. There had been such a marriage before. The early Christian liturgical music had been Greek, Syrian and Jewish in origin.[21] But now this connection is reaffirmed on a new level. It begins to be clear that the concept of a unique "Western" or "European" music, separated from the rest of the world's music by impassable barriers, is simply a figment of narrow prejudice. On the contrary, streams rising in many places in the world can flow into one another. Bartok would later show this to have happened with Asian and Hungarian folk music The same truth would be affirmed by the rich infusion of African music in the music of countries like the United States, Cuba and Brazil.

6. THE ROMANTICIST BATTLE FOR FREEDOM

"All at once the votaries of the different arts felt that they were brothers. Musicians studied the literature both of their own country and of other nations; poets (such as Hugo, Gautier, Mérimée, Boret) drew and painted. Poems were read in painters' and sculptors' studios; Delacroix's and Devéria's pupils hummed Hugo's ballads as they stood at their easels. . . . The authors Dumas and Hugo, Delacroix the painter, the sculptor David d'Angers, the musical composers Berlioz and Zuber, the critics Saint-Beuve and Gautier, Frederick Lemaitre and Marie Dorval the scenic artists, and corresponding to them, the two great daemonic virtuosi Chopin and Liszt—all these make their appearance together. One and all proclaim the gospel of nature and of passion, and around them assemble groups of young men who apprehend and cultivate literature and art in a spirit akin to theirs. . . . These young Romanticists felt like brothers, like fellow-conspirators; they felt that they were the sharers in a sweet and invigorating secret; and this gave to the works of the school a flavour, an aroma like that of the noble wines of a year when the vintage has been more than ordinarily good. Ah! that bouquet of 1830! There is no other in the century which can be compared with it."

—GEORG BRANDES, *Main Currents in Nineteenth Century Literature*

I

Expressing in art the spirit of a revolutionary age is a quite different matter from calling for a revolution in art. The democratic revolutionary upheavals at the end of the eighteenth and beginning of the nineteenth century had advanced themselves as representing the interests of all society, of all human progress against the outmoded institutions holding it back. They spoke for the peasantry and serfs oppressed on the great estates, for the city working people, for the artisans, merchants, industrialists, and more forward-looking of the aristocracy themselves, against the stifling grip of court and aristocrat institutions upon political, social and economic life. Their breadth of views is revealed in such documents as the American Declaration of Independence, Constitution and Bill of Rights, and the French Declaration of the Rights of Man. There were accompanying movements against anti-Semitism, and for universal suffrage and the rights of women, along with expressions of anti-feudalism, patriotic love of country, and appreciation of the universal kinship of humanity.

The leading figures in both politics and culture, raising the cry of individual freedom, saw that the condition of this was the freedom of others. An individual's freedom rested on his ability to join with the forward movement of society itself. And so rose the typical classic art of the period, with its unity of "inner" and "outer"; its tremendous development on the one hand of individual human portraiture, and its ability, on the other hand, to see these psychological riches, with their inner conflicts, as arising out of the real-life conflicts enveloping all society. It was a "learned" art which did not advertise its learning, but rather represented as well a turn to the "popular"; one which prided itself on its direct contact between artist and public, wherever this was possible, and on the communal sharing of ideas. It may have produced what from a later point of view seemed a "revolution in art." But its creators saw themselves as the inheritors of a rich tradition from which they took what they needed, and which they could carry further in response to the demands that life made upon art. There was no such spirit as that which would be expressed in Victor Hugo's romantic manifesto, the preface to *Cromwell,* of 1827: "Let us take the hammer to theories and poetic systems. Let us throw down the old plastering that conceals the facade of art."

Quite different then was the atmosphere in which the romantic movement of the 1830's and 1840's grew. The impelling event in France, causing a rift in the reactionary pall over Europe, was the revolt of July, 1830. It gave the boot to Charles X, one of the creatures of the Holy Alliance. But the leaders of the revolt, having rallied the people with the promise of a republic, turned about to put on the throne the "liberal" and parliamentary monarch Louis Philippe. They then turned furiously and murderously against the working people who had been the lifeblood of the revolt and still demanded a republic. The politicians' real aim had been merely to widen the base of rule among people of property against the narrow oligarchy of bankers and industrialists that had supported Charles X, and having made this gain, they turned reactionary. In the arts, Hugo's drama *Hernani* (later set as an opera by Giuseppe Verdi), had been in 1830 a rallying center for all rebels. But in 1832 censorship showed again its mindless face. Hugo's drama *Le Roi s'amuse* (later set by Verdi as *Rigoletto*) was banned by Louis Philippe. The hypocrisies of the period were accurately set down by Stendahl, who had an inside view as a government official, in his unfinished novel *Lucien Leuwen.*

France was still the center of a ferment of thought. Thousands of refugees came from other absolutist lands and lands denied their independence, like Heinrich Heine from Germany and Adam Mickiewicz from Poland. But in the avid discussion, the intellectual issues no longer had the clarity of the eighteenth century rationalist attack upon the institutions of court and aristocracy. To the bourgeois, victorious, the aristocracy appeared less the enemy than a source of strength and support, while the nightmare arose of the propertyless, the working class, demanding a republic and equal rights, including the right not to be thrown upon the scrap-heap in the periodic economic crises. Among artists there was universal dissatisfaction with the present order and yearning for "freedom." But what was the path to freedom? The servitude in livery to the courts had been done away with. The artist was now, at least in theory, a thinker, teacher, public figure, bearer of enlightenment. But he was now also hopelessly entangled in the meshes of the marketplace.

The freedom-yearning took many fantastic forms. Franz Liszt, in his book, *The Gypsies and their Music in Hungary* (a book at least signed by him), saw the Gypsies as representing the spirit of freedom, with their contempt for civilization. "They reject," he said, "all despotism of law." He also attacked the Jews as an "alien" force in Europe, and this anti-Semitic banner would be waved higher by his son-in-law, Richard Wagner. Liszt flirted with the Utopian Socialist theories of Saint-Simon. Wagner was influenced for a while by the anarchist theories of Michael Bakunin. Questioned was democracy, which was seen as synonymous with bourgeois marketplace society. Quite obviously the institutions through which democracy expressed itself were being like everything else, bought and sold. Science, the great enlightener to the eighteenth century, also was now suspect, appearing to be responsible for the bleakness of industrialism. Most important to the artists, art itself appeared as a kind of freedom, not put at the service of life but seen as a way of life. Here the artist could express himself and carry out his private revolution, defying the "dictatorship" of past theories and methods.

Thus a division appeared in the music generally described as nineteenth century romanticism. To the extent that the composer, like Verdi or Dvorak, allied himself to a movement for national freedom, affirming his own ties to the nation, his music took on a folk or popular character, and something of the classic union of "inner" and "outer." On the other hand, the composer who, while vainly trying to free his art from the tentacles of society, renounced society in theory, became the musical "revolutionist." Society could be left to the politicians. In art he could express himself and proclaim, secretly or symbolically, his untrammeled freedom. And the victories of this "revolution" were in the realm of an increasing inwardness, at the expense of a classic grasp of outer reality. The garment of social responsibility is not thrown off easily. But it begins to slip. And the process is initiated which will culminate in the lonely whispers and outcries of twentieth century atonal music.

The romantic art based on such views had necessarily to be narrower in its intellectual life than the classic art, which had fed on the eighteenth century social criticism and rational philosophy. As art put itself in opposition to society, it was no longer educated by society. Because of the psychologically inward turn, the classic forms could no longer be recreated, however the composers idolized a Beethoven and glamorized him as a romantic defier of all conventions. And the artist, instead of feeling that he was moving hand in hand with society, now appeared before it as either a mouse or a lion. He pleaded for his right to exist, like a delicate child buffeted by the harsh violence of practical life, or demanded that society worship him as a magician or demi-god. As the artists alienated themselves from the life of their fellow human beings, their own inner conflicts and frustrations appeared increasingly mysterious in origin. Medieval and ancient magical beliefs that had appeared to be exorcised by the enlightenment now reappeared; bats, owls, fairies, ghosts, sorcerers, doomed wanderers, primitive nature gods, the Witches' Sabbath, the Day of Judgment. They took on a new psychological aura, as symbols of fears and yearnings for which no realistic clothing could be found. Dark caverns of mental life were explored up to the shadowy borderland of consciousness, and a private anguish was disclosed that was deeper than any that had appeared in art before. This new inner sensitivity was the great achievement of romanticism in music, and although it was a one-sided development, no later music, however it sought to return to the outer world, could afford to ignore its discoveries.

II

In following its inward path, romantic musical form built with motifs that were indefinite, speech-accented, declamatory, ending so to speak "in the air," and calling for more to follow. If we listen to the slow introduction of Haydn's *Symphony No. 114 in D,* we find such a mysteriously portentous statement, sounding like later romanticism. But in the Haydn symphony, the *Allegro* of the movement proper restores the "outer life" balance. If we then turn to one of the great early examples of romantic musical form, Hector Berlioz' overture, *Les Francs-Juges,* of 1827, we find that this kind of declamatory theme dominates most of the work.

Thus one aspect of romantic musical form is the undefined, unrounded character of its themes, as against the classical use of a theme as a clear structural and psychological "building block." The romantic theme seems to rise somewhere in the borderland of consciousness, make its presence felt, and fade away incomplete, like an unanswered question. A beautiful example of this is the opening of Schumann's piano *Fantasy in C, Op. 17,* which makes us feel also that we had suddenly burst upon a music that had been already under way. Even the simple song "Im wunderschoenen Monat Mai," that opens Schumann's great song-cycle, *Dichterliebe,* ends so to speak, "incomplete," up in the air, as if the "heard" tones (and this is also a Schumann concept) had to be carried on by the "unheard" tones found only in the listener's mind.

Another aspect of romantic form is that it presents what might be called the birth-pangs of its themes as well as its themes themselves. An example is the opening of Berlioz' *Symphonie Fantastique,* of 1830, one of the monuments of musical romanticism. Out of a first brooding statement, hardly a theme at all, a slow, hauntingly beautiful melody evolves, which winds its way without coming to a close. A faster theme then appears, introducing another mood. But then the slow music returns, as if the faster music were only an "outside" intrusion upon the brooding inner consciousness. A moderately faster theme then appears, and it is followed by still another melody, which is a remarkable transformation of the very opening music, and is also the key theme, the *idée fixe* of the symphony. Thus the theme is born which runs like an obsession throughout the entire work. Berlioz' *Harold in Italy* offers an equally beautiful example of a thematic melody slowly being born, and in fact always reshaping itself.

Still another aspect of romantic form is that it tends to eliminate the significance of the classical divisions between exposition, development, recapitulation and coda. We can if we like analyze the first movement of the *Symphonie Fantastique,* in terms of such divisions, but they would not have the real psychological or structural meaning that they have in Haydn, Mozart and Beethoven. This is not a matter of the classical composer following rigid models, which the romantic tosses away in the name of "freedom." Classic art thinks in terms of such great blocks of sound, sharply defined and contrasted to each other. It builts its monumental unity out of such oppositions and their resolution, for this is also the way in which it sees the movement of life. But the romantic achieves unity in a different way, through homogeneously "knitting" the parts together, so that each one seems to flow into the other. It seeks the continuity of a stream of consciousness, rather than the contrasts of opposite sides of the real world in conflict. It sets up a central consciousness, that of the composer, at which the outer world pulls and upon which it impinges. It is meditative, *parlando,* speech-accented style now dominating the entire form of a work. Enriched by a sensitive, exploratory harmony and new richness of evocative tone color, it carries a tremendous psychological power, capturing the mind of the listener. Where a Beethoven symphony seems to tell the listener that "this is real life," "this is what you yourself have been thinking and feeling," a Berlioz symphony (as the Wagner operas do on a grandiose scale), takes the listener out of his life into a strange world, which makes the real world suddenly seem unreal. Romantic form is the mirror of its subjectivism.

Again, romantic form intensifies its homogeneity, or principle of one continuous flow of thought, by merging the various movements of a work into one, as in the Liszt piano concertos or *B minor Sonata,* or by carrying the same theme into different movements, as in Berlioz' *Symphonie Fantastique.* And often its various themes are transformations of one another. Of course many classic works reveal, upon analysis, a subtle linking of themes, as in the processional rhythms and melodies heard throughout the Beethoven *Fifth Symphony.* In the first movement of Beethoven's *Kreutzer Sonata* for violin and piano, the opening phrase seems to haunt all the motifs and episodes. But even in this highly declamatory music, Beethoven preserves a feeling of opposite and contrasting images of life. The romantic transformation of themes however, of which Liszt, Berlioz and Wagner are such great masters, is a qualitative step beyond this, and its effect is that of one human image taking on various costumes and roles, like an actor. Thus where a classic work appears to be as much shaped by life outside as by the composer, a romantic work appears to be a subjectively created world. The subjectivity of Berlioz' *Symphonie Fantastique* is plain in the program which the composer attached to it. A young man, disappointed in love, takes opium, and falls into uneasy, nightmarish dreams, in each of which the obsessive image of his "beloved" appears (musically symbolized by the key theme). The various movements are titled "Reveries and Passions," "A Ball," "In the Fields," "March to the Scaffold," and "Dream of a Witches Sabbath." And the music is in a sense autobiographical; not that Berlioz took opium or dreamed these dreams, but that he went through that same obsessive experience. He had fallen madly in love with the leading actress of an English travelling company which in 1827 had given Paris its first adequate picture of Shakespeare. He writes in his memoirs, "I had spent some months in the kind of hopeless stupor of which I have only faintly indicated the nature and the cause, dreaming ceaselessly of Shakespeare and of the fair Ophelia of whom all Paris raved."[1]

The romantic approach to form, with its reappearance of themes from one movement to the next, may appear to make for a tighter unity than classic form, but this is not so. In a Beethoven sonata or symphony, the last movement will come as the psychological summation and resolution of the conflicts of the entire work. In a Berlioz work, it is merely the closing episode.

III

Of national expression in Hector Berlioz (1803-69), there is little to say because for all his genius, being one of the most inspired and inventive composers of the century, his scope was too limited by the unceasing war for artistic survival that he carried on against society. In his memoirs he wrote of his life in Paris as "the bitter war against men, ideas and things which I waged almost from the moment I arrived there, and have carried on ever since."[2] He could not make himself the voice of the French nation as his more social-minded and democratic contemporary, Victor Hugo, was doing in literature. He welcomed the revolution of 1830, but was disinterested in that of 1848, which set up a short-lived republic. What was happening to the people of France apparently mattered little to him. Uppermost in his mind was what would happen to art and to him. "Poor forsaken artists! What a republic of rag-pickers and pickpockets."[3] As it happened, the republic treated him quite decently, although Berlioz offered his services without hesitation to the adventurer Louis Napoleon who kicked over the republic, made himself Emperor, and dragged the country into a series of wars.

Folk or popular music plays a small role in Berlioz' art, although he could write the charming baroque-sounding "farewell chorus" of the shepherds in the oratorio, *The Childhood of Christ.* Even the peasant choruses in *The Damnation of Faust,* and the music of the builders, sailors and farmers who march before Dido in the first scene of *The Trojans at Carthage* (the second part of the grand-scale opera, *The Trojans*) have no folk character, and no appreciation of the fact that the common people have an independent presence and character of their own. It is of course possible to create a profound national expression without recourse to folk or popular motifs. There are many sides to the nation. But Berlioz' limitation, showing itself most glaringly in his dramatic and stage works, is his inability to get out of his own skin, to create varied musical characterizations that are equally searching, strong, convincing, and independent of one another. It is Faust who dominates musically the opera, *The Damnation of Faust;* Romeo's pathos of love which dominates the dramatic symphony, *Romeo and Juliet;* the rapture and tragedy of Dido's love which dominates the music of *The Trojans at Carthage.* The musical area out of which Berlioz shapes his melodies seems to have been provided by Gluck, Italian composers who influenced French music like Spontini, Cherubini and Rossini, and French minor theatre composers like Gretry, Mehul and Dalyrac. Berlioz' melodies have a surpassing distinction and beauty, a self-evolving romantic structure, and a far-reaching linear span unique among composers of the century. Yet they tend to repeat each other emotionally, with recurrent moods of "the man alone," of deep, unsatisfied longing, and the poignant seeking for love.

In a relatively weak work, Berlioz created what may be called a pseudo-national patriotic expression—the *Funeral and Triumphal Symphony*, which he was officially commissioned to write, at his own suggestion, in 1840. It was planned as a big "open air" work for military band and chorus, to be performed at a ceremony ostensibly commemorating the heroes who died in the 1830 revolution. The actual purpose of the ceremony was to lend a patriotic gloss to the Louis Philippe monarchy. Berlioz' *Symphony* starts with a funeral march, which was perhaps composed with the funeral march of Beethoven's *"Eroica" Symphony* in mind, but there is a world of difference between the two works. Berlioz has none of Beethoven's ability to project a great philosophical view of death, to link the listeners with his hero in the struggle for life, lament and consolation he portrays. Berlioz' lamenting themes, projected over an inexorable rhythm of drum-beats, are inspired music, but calculated to stun or awe the listeners. He would use the same approach for the funeral march that he composed for *Hamlet*. Wagner picked up the idea for Siegfried's funeral march in *Götterdammerüng*. Here too the lamenting motifs proceed over a repeated rhythmic figure that rises to climactic power. The effect is to make the listeners feel that they are observing the death not of a human being like themselves, or of a beloved leader, but of a myth-hero or demi-god. The second movement of Berlioz' *Symphony* is an instrumental recitative, a sensitively written "oration without words." Then the chorus joins the band for a closing hymn or "Apotheosis," and it is here, where the image of the people should carry this "national expression" to its heights, that the music falls dead.

It is interesting to quote in this respect Jacques Barzun's book *Berlioz and the Romantic Century,* which is full of information and ideas but tends to take towards Berlioz the attitude of a defense attorney in a courtroom trial. Barzun writes of this section, "The revolutionary ideal of art for the masses, which

Berlioz inherited in purified form precisely because he was not contemporary with its beginnings, has often been invoked and talked about; it is another thing to put it into practise. For in spite of the broad human feeling required, the artist must tread a very narrow path if he is not to fall into alternative dangers—on the one side, queasy condescension to his untutored audiences; on the other, vulgar platitude."[4] Describing the music furthermore as "a people's music" and "democratic art," Barzun then says, "generally the Apotheosis remains musically primitive and solidly unpretentious."[5] This is a roundabout way of apologizing for the fact that it is really trite stuff. The very quandary of which Barzun speaks, namely "condescension to his untutored audiences" versus "vulgar platitude," would be faced only by a composer who had no understanding of the "masses" and felt no kinship with them, which happened to be true of Berlioz. He could employ his best powers in impressing them with a funeral march, but had to fail when it came to having them speak in their own voice. It is worth remembering that when Mozart wrote "for the masses" in *The Magic Flute,* he produced the greatest music of which he was capable. And contemporary with Berlioz, Daumier was producing for the "masses" supreme examples of French pictorial art.

In 1842, almost contemporaneous with Berlioz' "popular" symphony, the young Giuseppe Verdi in Italy showed what a genuine piece of music "for the masses" could be, in an "unpretentious" way. His opera, *Nabucco,* written under the Austrian censorship, tried to express the yearning for freedom of the Italian people through an analogy to the Jews striving for liberation from their Babylonian captivity. The analogy is summed up in the third-act chorus of the Hebrews, "Va pensiero sull' ali dorate," telling of how their thoughts fly back to their native land so beautiful and lost to them—"O mia patria si bella e perduta." The high priest Zechariah calls, "Arise my suffering brothers!" The chorus answers, "Yes—the shameful bondage shall be broken." The music of this chorus is one of those seemingly simple but imperishable popular-style melodies which only a man whose affections are with the common people can write. Once heard, the song was on almost everybody's lips, and unlike Berlioz' Apotheosis, it has remained a beloved Italian song, like a new addition to folk song, to this day. It is this kind of identification with the people and nation that Berlioz could never attain.

IV

In Germany, Robert Schumann (1810-56) created through his piano works and art songs a perfect expression of romantic introspectiveness, with a far greater infusion of folk elements than can be found in Berlioz. Schumann's mentality was that of the private or secretive revolutionist, leaving politics and the affairs of real life to the politicians, and carrying on battles for freedom in the realm of art and imagination. He invented his own band of conspirators, the *Davidsbündler* or "League of David." They were sworn enemies of the Philistines, or those who defiled art by treating it as a practical commodity and lowered it to marketplace standards. Schumann gave names to these imaginary *Davidsbündler.* He hinted that some were projections of different sides of himself by signing their names like the impetuous Florestan and dreamy Eusebius, to his music and critical writings. Honorary members of the band were a select few living musicians, like Paganini and Chopin. And it is as part of a private secret of Schumann's own that the popular motifs enter Schumann's music, like the *ländler,* waltzes and melodic turns of German folk song. They do not seem to come to him from the people directly, from the countryside, villages and city streets. Rather, the intermediary is their use in other composed music, notably that of Franz Schubert, and their use now takes a deeply subjective turn.

A beautiful example of this indirect national feeling is the chain of twelve short pieces, *Papillons, Op. 2,* begun in 1829. Dance measures are heard almost throughout, with the lilt of the folk *ländler.* But where Schubert's sets of *Ländler, Walzer* and *Ecossaisen* are in popular style, intended to be played in the home and danced to, Schumann's music is not for dancing. Its rhythms appear as a kind of evocative dance imagery, a "dance symbolism." The melodies take on a *parlando-rubato* or speech-inflected quality. They are interspersed with meditative recitaives, and each piece seems to send out tendrils which link it to the next. An extended section at the end gives the work an all-over unity; a little "tone poem," putting an old folk waltz in conflict with a frolicsome march, with six soft bell chimes heard at the close. Over this concluding section Schumann wrote, "The noise of the Carnival night is stilled; the tower clock strikes six." And this introduces us to one of Schumann's protesting or secretly revolutionary symbols, symbols that would be recognized only by the sensitive *Davidsbündler* fraternity. The

Carnival had been a traditional holiday period, descended from ancient pagan festivals like the Roman Saturnalia, and becoming in the Middle Ages a time for masks and mockery. Permitted by the authorities as a kind of "blowing off of steam," it was also feared because of the dangerous "license" it seemed to engender. To Schumann it became a symbol for rejection of authority.

The Carnival is always associated in Schumann's mind with his secret protest and highly personal use of the folk waltz and *ländler*. In the *Faschingsschwank aus Wien, Op. 26*—"Carnival jest from Vienna" (1839)—Schumann slyly inserted some bars, disguised, from the *Marseillaise,* a piece banned by the Austrian censors. The most brilliant of the "Carnival" works, and most effective in the concert hall, is *Carnaval Op. 9* (1834-5). Here the "Carnival" is combined with his "David's band" symbolism. In the twenty-two short sections, waltz measures abound. After a gay opening march, a series of musical-psychological images appear, bearing symbolic titles, or names of the *Davidsbündler,* such as Eusebius, Florestan, Chiarina (who is his future wife, Clara Wieck), Chopin, and Paganini. At the end comes a defiant processional of the *Davidsbündler* against the Philistines.

Perhaps the deepest music in this vein is the *Davidsbündlertänze, Op. 6* (1837), which is however so hushed and intimate a work that pianists find difficulty in making it "sound" in a concert hall. Schumann said of its eighteen closely-knit pieces that here there were "faces," not "masks." In other words, the Carnival wit and jesting are abandoned. He also said of it that it embodied his happiness at the time of writing it, but the pervading mood is one of deep pathos. Waltz measures are mainly heard at the opening and at the close. It is as if the waltz or dance movement had dissolved into the most inward reflections. There is no defiant march gesture at the close. The last piece but one is a slow, touching waltz, which works up to what seems to be a bravura, declamatory ending, but then another slow waltz, in poignant harmonies, ends the work. It is the high point of what we can call Schumann's subjective use of folk music, the "popular" turned secretive, the lilt turned inward, and giving his music an affecting unrest like that of no other composer of his time.

The characteristic Schumann melodies have this romantic "open" form, with a close which is not quite a close, setting off reverberations and chains of thought in the listeners' mind.

Typical are the eight *Fantasiestücke Op. 12* ("Fantasy pieces" 1837) which also present the psychological motifs that recur in his music. Thus *Aufschwung* ("Soaring") is his "freedom" proclamation, the poetic imagination taking wings. *Warum?* ("Why?") is a reiterated question, with a gentle answer that does not settle the issue, all built with affecting speech-like inflections. *In der Nacht* ("In the night") with its urgently reiterated bass motif, is a compulsive nightmare and obsession piece. *Ende vom Lied* ("End of the song") is Schumann's heroic and defiant march motif, here dissolving into meditation.

Yet Schumann never allows himself to drown in subjectivism. For all the subtlety and richness of his harmonic web, with which he intensifies this inwardness of feeling, he never permits his melodies to lose their firmness and distinction of contour. It is as if he were keeping one foot in the outer world. As Schubert had done, he builds his large-scale forms with the stuff of song. Thus the first movement of his great *C major Fantasy Op. 17* (1836), a romantic compression of sonata form, is built with these singing melodies, and the last movement may be called a "love song" in a nocturne setting. In another of his greatest piano works, *Kreisleriana Op. 16* (1838) all the eight movements are in extended song form, like the Schubert *Impromptus,* but connected to one another by a subtle transformation of themes, and by the psychological links of a deepening pathos.

We can trace Schumann's melodic-creative process in the variations that make up the *Symphonic Etudes Op. 13* (1834). Here the starting point is a simple folk-style tune from the pen of a musical amateur, and as Schumann weaves it into his personal harmonic-rhythmic fabric, typical fresh Schumannesque melodies evolve. And very much like the chains of melody in the piano works is the great song cycle to texts of Heine, *Dichterliebe Op. 48* (1840-44). As in many piano compositions, a heroic "march gesture" dissolving in pathos closes the work. The sixteen songs, so different from one another, give the impression of springing from two or three common roots. The starting point is the simple, folk-style melody of the first song, turned "inward" by its indefinite close and the pathos of the accompanying piano figures. And others that follow may be called, without stretch of the imagination, "variations" on this melody, for example, No. 5, "Ich will meine Seele Tauchen," No. 8, "Ich wüssten's die Blumen," No. 10, "Hör' ich das Liedchen klingen," and No. 16, "Die alten, bosen Lieder." And the basic law which Schumann observes is that each new melody, woven out of previously used material, gains its freshness because it is a response to a different human situation.

Schumann sensed the weakness in his own romanticism. He respected the great classic tradition which culminated in Beethoven and Schubert. In some works of the 1840's, like the *E flat Piano Quintet, Op. 44* and the symphonies, he moved away from the intimacy of his piano music and songs. The symphonies fell short of the epic quality of the classic models, but did attain a bubbling joyousness that was a new and lovely side of his art. The problem he faced was a real one; that of romantic music becoming too introvert an expression, with an accompanying softness of structure.

The same question was raised by Felix Mendelssohn (1809-1847), who was somewhat kin to Schumann in temperament. Mendelssohn's *Hebrides* and *Midsummer Night's Dream* overtures, and *Violin Concerto,* are little masterpieces of romantic form, if not as penetrating as Schumann in their emotional life. And he also began to restudy the classic models. He was of Jewish parentage, although his family had converted to Protestantism when he was a child. The purpose was to provide the children with a ticket of entry into education and cultural life.

Mendelssohn did embrace eagerly the German heritage, while playing a notable role in musical life. As pianist and conductor he fought to keep alive the consciousness of Beethoven's greatness, which was in danger of being forgotten. His revival, in 1829, of Bach's *St. Matthew Passion* was a turning point in the rediscovery of the great German heritage contained in Bach's unpublished works. Yet this achievement also aroused jealousies. German society never allowed him to forget that to it, he was still "the Jew." The medieval ideological pretense for assault upon the Jews, that of religious difference, was no longer usable. But nineteenth century bourgeois society had discovered a new weapon, a mythology of "race," "blood" and "national purity," according to which the Jews represented an "alien contamination." It is possible that the awareness of a spotlight on his activities helped limit his musical exploration. Subsequent criticism has been too harsh in attributing Mendelsohn's turn towards classic forms to an attempt at "Victorian conformity." If in some of his more ambitious works he attempted a "grand manner" that he did not feel in the depths of his being, he thought that this manner was something that music should not relinquish. And in works like the oratorio *Elijah* (1846) and the *F minor String Quartet, Op. 80* (1847) there is deeply moving music.

The problem raised by romantic subjectivity, with its dissolution of classic form, would emerge in the open, in the third quarter of the century, with the appearance of two distinct camps in German music. One embraced the romantic innovations of Berlioz and Liszt, idolized the rising genius, Wagner, and saw itself as carrying through a revolution giving birth to the "music of the future." The outstanding figure of the other camp was the young "conservative," Johannes Brahms, with his humble, self-effacing respect for the mighty tradition of Bach, Haydn, Mozart, Beethoven and Schubert. And unlike the composers of the "music of the future," Brahms had a warm feeling for German folk music, which linked him closely to Schumann.

Brahms belongs in another chapter, with the composers who represented a critique of the extremes of romanticism. But it is worth describing how Schumann discovered the genius of Brahms, who was then twenty years old. He wrote a notable welcoming article in 1853 in the Leipzig *Neue Zeitschrift für Musik*. Its closing words were, "His comrades hail him on his first journey out into the world, where wounds perhaps await him but laurels and palms besides. We welcome him as a stout fighter. Every age is dominated by a secret coalition of kindred spirits. Do ye who are its members draw the circle closer, that the truth of art may shine ever more brightly, spreading joy and blessing on every side." This tells much about Schumann. There is the brave call to battle, for Brahms has been welcomed to the *Davidsbündler*. And yet implied in such a term as "a secret coalition of kindred spirits" is the pathetic realization that the "things of the spirit" are frail when they take on in battle, unaided, the material world.

V

It was Richard Wagner (1813-83) who expanded on a colossal scale the romantic inner sensitivity, stream of consciousness and individualist self-projection. He looked upon the past of German music as nothing more than the path of preparation for his own genius. Instead of making art a refuge from the material world, he demanded that this world serve him, and proclaimed his art as the embodiment of the German national spirit itself. The national picture he presented was one in which everything that was irrational in the past, including primitive magical beliefs, tribal violence, the mystique of race and "blood," and the worship of the god-hero, was refurbished as a newly discovered truth. Erased was the presence of the working people or the recognition of the peasantry as human beings. But this was the wave of the times, for the national unity of Germany was being achieved by the Hohenzollern monarchs, the militaristic and feudal-minded landlord–Junkers, and the Krupp armament works, on the wreckage of the old humanist traditions and the idea of the "universal brotherhood of mankind."

Wagner had allied himself with the democratic revolutionary movement of 1848-49, and after its defeat was forced to flee Germany. But what impelled his radicalism was irritation at philistinism rather than democratic ties. In the creative works of an artist we can read his human and social sympathies, and in the operas Wagner composed in the 1840's, like *The Flying Dutchman* (1841), *Tannhäuser* (1845) and *Lohengrin* (1845-48) there is no hint of democratic, humanist or anti-feudal thought. There were models of the latter kind existing; Beethoven's *Fidelio,* for example, or Rossini's *William Tell* of 1829. In the 1840's the young Verdi was satirizing the aristocracy in the comic opera *Un giorno di regno,* was turning for libretti to the dramas of Shakespeare, Schiller and Hugo, and was raising the cry for Italian freedom in works like *Nabucco, I Lombardi,* and *La battaglia di Legnano.*

Wagner's starting-point for opera was the mindless Germanism of Weber. In Wagner's early works some of his special characteristics are already revealed. Magic and the supernatural appeal to him. They are to be taken seriously by his audiences, as a "higher reality" with a hidden significance. The typical Wagner heroine has been created, the woman who must abase herhelf before the man-god, like Elsa in *Lohengrin,* or die for the hero's salvation, like Senta in *The Flying Dutchman* and *Elizabeth* in *Tannhäuser.* There is already a psychological self-projection. Thus in connection with the *Flying Dutchman,* where the hero is saved by a woman's sacrifice from the curse put upon him, Ernest Newman writes, "Wagner was always very sorry for himself, regarding himself as a man particularly ill-used by fate; and in those early days of his he was mainly possessed by two great longings—for rest and comfort, and for an ideal woman's love."[6]

Wagner is neither a prolific nor generally a distinguished

melodist, his original melodies often showing a blatant obviousness or sickly sweetness, like the Grand March and "Song to the Evening Star" in *Tännhauser,* and the "bridal chamber" duet in *Lohengrin.* He takes important motifs from other composers, like Marschner, who inspired Senta's ballad in *The Flying Dutchman,* and Beethoven who, near the opening of his third *Leonore* overture, provided the main theme of the third act prelude of *Lohengrin.* He is developing an operatic style of continuous melodic declamation in connection with which the orchestral fabric plays a major role. His use of repeated motifs begins to attain an effective psychological power as they reappear in new contexts, and grip the mind of the listeners like an artfully created "stream of consciousness." He is an inspired harmonist, supporting his harmony as well with a fine sensitivity to the combination of instrumental timbres. Masterpieces of the new romantic inwardness are the sustained melodic-harmonic arch of the *Lohengrin Prelude,* and the stormy sea-picture of the *Flying Dutchman Overture.*

The operas of his maturity reach much loftier musical heights. Yet with the exception of *Die Meistersinger* they are all badly damaged works to most modern audiences. What seemed at the time of writing to be their most important innovations, the philosophy-inspired, absolute unity of drama with musical clothing, and their planned musical architecture from the first note to the last like colossal symphonies, are now most open to question. Long, arid and uninspired musical stretches appear in them. Their philosophically bolstered symbolism now appears more dated than the melodrama of Italian opera against which the invectives of the Wagnerians were hurled. In 1865 Wagner wrote to the young King Ludwig of Bavaria, whose treasury made possible the Wagner productions at Bayreuth, "I know that you, my glorious Friend, were sent to me by God so that my faith might become religion."[7] In 1866 he wrote to the same patron, "Without Germany's greatness my art was only a dream: if this dream is to become reality, then as a matter of course, Germany must achieve its predestined greatness."[8] It was in the spirit of a national-religious ritual clothed in art that he conceived the four operas of the *Ring* cycle, and the muddled theology of *Parsifal,* but comparatively few accept them on these terms today. The operas are listened to subjectively, for the emotions stirred up by the more inspired passages, and meanings are read into them different from those intended.

The Wagnerian magic was particularly powerful on critics who were in their young manhood when Wagner still seemed to be the great revolutionist of art, the heroic defier of established authority. George Bernard Shaw felt this when he was a music critic in London, and it affected him so deeply that he was unable to see any musical virtues in Brahms for many years, since Brahms was Wagner's "enemy." In similar fashion, the great scholar and critic, the late Ernest Newman, in his monumental life of Wagner departs from the scholarly objectivity he shows in every other aspect of music. Wagner's enemies become his enemies, and he himself is contaminated by Wagner's anti-Semitism. Jewish women in the book are referred to as "Jewesses," as if they were a lower order of being. Whenever he can connect "Jew" with something unpleasant, he is sure to do so, "a rich Jew banker," "an evening spent among Polish Jews of forbidding aspect and suffocating aroma," "the rich Jew" (Meyerbeer), or "Authors in those days were very much at the mercy of the publishers, and the German Jew Schlesinger was a particularly good business man." These are Newman's writing, not quotations from Wagner.

Thus Newman rationalizes Wagner's colossal self-centredness. "Nature's crowning foresight was to make him at once luxurious and self-indulgent in his tastes and completely indifferent as to the way in which he found the means to indulge them. Richard Wagner would never die of hunger, or even live in penury, so long as friends had both kind hearts and money, and optimistic tradesmen were willing to give credit. The moralist may regret the insensitiveness of Wagner in these matters; the historian is bound to recognize that without that insensitiveness Wagner the artist would have gone under."[9] But Newman the scholar should have known that practically every other great composer of the age, such as Schumann, Verdi, Brahms, Dvorak, born with no greater material advantages, managed to fulfill his genius without living as Wagner did. Peter Cornelius, Wagner's disciple and admirer, put it more simply. "Wagner never gives a moment's serious thought to anyone but himself."[10] The real lesson, ironically, is presented in the dramatic-philosophical theme of Wagner's own *Das Rheingold;* namely, that he who steals the magic gold, the world's treasure, for himself, making it a means for his own power and domination, must be one who renounces all love. This social-minded thought, which so impressed Shaw, was probably one of the few carryovers in

Wagner's later years of the early impression made upon him by the anarchist Michael Bakunin, and it offers a clue to what happened to Wagner. It would be wrong to say that Wagner was incapable of affection and love, but generally, in the war between his own desires and some consideration for others, it was his own desires that won. And in the end, the Wagnerian spell was broken for Newman, although it took the Nazi bombs dropping on the men, women and children of London to do this. In the first two volumes of his biography, completed respectively in 1932 and 1936, there is practically no criticism of the anti-Semitism or other racist and chauvinist theories which permeated Wagner's voluminous writings. But near the end of the third volume, completed in 1940, Newman applies his critical intelligence, writing. "He had to an extraordinary degree the national faculty for duping himself with his own words, for mistaking his artfully constructed verbal fantasies for objective realities, for seeing only what he wanted to see, and convincing himself of the truth of whatever it suited him to believe at the moment."[11] In the fourth volume, completed in 1946, Newman provides a clear analysis of the roots of Wagner's racist theories and their relation to Hitlerism.[12] The truth is that much of Wagner's actual phraseology, as when he described the "princes of the nation" as the "natural protectors of the folk," or claimed that the "regeneration of the European Folk-blood" would be effected by the German as "creator," found their way into Hitler's *Mein Kampf*. But the question which Newman still did not take up was whether a composer who "dupes himself with his own words," and has regard for no one but himself, writes the same kind of music as one who has some feeling for objective reality, and has some care for the troubles of others. Newman's idolatrous picture of a man who had to fight the world tooth and nail in order to deliver himself of the great gift to humanity that had been implanted within him, ignores the fact that such a purely self-centered struggle must affect the art itself.

The real conflict is not between the "monster" in life and the "genius" in art, but within the life and within the art. In spite of the proclamations about his work that it represented the "art of the future," Wagner tended to sacrifice the future in the interests of dominating the "present" of his own time. Or, in other words, where a Verdi for example based his art and thinking on what was most permanent and capable of growth in the present, namely a democratic and independent Italy, Wagner based his life and art on what was most transitory in the present, namely the rule of the autocratic German princes, abandoning his early democratic leanings. And so he badly contaminated his future, as we can see in the deep reservations audiences have to make today while appreciating his works. He contaminated his own hope, that his art would be a great national monument of the German people, by choosing a concept of the German nation that was most chauvinistic, nationalistic, racist, unscientific, scornful of all other peoples, and as must necessarily happen, contemptuous in the end of the common people of Germany themselves. It is painful to read the epithets he spewed at not only Jews, but Frenchmen, Italians and Slavs, although Frenchmen were among his warmest admirers, Russia gave him a friendly welcome when he was unrecognized elsewhere, and Jews turned out to be among the most valued interpreters of his art.

In fact, the outstanding interpreter of his music, whom Wagner chose to conduct the first performance of *Parsifal* at Bayreuth, was an "alien" Jew, Hermann Levi, although Wagner continued to write anti-Semitic diatribes and embarrassedly refused to introduce Levi to some of his patrons. In addition Wagner suspected that his own actual father was a Jew, Ludwig Geyer. It is painful to read that in the war of 1870, he hoped that the Germans would bomb, burn and destroy Paris, and he wrote a stupid farce expressing great hilarity over the misery and starvation of the Parisian people.[13]

Contempt for the common people and working people stands out in his librettos. The scene which opens *Das Rheingold,* in which the Rhine maidens pretend to make love to the dwarf Alberich, is not legend or philosophy, but a typical example of Wagner's brutish and heavy-handed humor, portraying a country bumpkin being teased by three loose-minded flirts who dangle their charms before him and then sneer at his ugly appearance. The giants, Fafner and Fasolt, who build the castle of Valhalla for Wotan and the gods, are portrayed as repulsive morons; a typical bourgeois view of working people. And the music given to such people bears out Wagner's lack of common sympathies, so different is it from Verdi's tender musical portrayal of the Gypsy woman, Azucena, in *Il Trovatore,* or the peasant characterizations, so rich in folk music, of Smetana's *The Bartered Bride.*

Wagner sacrificed the kind of clarity and rationality he might have achieved through an acceptance and understanding of the objective world, by choosing to erect a gigantic fantasy in opposition to reality. His operas are high-minded in intention. One quality stands out. They are the first operas or music dramas in history to be conceived as complete and controlled works of art from beginning to end, with a unifying concept involving every phrase of music and every move on the stage. This view of opera has had a permanent effect upon music, influencing composers who had a quite different approach to life and people.

Yet Wagner's operas are in fact incompletely realized works of art, because of the opposing elements in them which clash with one another, and it is this that causes great gaps to appear in them with the passage of time. There is first of all the philosophically-bolstered fantasy, which provides the basic plot outline and structure of the operas. Secondly, there is the Wagnerian subjective projection of his own psychology, his introspectiveness, visions of himself, drives and yearnings, conflicts and egoistic human relationships, which gives the music its compelling emotional life. And third there is the impact of the objective world, which is felt more in some operas than in others. Even *Tristan and Isolde,* the most perfect of the operas in all-over homogeneity has such a clash. The fantasy is based on an old legend according to which the love between Tristan and Isolde rises out of the fact that Isolde's maid, Brangaene, substitutes a magic love potion for the death potion that Isolde wants to offer to Tristan, as well as to drink herself. But the opera has nothing to do with the Middle Ages. Philosophically transmuted, the potion becomes "fate," which draws the ill-starred lovers together against their will. And in the second act the Wagnerian anti-realist philosophy is fully expressed when Tristan cries out that day is made of "lies," night is "truth," reality is unreality, the moment of love is eternity, after which the renunciation of reality engenders the "death wish." It is all irrationality, for people, including Wagner, cannot live by this philosophy, and so they must think one way and live another. But most of the compelling power of the opera comes not from the philosophy but from still another source, the subjective projection by Wagner of his own drives; namely the actual passion of two people, one of whom is another man's wife and the other is that same man's friend. This is a triangle that occurred more than once in Wagner's own life. And of course in real life, it did not end as in *Tristan,* with the lovers dead. Love was not quite so tragic or all-embracing. Wagner found too many women attractive at the same time. But there is in the music the powerful portrayal of the yearning and soaring ecstasy of the love act itself.

In the four operas of the tetralogy, *Der Ring des Nibelungen,* confusion is carried out on a grand scale. The "prologue," *Das Rheingold,* is constructed about a meaningful social thought, perhaps borrowed from Bakunin. It is the inevitable curse that follows upon the gold stolen from nature (represented by the Rhinemaidens), and the corruption it brings to those who handle it. But subjectivity enters with the introduction of Wotan, king of the gods, and his consort, Fricka. He is proud of the castle he has had built, and she complains of the cost. We discover the hero Wagner, with great visions, afflicted by a nagging, over-practical wife. Also characteristic of Wagner's mind is the self-righteousness with which Wotan plans to change his bargain with the giants who did the building (what right to they have to insist that the hero Wagner pay his bills?) and to rob the dwarf Alberich of the Rhine gold (after all, didn't Alberich steal it in the first place?) Yet along with the social theme of the curse that follows the gold, there is the marvellous portrayal of primitive myth itself, with its nature gods that embody mankind's first speculaitons about the outer world. Man himself, in this opera, has not yet come upon the scene. Among the magical sections of the score are those which depict the gods suddenly aging, as "Spring" is lost to them, and their rejuvenation when the goddess of Spring is restored to them. And there are the sensuous humanizations of nature in the water pictures that open and close the drama.

With *Die Walküre,* the social theme of the curse that follows the stolen gold fades to the background. While we are still in fantasy-land, mortal human beings enter the scene and the gods act like them too, the whole faintly resembling the bourgeois family. Wotan follows with approval the fortunes of his illegitimate children, Siegmund and Sieglinde, who elope with one another even though she already has a husband. And of course the meanest person in the opera, to Wagner, dramatically and musically, is the husband, Hunding, who insists on holding on to his wife. In the second act Wotan's scolding wife enters shrewishly jealous of his promiscuity and insisting that in the combat to come between Siegmund and Hunding, Siegmund must die because of his moral lapse. So the hen-pecked Wotan sadly instructs his legitimate daughter, Brunnhilde, who is one of the Valkyrie that carry dead heroes to Valhalla. But there is a rather close father-daughter relationship (it is not surprising that Freud found so many ideas in Wagner), and Brunnhilde, sensing Wotan's real desires, tries vainly to save Siegmund. She must therefore be punished, and sadly Wotan puts her into a magic sleep behind a ring of fire, to lie there until a hero will come and wake her. Wagner is both the young impassioned Siegmund and the aging promiscuous Wotan. The tempestuous music near the end of the first act is stirring, except for Siegmund's rather sickly love song, "Winterstürme wichen." The touching scene in the second act beween Siegmund and Brunnhilde, presenting the pathos of youth in the shadow of death, is Wagner at his most sensitive. Deeply moving is Wotan's tragic farewell to his daughter, who is lost to him forever.

Siegfried, introducing the son of Siegmund and Sieglinde, returns largely to philosophical fantasy, with a Schopenhauer-oriented thinking now replacing Bakunin. Wagner projects himself as both Wotan and Siegfried. As Wotan he expresses his "world renunciation." Wotan is doomed, not because of the stolen gold, but because that is fate. He "wills" his own destruction. And as the young Siegfried, Wagner personifies his own drive to power. Siegfried the hero rides roughshod over anyone in his way, with a typical portrayal of the morality of strength, brandishing his muscles like a bully, scornful of and sneering at the weak, boasting of his own high-mindedness while, without a qualm, he puts to the sword whomever annoys him; a future storm-trooper. There is a father-son scuffle (actually in the complicated genealogy of the operas Siegfried is Wotan's grandson) which fits neatly into the Freudian "family." And at the end, when Siegfried bursts through the magic fire and wakes Brunnhilde, we learn, as in *Tristan,* that love brings doom, but that the ecstasy of love is the answer to death and doom. Beautiful especially is the nature music of the forest scene.

In *Götterdämmerung,* the fantasy and the gods fade to the background. Brunnhilde is no longer the daughter of a god but a weak, bewildered and betrayed wife. In turn she betrays the hero Siegfried to his enemies, who stab him in the back, and she in turn must follow the path of the other Wagner heroines.

The man-hero is dead and she must immolate herself on his funeral pyre. Siegfried's colloquy with the Rhinemaidens is another example of Wagner's loutish humor, showing the male hero threatening the women with his sexual prowess. There are haunting "supernatural" scenes, like that in which Waltraute, Brunnhilde's sister, announces the doom of the gods and begs Brunnhilde to return the ring made of the Rhine gold, or that in which the ghost of Alberich appears stirring his son Hagen to avenge his death. But what Wagner has effectively, if probably unwittingly, captured is the transition from the world of myth to something of the real world of tribal society, or the world of the old bloody German sagas. The "twilight" of the gods is the end of fantasy, the beginning of history. The style of the music changes, and there are more varied real-life characterizations, with (as Shaw noticed, to his disgust) somewhat more traditional operatic methods employed.

Wagner's self-centredness, his gingerly approach to real life, his removal from the ordinary people, operate to constrict his fund of creative melody. Far more than most composers of his genius, he draws heavily for his motifs on past composed music. In *Das Rheingold,* where many of the key motifs are presented that will run through the entire tetralogy, the "Rhine" music, as Philip Radcliffe points out,[14] could have been inspired by Mendelssohn's overture, *The Legend of the Fair Melusina.* The beautiful "renunciation of love" motif heard before and after Alberich steals the gold (the names given these motifs are not Wagner's) is the melody of Chopin's *C minor Etude, Op. 10 No. 12.* The "treaty" motif, heard first when Wotan tells Fricka of the contract he has made with the giants, is the main theme of the first movement of Liszt's *Dante Symphony.* The "smithy" motif heard as Wotan and the fire-god Loge descend to the caverns of Alberich, comes from the scherzo of Schubert's *Death and the Maiden Quartet.* In *Tristan and Isolde* the germ of the opening theme, an epitome of the romantic "sigh," may be heard at the beginning of "Romeo's Reverie" in Berlioz' *Romeo and Juliet,* as well as in the first movement of Liszt's *Faust Symphony.* The beautiful melody sung by Hans Sachs at the close of his *Fliedermonolog,* in the second act of *Die Meistersinger,* can be found near the close of the slow movement of Brahms' *F Minor Piano Sonata, Op. 5.*

The debt of Wagner to his father-in law, Franz Liszt, seems to have been extraordinary. It is traced by James G. Huneker, who writes, "the published correspondence of the two men prove that Wagner studied the manuscripts of the Liszt tone poems carefully, and, as we must acknowledge, with wonderful assimilative discrimination." Pointing out many thematic similarities, he adds, "to search further for these parallelisms might prove disquieting. Suffice to say that the beginnings of Wagner from Rienzi to Parsifal may be found nuggetwise in this Lisztian Golconda." He recounts an anecdote of Liszt and Wagner attending the rehearsals of *Die Walküre* in 1876. At one point Wagner said, "Now, papa, comes a theme which I got from you." Liszt answered, "All right, then one will at least hear it."[15]

There is nothing reprehensive about such borrowings. They are merely cited to show the bent of Wagner's mind. Since he erected a subjective fantasy against reality, he tended to find musical ideas not in the folk and popular music of the people about him, but in the past of composed music itself, like a novelist who will find clues to his characterizations less in the real life about him than in the characters of past novels. Wagner made a most creative use of his motifs, both those borrowed and those invented. He is one of the greatest of musical psychologists; not in the sense of being able to create convincing characterizations which are sharply different in their music from one another, and different from himself—Verdi is a far greater master of this—but in the introspective sense, of capturing the process of flow of association in the background of consciousness. His mastery of harmony and feeling for mental responses enable him to repeat a theme incessantly, while creating, instead of monotony, an almost hypnotic effect. He almost compels his listeners to surrender themselves to him, by his projection of these motifs, linking them with what the listener sees, fixing them in the mind by repetition and then drawing upon them in ever-changing combinations, thus evoking a stream of haunting associations and memories.

The use and repetition of key motifs recalls the fabric of the classical symphony, and in fact Wagner's operas have often been described as colossal examples of symphonic architecture, both in this thematic repetition and in the arch-like process of key movement, away from and back to the opening tonality. But the repetition of *leitmotifs* in a Wagner opera does not have the cumulative effect of the development of themes in a Beethoven symphony, where the significance of each new passage rests directly on its relation to the one that had preceded it. Each reappearance of a Wagnerian *leitmotif* does not depend for its impact on what had happened musically immediately before, nor on the immediately preceding appearance of that same motif. In other words, Wagner's key motifs are psychologically evocative, not structural elements. As in a stream of consciousness, there is no attempt at a logical recasting and ordering of experience. Each moment psychologically wipes out the preceding one.

Actually Wagner's construction is the height of the romantic "open" form, substituting a sensitively woven continuity for a classic architecture built with the clash and resolution of opposites. The great finales, like the closing pages of *Tristan, Das Rheingold, Die Walküre* and *Götterdämmerung,* appear to be gigantic recapitulations and codas, but they make effective pieces in themselves, which is not true of any recapitulation and coda of a classic symphony. Ironically, although Wagner's theories attacked the "set" forms of Italian-style opera, such as overtures, arias, duets, dances, ensembles, the inspired sections of his own work operate as such parts within the whole but somewhat disguised. They come in the moments when the vocal declamation suddenly takes on a haunting melodic beauty like a great romantic art-song, with the orchestra often adding a magical sensuous-harmonic web, or when the motifs suddenly coalesce in a fresh melodic-harmonic fabric which captures perfectly the inner mood of that moment of the drama. Even Wagner in his lifetime countenanced the concert performance of excerpts from his music dramas, although of course they can never be a substitute for knowing the whole drama.

The Wagnerian form, then, is not the "opera of the future." It is a masterful creation embodying his own view of life and people. And nothing proves better the organic ties in his work between content and form, than *Die Meistersinger.* Here the feeling for real life and people, which had been secondary in the other operas, becomes primary. The view of the Middle Ages in terms of its own myths, of *Tannhäuser, Lohengrin, Tristan,* (and later to recur in *Parsifal*) vanishes, and instead the society of sixteenth century Nuremberg appears. With the myths, disappear a host of "Wagnerisms." There is a rounded overture, the nearest to a "classic" form in all his music. There is a chorus, another element forbidden by Wagner's theories. There are "set numbers," such as the chorale at the beginning, the dance of the apprentices, the prize song, the Meistersinger march, and even one in which the characters defy another of Wagner's pet theories by singing at the same time; namely the last-act quintet. *Leitmotifs* play a less important role, and there is an abundance of songful melody in popular and folk style.

The view of sixteenth century Germany is narrow. One would not know from the opera that this was the age in which Germany was rocked by the battle over Lutheranism, and by the peasant revolt. There are subjectivisms. Wagner sees himself as both Walter, the knight whose song art defies rules, and as Hans Sachs, the shoemaker poet, who, the plot indicates, could have won the heroine from Walter had he so wished. At the close, Sachs delivers a nationalistic oration for "German art." The lampooning of Wagner's enemy, the critic Hanslick, in the person of Beckmesser, is brutish and heavyhanded humor. But the atmosphere is real, the people are well defined, and the music has a sense of open air that places it at the opposite from that greatest of "night pieces," *Tristan*. First conceived in 1845, when Wagner was still talking of "love of humanity," it was seriously taken up in 1861-62, and planned as an "easy" work which, unlike his other operas, could be put on at the "smallest theatres." It may very well be the work for which in the end, he will be most cherished.

7. OPERA, TONE POEM AND POLITICS

"However people of our upper classes (feeling that their ascendancy can only be maintained as long as they separate themselves—the rich and learned—from the laborers, the poor, and the unlearned) may seek to devise new conceptions of life by which their privileges may be perpetuated, —now the ideal of returning to antiquity, now mysticism, now Hellenism, now the cult of the superior person (over-man-ism),—they have, willingly or unwillingly, to admit the truth which is elucidating itself from all sides, voluntarily and involuntarily, namely that our welfare lies only in the unification and the brotherhood of man.

"Unconsciously this truth is confirmed by the construction of means of communication,—telegraphs, telephones, the press, and the ever increasing attainability of material well-being for everyone—and consciously it is affirmed by the destruction of the superstitions which divide men, by the diffusion of the truths of knowledge, and by the expression of the ideal of the brotherhood of man in the best works of art of our time."

—Leo N. Tolstoi, *What Is Art?* (1897)

I

Comparing Giuseppe Verdi (1813-1901) to Richard Wagner, both born in the same year, there is no doubt that Wagner was the greater musical innovator while Verdi was the more admirable human being. The latter point is not unrelated to their musical achievement. Wagner's extreme self-centredness affected the form and content of his works. The philosophical and subjective fantasy which he erected against reality has contaminated his greatest works to modern audiences, while Verdi profited by his sympathies for his fellow men, and by the fact that all his mature life he tried to live with, understand, and even change the real world.

At the opposite extreme from Wagner's egotism is Verdi's modesty, typified in his remarks about his way of work. "Please don't think that when I speak of my extreme musical ignorance, I'm merely indulging in a little blague. It's the truth, pure and simple. . . . I'm talking about erudition, not about musical knowledge. I should be lying if I denied that in my youth I studied long and hard. That is why my hand is strong enough to shape the sounds as I want them, and sure enough for me generally to succeed in making the effects I have in mind. And when I write something that doesn't conform to the rules, I do it because in that case the strict rule doesn't give me what I need, and because I really don't believe that all the rules that have been taught up to now are good."[1]

Born a peasant, Verdi strove all his life for the independence of Italy and the welfare of the peasantry, seeing the two as one. He involved himself in his nation's struggles as artist and citizen, and because of his immersion in the events taking place about him, he became a perceptive analyst of politics even though in this field, as in musical erudition, he would constantly apologize for his ignorance. Verdi knew that the direct enemy of Italian unity and independence was Austria. But he also learned that the Italian people could not depend on most of the Italian aristocracy. He also learned the bitter lesson that other countries, such as France, Germany and England, for all their high-flown proclamations about freedom and progress, would put every obstacle in the way of another rival for trade and markets coming on the world scene. Verdi's early operas were alive with stirring calls for the independence of Italy, such as the chorus of the Jews seeking their homeland in *Nabucco* (1842), the chorus "O Signore dal tetto natio" in *I Lombardi* (1843), the outlaw-hero symbolism of *Ernani* (1844), and the beautiful chorus set to Shakespeare's words, "Alas, poor country," in *Macbeth* (1847).

The revolutionary year, 1848, which brought a republic to France, also saw a wave of democratic struggle in Austria, Germany and Italy. But in Germany and Austria the insurrection was defeated. In France, the middle class, seizing control, turned against the working people, thereby spelling the doom of the republic itself. The government proceeded to invade Italy, halting the progress of the Italian revolution, and protecting the favored position of the Papacy. It was this year that Verdi wrote in a letter, "God forbid that we should rely on our kings or on foreign peoples!"[2] He also wrote a hymn for the Italian leader Mazzini, saying "May this hymn, amid the music of cannon, soon be sung on the Lombardian plain!"[3]

It was the army of the common people, led by the democrat and socialist Giuseppe Garibaldi, which finally won the freedom of Italy, but pressures from "outside" forced a monarchy upon the country, with limited rights for the propertyless and a favored position for the aristocracy. Such an Italy could more easily be a puppet of other powers. Following the compromise of 1859, Verdi wrote, "After such a victory, what an outcome! Poor disappointed youth! And Garibaldi, who has sacrificed his long standing convictions in favor of a king, and still has not achieved his goal."[4] Verdi procured guns for Garibaldi's troops. In 1861, Verdi was elected to the first Italian parliament, and served better than most, although he continually exclaimed that he "knew nothing about politics." He finally resigned in 1865, feeling ill at ease among the professional politicians.

Always in Verdi's mind was the continued misery of the poor, a misery that was forcing thousands to emigrate from a "free Italy" to the Americas. And he was sensitive to the troubles of other peoples. In 1862, invited to produce a new opera in Russia, he travelled there and was received royally. But he could not help noticing that coachmen sometimes froze to death "while waiting for their masters, who are carousing in warm and splendid apartments."[5]

In 1867 the French troops, this time sent by the Emperor Napoleon III, again invaded Italy, to keep Rome outside of a united Italy. Verdi thus had many reasons to feel resentment at the French. When asked at one time in France to use a libretto which seemed to be a slur at the Italian people, he said, "Good Lord! There are virtues and vices in the history of every people, and we are no worse than the rest. In any case, I am first of all an Italian, and I will not make myself an accomplice to any offense to my country at any price."[6] Yet chauvinism was no part of his makeup. He gave 2000 francs for the relief of French soldiers wounded in 1870. And similarly he tried to do everything he could for the Italian peasantry, proudly writing in 1879, "I've helped out at a concert which produced 37,000 lire for the poor."[7]

The peasantry do not play a prominent part in Verdi's operas. The theme which appears most frequently in his operas, other than the patriotic call to independence itself, is that which was most needed to unify the Italian people about progress; a critique of the arrogant and hidebound mentality of the feudal-minded nobility. For this purpose he often based his operas on dramas by those writers, old and new, who appeared to be the most intellectually liberating forces in his time; Shakespeare,

Schiller, Hugo, Dumas the son. Unfortunately the writers he had to depend on to reshape these dramas into usable librettos were mostly second-rate dramatists. His characters were musically real and convincing, whatever level of society they belonged to. He treated kings not as exalted personages but as troubled people, sometimes dissolute, like the king (changed by the censor to a duke) in *Rigoletto.* His favored heroes and heroines were often commoners, people with no rights and scorned by snobs or their feudal-minded superiors, like the retired soldier, Miller, and his daughter, in *Luisa Miller;* Azucena in *Il Trovatore;* the courtesan Violetta in *La Traviata;* the court jester, Rigoletto, and his daughter. The comedy masterpiece of his old age, *Falstaff* (1892), based on Shakespeare's *The Merry Wives of Windsor,* is such a heart-warming portrayal of ordinary townspeople. In *Simon Boccanegra* (1856, revised 1880-81), he took up a theme close to his heart; the leader, born a commoner, who tries to bring together the warring factions who tear a nation apart. The tragedy of *Otello* (1886) is closely related to his feelings about Italy. This is not to intimate that Othello is in any way a symbol for Garibaldi and his followers. But the opening patriotic choruses of victory give us a link to the emergence of a free Italy, and Othello is a defender of the nation, victimized by a crafty, ambitious politician precisely because he himself is so open, honest, lacking in deceit.

Verdi's treatment of love is profound. One of the most striking differences between him and Wagner, revealing a human being with a feeling for others than himself, is the respect he shows for women and an understanding of their problems in a male-dominated society. It is seen both in the role they play in the drama and in the music that brings them to life. Even when they sacrifice themselves, like Gilda in *Rigoletto* or Violetta in *La Traviata,* they are not slaves of men, or idealized myth figures, like Wagner's, but real human beings and often the moral superiors of the men. Love itself is handled not as a blind obsession or in its purely erotic aspects, but in the complex forms that such relations take between two people. His love duets—or rather love scenes, since the duets are often an integral part of a larger structure including dramatic arias and monologues—thus differ widely in the human situations they portray musically. In *Rigoletto,* the duke is playing an amorous game, while the youthful Gilda throws herself into love heart and soul. In *La Traviata,* the young man impetuously thinks of nothing but his passionate desire, while the woman, wiser, feels a tragic inner conflict. In *Un Ballo in Maschera,* the king (changed to the "Governor of Boston" by the censors) feels only the possessiveness of love, while Amelia, also deeply in love, is torn between this and moral obligations; not obligations to social strictures, but to other people whose lives are involved. In the duet that ends the first act of *Otello,* the overwhelming poignance of love is joined and heightened by the musical foreshadowing of the tragedy to come.

The roots of Verdi's melody lie in Italian popular song; the countryside folk song, the band music he heard in childhood, and most of all, the melodic fund of his predecessors such as Rossini, Gaetano Donizetti (1797-1848) and Vincenzo Bellini (1801-35). Rossini, the great sensation at all the courts of Europe, mysteriously stopped writing opera in 1829 when with *William Tell,* he was revealing a new social breadth in his work. Donizetti wrote sixty-seven operas, pouring them out too rapidly to give any but a few, like *Lucia di Lammermoor* and *Don Pasquale,* his most concentrated powers. Bellini tragically died young. But all of them carried on the great Italian tradition of melody that, for all the brittle floridity it sometimes took on the operatic stage, never lost its popular roots. Thus they gave the people a new fund of song, fresh yet familiar in substance, as for example the inspired love airs that adorn Donizetti's operas. This became a popular music or, to take a term Bartok sometimes uses, "semi-folk."

The tradition was continued by Verdi, who however saw the need, at the same time, for an operatic style of deeper psychological penetration, one more varied and distinctive in human characterization and in its reflection of emotional conflict. He was prolific in indestructible, rounded and rhythm-dominated popular melodies, like those heard in *Ernani* and *Il Trovatore,* which give these works a vigorous sense of outer life. But he also developed along with this his great monologues, a primarily speech-inflected music, made up of the traditional recitative of Italian opera merging with the aria in a declamation of melodic richness and inwardness of feeling. In them the orchestra plays a major role in support of the voice. This is not a "tone poem" role, as often in Wagner, one taking on the main burden of the music, but an "obbligato" role in which the orchestra joins and yet is opposite to the voice, with each line of music necessary to the other. Among the great examples of this kind of writing are the "sleep walking scene" in the early opera *Macbeth,* the monologues that build up the characterization of Rigoletto, and the monologues of Iago and Otello in *Otello.* And of course the supreme creation of Verdi in this style of melody-infused speech, turned to comic purpose, is the whole of *Falstaff.* In between the simple air and the melodic declamation, come the set forms of aria, duet, and larger ensembles—like the *Quartet* in *Rigoletto* and the *Quintet* in *Un ballo in maschera*—handled with great plasticity, and developed in terms of emotional conflict and crisis.

Unlike Wagner's projection of a revolutionary new style, but more like Beethoven's adaptation of the forms inherited from Mozart to his own use, Verdi adapted the operatic procedures of his Italian predecessors and of Mozart to the task of creating a thoughtful, convincing and realistic human portraiture in music. Thus his great characters, like Lady Macbeth, Rigoletto, Violetta, Gilda, Otello, Iago, Amelia, in *Un ballo in maschera* and Aida remain in the mind as distinct personalities each different from the other, not only because of their role in the drama but even more because of their characteristic musical expression. It is an expression going far beneath surface mannerisms to record the basic conflict that makes each characterization a different generalization of human life.

Verdi's art is a stage in the development of operatic realism. Opera is now engaged in the task of putting flesh and blood upon typical events and personages of history, and history itself is seen in terms of its lessons for the struggle in behalf of progress in the present. Thus in a letter of 1880, when Verdi is engaged in revising *Simone Boccanegra,* he mentions two "magnificent" letters of Petrarch, one of them written to the actual Boccanegra of history, raising the concept of a single Italy. "This idea of an Italian fatherland at that time was quite sublime. All this is political, not dramatic; but a skillful man could certainly turn it into drama." Clearly Verdi is eager to create operas about political ideas, with only the reservation that the politics must be turned into the stuff of art, namely "drama" or human relationships. The same letter gives the reasons that Verdi, so profound a realist, did not join the movements of the time which called themselves musical "realism." Such trends turned operatic music towards the portrayal of a stream of consciousness, following Wagner, or made it subservient to fast-moving, violent and often bloody action. To grip the audience at each moment was more important than to make the audience think, and in this drive towards "naturalness," or a superficial realism—better called naturalism—the set forms or structural units of opera, like recitative, area, duet and ensemble were denounced as "artifices." But to Verdi such "artifices" were precious, for if they seemed to halt the action, they nevertheless enabled the composer to penetrate deep into the inner life of his characters, and at the same time to escape the subjectivism of the "stream of consciousness" school. Although violence is part of the plots of Verdi's operas, he is most interested in the unfolding of human problems. Here he is referring to one of the despised "artifices," the *cabaletta,* or brilliant, fast and florid concluding section of the aria. He says that if a young man appeared who could write good *cabalettas,* "I would go to hear him with all my heart, and let the harmonic fancies and the refinements of our learned orchestration go. Ah, progress, science, realism! Be a realist as much as you please but . . . Shakespeare was a realist, only he did not know it. He was a realist by inspiration; we are realists by design, by calculation. And so, after all, system for system, the *cabalettas* are still better. The joke of it is that in the fury of progress art is turning around and going backward. Art without spontaneity, naturalness, and simplicity is no art."

A powerful, emotionally and dramatically realistic example of Verdi's own use of the *cabaletta* is that beginning *"Sempre libera"* which concludes the great aria of Violetta in the first act of *La Traviata.* It becomes the emotional climax and resolution of the entire preceding love scene, and of the conflicts that have been aroused in the heroine.

Using such musical "blocks" as the simple air, the monologue, the speech-inflected or *parlando-rubato* developmental aria and duet, and the *cabaletta,* Verdi worked out a finely-conceived larger architecture making an entire scene into a musical unit. This is not done with the repetition of musical themes or motifs. Sometimes he does employ a recurrent motif in an opera, like the "curse" theme in *Rigoletto,* the "fate" theme in *La Forza del Destino,* and the "kiss" theme in *Otello.* These are in no way Wagnerian *leitmotifs.* They have no "stream of consciousness" function. They are the means with which Verdi at crucial moments will tie up a present event with a past one. Verdi's unity is achieved through a masterful pacing of the musical flow, a slackening or heightening of tension, and a drop or increase in dynamics, thus developing the emotional life of his characters, bringing them into opposition, and carrying this conflict to its peak or resolution.

An example of such a well calculated musical structure is the second scene of the first act of *Rigoletto,* which may be likened in formal terms to a gigantic recitative followed by a gigantic aria, except that each part is expanded to embrace many sections and different voices. It opens with Rigoletto meditating on the "curse" with which the preceding scene had ended. The "recitative" or *parlando* style continues in the duet between Rigoletto and the assasin Sparafucile, and reaches a climax in Rigoletto's great monologue, "Pari siamo." Then what we can call the "aria" section of the scene, or the more rhythm-dominated and tuneful music, begins; the sweetly melodic duet between Rigoletto and Gilda (baritone-soprano), followed by, as Rigoletto leaves, the love duet between the Duke and Gilda (tenor-soprano). Its climax is Gilda's aria, "Caro nome." Then the "action" comes, the abduction of Gilda, gotten over as quickly as possible, and the scene ends with a reflection of its opening, as Rigoletto, in dismay, recalls the "curse."

A remark made by Verdi throws a revealing light upon his concept of operatic form. A soprano had asked him to compose a special aria for her in *Rigoletto.* (Mozart generally did such a chore quite willingly, but that was a different age and style, and Mozart achieved perfection quite differently). Verdi answered, "And where is it to be placed? Verses and notes can be written, but they would make no effect without the right time and place. . . . My idea was that *Rigoletto* should be one long series of duets without airs and finales, because that is how I felt it."[9] This should not of course be taken too literally. In *Rigoletto* and his other operas Verdi did not write only duets. The point is that Verdi conceived an opera as an unfolding of the individual emotional life of his characters, developed at the same time in terms of their relationships to one another. And in this concept duets play a central role. The great Verdi duets of this nature are a unique achievement, quite different from the sharing of a melody between two voices that can frequently be found in his Italian predecessors, in Mozart, or in other parts of his own work.

In these great duets, often lasting a full half hour, intertwining the stuff of both declamation and song, two characters in colloquy lay themselves bare. Some of these great "duet" scenes are that between Violetta and Germont in the second act of

La Traviata, that between Leonora and the Padre Guardiano in the second act of *La Forza del Destino* and that between King Philip and the Grand Inquisitor in the third act of *Don Carlo.* The entire second half of *Aida* is constructed about a series of such rich duets.

As an example of the grandeur of Verdi's architecture, *La Forza del Destino* (1861-62) will be discussed here, because it brings together many facets of his national thinking and is also one of the more underrated of his works. It has a remarkable symmetry, which is disclosed when we ignore its act divisions and see it as built in six great scenes, corresponding roughly to the divisions of a colossal symphony. They are (1) movement of dramatic conflict; (2) scherzo; (3) slow movement; (4) slow movement; (5) scherzo; (6) dramatic closing movement. Its lack of full appreciation is due to the fact that critics, classifying Verdi as a great "popular" melodist, refuse to recognize that he is also an intellect. They do not look behind the surface melodrama to discover his real aims. A Verdi stereotype is manufactured, and when the music does not conform to it, performances are mangled and vulgarized to fit the stereotype. Thus the Metropolitan Opera Company in New York, in its production of this opera hacks out some of the finest music and most significant scenes, on the grounds that they do not seem "essential to the plot." It takes as basic the "blood and thunder" which Verdi actually used as a springboard for deeper matters. Even so friendly a critic as Francis Toye describes the opera as "a curious jumble," and, taking a clue from the fact that it was commissioned by the St. Petersburg opera and first produced there, says that it remembles "Russian shapelessness and incoherence."[10] It is true that the original drama, written by a liberal Spanish diplomat, the Duke of Rivas, is no artistic masterpiece, and suffers from having too many accidents and coincidences. But it attracted Verdi because it gave him the material to develop four great national themes central to his mind; the backward mentality of the feudal aristocracy, the division within the Church, the patriotic call for independence, and the misery of the common folk. To each of these he gave its own inspired musical clothing.

The first scene—dramatic first movement—gets over much of the plot as rapidly as possible, so that Verdi can devote more time to other matters. Its theme is the bigotry and bloody-mindedness of the old feudal minded aristocrats, with their artificial, destructive concepts of "family honor" and their caste consciousness. The heroine, Leonora, is in love and about to elope with Alvaro, who comes from a noble family of India. But her father, the Marquis of Calatrava, despises the lover for his color. He surprises the two together, and when the lover throws away the gun he is carrying, to leave himself unarmed, it accidentally goes off and kills the Marquis. The ill-fated lovers separate. The music is in the swinging, dramatic-melodic vein of works like *Ernani* and *Il Trovatore.*

The second scene—scherzo—which takes place in a village, is entirely different musically, as it is in thought. All it tells us, concerning the plot, is that Leonora is wandering, disguised in men's clothes, and that her brother, Carlo, disguised as a student, is bent on tracking down her and her lover, so that he can wipe out in blood the stain in the family. But the scene is the first great portrayal in the opera of the common people, and of the independence theme. It is a perfect giant-size scherzo. It starts with a chain of dancing folk and popular style melodies, with voices skillfully woven in as on the scene come muleteers, peasants, a wandering peddler, the town mayor, and a Gypsy woman, Preziosilla. It is she who becomes the stirring embodiment of the theme of struggle for freedom, and she sings of fighting the Austrians, who are a "plague to Italy." There is a "trio" section as in a symphonic scherzo, here consisting of a prayer, as chanting pilgrims pass outside. Then the "scherzo" resumes with dance-like music, including the opening dance theme and a rollicking "student song" air by Carlo. There is a beautiful coda, as the villagers say "good night" followed by a magical, quick recapitulation of the main musical themes previously heard.

The third scene—slow movement—takes up the theme of the Church; one of great importance in Verdi's mind, since the Papacy and Church hierarchy with little exception had put constant obstacles in the path of Italian democracy and unity. He aims to show the two contrasting sides of the Church, in the form of two characterizations; the mean and querulous Fra Melitone, and the wise, tender and deeply sympathetic Padre Guardiano. The place is at first outside, and then inside, a church and convent, where Leonora comes for refuge, asking permission to live as a hermit nearby. It starts with Leonora's aria; then after her peevish reception by Melitone, moves into one of Verdi's greatest "duet" passages, namely that between her and the Padre Guardiano; reaches a musical climax in the antiphonal music between the Padre and the monks' chorus, and ends with a coda as Leonora's voice is heard floating over the chorus.

The next scene—a slow movement with interspersed dramatic passages—is at an army camp in Italy, where Spanish soldiers are fighting the Austrians. The hero Alvaro is now a soldier. Carlo is in the same camp, obsessed with the insane desire to avenge his father, and to kill the two lovers, regardless of their innocence of any wrongdoing. He represents Verdi's portrait of the feudal mentality. Carlo does not know that Alvaro is the culprit he seeks, but after Alvaro saves his life in a skirmish, Carlo discovers Alvaro's true identity. The music has a symmetrical form, the scene starting with Alvaro's recitative and aria, reaching a climax in the famous duet *"Solemne in quest' ora,"* and ending with Carlo's recitative and brooding aria.

The following scene opens with a short, melodramatic duel between the two men, and then becomes a wonderfully rich scherzo movement, as the common people enter. The place is an army camp, and the soldiers, with the woman camp followers, are presented in rousing popular style march and dance melodies. Preziosilla, the fiery and witty spirit of freedom, sings a patriotic air, musically providing an interesting change to a modal idiom perhaps Gypsy, or Slavic. There is a cry for a "united Italy." Then the peddler enters, with still another change of folk idiom, his music having a plaintive, "street cry" quality. Verdi exposes the seamy side of army life, as the peddler preys upon the soldiers, offering them a few pennies for the spoils which they have laid their hands upon. The bargaining is accompanied by dancing, folk-style music. Then comes the scherzo "trio," the sad lament of the peasants, crying that war has torn up the land and brought starvation upon them. A group of recruits enter who have been pressed into the army, torn from their homes. The rousing opening music returns, as the women try to cheer them up, and this turns into a lively *tarantella,* which adds still another folk pattern to this remarkable "peoples scene." Then Melitone enters, with a sardonic monologue, quarreling with the soldiers, and the scene ends with a song by Preziosilla, accompanied by drums (a later addition by Verdi and somewhat weaker than the previous music in the scene).

The scene as a whole is unique in Verdi; a portrayal of the common people not simply as "chorus," but as a group of differentiated human beings, and achieving this with a remarkable variety of popular and folk-style idioms. There is a close resemblance between this scene and the great crowd scenes in Mussorgsky's *Boris Godunov,* down to the cry of the peddler, which foreshadows the haunting music of Mussorgsky's half-crazed mendicant. The fact that this opera was produced in St. Petersburg, about six years before Mussorgsky began *Boris Godunov,* indicates that the influence might have been a direct one.

The closing scene of the opera takes place outside the church and convent where Alvaro has also found refuge, not knowing that Leonora is living nearby as a hermit. There is another powerful crowd scene as the hungry people clamor for bread, and Melitone unwillingly feeds them, while abusing them. He is rebuked by the Padre Guardiano, and a masterly short duet between the two churchmen follows, a perfect piece of succinct dual characterization. Then, as Carlo enters, finally having tracked down his victim Alvaro, the dramatic-melodic final movement of the opera begins. It moves through the powerful duet between the two antagonists, with its swinging, rhythm-dominated melodies; Leonora's aria, and the grand and poignant closing trio. Although Verdi subsequently composed such great works as *Don Carlo, Aida, Otello* and *Falstaff,* he never went further in the directions opened up by *La Forza del Destino;* the block-like, broadly conceived symphonic structure, the delving into the varieties of folk music, and the Shakespearean bringing together of many sides of life.

The historic limitation of Verdi's music dramas is their recourse to melodrama such as the coincidences, the accidental changing of babies at birth, the mysterious poisonings, the overused motif of love across the warring camps. Thoroughly realistic in temperament, deeply immersed in the struggle for Italian independence and progress, he nevertheless had to deal with contemporary ideas and problems through implication. He was unable to take the step of addressing himself directly in opera to the faithful portrayal of history or of the actual life of the Italian people. One reason is that not only in his formative period, but for most of his creative years, he had to work under one or another form of censorship. Another perhaps was that he was so much of a lone figure in Italy. There was no galaxy of composers, writers, painters and critics, like that which in Russia was bringing into being a vigorous and many-sided national art, one that was tackling every problem freshly.

There may also be a subjective aspect to the melodrama. It is his dwelling upon, trying to view in terms of human personality and ethics, a national and historical problem to which he could find no practical solution—the contradictions within Italy itself, both during the struggle for independence and after victory. Evil appeared in the very process of gaining triumph. It was clearly apparent after the 1860's, in the self-seeking politics which ignored the continued misery of the poor, so that in 1879, he could cry to the government to "bother about the daily bread that people must have to eat."[11] Certainly there is no direct connection between this and the melodramatic events of his operas. But the tragic theme behind these events, like that behind his melodramas is that of love, the most human aspect of life, corresponding to the deepest yearnings of people, destroyed by mean ambition and cold-hearted malevolence.

II

If Verdi spoke for a national struggle that was at least in part victorious, the Czech composers spoke for one, the victory of which could only be a distant hope. The first major composer to express the national consciousness of Bohemia, striving for freedom from the yoke of the Austrian Empire, "prison house of nations," was Bedrich Smetana (1824-84). Behind him was a long line of gifted Czech composers. But the turning point he represented in Czech musical life was that he could live and work at home, serving his own nation. The son of a brewer in the service of a nobleman, he turned to music for a career despite the wishes of his father, who rightly saw it as the worst paid of professions.

Smetana started a modest music school in Prague, but his first attempts to foster a Czech music seemed hopeless in the reactionary atmosphere that followed the crushing of the democratic revolutionary movements of 1848. France, Germany and Austria had taken fire, and also Hungary and Bohemia. But the movement was shot through with racialisms. The middle class revolutionary forces in Germany and Austria, even in the brief period when they had hopes for a parliamentary government, had little interest in the freedom of other peoples. The Tsarist Russian Empire, likewise a "prison house of nations," was making a bid for the allegiance of all the Slav peoples. The Hungarians, seeking freedom from Austria, were willing to be used as a police force to fight Italians and Slavs. The independence movement in Bohemia found itself crippled by the presence of a large German population, German in allegiance, and many Czechs found rule by Austria more appealing than the intense "Germanization" threatened by a rising, autocratic, unified Germany. By making an adroit use of these complex racialisms and antagonisms, the Austrian Empire was able to tighten its political and cultural hold upon its subject peoples. It was not until the victories of the Italian independence movement came in 1859 that the frightened Austrian court allowed the Bohemians a limited parliamentary representation. In 1867 Hungary demanded and won a relatively independent position, although as part of a "dual monarchy," Austria-Hungary, in which the Hungarian ruling force was the landed aristocracy while the peasantry lived in abject poverty. In Bohemia the Austrian reins alternately loosened and tightened, but there was at least intellectual elbow room for a few determined figures, like Smetana, and following him, Dvorak, to create one of the great European national musical movements.

In 1856 Smetana had gone to teach music in Sweden, where he had won considerable eminence, but the more liberal atmosphere of the 1860's impelled him to return home. From 1861 to his death he became the impassioned fighter for a Czech national musical art, as journalist, conductor, teacher and artistic director of the Prague Opera. Among his big works were a series of operas, including *The Brandenburgers in Bohemia* (1863), *The Bartered Bride* (1863-6), *Dalibor* (1866), *Libuse* (1872), *The Two Widows* (1874), *The Kiss* (1876); the great cycle of six tone poems collectively entitled *My Fatherland* (1874-49); and the heartbreakingly beautiful *String Quartet in E minor*, "From My Life," (1876).

All of these works were imbued with a fiery patriotic feeling, yet devoid of any racism or national chauvinism, and based on a tender affection for people. They won him the love of great numbers of Czechs. Yet they also aroused hostile and bitter criticism. The Czech landed aristocracy was lukewarm in its desire for independence, and resented seeing its peasantry, who had only recently been serfs without rights, depicted as human beings with dignity. The Bohemian German population played a strong role in cultural life and attacked a Czech-conscious music as a provincialism. There were on the other hand narrow Czech nationalists who saw no reason for learning anything from abroad. They accused Smetana of "Wagnerism" whenever he used the repetition of musical motifs, or the harmonic and orchestral lessons of German orchestral music, to portray human psychology. Bickering and mean intrigues constantly hampered his work. Something of this atmosphere is recorded by a Czech art historian, who was attending lectures on the history of music by a Dr. Ambros, at about the time *Dalibor* was staged. This happened to be an opera vulnerable to attacks by chauvinists from both sides; by the Germans, for its Czech patriotic theme, and by the "anti-Wagnerians," for its *leitmotif* fabric.

"Dr. Ambros, a small man with a huge grey beard and as lively as quicksilver, tripped in. He put down the book he was carrying, and sat there, silent. No, not actually silent, he kept coughing and clearing his throat. After a while he spoke, as though deep in thought. 'Dalibor was a failure yesterday at the Czech Theatre!' There was a pause. In a little while he brought out another few words: 'And yet every note is a pearl.' Again silence. Finally: 'That Smetana – a whale in a fishpond!' That was all. Then he continued his lecture where we had left off last time." The writer adds, "If the fishpond had even been a clean one!"[12]

Smetana stood his ground, never compromising, although even making a living was difficult for there was little money in Prague compared to what could be earned by a gifted musician abroad. In 1863 he helped form a union of Czech artists which exists to this day. He and his music played a central part in the demonstrations for Czech autonomy which took place in 1868. In 1874 he was afflicted by deafness, and retired from public life. Some years later he fell victim to a cerebral disease, and he died in a sanitarium. Yet his life was not a tragic one. It was after deafness struck that he wrote *Vltava* ("The River Moldau") with its radiantly lovely melodies, and the opera *The Kiss,* with its sweet tenderness and gentle humor. Even the autobiographical quartet *From My Life,* which depicts the devastating blow of his deafness, with pages to which one can hardly listen without weeping, is not a work of self-pity. It is a strong work; a musical self-portrait which looks back on his life as a good one, with its youthful yearning and love of art, its exhilarating dance episodes, its bliss of first love, and its joy in discovering the national path of musical creation. And the style is a perfect mirror of his musical personality, in its introspectiveness, and poignant, declamatory phrases interwoven so perfectly with the vitality of folk-style song and dance melody.

The absence of chauvinism from Smetana's national thinking is confirmed by the breadth of his musical roots. He grew up musically on the innovations of the early romantics like Mendelssohn, Liszt, Schumann, Chopin, and the young Wagner, welcoming and sharing their urge for individual freedom, their defiance of all academicism, and their inner sensitivity. And he also worshipped Mozart. It is worth remembering that Prague had been musically Mozart's "second home," far more appreciative of his great operas than Vienna, and Prague music lovers had looked on Mozart as one "of their own." If romanticism and Mozart seem to be a strange combination, the clue to the way in which Smetana could make them both part of his style lies in the fact that he preserved the sensitivity of romanticism without its bombast, turgidity, and grandiose self-projection.

Smetana was not one of those peasant-born composers with folk music, so to speak, in the blood. He learned comparatively late the beauties of Czech folk music. At first he would call the national dances "jig-jogs," teasing friends like the poet Jan Neruda or the musician Ferdinand Heller, who were folk dance propogandists. But then he began to feel the plastic possibilities of this music, and while writing *The Bartered Bride* would bring each new section to these "specialists," saying with a smile, "Another jig-jog," but deeply concerned over whether they thought he had struck the essential folk quality.[13] He rejected the easy path of simply transcribing existing folk songs, which was the only way the German-minded theorists could understand the use of folk music. "Smetana again opposed this, saying that in this way a medley of various songs, a kind of quodlibet would come into being but not an artistic work with any continuity."[14] In other words he rejected "folk style" if it were only to be a light divertissement, contrasted to "serious music." If Czech folk music were to be used for creative composition, it had to show itself as material fit for great emotions, for sensitive character portrayal and organic form. Perhaps the special radiance of *The Bartered Bride* is due to the fact that it was written precisely in this period of joyous discovery of what could be done with the music of the Czech people.

There are two sides to Smetana's approach to national art. One offers realistic images of the Czech common people in terms of domestic and village life, removed from the big currents of history, but treating the characters with great warmth and dignity. The other, the call to Czech freedom and independence, is presented in terms of the heroic, semi-historical and semi-legendary Bohemian past. In the first category fall such operas as *The Bartered Bride, The Kiss, The Two Widows,* and the two great "nature pictures" from the tone poem cycle, *Ma Vlast, The River Moldau* and *From Bohemia's Meadows and Groves.* In the second fall such as operas as *Dalibor,* which deals with a knight in the Middle Ages who takes up the cause of the peasantry against the Bohemian king, and *Libuse,* telling of a legendary Bohemian princess who married a peasant. Also in this group are the other four tone poems of *Ma Vlast—Vysherad, Sarka, Tabor* and *Blanik.* The last two emerge from the legendary into real history, evoking the memories of the heroic Taborites, followers of Jan Huss, who fought for peasant rights and against church corruption in the fifteenth ceuntury.

The difference in approach is reflected in the difference in musical style. The first group tend towards a greater clarity of texture, a rhythm-dominated music with a liberal use of rounded folk-style melodies and dance rhythms such as polkas and *furiants.* The second, with their romantic, dream-like visions, tend towards a more subjective style with a richer harmonic texture, kin to the romantic tone poems; a *parlando* or declamatory musical line, and a liberal use of repeated symbolic and psychological motifs, like the Wagnerian *leitmotifs.* If they show a less obvious use of folk patterns, the motifs, like those of the prison scene or marches of *Dalibor,* nevertheless have an indefineable Czech feeling, perhaps drawn from more ancient or medieval sources, like the great tradition of Czech and Moravian popular hymns. And in one instance, the source Smetana draws upon is clear; the great Hussite hymn "All ye warriors of God," which figures in *Tabor* and *Blanik,* and in the prophetic finale of *Libuse.* It was the more subjective works which inspired the attacks of the "anti-Wagnerians" upon Smetana. But although he admired Wagner, the spirit of his legendary works is quite different from that in Wagner. It is not a dream-life upheld against reality, but a dream of the future, growing out of the struggles of the present, and bolstered by the heroism of the past. It is subjective music but not subjectivist and egocentric; the composer's deepest hopes are bound up with the future of his country and people.

The most cherished of Smetana's operas, at home and abroad, is *The Bartered Bride.* It is his most classical work, in which his love for nation and people takes its most objective form, fully realized in word and music, creating a captivating play of real people in real society, with an open air feeling. The story handles a much-used theme, but one always valid, for it comes up again and again in real life; the struggle of two young people for the right to love and marriage, against the pressure of those who want them to sell their happiness and freedom for money. The characters are beautifully and distinctively re-created in music, the heroine Marenka especially emerging with real tenderness, depth and high spirits, and being given some of Smetana's great arias, combining *parlando,* or arioso style, with rounded rhythmic melody. The score abounds in rousing folk dances and choruses, and displays as well Smetana's plasticity in handling folk idiom. The overture, for instance, begins with typical folk melodies being born, so to speak, out of their harmonic-rhythmic roots. Beautifully constructed, it is like a Czech version of the overture to *The Marriage of Figaro.* Indeed the whole opera, if lacking Mozart's brilliant play upon two levels of music and meaning at once, is Mozartian in its concept of form, adroitly repeating and varying its melodies to create solid, architectural blocks of music, which are at the same time responsive to every change of mood. *The Bartered Bride* has a thoughtful and serious lesson; the humanity of the common people and their place in the nation. Its Mozartian quality discloses the truth that the nineteenth century Czech national music, far from being a provincialism, was a natural growth out of the classic tradition which, far from being purely German or Austrian, had been a product of many peoples including the Czech.

Dalibor is a moving and beautiful opera, composed in Smetana's more visionary and subjective style. Its first act for example, may be called a masterly, integrated tone poem with voices, a cumulatively developing musical structure woven out of the motifs presented in the very opening, and their transformations. *The Kiss,* a late work, shows a nostalgic and *parlando* use of folk style, full of fine melody and richer in orchestral fabric than *The Bartered Bride,* and it also makes a notable advance in the close unity of musical phrase with Czech speech. It parallels the developments in "speech song" being made at the same time in Russia, and it is worth noting that Smetana, who admired the German tradition but fought against the Germanization of Czech culture, also provided a bridge between Central Europe and Slavic culture. He resented the policies of the Austrian government, "to throw all the nations of Austria into one pot—that of Germanization—in order to rule over all of us."[15] When he instituted the first regular symphony concerts in Prague, he wrote, "The programmes are to include masterpieces by the tone heroes of any and every nation, but particular consideration will be given to the works of Slav composers. Have performances by Russian, Polish or Southern Slav composers ever been heard at performances in Prague? I hardly think so. Indeed it is a great rarity to meet one or the other of our own people's names on our programmes. . . . As a Czech I arrange Czech concerts."[16]

The six tone poems of *Ma Vlast* ("My Country")—should be known as a unit. Not only do musical motifs reappear from one work to the next, but the entire cycle becomes a composite picture of what is meant by a nation's cultural heritage, linking together the past, present, and hope for the future. It is a ringing answer to the overlords who, in order to oppress or enslave a people, will try to wipe out from their minds the memories of their own heroic and independent past. Musically, the cycle shows the sensitive integration between the Czech motifs of the medieval and ancient past, and those of the present. *Vysherad* opens with a harp motif, recalling the ancient bards at the legendary Bohemian courts. In the middle section folk-style music appears, and this is transformed into a sad memory of ancient glories. *Vltava* ("The Moldau") is on the surface a nature picture, portraying the Czech river rising from its source, passing villages and meadows in the brightness of daytime activity and the quietness of night, and falling over cascades, until it flows majestically past Prague. But built with the repetition and development of one of the loveliest of folk-style melodies, linked to the past by the reappearance of the bardic "Vysherad" theme, it evokes a picture of the Czech people, rising out of slumber, dancing in the fields, moving through turbulent struggles, and becoming part of an unstoppable movement for freedom. *Sarka,* depicting the legendary Czech Amazon queen, is full of a wild spirit of independence. *From Bohemia's Meadows and Groves* is again a nature-folk picture, festive in mood, showing once more how folk-style themes become malleable elements in Smetana's hands, "born" out of the elements of harmony and rhythm. *Tabor* is a sombre battle scene, recalling the band of Taborites who fought under John Ziska, and built with moving transformations of the old Hussite hymn. *Blanik* evokes the mountain under which the Hussite warriors sleep. The music takes up the thread from the preceding tone poem, turns it into quiet "sleep" music, with a pastoral feeling; then moves into a rousing march, followed by a triumphant statement first of the Hussite hymn and then of the "bard" motif with which the entire cycle had started.

III

In Russia, within the space of ten years, a galaxy of composers was born who would create through their combined efforts the most challenging national movement of modern times, with forms of startling originality and world influence, the implications of which have come to be recognized only in the twentieth century. In St. Petersburg Mily Balakirev (1837-1910), organized in 1862 a Free School of Music, devoted to bringing concerts and musical instruction to the poor. Around him, attracted by his opposition to academicism, his propaganda for Russian folk music, and his championship of the stimulating romantic currents represented by Schumann, Liszt and Berlioz, gathered four others. With Balakirev they came to be known as the "Mighty Five," or the "Invincible Band." They were Cesar Cui (1835-1917), Alexander Borodin (1835-87), Modest Mussorgsky (1835-81) and Nicholas Rimsky-Korsakov (1844-1908). Out of the Moscow school, somewhat more conservative in its theories, rose Peter Ilich Tchaikovsky (1840-93).

They all were composers of sharply different temperament and musical style. Yet what they shared in common was their identification with their land. Thus Tchaikovsky wrote in a letter from Italy, "It is gloriously beautiful. And yet–shall I tell you or not? When I walk by the sea I am seized with a desire to go home and pour out all my yearning and agitation in a letter to you, or to Toly. Why should a simple Russian landscape, a walk through our homely villages and woods, a tramp over the fields and steppes at sunset, inspire me with such an intense love of nature that I throw myself down on the earth and give myself up to the enchantment with which all these humble things fill me?"[17]

The special qualities which their work collectively embodied were those which Russia itself represented in nineteenth century history. A vast land with great resources, it had made little contribution to world science and art between the Middle Ages and the nineteenth century, with exceptions like the work of the brilliant scientist Mikhail Lomonosov, just as it had made little progress in industrialization and education. First keeping it backward were invasions by the Tatars and Mongols from the East, and Germany and Poland from the West; then the formation of a rigid class of landed aristocracy, which forced serfdom upon the peasantry. These manacles were only broken in 1861. But the peasantry had never been a beaten or resigned people. There had been constant unrest and rebellion, which showed itself as well in a vigorous oral traditoin of poetry, story and song.

The clue to the unique qualities shown by nineteenth century Russian art, music and literature lies not in mysticisms about the "Slavic soul" but in the fact a country so great in potential was covering the ground in a century that others had covered in four centuries, with transformations so rapid that all traditional values were thrown into question. "Advanced" countries like England and France looked upon Russia as a fallow field for their own investment, and at the same time feared it as a potential rival. They instigated the Crimean War of 1853-56 to keep Russia from developing as a Black Sea naval power. The frightful losses in this "little war" by the Russian common people, largely the peasantry, burned itself in the mind of writers like Tolstoi. And it was the weakness which Russia showed then which was probably an impelling reason for abolishing serfdom. But this only changed the nature of the peasants' misery. As Lenin wrote, "The patriarchal countryside, only recently emancipated from serfdom, was literally given over to be sacked and looted to rapacious capital and the tax collector."[18] With the development of capitalism, the aristocracy retained its power as part of the governmental bureaucracy under the Tsar, but some of the gentry found themselves penniless, their estates having been sold piece by piece to merchants. Feudalism, capitalism, the old traditional religion and the "benefits of science," all were thrown into question, for the great mass of people suffered the oppressiveness of the worst aspects of capitalism combined with the worst aspects of feudalism.

Thus the Russian national movement differed from the Czech, for example, where the struggle was against an external enemy, the Austrians. Who was oppressing Russia? An article written by the great critic, N. A. Dobrolyubov, in 1860, in the form of a review of Turgenev's novel *On the Eve,* both throws light on this and offers an example of the boldness with which leading writers expressed themselves despite the censors. "We, thank God, are not enslaved by anybody, we are free, we are a great people who more than once have decided with our arms the destinies of kingdoms and nations; we are the masters of others, but we have no masters." But this, of course, is irony. He concludes with the profound implication that true patriots would have to look "inside" for what was stifling the nation's progress. "An external enemy, a privileged oppressor can be attacked and vanquished far more easily than an internal enemy, whose forces are spread everywhere in a thousand different shapes, elusive and invulnerable, harassing us on all sides, poisoning our lives, giving us no rest, and preventing us from surveying the battlefield. This internal enemy cannot be combated with ordinary weapons; we can liberate ourselves from him only by dispelling the raw, foggy atmosphere of our lives in which he was born, grew up and gained strength, and by surrounding ourselves with an atmosphere in which he will be unable to breathe."[19]

Hostility to science, education and democracy, a stifling police censorship, an importation of culture from Germany, France or Italy, a suspicion of anything national unless it was merely quaint and spoke of the "good old times," a resentment of any portrayal of the real life of the working people, were some of the means through which Tsardom and aristocracy kept their grip upon the nation. And the effect of the national movement in music as in the other arts was to dispel this "raw, foggy atmosphere."

Certainly of the leading Russian national composers, none could be accused of even remotely explicit radical political ideas, except for Rimsky-Korsakov, who in his quiet way held sharply critical views of Tsardom. A naval officer before he turned wholly to music, he writes in his memoirs of a mission on which his ship was sent in 1863, when there was a Polish uprising and the Baltic coast had to be guarded against arms being smuggled to the Poles. "In spite of the secret sympathy in the young hearts of us (the members of the midshipmen's cabin), for a cause that seemed righteous to us, the cause of a distant and kindred nationality oppressed by her sister Russia, we were forced to set forth willy-nilly, at the authorities' orders, to serve the oppressor faithfully."[20]

But the composers, whatever their politics, set one standard for their work; that it reflect truthfully the real life, character and history of the Russian people, and be of service to them, even if the works could not reach the great mass of people during the composer's lifetime. This itself brought them into constant conflicts, not of their own devising, with the authorities. Thus when in 1868, Mussorgsky's imagination was fired with the idea of setting to music Pushkin's *Boris Godunov,* it happened to be a drama which only two years before had been first passed by the censors for stage performance, forty years after it had been written. And even then, the censors excised some scenes. Completing the first draft of the opera in 1869, Mussorgsky had a five year fight to get it produced, and then some scenes of the opera had to be omitted. In 1872 Rimsky-Korsakov had censor difficulties with his opera *The Maid of Pskov,* dealing with the times of the Tsar "Ivan the Terrible." Tchaikovsky's opera *The Oprichnik* was forbidden by the censors in 1880, for political reasons. In 1891, while on a visit to the United States, he wrote in a letter, "Went to Knabe's to thank him for the beautiful present (a statue of Freedom) which he sent me yesterday. Shall I be allowed to take it into Russia?"[21]

A letter written by Tchaikovsky in 1878 gives a revealing picture of "The Five." It is too harsh in its judgments. Its importance however is that it underlines the complex problem of what a truly national music requires. Tchaikovsky knew that the path he had worked out for himself, that of recreating in Russian terms the forms of symphony, chamber music and sonata, and taking up the host of professional musical skills that were at hand, was profoundly necessary. In the name of a Russian national music, "The Five," under the leadership of Balakirev, were discarding too many necessary tools. And yet he recognizes the power in Mussorgsky, even though this art is too different from Tchaikovsky's own for him to grasp its full contribution.

"Rimsky-Korsakov is the only one among them who discovered, five years ago, that the doctrines preached by this circle had no sound basis, that their mockery of the schools and the classical masters, their denial of authority and of the masterpieces, was nothing but ignorance. . . . From contempt for the schools, Rimsky-Korsakov suddenly went over to the cult of technique. . . . Either he will turn out a great master, or be lost in contrapuntal intricacies. C. Cui is a gifted amateur. His music is not original, but graceful and elegant; it is too coquettish—'made up' so to speak. . . . Borodin—aged fifty—Professor of Chemistry at the Academy of Medicine, also professes talent, a very great talent, which however has come to nothing, for the want of teaching, and because blind fate has led him into the science laboratories instead of a vital musical existence. . . . With regard to Mussorgsky . . . his gifts are perhaps the most remarkable of all, but his nature is narrow and he has no aspirations towards self-perfection. . . .Mussorgsky plays with his lack of polish—and even seems proud of his want of skill, writing just as it comes to him, believing blindly in the infallibility of his genius. As a matter of fact, his very original talent flashes forth now and again. Balakirev is the greatest personality of the entire circle. . . . Now he spends all his time in church, fasts, kisses the relics—and does very little else. In spite of his great gifts, he has done a great deal of harm. For instance it was he who ruined Korsakov's early career by assuring him he had no need to study. He is the inventor of all the theories of this remarkable circle which unites so many undeveloped, falsely developed, or prematurely decayed, talents. . . . What a sad phenomenon! So many talents from which—with the exception of Rimsky-Korsakov—we can scarcely dare to hope for anything serious. But this is always our case in Russia; vast forces which are impelled by the fatal shadow of a Plevna from taking the open field and fighting as they should. But all the same, those forces exist. Thus Mussorgsky, with all his ugliness, speaks a new idiom. Beautiful it may not be, but it is new. We may reasonably hope that Russia will one day produce a whole school of strong men who will open up new paths in art."[22] (Plevna was a fortified town which, during the Russian-Turkish war of 1877, the Russian armies tried vainly to capture for five months, although, as it turned out, they had no strategic use for it).

Balakirev, Rimsky-Korsakov, Borodin, Tchaikovsky, all were deeply attached to the nation and loved and studied its folk music. What was unique about Mussorgsky however was his complete identification with the peasantry. This may be seen in his style, with its recreation of melody out of its roots in speech, so that speech seems naturally to move into song. It is a different kind of vocal line from that of French operatic declamation, Italian recitative, Verdi's monologues, and the musical declamation of a Wagner or Hugo Wolf. The difference is not simply a matter of language; that the others are Italian, French and German, while Mussorgsky set Russian speech. Previous composers of opera and song had generally set language which had first passed through the refinement of poetic forms. Mussorgsky tried to write "As living people speak. . . . If the expression in sound of human thought and feeling in simple speech is truly reproduced by me in music, and this reproduction is musical and artistic, then the thing is in the bag. . . . Whatever speech I hear, no matter who is speaking (nor what he says) my mind is already working to find the musical statement for such speech."[23]

The "simple speech" Mussorgsky had in mind was by no means ordinary conversation. It was poetic, but in a direct, earthy way, comparable to the poetry of folk speech, with its frequently musical qualities and vivid imagery drawn from everyday life. Many great writers have discovered this quality of peasant speech, such as, within the Irish national literary movement, John Millington Synge and Sean O'Casey. George Thomson tells of an Irish peasant woman's eloquence while talking of her family abroad. "As she spoke, she grew excited, her language became more fluent, more highly-coloured, rhythmical, melodious, and her body swayed in a dreamy, cradle-like accompaniment. Then she picked up her buckets with a laugh, wished me good night, and went home."[24] Another parallel is offered by the poetic, yet earthy speech of the American Negro folk blues, which engenders its own seemingly natural, effortless musical expression. By "reproducing" such speech in music, Mussorgsky meant something quite different from setting it to melody or heightening speech inflections with musical pitch. He started with the patterns of folk music itself, exploring and expanding particularly its *parlando* or speech-inflected melodic shapes. What emerged then was a richly melodic music, with a freight of emotion carried in the musical line, not simply in the heightened words. This is the kind of music Calvocoressi speaks of when he says, "There is a world of difference between negative realism, which consists in avoiding all that would be non-realistic, and positive realism, which consists in discovering striking processes of evocation and expression—entirely a matter of creative imagination."[25] To this Mussorgsky added a genius for feeling out and using the special qualities of an enormous variety of patterns that were contained in the general area of "folk." He wrote melody based on various modal scales, some of it Oriental; rounded song in major-minor modalities; melody in the style of more courtly or middle class popular song, with folk connections; melody in the patriotic anthem style, in the modes of ecclesiastical music. With this he created a gallery of profound psychological musical portraits, by no means limited to the peasantry.

A song such as *Yeremushka's Cradle Song* (1868) illustrates the unchartered territory Mussorgsky was exploring through the gates of folk song. In the text a peasant woman is brooding over her child while rocking it to sleep. An *ostinato* of repeated, descending two-note phrases both is the germ of the mother's song, and conveys the rocking of the cradle. Out of the barest of means, a human image or living melody is created. The scale is folk-modal, and irregular, typical of *parlando-rubato* folk song, with a note a half-tone higher or lower sometimes substituted for that in the basic pattern. Then another melody enters, contrasting in shape, more rhythm-dominated, with a hint of folk dance. A variant of the opening then ends the song. We can say that Mussorgsky, instead of modulating in classic style, is playing two different folk scales against each other. Every phrase of the song is in folk style. Yet the song is not a simulated folk song, but a full-fledged "art song," a psychological portrait with a feeling of both "outer life," — the mother rocking the child to sleep—and "inner life," namely the sad thoughts of the mother.

As the great wealth of his songs reveal, folk music to Mussorgsky was not an undifferentiated mass of useful "peoples" musical material but a kind of lexicon of musical phrases and patterns able to evoke the most varied kinds of people and situations. They can embrace the whimsicality and capricious imagination of children, in the song cycle *The Nursery;* the breathless patter of a peasant making an address of love, in *Lovely Savishna;* the wild outcry of misery at the heart of a dance, as in *Gopak.* The dominating pattern is *parlando;* the rhythm is "internal," often changing from phrase to phrase, with a remarkable evocation of shifting body movement and gesture. A model of this fluid interweaving of *parlando* and dance patterns is the song *Trepak,* or "Death of a Peasant," from the cycle *Songs and Dances of Death.* In it the plastic elements of Russian folk song are used for a heartrending portrayal of the miseries of peasant life.

With the one act he composed of the opera *The Marriage,* in 1868, Mussorgsky, as he said, "crossed the Rubicon"[26] towards his goal of writing music "as living people speak." The style was as he himself remarked, "musical prose." But it led the way to the immense achievement of *Boris Godunov,* which he took up that same year, completing the first version a year later. In 1871-2 he remodelled it.

The leap forward, not only in his work but in the entire history of opera, represented by *Boris Godunov* lies in its tremendous portrayal of the Russian folk. It is a great collective tragic portrait. The folk is seen in its mercurial changes of mood, its uneasy passive resistance when prodded, its buffoon mask offered to official Society, and its secret resentments breaking out into violence. It is sometimes differentiated into various groups—men, women, children, and pilgrims—and sometimes coalesces into a great mass moving across the face of history. Individual characters also emerge to speak for different aspects of the folk, like the wandering friar Varlaam who had run away from a monastery, the woman innkeeper, the nurse in the Tsar's palace, and the half-crazed mendicant, whose sad song ends the opera. And in this same category can be put the powerful character of Pimen, the patriarchal monk chronicler, in his own words, "of truthful records so that future generations may know the past history of their land." He is not actually a folk character, and yet he represents the conscience of the nation. Against this panorama the noble personages of the opera act out their roles; Boris, who has murdered a child to gain the Tsar's throne, and who fights the nobles, whom the people hate, but adds to the people's burdens; the young monk Grigori, who becomes "the false Dmitri," declaring himself to be the former Tsar's son and claiming the throne, gathering an army in Poland to challenge Boris; Prince Shuisky, the crafty statesman, who both serves Boris and connives against him. And the common people are not merely "background." Their unrest and misery provide the moral base against which the duplicity, self-centredness and self-questioning of the leading personages are thrown into high relief.

Folk material is handled with the utmost variety. The orchestral introduction is a polyphonic elaboration of a folk-style melody. The opening chorus is a rounded folk-style song, which is developed to an intense, pleading climax. The "Coronation scene" employs an actual folk song, one that Beethoven had used in the scherzo of his *Second Rasoumovsky Quartet.* The inn scene starts with one strophic folk-style song followed by another, the innkeeper's song and Varlaam's "In the City of Kazan." Then Varlaam, as he sinks into a drunken half-sleep, goes into a more harmonically "primitive" folk-style song, like a cry from the heart. In the palace scene the song of the nurse is also in more "primitive" folk style, that of a tale told in endless, repeated, alternating phrases, and similar is the "game" song sung by the nurse and the Tsar's son.

Melodic motifs recur in the score, but in key psychological moments rather than as part of its continuous texture, more in the manner of Berlioz' *The Trojans,* Verdi in *La Forza del Destino* or Smetana in *The Bartered Bride* than in Wagnerian style. Notable is the motif which accompanies "the false Dmitri." It is heard first in the scene in Pimen's monastery cell, reflecting the dreams of glory rising in Grigori's mind. It is also heard in the monologue of Boris, when he learns of the threat to his rule. It has a patriotic, "national anthem" character. Calvocoressi writes, "It affects many forms and colors; it is in turn tragical, poetically mystical, impassioned, sardonic and martial."[27]

Like all the great opera composers, Mussorgsky seeks means to give various scenes a musical-structural unity, and one of the greatest examples is the "revolutionary scene" in Kromy forest, which, following Mussorgsky's intentions, should close the opera. Its structural origin may be found in Mussorgsky's early tone poem, *St. John's Night on Bald Mountain,* which he conceived in 1860, took up seriously in 1866, completed in 1867, and rewrote for inclusion in his comic opera, *Sorochinsky Fair.* The tone poem is based on the folk-tales of the "witches sabbath." It opens with a whirling *ostinato* phrase depicting the gathering of the witches, moves into a wild fantasy using typical phrases from both Russian folk and ecclesiastical music, and ends with soft, lovely phrases depicting the dawn. The "Kromy Forest" scene in this structure broadened, far richer in full-throated melodies and human images, even sharper in its contrast of melodies representing different scale and harmonic patterns. Here the whirling *ostinato* with which the scene starts depicts the milling crowd. Boisterous, melodic-declamatory phrases are heard from the chorus, reaching a peak of excitement as the people discover a nobleman and tie him to a tree. The women sing a sweet, rhythm-dominated folk-style song, taking on a sardonic character with the mocking words, "hail to the boyar!" The two friars, Varlaam and Missail, then enter, and the musical pattern changes to a folk song in ecclesiastical mode. There is another change, as two Jesuits enter, with their melody reminiscent of Catholic chant. "The "false Dmitri" then appears with his troops, haranguing the people, while the music takes on a martial patriotic character, including the use of his own motif. Then, as the crowd marches off with him, to the military music, there is an extraordinary transformation of the "praise to the boyar" motif, which had formerly been sardonic, and now is serious and martial. And just as the tone poem had ended with the soft "dawn" phrases, so now the opera scene ends with the prophetic song of the half-mad mendicant, alone on the stage, a sad, chromatically descending melody over an *ostinato* phrase which itself is like a sigh of pain. It is worth noting that the same all-over form of this scene was taken over by Stravinsky for the opening "Carnival" scene of his ballet *Petrouchka.*

Mussorgsky's grandmother had been a serf woman, and his immediate family was of the impoverished gentry. The career planned for him had been the army, and leaving this, he got a dreary, poorly paid civil service post. He was a sociable person, good company and full of high spirits. His fellow composers recognized his genius, and yet none of them fully comprehended what he was doing. They saw crudeness or clumsiness in some of his most inspired innovations in the harmonic and instrumental setting of varied folk idioms. They shared his national feeling and love for folk music, but did not go so far as he in his identification with the peasantry, and in the active role he saw, with deep insight, that they played in history. We can see this in the comparatively lesser, "background," role that the common people play in Borodin's *Prince Igor,* Tchaikovsky's historical opera *Mazeppa,* and Rimsky-Korsakov's historical opera *The Tsar's Bride.*

Mussorgsky and his friends fought to have *Boris Godunov* produced, and when the Imperial Theatre in St. Petersburg unwillingly staged it in 1874, it was a great public success, although critics hammered at it viciously. After two years it disappeared from the repertory. Rimsky-Korsakov shrewdly surmised that "the opera had displeased the Imperial family; there was gossip that its subject was unpleasant to the censors.[28]

Mussorgsky was broken by an oppressive society which recognized in his art an enemy. Making a living out of his art was impossible. The civil service post was exasperating in its pettiness and meagre pay. As he wrote, "But now I am destined to wither and grow sour among the Chaldeans, with wasted labor and time spent on business that would be done better without me. I am destined to be aware of the whole fruitlessness and needlessness of my labors in the Forestry Department. . . . It is horrible."[29] He could not make the compromises between art and livelihood or social position that others made in his time. He was too much aware of the fact that to create the art demanded by his times was a full-time job. "How have society's demands on modern Russian artists grown! A great proof of the discontent in these terrible times throughout all classes. And how intolerable are the *old-believer* artists, stagnating in their closet labor and their four-walled dreams!"[30]

The lack of understanding among his associates must have aroused bitter or conflicting feelings. Perhaps closest to him in the last decade of his life was the art critic, Vladimir Stasov, and even Stasov seems to have suffered from a weakness that afflicted the entire group, namely that of interfering in too cocksure a manner in someone else's creations.[31] In the middle 1870's Mussorgsky alarmed his friends by becoming careless as to the way he lived and seeking sustenance in alcohol. But they all had troubles and problems of their own, and lost touch with him over periods of time. He never stopped working on the grand musical projects he had outlined for himself. But suddenly he was dead at the age of forty-two, leaving fragments of a comic opera, *Sorochinsky Fair,* and another great but unfinished masterpiece of historical opera, *Khovanshchina.* Its setting is in the Russia of the youth of "Peter the Great," the close of the seventeenth century, about a hundred years after the time of *Boris Godunov.* Mussorgsky had planned still a third opera, that would carry his portrayal of key periods of Russian history into the late eighteenth century. It was to deal with the Cossack revolt against serfdom led by Pugachev in 1773. Never before Mussorgsky had any composer projected so grand and sweeping a portrayal of a nation's history in music drama, and in fact no one has since thought in such terms.

Khovanshchina presents a panorama of nobles, showing them as violent, intriguing, and bloody in their methods. The feudal-minded Prince Ivan Khovansky and his brainless son, Prince Andrew, represent the "ancient, gloomy, fanatical, dense Russia," in the words of Stasov, who suggested the plot. Prince Vassily Golitzin represents the more modern, "Europe-minded" aristocrat, shrewd, but also self-seeking. Both conspire against the power of the throne, represented by the youthful Peter (who does not appear on the stage). The throne is supported by another noble, Shaklovity, who combines genuinely patriotic feelings with conniving and bloodthirsty methods. Another leading character, Prince Myshetzsky, who has changed his name to Dosefei, has become the leader of a religious sect, the "Old Believers." They seek a return to ancient communal practices, looking with horror on both the immorality of the feudal-minded nobles and on any plans for "modernization" or progress. With deep insight Mussorgsky sees that the "new," the "open door on the West," is necessary for the nation to move forward, and that the "turn to the past" would lead only to stultification; yet also that the "new" is represented by self-seeking men who see in the common people only a means to support their own ambitions. There is also what was lacking in *Boris,* a fine woman characterization. It is Martha, passionately in love with Prince Andrew and cast off by him, who joins the "Old Believers." When Stasov criticized Mussorgsky's drama as dealing too much with the nobles, the composer wrote, "I wished to show one aspect of that period—that the nobles ran away to the people."[32] He entitled the opera, "A people's musical drama in five parts."

This is carried out fully in the music. Mussorgsky separates the common people into three groups. One comprises the Moscow populace. Another comprises the soldiers or *strelzi,* an armed detachment that had originally been set up to guard the throne, but who are being used for his own purposes by Khovansky. The third consists of the "Old Believers," who in their fanatical search for a moral life set themselves against civilization.

The first act presents a spacious panorama of Moscow in agitation, more diffusely written than the great scenes in *Boris* but going beyond them in wealth of characterization. The *Prelude* is a magical tone poem, evoking dawn in Moscow, sensitively orchestrated, intensely Russian in melody, a gem in itself and also an integral part of the act. For the end of the act, with its subdued chanting of the Old Believers, and deep bell sounds, is like a subtle reversion to the mood and sound of the opening. As the curtain rises on three gossiping armed guards, we get a beautiful example of Mussorgsky's ability to make "speech" phrases imperceptibly grow into full-fledged folk melody. At different times the Moscow populace, the *strelzi,* and the Old Believers are on the stage, the first given a beautiful, plaintive folk-style chant, the second a more boisterous, rollicking folk style, and the third a haunting ecclesiastical style. And as the drama of the individual characters is set in motion, in the same act, we find not only Mussorgsky's effective musical-speech setting, but a different idiom for each personage; the scribe has quavering, pathetic accents, Prince Ivan Khovansky is given a martial tone, Martha is given rich, impassioned folk-style melody, Shaklovity a court-style melody, and Dosefei a declamation of great grandeur like that of Pimen in *Boris.*

Likewise through the remainder of the opera, there are not only splendid crowd scenes, but also monologues which shape themselves into richly melodic arias, and represent a forward step for Mussorgsky. Like many other theorists, he finds that the pressure of real life forces him to change methods that he had previously found satisfactory. Perhaps he was influenced in both his aria style, and in such exotic touches as the fourth act Persian Dances, by Borodin's *Prince Igor,* which remained unfinished, but which Mussorgsky knew well. The opera must be known with the sections included that were excised by Rimsky-Korsakow in his edition. Rimsky-Korsakow has been much berated by modern critics for his cuts and other changes, and perhaps unfairly. They were probably due less to musical insensitivity than to his shrewd eye for what might not pass the censors and critics. One of these cuts included a stirring scene of the Moscow people, at first enraged and then frightened, in the first act; another was that of the *strelzi* and their women, in the third act.[33]

A number of twentieth century composers were directly influenced by Mussorgsky. The long *ostinato* passages which become an integral part of his form, and are directly connected to certain more "primitive" folk styles which he wanted to preserve, were such an influence; also his revelation of the various scale patterns that lay behind folk melody, and the way in which they could be juxtaposed in a single musical fabric. Unfortunately these lessons derived from Mussorgsky were often taken up as purely technical or exotic devices, leaving behind what was most important in Mussorgsky's mind, the deep and realistic portrayal of the nation and its people. One passage from his letters should be kept in mind whenever Mussorgsky's innovations are discussed as simply technical matters. "You know my motto: Dare! Forward to new shores! . . . The time has passed for writing at leisure; one must give one's whole self to the people—that's what is now needed in art."[34]

8. THE SEARCH FOR CLASSICAL BALANCE

"This system . . . has therefore produced the opposite of what the old craft-system produced, the death of art and not its birth; in other words the degradation of the external surroundings of life, or simply and plainly unhappiness. Through all society spreads that curse of unhappiness: from the poor wretches, the news of whom we middle-class people are just now receiving with such naif wonder and horror: from those poor people whom nature forces to strive against hope, and to expend all the divine energy of man in competing for something less than a dog's lodging and a dog's food, from them up to the cultivated and refined persons, well lodged, well fed, well clothed, expensively educated, but lacking all interest in life except, it may be, the cultivation of unhappiness as a fine art.

"Something must be wrong then in art, or the happiness of life is sickening in the house of civilization."

—William Morris, *Art Under Plutocracy* (1883)

I

Johannes Brahms (1833-1897) had on the surface no political views more liberal than Wagner's. Coming to maturity at a time when Germany was being unified into a great power by the autocratic Prussian monarchs, the Junkers and Krupps, with Bismarck as their statesman, he had no doubts that this was the best of all possible paths. He devoutly admired Bismarck. Brahms' biographer, Walter Niemann, writes of his opinions, "Not only were they thoroughly conservative, monarchical, and imperialist, but they knew no doubts or hesitations. He was mortally offended at any criticism of the German Emperor."[1]

While Brahms did not proclaim any racial theories, as Wagner did, he had more than a touch of chauvinism, which took the turn of a narrow German provincialism. He enjoyed Italian scenery, but he never cared to visit France or England. Visiting Denmark at one time, after its defeat at the hands of the Prussians, and being asked whether he had seen the museum of the famous Danish sculptor, Thorwaldsen, he answered tactlessly,

"Yes, it is quite extraordinary. It is only a pity that it is not in Berlin."[2] Needless to say, the atmosphere in Copenhagen became quite chilly for him. Where Wagner read voluminously, turning everything however to his own irrational and subjective uses, Brahms seems to have been, of all the great composers, the most lacking in broad cultural interests, whether concerning the world at large or his own Germany and Austria. The thought central to Beethoven's personality, and taken up in a grotesque perversion by Wagner, that an artist had to know what the past of society made it possible for him to know, that he was a "teacher of the nation," was foreign to Brahms. While Wagner sought to bind his art to the victory of the autocratic and racist "Greater Germany," making his art its symbol and representative, Brahms left politics to the politicians, and was quite willing to let them rule his outer life, while his inner life was his own.

Quite different was their search for German roots. Brahms had no use for Wagner's tribal sagas and medieval magic, his dream visions and his philosophies which made such grandiose opera-poetry but had no relevance to the real world. Brahms never suffered from self-delusions. Since his vocation was that of a musician, to him the monuments of Germany were the great musicians; Johann Sebastian Bach, Handel, Haydn, Mozart, Beethoven, Schubert. Their work at least was solid and real. Brahms worshipped them, studied them, and tried to digest their art and make it his own. It was a humble worship, and he resented any attempt to place his music on a level with theirs, saying at one time, "Do you know, there are asses in Vienna who take me for a second Beethoven?"[3] But he was unable to see these giants as real people, in their historical setting. They were ancestral gods. Where Wagner saw his art as the culmination of the past, Brahms realized there had been an element of greatness in the classic past which was missing in the present. The reason, its social thought, eluded him. It is a sad picture; this mind, so innately sensitive, thoughtful, sceptical of all myths and fantasies thrown up against reality, preferring to keep his feet solidly planted in the "world of necessity," yet having so little to feed on.

Both were intellectual children of reaction. Brahms, born in Hamburg, preferred to live after 1863 in the culturally more genial milieu of Vienna. But while Metternich, the engineer of the Holy Alliance was gone, there was little change in political atmosphere. Decsey describes it in these terms. "It is the period of the deepest reaction, of senile middle age. It (Austria) is segregated from Europe, chained to a silence and devoid of ideas. . . . The word 'freedom' sounds like high treason; authority weighs down all forms of life."[4] And similarly from the mid-century to the First World War, dominant was the adulation of the court, and the clerical censorship, with an intellectual life permitted to soar in every realm but that which pertained to the way people lived and were ruled. Where Wagner flitted about this reaction, pretending that he was shaping it instead of that it was shaping him, carrying on skirmishes and battles, Brahms lived a quiet, outwardly uneventful life. Where Wagner found "freedom" in reshaping music and could fill out his grandiose projects only by allowing pretentiousness to alloy his inspiration, Brahms set himself the most rigorous standards, based on his searching study of the past of the art. Nobody, not Mozart, Beethoven, Schubert, all of whom surpass Brahms in the sheer breadth of life and ideas in their art, can show an output like that of Brahms' life work, in which the thin, the shallow, the trivial, the perfunctory are almost completely absent. His first published compositions, the two *Piano Sonatas Op. 1* and *Op. 2,* are big, solid, deep and thoughtful works. And so it is; from the *F minor Piano Sonata, Op. 5,* already a masterpiece, on to the *Clarinet Quintet Op. 115,* the last piano pieces, and the "Four Serious Songs," there is hardly a weak work. The most ruthlessly self-critical of composers, what he destroyed would have enriched the career of any other musician of his time.

Although he got his lessons from the study of the past, there is no formalism in his work, no substitution of technique for a lack of ideas. It is an art full of deep feeling. In it lies one of the deepest melancholy expressions in the history of music. The tragedy is not unalloyed. There are in his music declamatory protests, violent struggles, assertions of strength, a light and tender playfulness, and sometimes a real joy. But the protests, like the heartrending outcries, more often than not end in resignation; the playfulness generally has a nostalgic, melancholy tempering; the joyous *finale* is not a resolution of the preceding conflicts but a proclamation that life is worth living in spite of them, or else a temporary wiping of troubles out of mind.

Nietzsche described Brahms' character as "the melancholy of impotence."[5] This cannot refer to any lack of strength or creative power. It does point up Brahms' inability to find a pathway to satisfy his deepest yearnings. The desire to love and be loved is unquestionably communicated by the passionate emotion of his songs. But he lived a rather lonely, outwardly loveless life, sometimes driving people away from him by his pride and his harsh and brusque manner, as if he had made a resolution never to show a weakness. He is perhaps the most enigmatic figure among the great composers. He never made any proclamations like Wagner of the supremacy of the German *"volks* spirit," or of his art as representing the "folk blood." But where folk music enters sparsely in Wagner's writing, Brahms' music is almost saturated with it. Here again we can guess at a deep attachment to the common people, a desire to be close to them. And yet, far more than in Schumann's music, folk melody is turned to the most subjective uses. In 1896 Dvorak, visiting the ailing Brahms, left lamenting, "Such a man, such a soul—and he doesn't believe in anything, he doesn't believe in anything."[6] This could have referred to religion, for Dvorak was a devout believer, while Brahms, as Latham observes, "At an early age had lost his belief in the Christian God, and never recovered it."[7] But there is also an implication of a loss of faith in people; in other words, that Brahms found nothing outside of himself to sustain him, such as Dvorak possessed in his attachment to the Czech people and their struggle for freedom.

The baroque and classic tradition was a bulwark to which Brahms clung. It was a psychological necessity to him, not an academic refuge, for otherwise he could not have been able to use it so creatively. It takes in his hands a romantic, subjective turn. A striking example is his *Piano Concerto in D minor, Op. 15,* composed in 1854-58. Begun as a symphony, then rewritten as a sonata for two pianos, and finally emerging as a concerto, the model its first movement follows so closely is that of Mozart's *C minor Piano Concerto, K. 491.* Brahms rejects the Liszt and Mendelssohn romantic "reduction" of the concerto form. As in the classical concerto, he divides his thematic material beween two full expositions, the first for the orchestra and the second bringing in the piano. Then he proceeds through a classical development, recapitulation and coda.

What is notable is that even in shape Brahms' themes resemble those of the Mozart *C Minor Concerto,* and similar also is the manner in which they answer one another, and in which the piano first enters. It is almost as if Brahms had "re-done" the Mozart first movement. But the difference in emotional life, or in "human portrait," is fundamental. Although the Mozart concerto is one of his most dramatic and from the start, passionate, even "romantic" works, its melodies have the classical rounded quality, and clarity of contour. There is a balance between rhythm-dominated and *parlando* music. Brahms' themes have the typical romantic indefiniteness of contour, seemingly always ending "in the air," calling for further evolution, with new themes growing out of what seem at first to be transitional passages. The entire first movement is in a style of impassioned declamation, alternating with equally unrounded, yearning themes. Similarly the second movement carries on the Mozart concept of a dialogue, as of equals between the piano and orchestra, but it is altogether inward and brooding, with its melodies only slowly, hesitatingly taking on firmness of shape, and then being dissolved again in the harmonic web.

It has been noticed that the Brahms *Violin Concerto* is modelled after the Beethoven *Violin Concerto.* Similarly the *German Requiem, Op. 45,* composed over the period 1857-68, shows how much Brahms has absorbed from Bach. As in the Bach Cantatas, Brahms uses a German text based on the Lutheran Bible, and follows each verse with the appropriate musical expression and imagery. Like Bach, he draws upon the Lutheran chorale and upon folk music. Thus in the great second movement, "Behold all flesh is as the grass," we hear an illustrative funeral-march theme, which will later serve as a bass for the chorus singing a chorale, and it is followed by the lilt of a *ländler,* although turned into poignant, "inward" expression. In the sixth movement, for baritone and chorus, a dramatic modulation followed by the entry of the chorus illustrates the words "for the trumpet shall sound." But in this work again, if the model is Bach, nothing sounds like Bach. Even the fugal writing has a typically romantic richness of chord structure, at the expense of the baroque freedom of melodic counterpoint. A borrowing from Beethoven offers a clue to Brahms' tie to the late, most "inward" period of Beethoven. It is the first theme of Brahms' *Fourth Symphony,* which comes from the slow movement of the *Hammerklavier Sonata for Piano, Op. 106.* It is not Beethoven's main theme however that Brahms uses, but an unrounded, yearning variation of it, as it re-enters (bars 78-84) to open the development section.

The subjective turn given to the classical heritage is seen

in Brahms' reluctance to handle the big orchestral forms, of symphony and concerto. He avoids "public oratory," much preferring the comparative intimacy of chamber music. His *First Symphony* was not completed until 1876, when he was forty-three. The resemblance of the main, march-like theme of the last movement to the "Ode to Joy" of Beethoven's *Ninth* was immediately noticed (Brahms remarked, when questioned, "Any fool can see that.") But up to the point that this theme enters, the entire symphony is in a style of powerful, explosive declamation, answered by tender, yearning themes. It is all *parlando*, with no "outer-world," rhythm-dominated melodies.

Each of the four symphonies has a different balance between "inner world" and "outer world" elements. Thus the *Second and Third* are folksier, with a more "outer" turn, than the *First* and *Fourth*, although the gently "pastoral" *Second* has for its slow movement one of the most heartrending tragic expressions in Brahms. And in all of the four we find the typical and unclassical complexity of Brahms' style; a complexity which caused him to be looked upon as a cold, "over-intellectual" and even mathematical composer, but which actually reflected the introspective complications of his own emotional life. Rarely can he make a direct and forthright statement. Every thought brings up a counter-thought, every feeling evokes its opposite, and everything is said with reservations.

A striking example is the *Third Symphony in F major,* Op. *90,* completed in 1883. It opens with one of Brahms' most propulsive, declamatory themes, but only a few bars later, the urgency is dissipated in reflective music. Then comes the "second subject," a sweet, lilting melody in a folk waltz or *ländler* style, but this too soon loses its momentum. A fiery transformation of the first theme follows, and this ushers in the development section, romantic-style, without appreciable break or demarcation. But in the development the storm again quiets down. So the music proceeds, with its propulsive force constantly halted by meditation. The recapitulation leads to a violently proclamatory code, but at the very end, the first theme emerges wholly chastened and robbed of its strength. And this assertive strength subsiding in nostalgia is the emotional pattern of the entire symphony. Thus the slow movement starts with a simple folk-style melody, but its sweetness and transparency are soon turned into a brooding meditation. For the third movement Brahms rejects altogether the traditional dancing *scherzo,* instead taking the sweet melody of the *Romanze* of Schumann's *Fourth Symphony* and offering a nostalgic transformation of it, like a flower laid sadly on Schumann's grave. The last movement seems to be making up for the lack of a *scherzo.* It starts with a brightly dancing, even rollicking theme. Yet almost immediately after, there is an ominous answer by the low strings and bassoons. The first theme returns, building up to some of the most exultant passages in Brahms' music. But at the close comes the magical transformation in the form of a long coda, full of lovely, autumnal sadness, with in the last bars, subtly suggested, a quiet, reflective version of the motif that had opened the symphony in so stormy a fashion.

It is this kind of complex, inner, brooding turn of thought which determines Brahms' handling of folk and popular music. Brahms wrote a considerable amount of music in popular style for home consumption; pieces for piano four-hands, or for voices and piano, requiring no great virtuosity. Among them are the two sets of *Liebeslieder* waltzer, the Gypsy songs, the piano waltzes, and arrangements of folk music like the *Hungarian Dances* and the volumes of German *Volkslieder.* Even in these we can sense Brahms' more nostalgic, reflective turn of thought; if we compare the *Liebeslieder* waltzes, for example, to the Schubert waltzes and *ländler.*

His folk song settings are not what the modern folklorist would call "scientific;" that is aimed at preserving their "primitive" or countryside character. Rather, with his retouching of the melody, and his harmonizations, they begin to sound like typical Brahms songs. But they remain folk melodies, and if we compare one such folk song setting, *Sandmännchen* (from a group of "Folk Songs for Children"), to some of Brahms' simpler original songs, like the waltz-like *Vor dem Fenster, Op. 14,* or *Sonntag, Op. 47,* we can discern how the turns of folk-style melody become part of Brahms' creative thinking. This is true as well of some of his most deep, subtle and introspective songs. Many of the German folk songs, as set by Brahms, are based on the notes of the "common chord;" *Die Sonne scheint nicht mehr* and *Mein Mädel hat einem Rosenmund,* for example. And two of his very great "art" songs, *Die Mainacht, Op. 43* and *Sapphische Ode, Op. 94* start with this same kind of folk-style, common-chord melody. But as these songs continue, the melody undergoes chromatic changes and modulations, losing its folk simplicity and turning into a personal evocation of inner unrest.

So it is with much of the big-scale instrumental music. Karl Geiringer sees folk song as the parent of the typical Brahms melody.[8] The brooding *"Edward" Ballade* for piano, *Op. 10 No. 1,* is a transformation of a folk ballad known in many North countries; Scotland, Germany, Finland.[9] The slow movements of his first two published works, the *Piano Sonatas Op. 1 and Op. 2,* are made up of variations on a German folk song. In the great *F minor Piano Sonata, Op. 5* the slow movement starts with a distant transformation of a folk song, *Steh' ich in finst'rer Mitternacht,* the actual melody of which emerges near the close of the movement. A folk-style theme which haunted Brahms is that of his lullaby, *Wiegenlied, Op. 49,* which has attained the status of an almost world-wide beloved "folk song." Undergoing a rhythmic and harmonic alteration, it becomes the *A flat major Waltz, Op. 39 No. 15,* the most popular of his waltzes. Transformed again, but still recognizable, it opens the slow movement of his great *Piano Quintet in F minor, Op. 34,* where it undergoes a brooding and lyrical development. It appears again as the sweet and tender second subject of the first movement of the *Second Symphony,* helping to give this movement its folksy and pastoral feeling. In the slow movement of the *Violin Concerto,* the main theme, sung by the oboe, is again a "common-chord" folk style melody, very much like the opening of *Sapphische Ode.* But as taken up by the solo violin, the melody goes through increasingly reflective and poignant transformations. Troubled syncopations enter in the middle section of the movement. The opening melody then returns, and the violin takes it through modulation upon modulation, spinning one of those wonderful Brahms nostalgic or "autumn twilight" codas. And this pattern—simple folk-style melody, troubled middle section, reprise, chromatic, modulating autumnal coda—occurs again and again in Brahms. A beautiful example is the slow movement of the *First Violin Sonata, in G, Op. 78.*

Even though Vienna was only his adopted home, Brahms shared another characteristic of two great Viennese composers, Haydn and Schubert; a love for Hungarian music. It is the Hungarian Gypsy style that Brahms takes up, not only in his *Hungarian Dances* but in the "happy endings" of many big works, announcing an abandonment of sadness for a merry jaunt among the "folk." Such is the spirit of the closing movements of the *Violin Concerto, B flat Piano Concerto, A minor String Quartet, A major Piano Quartet,* and *G minor String Quintet.* Perhaps the most remarkable of these "Hungarian" finales is that of the *G minor Piano Quartet, Op. 25,* in which Brahms masterfully recreates the actual sound of a folk orchestra, down to the improvisation-like cadenzas. But he will also use Hungarian folk material for "inner" probing. Hungarian is the main theme of the slow movement of the *C major Trio, Op. 87.* Niemann speaks of the "progressive inward clouding, which increases with every variation, of the simple folk-spirit of the ideas in the ballad-like theme."[10] Also Hungarian is the slow movement of the poignant *Clarinet Quintet, Op. 115,* in the middle part of which the clarinet embarks upon a series of haunting arabesques, in the florid, improvisational, *parlando* style of a Gypsy folk musician.

Thus Hungarian, like German and Austrian, folk material is turned by Brahms into the most intensely troubled, subjective and personal expression. It is not music which can be described as portraying "the mind of the folk." The folk might recognize their typical melodies in their early, simple appearance, but would not think of Brahms' music as a whole as essentially "their music." The complex emotional life which his use of this music reveals is his own combination of a deep attachment to the common people with an awareness of alienation from them.

II

The situation is quite different with the peasant-born Antonin Dvorak (1841-1904), who always preserved a complete identification with the Bohemian folk, and even in his most ambitious handling of "peasant" material, retained throughout a quality that the folk would recognize as "their own." Typical is an incident recounted by Dvorak's son. "At Vysoka, he told the miners that he was going to write an opera and that in one act there would be real miners and that they would work in the mine with exactly the same machines as they worked in the Príbram and Brezohorské mines. And then Father promised them that at the premiere of the opera the National Theatre must give him the whole auditorium where the miners from Pribram would take their places as the main part of the audience so that they might give their opinion about how far the act gives the impression of reality."[11] It is characteristic of Dvorak's entire career that he should thus offer a simple thought, almost like something which any one should take for granted, which was nevertheless a revolutionary concept in the history of music. For who before then had thought of the working people not only as the subject of an opera, but also as its critical audience, so that they could test its reality against their own lives?

Brahms gave Dvorak a helping hand. In the 1860's Dvorak had been a viola player in Prague, first in a restaurant orchestra and then in the orchestra of the new Czech National Theatre, where Smetana was raising the banner of Czech national opera. By 1875 Dvorak had won a local reputation, and the approval of Smetana, with his early works. But there was still little money to be made in Prague, and there was also the bickering between the Czech-conscious and German-speaking groups. A composer had to win an international success for solid standing at home. At this time Brahms was a member of an Austrian State Commission, which gave grants to "young, poor and talented painters, sculptors and musicians." Brahms recommended Dvorak for such a grant, and also, in 1877, sent to his Berlin publisher, Simrock, Dvorak's *Moravian Duets.* On Brahms advice Simrock published them. Then, when they proved to be sellable, Simrock suggested that Dvorak compose something like Brahms' *Hungarian Dances.* Dvorak came forth with the first set of *Slavonic Dances, Op. 46,* in 1878, and it became a best seller.

It was next, on the international arena that Dvorak fought for the recognition of Czech culture, showing that Czech folk music could be used for compelling communication in the most ambitious musical forms. Simrock could not see why this young man from the provinces could not devote himself to the vein of attractive folksy pieces like the *Moravian Duets* and *Slavonic Dances,* which were a publishers' gold mine. But when he offered this advice, Dvorak answered, "Not to write symphonies and large vocal and instrumental works, but only publish here and there some songs, piano pieces or dances . . . this, as an artist who wants to make his mark, I cannot do."[12]

There were other arrogant attitudes to be combatted. Although the great German conductor, Hans von Bulow, and the Hungarian-born Hans Richter, took up Dvorak's music, there were critics who screamed subversion when Dvorak wrote the Hussite overture based on the old Hussite hymn. Simrock, as Dvorak's publisher, blithely Germanized the composer's name from Antonin to Anton, to the composer's annoyance, and also ignored, as a piece of provincial foolishness, Dvorak's request to have his music printed with Czech titles as well as German. Dvorak wrote, "Do not laugh at my Czech brothers and do not be sorry for me either. . . . I only regret that you are so badly informed. That is how all our enemies are. . . . Let us hope that nations which possess and represent art will never perish, no matter how small they are. Forgive me but I only wanted to say to you that an artist has also his country in which he must have firm faith and for which he must have an ardent heart."[13] The turning point came with Dvorak's visits to England, starting in 1884. His reception as a composer was so enthusiastic that between then and 1890 his yearly visits became almost an institution of English musical life. Along with the success of his symphonies, he linked himself with big choral works to the great English tradition of popular chorus festivals. From this point on he became recognized as a major world figure.

As with other composers who raised the goal of national expression and the creative use of folk music, the knowledge of how to use this music with full freedom and plasticity came slowly, along with the mastery of the craft of composition itself. Dvorak's earlier works, up to about 1877, like the *String Quintet in G* and the *Symphony No. 3 in F,* (actually the fifth symphony he wrote, and the third to be published, for four early symphonies remained unpublished and un-numbered at the time of his death) are neither emotionally penetrating nor outstanding in their folk character. They are sweet, attractive and melodious in the tradition stemming from Schubert and Mendelssohn, with an added Czech "air" about them.

The set of *Slavonic Dances, Op. 46* (1878) marked a leap forward. On the surface unassuming "dance poems," they differ from Brahms' *Hungarian Dances,* which used actual folk or Gypsy tunes, in that every melody is Dvorak's own invention. And yet they sound completely folk, with strong, imperishable melodies that seem to have always existed. Dvorak has learned to think in folk style, like a peasant improviser who has discovered how to write his inventions down. Alternately boisterous and dreamy, they are permeated with an "outer world," open air feeling, lacking the subjective turn that takes the Chopin *Mazurkas* one step away from the folk. And they also indicate the special bent of Dvorak's folk approach. Unlike Mussorgsky, who favored the *parlando* aspect of folk music, Dvorak favors the rhythm-dominated side of folk art, with wonderful evocations, in his "dancing songs," of the intricate play of human movement. The new folk voice attained is immediately apparent in the following big works; the *E flat String Quartet, Op. 51* with its "Dumka" second movement, of 1879, and three works that appeared in 1880, the *Gypsy Melodies* for voice, the *Violin Concerto,* and the *Symphony No. 1 in D* (actually the sixth symphony he wrote). They are altogether infused with Czech folk-style melody, representing a "new sound" in instrumental music based on the classic forms, and developed into a beautiful spun-out lyricism.

The next step was to deepen his art in the realm of dramatic and even tragic emotion, enriching the harmonic and polyphonic texture and tightening the construction. The folk character seems to diminish, while lessons learned from Brahms appear paramount. Works of this nature are the *C major String Quartet Op. 61* (1881), the *F minor Trio Op. 66* (1883) and the *Symphony No. 2 in D minor* (1885). Yet the voice is authentically Dvorak's. We can see this if we compare the slow movement of the great *Second Symphony* (actually Dvorak's seventh symphony), to its Brahms counterpart. In Brahms the tragic expression is more harrowing. In Dvorak, there is an unflagging rhythmic impulse which checks the inward turn of melodic phrase, and tempers the sadness with a touch of "outer world" serenity.

The following step was towards a folk-saturated music on a new level of subtle emotional play, with a complete freedom in handling the classic forms, making them, so to speak, "dance to his own tune." The second set of *Slavonic Dances, Op. 72,* of 1886, seems to mark the change. There is a more refined manipulation and variation of folk material than in the first set. It also reveals a broadening of folk interests. Here he also uses Ukranian, Polish and Yugoslav styles along with Czech. Dvorak established Slavic ties also in other ways; his opera *Dmitri* (1881-83) which used for its plot a sequel to *Boris Godunov,* his welcome of Tchaikovsky to Prague in 1888, and his visit to Russia in 1890. Together with his warm-heated reception in England, we have here the outer circumstances reflected in the triumphal succession of fresh and folk-inspired masterpieces; the *A major Piano Quintet, Op. 81* (1887), the *Symphony No. 4 in G, Op. 88,* (1889), the *"Dumky" Trio Op. 90* (1890-91). They announce that Czech music has conquered the "big" instrumental forms and emerged as a world voice. It is no longer a provincial off-shoot of the German symphonic and chamber music tradition.

The *Fourth Symphony,* like the *Piano Quintet,* represents the complete recreation of the classic form in terms of folk style. Amazing in the symphony is the abundant melodic growth out of a few fertile phrases. The first movement for example has many differentiated themes but can also be called monothematic. Out of the opening slow motif in the bass, is born the following flute theme, and out of these rise not only all of the melodies of the movement proper, but also the passage-work, accompaniment figures, ornament and counterpoint. Dvorak has mastered the secret of melodic creation from the plastic core of folk music, and from this core the entire texture of the music unfolds. Similarly in the slow movement, the opening melody is answered by a variation of itself, and a lovely flow of music is then engendered, distinguished by its wonderfully flexible rhythm, and by the enchanting soft colors of the instrumentation. The third movement is a rousing Czech waltz, and the last movement is a theme with variations, combining joy in life, a touch of sombre thought, and a blithe wit. Like the Schubert *C major Symphony* and the Beethoven *Seventh,* the Dvorak *Fourth* is one of those expressions of joy which embodies the whole man.

The most original work is the *"Dumky" Trio.* The "dumka," a favorite form with Dvorak, is a Ukranian "lamenting" folk pattern, with a slow beginning followed by a faster section. In this trio the classic "sonata form" and four-movement layout are abandoned, and yet a similar variety of mood is re-created in terms of six movements, each a "dumka," each following the traditional folk pattern and yet each different from the others. The first two "dumkas" have the sharp dramatic contrasts of a classic "first movement." The third is a slow movement of heartrending sadness, and even the faster second section brings only an added poignance, underlined by the folk-style slides or *glissandos.* The fourth is an ebullient *scherzo.* The last two make up a stirring *finale.* It is a finely wrought "learned" work, and yet with a folk feeling in every phrase, as if an inspired village musician were improvising with a century's musical development at his fingertips.

Having won these victories for Czech music, Dvorak found himself engaged in a new, remarkable endeavor; that of helping foster a national music in the United States. His experiences in the course of his short teaching visit, from 1892 to 1895, are a testament to the fundamental humanity of his Czech national outlook; an affection for his own common people which grew to embrace all common people. It was the opposite to the wave of jingoistic nationalism and racism that was then sweeping the United States, temporarily driving underground the currents of democratic feeling that had won the Civil War and brought about the abolition of Negro slavery. The Populist movement was trying vainly to cope with the enormous strength of the giant industries, which were rapidly becoming trustified. In the South the Negro people were being assaulted, driven into land peonage, robbed of voting rights, of representation in legislature and of civil liberties, all with the agreement and encouragement of Northern industry, which preferred to rule the South as a colony of cheap labor and no democracy. Millions of immigrants were being encouraged to come from other lands, to turn the wheels of the mushrooming industries, and at the same time labor had to be "kept in its place." Racism spread through the North as well as the South, its main attacks levelled against the Negro people but taking in its sweep Irish, German, Italian, Jewish, Slavic, Chinese and all others whose labor was needed but not their cultural heritage or their democratic hopes. Theodore Roosevelt, in 1895, attacked the Negro people as a "perfectly stupid race."[14] Thomas Bailey Aldrich, the genteel editor of the *Atlantic Monthly,* railed against the "wild motley throng" that was passing through our "Unguarded Gates."[15] Avaricious eyes were being turned to the raw materials and potential riches of the Caribbean Islands, as well as of Central and South America, and the Philippines. Bolstering such urges was a racist nationalism taking the form of an Anglo-Saxon "mystique." This proclaimed that inherent in Anglo-Saxon "blood" was a natural superiority, destined to bring "law and order" to other peoples whose inferiority was clear to behold in their darker skin. It was part of a larger world movement reflecting the appearance of cartels and monopolies, and the accompanying "great nation" power politics, the new imperialist drive for markets and raw materials over the world. War was in the air. This spirit could be felt in the tightening repression by Russia of Finnish autonomy and by Austria of Bohemian freedom, in the anti-democratic and anti-Semitic movements in Germany, the Dreyfus case in France, and in the Western inroads in China. It gave birth to a poisonous jingoistic and nationalistic frenzy.

The invitation to Dvorak came from a woman who was herself a remarkable person, Mrs. Jeanette M. Thurber, the wife of a wholesale grocer. A lover of music, she tried to encourage a native American opera, and set up a "National Conservatory" in New York which gave free musical instruction to those who could not afford to pay. In May, 1893, a newspaper advertisement invited Negro people to enroll in it.[16] Although the salary she offered Dvorak was fantastically large compared to his modest income from the Prague Conservatory, what actually impelled Dvorak to accept was the democratic spirit of the task itself. He wrote shortly after his arrival, "The Americans expect great things of me and the main thing is, so they say, to show them to the promised land and kingdom of a new and independent art, in short, to create a national music. . . . It is certainly a great and splendid task for me and I hope that with God's help I shall accomplish it."[17]

He was excited by precisely the aspect of the land, the Whitmanesque picture of the brotherhood of peoples, that the Aldriches were deploring, writing in 1893, "Here in America there are *names of towns and villages of all nations under the sun!*"[18] Welcomed as a great celebrity by the musical world, he refused to behave as one. He spent the summer of 1893 in a Czech farmer community in far-off Spillville, in Iowa, eager to see how his former countrymen were faring in the new world. Through back-breaking labor they had won for their children a better life than that of a Bohemian peasant. "All the poorest of the poor, and after great hardships and struggle they are very well off here. . . . And so it is very 'wild' here and sometimes very sad—sad to despair."[19]

Dvorak eagerly studied whatever he could find of characteristic American music, more interested in the folk and popular than in what he heard of academic composition. At the conservatory Henry Thacker Burleigh (1866-1949) who would himself become a composer of eminence, sang Negro spirituals for him. In a *New York Herald Tribune* article (May 21, 1893),

Dvorak wrote, "I am of the opinion that in the Negro songs I have found a secure basis for a new national school, and I have come to the conviction that the young musicians here need only careful guidance, earnest industry, support and encouragement on the part of the public in order to create a new musical school . . . the natural voice of a free and great nation."[20] Interviewed subsequently by the same newspaper, he said, "In the Negro melodies of America I find all that is needed for a great and noble school of music. They are pathetic, tender, passionate, melancholy, bold, merry, gay or what you will. There is nothing in the whole range of composition which cannot be supplied from this source."[21]

In this quiet way, Dvorak dropped a bombshell in the midst of the most deeply entrenched prejudice of the time. Not only was he pointing out that a great music could come out of the folk art of the Negro people, but he was also saying that it would be a great "American" music, putting his finger on the truth many will still not admit today, that the Negro people are an organic part of the American people and nation. The truth of course had been apparent to anyone willing to see. Negro culture had already become an integral, if unacknowledged part of American folk and popular art, through folk tale, minstrel show and published song. Dvorak took up the matter further in a *Harpers* magazine article in 1895, asking why, in a land of so much opportunity, and patriotism, so little was being done for music. He suggested that opera be performed in English, and that composers should study the music of the people, like folk songs, dances and street cries.

Feeling that it was only fitting to practise what he preached, Dvorak planned an opera based on Hiawatha, "bringer of peace" among nations, and failed to carry this out only because he could not obtain a usable libretto. And so what turned out to be his big "American work" was the *Symphony No. 5 in E minor,* "From the New World." There has been lengthy discussion since as to whether Dvorak used actual Negro or Indian melodies in it, most of the argument being carried on from the shallow viewpoint of agreeing to a folk influence only when an actual folk tune can be proved to have been incorporated. Dvorak denied having used American melodies in this way, just as he would have generally thought it uncreative to put an actual Czech folk song in a composed work. But he wrote, "Well, the *influence* of America must be felt by everyone who has any 'nose' at all."[22] In the first movement, the first theme, following the slow introduction, does not seem to be particularly American, but for a touch of characteristic syncopation. The pentatonic second theme hints perhaps at an "Indian" character, but could also be a Czech dance, with a bag-pipe drone. The third theme however, heard first from the flute, is a lovely "American" melody, actually based on "Swing Low Sweet Chariot," but rhythmically transformed, with a skipping rhythm typical of cakewalk, ragtime and the more syncopated spirituals like "I Want To Be Ready."

The melody of the slow movement, later arranged by a Dvorak pupil as the popular song, "Going Home," has a family kinship both to Negro spirituals like "Deep River," and to Dvorak's Czech melodies, like "Songs My Mother Taught Me." This double character is not strange, for the spirituals themselves had shown how easily an African musical tradition could combine with a "Western" hymn tradition, and one of the greatest American hymn traditions had been that brought by the Moravian people from Dvorak's homeland. The middle section of this movement represents unmistakeably Dvorak yearning for home, and in the center of it appears a touch of Czech folk dance. The *scherzo* again has a happy "meeting of two worlds," its first part being sweetly American in its lilting melody and the "trio" being a Czech waltz. The last movement begins with a grand processional theme that is also a transformation of the slow movement melody, and in its course other themes from the earlier movements appear, woven together into a jubilant tribute to the "New World."

Thus what we have is not an "American" symphony, but one by a "Czech Composer in America." It exhibits Dvorak's ability to seize upon the core of not only Czech but also any folk music, in this case American Negro, and create new themes from it. This is partly due to his plasticity of rhythm, and themes appear which may be Czech in original melody, American in rhythm. The process goes further, and magically, "American" themes turn into "Czech," "Czech" into "American."

In 1895, pressed to remain, Dvorak decided that his place was back among his own people. The works he composed fully or began in the United States do not constitute an "American" period or style. If anything seems to characterize them, it is that but for the joyous *"New World" Symphony,* they show a turn towards the deepening sadness of his late period. Examples are the beautiful slow movements of the *E flat String Quintet, Op. 97,* the *Violoncello Concerto, Op. 104,* and the particularly great *String Quartet in G, Op. 106.* Perhaps the prosperity and democratic aspects of American life had intensified in his mind the poverty and repression of Bohemia under the Austrians.

Dvorak never gives himself over to any overwhelming tragedy; there is always a gentle serenity. This late sadness can be felt in the tone poems, based on macabre Czech folk tales, like *The Midday Witch* and *The Golden Spinningwheel.* It is most poignant in the opera *Rusalka,* of 1900. This is a "fairy tale" opera, on the familiar folk tale of the water nymph who leaves her peaceful home, falling in love with a prince and becoming mortal, thus entering a world of unhappiness. Behind many of the old folk tales of water nymphs loved and rejected by princes, lay the actual situation of peasant girls made love to and wronged by noblemen. The opera is not spectacular, or bravura in its singing roles, but extremely beautiful in its tenderness of melody and sensitive "tone poem" character, with its merging of voices and orchestra.

One can guess at another cause for this deepening sadness. Certainly the hopes for independence and freedom were not as bright in the late 1890's as they had been in the 1870's and 1880's. Repression was sharper. In 1899, finally, the earlier liberal decrees were annulled, and the Czech language was abolished from the government offices and law courts of Bohemia and Moravia. The noose upon "subject peoples" throughout Europe was tightening, and the great powers were gathering their forces for a world struggle. In 1914, ten years after Dvorak's death, and after repeated incidents, the holacaust would come, using the peasantry of Central, Southern and Eastern Europe as the main sources of cannon fodder.

III

In the music of both Peter Ilich Tchaikovsky (1840-93) and Nikolay Rimsky-Korsakov (1844-1908), both of whom rose to full maturity in the last quarter of the nineteenth century, we can sense a reaction to the bleak hopes this period held for the freedom of peoples. Tchaikovsky is in his own way as enigmatic as Brahms. He was deaf to the beauty of Brahms' music, and wrote of the German composer, "He never speaks out his musical ideas to the end. . . . He excites and irritates our musical senses without wishing to satisfy them, and seems ashamed to speak the language which goes straight to the heart. . . . His style is invariably lofty. He does not strive after mere external effects. He is never trivial. All that he does is serious and noble, but he lacks the chief thing—beauty."[28] The interest of this passage is that it puts so well Tchaikovsky's own aims, to "speak out his musical idea to the end," to speak a "language that will go straight to the heart;" clarity and directness in contrast to Brahms' complex cross-currents of feeling.

Tchaikovsky incorporated Russian folk song lavishly in his compositions, but looked at it differently from Mussorgsky. He did not use it to evoke the constant presence of the peasantry and their role in the nation, past and present. He sought in folk music for a kind of melody of a distinctly Russian character, usable as the expression of all classes of society, and able to become the material for symphonic and chamber works built, although with great freedom, upon the classic heritage. And so he preferred folk music of the less "primitive" or exotic kind, using many of the rounded popular songs that, accepted as folk, were also known by the middle class and nobility. They also served as the creative source for his own wonderful melodies, which have become a national and even international popular possession.

A letter to the great novelist Tolstoi, thanking him for sending some peasant songs, indicates Tchaikovsky's view of the irregular scale and rhythmic formations of Russian folk music.

"Honored Count: Accept my sincere thanks for the songs. I must tell you frankly that they have been taken down by an unskilled hand and, in consequence, nearly all their original beauty is lost. The chief mistake is that they have been forced artificially into a regular rhythm. Only the Russian choral dances have a regularly accented measure; the legends (Bylini) have nothing in common with the dances. Besides, most of these songs have been written down in the lively key of D major, and this is quite out of keeping with the tonality of genuine Rusian folk-songs, which are always in some indefinite key, such as can only be compared with the old Church modes. Therefore the songs you sent are unsuitable for systematic treatment. I could not use them for an album of folksongs, because for this purpose the tunes must be taken down exactly as the people sing them. This is a difficult task, demanding the most delicate musical perception, as well as a great knowledge of music history. With the exception of Balakirev—and to a certain extent Prokounin—I do not know anyone who really understands this work. But your songs can be used as symphonic material—and excellent material too—of which I shall certainly avail myself at some future time."[24]

In other words, Tchaikovsky has no academic narrowness, and understands the value of the varied harmonic-rhythmic patterns to be found in folk music, so different from "accepted" Western music. But he does not follow this up in his own creative style, as Mussorgsky did, and to some extent Borodin. He is also trying to conquer a field which Mussorgsky ignored; that of the big instrumental forms, with their architectural demands. And for such works, based on a classic tonality and key change, he does find folk music, even in its transformed version, useful.

We can trace this process of creative melodic transformation in Tchaikovsky's work. One such folk song, for example, that he had heard at a picnic,[25] appears in the first movement of the *Second Piano Concerto in G major, Op. 44* (1880), composed for and dedicated to Nicholas Rubinstein. When Rubinstein died, Tchaikovsky wrote the *A minor Trio, Op. 50,* in his memory. And the same melody becomes the theme for a set of variations that makes up the second movement of this work. We hear, evolving from the simple folk tune, one melody after another, beautiful and touching the heart, including a lovely waltz of the kind that adorned his operas and ballets.

Rhythm plays a central role in Tchaikovsky's process of variation and melodic creation. Like Dvorak, and unlike Brahms and Mussorgsky, he tends to write a rhythm-dominated rather than *parlando* music. Even his slow melodies, like the *Canzonetta* of the *Violin Concerto,* the second movement of the *Fifth Symphony,* or Lenski's aria in *Eugene Onegin,* have an unflagging rhythmic movement. This helps give his music a feeling of outer life, and combined with the firmly-contoured beauty of his melodies, it helped to make him the foremost ballet composer of the century; in fact the first to raise the full-evening ballet to the level of great art. The combination of outer-life feeling with the deep sadness found so often in the melodies themselves is central to Tchaikovsky's personality.

We cannot truthfully call him a composer given over wholly to subjectivism and pessimistic reflections. There is a deep conflict in his personality and music, like that in Brahms, but taking a different form.

Like Brahms, Tchaikovsky had a deep yearning to love and be loved, but lived a rather lonely life. In fact Tchaikovsky, hyper-sensitive, found himself often irritated by the presence of people. Like Brahms, he was moved by religious services, but had no religious beliefs. "Thus from one point of view, I am firmly united to our Church. From other standpoints, I have long since lost faith in dogma. The doctrine of retribution, for instance, seems to me monstrous in its injustice and unreason. Like you, I am convinced that if there is a future life at all, it is only conceivable in the sense of the indestructibility of matter, in the pantheistic view of the eternity of nature, of which I am only a microscopic atom."[26]

He would often suffer from a frightful lack of confidence in himself, writing in 1877, "The real trouble is my depression—a wearing, maddening depression which never leaves me for a moment;"[27] and again in 1878, "It comes over me suddenly that no one really loves me; or can love me, because I am a pitiable, contemptible being."[28] This is no self-pity, nor is it a declaration that the world is "nothingness." It is a struggle to embrace life and to live as other people, which he regards as a supreme good. A theme always close to him is that of the heartrending beauty of love between two human beings, crushed by brutal forces outside of them. He had dealt with it in one of his great early successes, the Overture-Fantasia *Romeo and Juliet.*

He was acutely sensitive of the psychological block which prevented him from having normal love and sex relations. And it was probably his feeling that this inhibition was not "manly," that it could be cured by forceful measures, which impelled him into his sudden and short-lived marriage of 1877. What resulted was a horrifying experience which only intensified his self-deprecation, and drove him to the verge of suicide. Music became not an expression of personal misery, but a healing element, a pull to life. He wrote in 1878, "Physically I feel very well, at any rate better than could be expected; but mentally I am still far from sound. In a word, I am on the verge of insanity. . . . I cannot live without work, and when I can no longer compose, I shall occupy myself with other musical matters."[29] And in the big works of this critical time, the opera *Eugene Onegin* (1877-80) and the *Fourth Symphony* (1877-78), there is no "insanity," hysteria or surrender to personal anguish. A tragic character is brought to the *Fourth Symphony* by the motto theme, or "fate motif," which is introduced in the first movement and dominates as well the closing pages of the symphony. But this is also the richest in folk melody of his mature symphonies, and abounds in dance images, such as the waltz themes in the first movement.

Eugene Onegin and *Pique Dame* (1890) are Tchaikovsky's operatic masterpieces, both drawing on works of Pushkin for their drama. Abandoning the usual colorful historical spectacle, they depict the composer's own milieu, that of the Russian gentry, but a perceptive honesty and naturalness that made them in their quiet way a notable forward step in the relation of opera to the national scene and contemporary life. Tchaikovsky, writing to Taniev about *Eugene Onegin,* deprecated his innovation:

"Very probably you are quite right in saying that my opera is not effective for the stage. I must tell you, however, that I do not care a rap for such effectiveness. It has long been an established fact that I have no dramatic vein, and now I do not trouble about it. . . . I should like to call it 'lyrical scenes,' or something of that kind. This opera has no future! . . . but I can at least affirm that the music proceeds in the most literal sense from my inmost being."[30]

"From my inmost being" does not mean that the opera is autobiographical. Despite his own harrowing experiences, Tchaikovsky has been able to get out of his own skin, and throw light upon the problems of love, not in the abstract but realistically, as shaped by a particular stage of society. And he creates true drama in the contrast between the growth in nobility and stature of his heroine, Tatiana, and the deepening unrest and unhappiness of the egoistic Onegin. Onegin early in the opera rejects Tatiana's naively offered love, and in the end, is rejected by her, but for entirely different reasons from those that had moved him, namely her consideration and respect for other people's happiness. Tchaikovsky's deep affection for his characters is reflected in the subdued but beautiful lyricism of the music. It is sensitively fitted to the speech and at the same time inspired in melody, with a fine interplay between the voices and orchestra, and with an open, romantic flow that is never over-subjective, but keeps its grip on reality.

Pique Dame seems on the surface to have melodramatic elements but essentially it is the same realistic portrayal of a milieu, and its theme is, like that of *Eugene Onegin,* the tragic complications in the path of love. The penniless officer, Herman, whose need for money and passion for gambling destroy himself and the woman he loves, is a familiar figure in the Russia of the time. The apparently supernatural elements, the mysterious "secret" of the three cards which will turn up at a certain time and in a certain order, do not detract from the realism for they only underline Herman's obsession and growing insanity. As in Tchaikovsky's other operas, he here makes no great conquests in the realm of all-over operatic architecture. The beauty of the work is the naturalness with which the music fits the language and the characters, and its lyricism. This ranges from sweet folk-style melodies, such as those sung by the servants, to poignant arias, like that of Lisa before her death. This aria too is completely Russian music. It begins with the characteristic melodic shape, folk inspired, heard in the slow movement of the *Violin Concerto* and in the introduction to Mussorgsky's *Boris.* There are two extremes in the music. On the one hand, there is the haunting portrayal, with a discordant orchestra, of Herman's insanity, at the opening of the third act. On the other hand there is the little second-act "pastoral play," which speaks of Tchaikovsky's homage to Mozart. And this, in its sweetness, is not merely a light interlude. It is a part of Tchaikovsky's thought in this tragic opera. An expression of the happiness of true lovers coming together, it corresponds to the deep yearnings in Tchaikovsky's heart, as in everyone's heart. But it is a happiness that here (as in his ballets) he sees attainable only in fairy tale visions.

In the big-scale instrumental forms, it was only after hard and painstaking effort that Tchaikovsky achieved a version of the classic form suited to his own thought and feeling. He moved away from the classical pattern of an exposition presenting the main material, in two contrasting groups of themes, a development section carrying the conflict to a high pitch and a resolution of this conflict in the recapitulation and coda.

Instead, his first-movement form tends to present a motif, or group of related motifs, which immediately undergoes a considerable dramatic working up. Then wholly contrasting music appears, a long, beautiful, rounded lyrical episode. The middle section, corresponding to the classical development, carries the opening music to an even higher pitch of dramatic intensity. Again a version appears of the long lyrical episode. Then the recapitulation of the opening, and a coda, seem to resolve the conflict. But the point of this form is that the conflict is never entirely resolved. It adjusts itself to a view of two widely disparate and essentially irreconcilable aspects of life. What Tchaikovsky has actually done is adapt to the symphony a "fantasia" form which he had developed in his early *Romeo and Juliet* Overture. He uses this form in the first movements of the *Fourth Symphony*, the *Violin Concerto,* the *A minor Trio,* and the *Sixth Symphony.*

The *Fifth Symphony* comes closest to the classic procedure. It also has a finale unusual for Tchaikovsky. The "fate" theme that had dogged the previous movements is transformed into a heroic, patriotic processional. The most original in form of the symphonies is the *Sixth,* or "Pathetique." Its first movement is a big-scale version of the "overture-fantasia" form described above. It is not too farfetched to say that its theme is the tenderness and beauty of love, struggling against overwhelming destructive forces. The second movement, a waltz in 5/4 time, is the "dream happiness," tinged with sadness, of the ballet style. The third-movement march has a touch of fateful horror, perhaps suggested by the "March to the Scaffold" in Berlioz's *Fantastic Symphony.* As for the great lamenting *adagio* which makes up the last movement, we can confirm its message by the resemblance of its material to other sections of Tchaikovsky's music. It is the kind of music which accompanies the doomed old Countess, in the fourth scene of *Pique Dame.* It is a more intensely worked-up version of the kind of music in the duel scene, including Lenski's aria, in *Eugene Onegin*: "when the sun rises a new day will come, but I may be in yonder unknown, obliterated." Death is evoked, feared and hated, but it is a lament, not a cry of horror, and as the critic Edwin Evans points out, it is not music of self-pity.

Evans believes there is a hidden revolutionary significance in the *Sixth Symphony,* and he quotes a passage from Huneker which presents a similar conclusion. "Supposing that some Russian professional supervisor of artistic anarchy really knew what arrant doctrines Tchaikovsky preached! It is its freedom from the meddlesome hand of the censor that makes of music a playground for great brave souls."[31] There is no evidence in Tchaikovsky's diaries or letters for any such conscious program. But he did have conflicting feelings about the Russia of his time. He violently disapproved of the anarchist and nihilist groups, whose activities included attempts to assassinate the royal family. Yet he felt deeply the miseries of the people. In 1879, when an attempt had been made on the Tsar's life, he wrote in a letter, "I think the Tsar would do well to assemble representatives throughout all Russia, and take counsel with them how to prevent the recurrence of such terrible actions on the part of mad revolutionaries. So long as all of us—the Russian citizens – are not called to take part in the government of the country, there is no hope of a better future."[32]

He had a social mind. His favorite novelists were those with social minds; Tolstoi and Chekhov in Russia, Dickens and George Eliot in England. His symphonic works are deep personal expressions, in which the conflicts revealed are a parallel to the conflict in the real life of Russia in his time; the yearning for love, for human relations among people, and the protest against the harsh, oppressive and, as he saw them, mysterious forces stifling such hopes. And just as his operas, with their naturalness in viewing contemporary life, opened up a path different from those of the other Russian composers of his time, so his symphonies marked a stage in the development of the form, with their architectural strength, their absolute clarity, their long-drawn beautiful melodies, and their combination of integrity with the ability to capture the heart of great masses of people.

Only one nineteenth-century Russian symphony can stand alongside of Tchaikovsky's. It is the *Symphony No. 2 in B minor* (1872-76) of Alexander Borodin. As one would expect from a member of the "Mighty Five," it is close in its harmony, rhythm, melodic shape and orchestral color, to the earthy, irregular, and Caucasus-Asian elements in Russian folk music. Gerald Abraham writes of it, "No more thoroughly Russian music has ever been written."[32] But for all its tastefulness and perfection, it does not attempt the great dramatic and tragic problems which Tchaikovsky handled in the form. Borodin was one of the most universally beloved figures among Russian composers, as well as a scientist of great eminence. But perhaps one of his endearing characteristics proved also to be a limitation in the realm of composition. It was pointed up in a remark of Mussorgsky's: "O, if only Borodin could lose his temper!"[34]

IV

Of the galaxy of nineteenth century Russian composers, Nikolay Rimsky-Korsakov was probably the keenest political mind, the one most aware of what was going on in the world about him, and the outstanding satirist. He also embarked upon the sharpest criticism of the Balakirev school of national musical thought, a school in which he himself had been nurtured. He writes in his memoirs of the year 1874, "I played and scanned Bach a great deal and came to honor his genius very highly; yet in earlier days, without proper acquaintance with Bach, but merely repeating Balakirev's words, I used to call him a 'composing machine'. . . . I did not understand then that counterpoint had been the poetic language of that composer of genius . . . I had no idea of the evolution of the civilized world's music and had not realized that all modern music owed everything to Bach. Palestrina and the Flemings too, began to lure me." He describes some of the joking that often went on at Bach's expense, with Balakirev doing a dance to the music of a fugue, waving a different arm or leg each time another voice entered, and adds, "Possibly it was even witty; for a jest one never spares one's own father. But during my study of Bach and Palestrina, all this became repugnant to me; the figures of these men of genius appeared majestic, and as though staring with contempt upon our 'advanced' frenzy of obscurantism."[35]

It is a historic statement, raising questions much deeper than the values of eighteenth century and earlier music, which Balakirev had ignored in favor of the romantic "revolution." The deep-rooted question it raises is that of the relation between a national art and the world heritage. It points up the danger inherent in the approach of "The Five"; not so much a simple matter of the loss of useful techniques, as a possibility of cultural narrowness. The healthy resentment of a "borrowed culture," as of an "imposed culture," the healthy search for roots and traditions at home, all of it necessary for both a genuine national art and a world contribution, could be carried too far. It could turn into the belief that all necessary materials, all necessary lessons, and everything needful for the artist, could be found at home. In other words, it could become a "national narrowness." It could foster a school of artists who, for all their high intentions, could be missing the breadth that only a knowledge of the historic achievements of world culture could give them.

A compelling reason for this self-criticism was the fact that Rimsky-Korsakov, having finally left the Navy to devote himself wholly to music, was now responsible for teaching others, and was questioning whether he really knew enough to teach. His colleagues, who would refer to him as "Dear Sincerity," did not understand this ruthless self-examination, this remarkable picture of a "professor," with considerable musical achievements behind him, taking up again the humble role of "student." As he writes, when this change took place, "they began, indeed, to look upon me with a certain pity, as one on the downward path." It is true that there was nothing exciting about his transitional works, such as the numerous fugues and contrapuntal exercises, the *Third Symphony,* and a string quartet (of which he writes, "I felt somewhat ashamed"). And it is a general limitation of Rimsky-Korsakov's art that it does not penetrate deeply into psychology, and the undercurrent of tragic feelings. There is less of the "whole man" in his music than we find in Mussorgsky and Tchaikovsky. This weakens his serious historical operas like *The Tsar's Bride* (1898), a picture of moral corruption in the Tsar "Ivan the Terrible" and his court. But the great leap Rimsky-Korsakov made can be seen in comparing his symphonic suite, *Scheherazade* (1888) to his earlier beautiful work in a similar vein, *Antar* (1868), of which he says "it has no thematic development whatever; only variations and paraphrases." Under the shimmering fantasy-surface of *Scheherazade,* there is an unobtrusive but firm "bone-structure," based on his new, conscious mastery of harmony, counterpoint, and classical thematic development.

Stimulated by Wagner, whom he began to admire greatly as a musician, Rimsky-Korsakov began to use recurrent motifs more freely, somewhat like *leitmotifs,* put through cunning transformations. He also broke with the classical concept of orchestration, dethroning the strings from their traditional dominance, making them only sweet voices among the other instruments, and liberating brass and woodwinds both as solo voices and in ever-changing combinations. All this required a new sensitivity to harmony and even the harmonic use of instrumental overtones.

With his new equipment he carried further the study of the harmonization of folk music, including Asian music and ancient Russian "pagan" songs, with their irregular rhythms and modal and pentatonic scale patterns. He describes some of the difficulties. "I recorded songs from the mouths of our servant girls as had been born in districts distant from St. Petersburg. I rigidly avoided whatever seemed to me commonplace and of suspicious authenticity. Once, at Borodin's, I struggled till late at night, trying to reproduce a wedding song; rhythmically it was unusually freakish, although it flowed naturally from the mouth of Borodin's maid. . . . I had all sorts of trouble with the harmonization of the songs, recasting in every way imaginable."[36] He was especially interested in the old "pagan," ritual and pre-Christian songs, which linked up with his study of Asian music. There were fascinating examples of the latter to be heard in South Russia and the Caucasus. Typically Asian in *Scheherazade* are the free-flowing coloraturas, or melodies like arabesques, resembling the religious and storytelling chants of the East. He writes about the Crimea, "I was particularly struck by the quasi-incidental beats of the big drum, in false time, which produced a marvellous effect. In those days the streets of Bakhchiseray, from morning to night, rang with music, which oriental nations so love. . . . On our next visit (seven years later), there was no longer a trace of this left: the addle-pated authorities had decided that music meant disorder, and banished the gypsy-musicians from Bakhchiseray to somewhat beyond Chufut-Kale."[37] He gave new prominence in the orchestra to the percussion, using not only a variety of drums but also plucked strings and staccato woodwinds to create a web of percussive sound with its own harmony and melody, like an Asian orchestra.

Rimsky-Korsakov never uses such music for purely exotic effect. He creates a fanciful "far-away" world which at the same time embodies a tender love for people of other lands and places. It corresponds to a yearning for freedom and a revolt against philistinism and harsh "addle-pated" authority. In nine of his thirteen full-length operas he exploited the world of myth, legend and fantasy. And it is in these works that his innovations best appear; delicate chromaticisms and melodies suggesting modal and irregular scales, with appropriate freshness and novelty of harmony; dissonant chords used for color or for a sudden, sharp impact, sensitively orchestrated and sometimes creating a twilight, dream feeling, sometimes giving a witty twist to a familiar-sounding melody; a play of rhythms against one another, with different "chains" of rhythm-units moving simultaneously. It is operatic writing with the voices in the forefront, but the orchestra does more than accompany. A solo air or chorus tends to be a vocal-orchestral conception, with the voices themselves handled like instrumental timbres. The music of "impressionism" is more than foreshadowed; it is actually present as we can see in comparing, for example, the sea scenes of the opera *Sadko* to Debussy's *La Mer*. But there is in these fairy-tale works no flight from reality, no turn from the outer world to introspection and dream. We can trace in Rimsky-Korsakov's operatic legends a conscious connection to the real life and society of his time. In this respect he was fortunate, like other Russian composers, in having the work of such writers as Gogol and Pushkin to draw upon.

Thus in the opera *May Night* (1877-78), after a story by Gogol, fantasy involving the old "sun worship" and "Rusalka" or water-nymph legends is interwoven with a satiric comedy of Russian village life. The satire is aimed at the village Headman, Golova, who tries to rule the village with an iron hand. He is a typical portrait of "addle-pated authority." He constantly boasts that he was once chosen to be the guide of none other than the Tzarina herself. "I served her for three days and I was deemed worthy to sit next to the Tzarina's coachman on the coach box." The story deals with the tricks played upon Golova by the village youth, who include his own son, to shame him into letting his son marry a pretty maiden upon whom the old man himself has somewhat low-minded intentions. The score is made up of a variety of folk styles, including songs modelled after the ancient cult and ritual music, and beautiful examples of Rimsky-Korsakov's impressionist "fantasy" style, as in the water scenes bringing in the *Russalki*. There is also a subtle musical satire in the use of the traditional Russian patriotic or "anthem" style in the music acompanying the Headman Golova. It is constantly given deliberate dissonances and harmonic distortions, which reach a high point in the witty fugal passages in the second act that underline Golova's boasting.

Likewise in the fantasy opera *Sadko* (1895-96), there is a subtle allegory on the relations between the merchant class and the visionary artist-poet. The scene is the great medieval merchant city of Novgorod, the time being as the composer explains in a note to the score, in the "half legendary, half historical period when Christianity had just been introduced in Novgorod, the ancient peasant myths still operating in full strength." There are, he says, many anachronisms in the story, just as there are in the old *byliny.* These were the old narrative songs of the wandering, rebellious jesters or buffoons, on which the opera was based. The merchants are depicted by Rimsky-Korsakov as possessing a strong and independent spirit. They sing in the first act, "We have no great boyars nor great princes ordering us about, no feared army chiefs. Here at Novgorod everyone is his own master." But they are also stolid, smug and unenterprising. They lack the visions of Sadko, the poet, singer and explorer. But as the opera discloses, in the undersea scenes, when Sadko is about to marry the sea princess Volkhova, the artist can also lose himself in dreams, and loosen his grip on reality. And so at the end, Sadko comes home, back in the world of reality, while the world of magic and superstition is exercised. But Novgorod is also as a result of the poet's visions a transformed place, more open to explorations and new ideas. There is again in the music a subtle interweaving of many folk idioms. The entire opera gives the impression of a gigantic tone-poem for voices and orchestra. It employs a beautiful *parlando,* or arabesque music, accompanied by shimmering chains of rhythm.

The historic 1905 upheaval, of which there had been preliminary rumblings throughout the last quarter of the nineteenth century was touched off by the Russian-Japanese war of 1904, which exposed the incompetence of the Tsarist government. Unrest spread, turning into a revolutionary outbreak, when a delegation of people appealing to the Tsar to listen to their grievances was brutally shot down. The students at the St. Petersburg Conservatory, where Rimsky-Korsakov was teaching took part in the general agitation for democratic government. He tried to defend the students against the repressive police measures, and he was dismissed from the Conservatory. In protest, he resigned from the Imperial Russian Music Society. Letters and addresses supporting him came from all parts of the country. The police forbade performances of his music. He continued to teach his Conservatory pupils at his home. Finally the Conservatory won a measure of self-government, and he was reinstated. And it was at this time, 1906-07, that he composed his satiric fairy-tale masterpiece, *The Golden Cockerel.* Its story, taken from Pushkin, and dealing with an idiotic king rushing madly to war, was so pointedly relevant to the events of the time that even the censors could see its implications, and the opera was not performed until after Rimsky-Korsakov's death.

In the prelude to the opera an Astrologer appears, explaining that what will follow is a fairy tale with a lesson. The curtain then rises on the palace of King Dodon, who, tired of the wars he had carried on in his youth, now wants to rest and forget his enemies. His noblemen try to advise him with magic beans and other fortune-telling idiocies. Then the Astrologer enters and presents the king with a magic cockerel that will cry warning whenever the enemies approach. The king happily goes to sleep, but then the cockerel cries out. He sends his sons out to war, emptying the coffers of the kingdom to pay for it, and goes back to sleep. But again the cockerel cries, and the king must himself go forth to war. He arrives at a grisly battlefield, where his sons lie dead. A brightly colored tent is discovered, out of which steps the beautiful Queen of Shemakhan. She addles his brain with liquor and forces him to dance oafishly before her, while her servants jeer, "A king in rank and dress, but a slave in body and soul." War is forgotten, and he takes her back triumphantly as his bride. In the last act the people, anxiously awaiting news from the battlefield, learn that the king has gotten himself another bride. He enters with her, in a glittering procession, but then the Astrologer demands the Queen as his promised payment for the magic cockerel. The king angrily strikes the Astrologer dead, while the Queen berates him as a wicked monster. The cockerel then attacks the king, who falls dead, while the people moan, "Our dear king is dead, most wise, he ruled the kindom with his hands folded, lying at his ease . . . how long shall we live without a king?" Then, in the epilogue, the Astrologer assures the audience that everything was a dream delirium and perhaps the Queen and himself were the only real people.

The score of this short and compact opera is a beautiful interlacing of "Western" Russian folk and national melody, which is used for the activities of the king, and Asian or "Eastern" cantilenas which are used for the Astrologer, the Queen and the Cockerel. This sets off the fact that the latter are the "magic" beings, or the force which penetrates the King's foolishness and explodes his pomp. At the same time the King's music is touched up by witty dissonances. Among the memorable sections is the slumber music of the first act, which is an enchanting lullaby melody broken into by sensuous chromatic runs that indicate the nature of the King's dream. Remarkable is the opening of the second act, portraying the mysterious battlefield, with a sombre brass *ostinato* above which the dissonant woodwind cries like the shriek of ravens, and then the King's march music, in a

Russian "patriotic" idiom, is heard weirdly distorted. The Queen's scene is a long-spun "Asian" rhapsody for coloratura voice and orchestra. The dance music, contrasting the King's lumbering steps to the Queen's gracefulness, is again a satiric distortion of folk dance melody. And the most biting transformation of the king's "patriotic," anthem-like march occurs in the last act, when it becomes a bridal procession, its rhythms becoming sharp and violent, its harmonies and counter-melodies increasingly dissonant.

The music of *The Golden Cockerel* is a bridge to much *avant-garde* music of the twentieth century; the grotesquerie, mockery and wit of works like Prokofiev's *First Violin Concerto*, Shostakovich's *First Symphony*, Ravel's *The Child and the Sorcerers*, and Stravinsky's *The Soldier's Tale*. But lacking in much of the twentieth century music that essays such grotesquerie would be Rimsky-Korsakov's humanity, his breadth and ability to see many sides of life and music, his keen social mind, and his rich fund of tender melodic human images which gives so much substance to his comic caricatures. Unfortunately this musical wit would often degenerate into a bleak assumption of a pose of primitivism, as a form of disillusionment with civilization, or into a childish nose-thumbing at the musical past.

9. THE HUMANIST CRISIS IN THE TWENTIETH CENTURY

"It (humanism) is not so much a movement as an attitude which can be defined as the conviction of the dignity of man, based on both the insistence on human values (rationality and freedom) and the acceptance of human limitations (fallibility and frailty); from this two postulates result—responsibility and tolerance."

—ERWIN PANOFSKY, *The History of Art as a Humanistic Discipline*

I

The two composers of the late nineteenth and early twentieth century who inherit respectively the mantle of Giuseppe Verdi and Richard Wagner are Giacomo Puccini (1858-1924) and Richard Strauss (1864-1949). Both are a sizeable step below their predecessors. In neither is there a profound reflection of the life of their nation.

The Italy of Puccini's time was an independent monarchy which did nothing to better the life of the people and eventually handed its ruling power over to fascism. (The year Puccini died, saw the murder of the socialist Matteoti by the Italian fascists). In this Italy Puccini found no theme like that of the struggle for Italian independence which had fired the art of Verdi. Puccini is essentially the sweet singer of the yearning and pathos of love, as in the affecting melodies of *La Boheme* (1896) and *Madame Butterfly* (1904). Even in *Tosca* (1900), a drama of the persecution and murder of political liberals by the Roman police of 1800, what dominates the music is the love-inspired lyricism. The psychological issues, the inner conflicts that Puccini deals with, musically, in his operas, are less significant than those of Verdi. The area of social characterization is narrower, and the musical architecture is softened. The operatic style moves in the direction of a more superficial realism, the music being sensitively knit to the stage action, and adapted so that its finely knit continuity and flow allows the drama itself to proceed with an unimpeded naturalness. But the operas are irradiated by the tenderness of song which Puccini gives to his characters, and which reflects the regard he feels for them and for people in general.

Naturalism carried to much greater extremes, without Puccini's sweet affection for people but supported by a magnificent mastery of harmony and instrumental timbre, distinguishes the art of Richard Strauss. He provided, in his operas and tone poems, a brilliantly impressive impersonation of a social mind dealing with intellectual matters. But when a composer cuts himself off from the real life and issues affecting his people, deciding to carry on a "daring revolution" in the realm of musical form and avoiding what might be considered dangerous social matters, he also narrows the realm of human feelings about which he can speak with conviction.

The tone poems, appearing mainly in the 1890's, although they seem to range over a wide area of literature and philosophy, are brilliant examples of showmanship rather than deep thought. An example is *Thus Spake Zarathustra* (1896). A philosophy of life could be said to have been presented in the Beethoven, Brahms or Tchaikovsky symphonies, implied in their human portraiture and response to life. Strauss' tone poem however offers only a set of musical illustrations to a philosophical tract, with an impressive musical "sunrise," a clever fugue representing in its complexities the complications of science, and a waltz fitted to the statement, "joy is deeper than grief." It is as if Nietzsche had written a comic opera plot.

In *Don Quixote* (1897) the witty musical illustrations, including braying sheep, windmills and a ride through the air, only thinly disguise the fact that the music has no inner tie to the spirit of Cervantes' great masterpiece, with its sharp social satire and warmhearted, encyclopoedic representation of Spanish life. The form is also a brilliant novelty; tone poem, theme with variations, and concerto for solo instruments and orchestra combined into one. Yet after the first excitement is lost, one observes that the architecture sags.

Saddest of all the tone poems, because in certain ways it is perhaps the best of them, and certainly the most comic, is *The Merry Adventures of Tyl Eulenspiegel* (1895). Here Strauss touches on the folk realm. Tyl Eulenspiegel had been a German medieval folk hero, a comic Robin Hood, his buffoonery a mask for the resentment by the peasantry of their oppression by aristocracy, merchants and clergy. His popularity as a symbol had reached a peak at the time of the German peasant revolt. But in the tone poem, which moves like a blithe scherzo, the humor is aimed not at Tyl's and the people's enemies but at Tyl himself, the spokesman for the folk. He is presented as a childish trickster, upon whom the sledge-hammer of the law crashes down with awesome finality, while he can only squeak pitifully in answer to its charges. And just before the end, Strauss depicts Tyl's body "amusingly" dangling at the end of a rope.

The operas, which appeared in the twentieth century, are greater works, for there is less illustrative superficiality, and Strauss comes directly to grip with full-bodied human portraiture. In form they are "tone poem operas," the approach being a development out of Wagner's, with the magnificently colorful orchestra playing a central role, the vocal lines being open, speech-inflected and declamatory, and the development of melodic motifs, with their constantly changing harmonic-orchestral texture, giving the works a powerful inner and highly subjective psychological life. To music lovers seeking a continuation of the great German romantic line of Schumann, Wagner and Brahms, Strauss is clearly the nearest to a "great master" in this tradition. And no one can gainsay the artistry of these operas. But abandoned is the great humanist tradition which demands that an artist pay some heed to the life and troubles about him. At the time, the great task facing the German people was to carry through the struggle for a democratic republic, to get rid of the incubus of militaristic Emperors and Junkers supported by the Krupp armament works, to combat the upperclass jingoism, brutalization of life and drive to war. To one who ignored these matters, who did not hint in his works even of the presence of a German people, what intellectual life was left?

Salome (1905), based on the Oscar Wilde play, presents love in its most animalistic and perverted form, as a sheer physical sensuality turning quickly into hatred and appeased by murder. The king Herod and queen Herodias hate each other. Salome in turn sexually fascinates her foster-father, Herod, who in the end has her killed, and a young captain, who kills himself. She flaunts her body before the prophet John the Baptist, and when the prophet rejects her, she has him killed so that she can kiss the lips of the dead man. Adding to the brutality are the anti-Semitic characterizations, which the music cleverly underlines.

Elektra (1906-09) purports to deal with the Greek legend, but actually presents the neuroticisms of bourgeois family life out of which Freud was deducing an all-embracing psychology and theory of society. With the exception of a touch of tenderness in the reunion of Elektra with her brother Orestes, the driving emotional forces of the opera are Elektra's screaming, father-adoration and screaming, obsessed mother hatred, crying for blood. She has none of the nobility with which Sophocles had invested his Elektra, showing her as a person determined to live by principle rather than bow to tyranny.

In both operas, Strauss the composer rises completely to the demands of his themes, providing a perfect musical clothing for this dehumanized, obsessed psychology. It is a music that, with all its artistry, generates little human warmth, but has an almost visceral sensual impact on the listener. The limitation of such works is not that they are "immoral" or "indecent," but only that of such naturalism itself. What has previously been an "unmentionable" side of life is now thrown in the face of society, its very shock quality seeming to confirm it as "truth." And there is a limited validity to them, for these perversions are a part of life. But on the whole they tell us very little about life and people.

Throughout the history of art, sides of life had been disclosed which could be called unpleasant or ugly. But to inspire great art, such themes had to be part of a critical thought applied to society, resulting in an expansion of a human being's ability to understand and even rediscover himself in the real world about him. The devastating flaw in Strauss is the lack of such a critical mind. This is obvious in *Der Rosenkavelier* (1911), which is also the most genial expression of his personality. It is a comedy dressed in lovely but somewhat flabby melody. Strauss' narrow human and social sympathies had always tended to constrict his source of melody. His melodies tended to be sweet and on the verge of sickly sentimentality. A favorite strain is that of the Viennese waltz, which appears in strange places like *Thus Spake Zarathustra* and Salome's climactic dance in the opera. In the comedy *Der Rosenkavelier* sentimental waltzes abound, and in fact its main theme, as Moscow Carner points out[1] was probably borrowed from a waltz *Dynamiden* by Josef Strauss.

The setting of the opera is the late eighteenth century, the same milieu which Mozart, a truly critical mind, touched on in *The Marriage of Figaro*. Mozart and his librettist Da Ponte had been boldly critical of the aristocracy and had treated the servants with dignity, defending their right to love and marriage against the adulterous practices of their master. Strauss and his librettist Hugo von Hoffmansthal, however, tend to fawn upon the aristocracy while indulging in the safe practice of bourgeois baiting. There is a touch of chauvinism, the most corrupt characters being Italians speaking a broken German. The story is of the Princess von Werdenberg, wife of a Marshal, who soothes her unhappiness in marriage by a series of love escapades. The "tragic awakening" that gives "depth" to the opera is her realization that she is now getting too old to carry on such affairs. The youthful hero, Count Octavian, who at the beginning is her lover, is timidly happy when she releases him so that he can marry the naive girl Sophie. The role of buffoon is filled by the lecherous Baron Ochs.

The general picture is that of a society in which the people have nothing to do but carry on amorous games, and it contrasts adultery, as gracefully carried on by the Princess and Octavian, to the vulgar adultery carried on by Ochs. About this game of love the music throws a tender, rapturous glow, with sentimental melodies developed through rich harmonic and orchestral color to a drawn-out, blissful sensuousness and apotheosis. A touch of naturalism enters in the prelude, depicting a sex-spasm, just before the curtain rises disclosing the princess and Octavian in close communion. What remains an innovation in *Der Rosenkavelier,* as in all of these operas, is the psychological authenticity of its music. The neuroticisms and perversions of *Salome* and *Elektra* are the other side of the shallow and brittle human relations depicted in *Der Rosenkavelier.*

The subsequent operas betray a search for innocuous themes that have at the same time an impressive literary air, like a series of intellectual excursions. Perhaps the most ambitious is *Die Frau ohne Schatten* (1913-16). Its theme is essentially simple. An Empress is sad because she can have no children, and a peasant's wife is bitter at the meanness and poverty of her life. At the end the Empress learns from the peasant thoughtfulness towards others, which also enables her to have children, while the peasant's wife learns to love her husband and accept his conditions of life. This latter lesson, that the peasant must work hard and never complain of his lot, better fits the Middle Ages than the twentieth century. About the plot von Hoffmansthal throws a network of symbols—magic gazelles, magic falcons, a shadowless woman, an evil god with his spies and messengers, the voices of unborn children, golden fountains, golden bridges —all of whch add nothing to the meaning and only serve to give the impression that there are deep, unfathomable mysteries to the tale. Strauss follows suit, inventing *leitmotifs* for every magic symbol and psychological situation, and weaving them, with his usual technical mastery, into a refined and impressively complex musical texture. But the thread of Straussian melody gets to be drawn rather thin.

The whole Strauss picture is a sad one. Through the sheer bulk of his works, and the musical craft they display, he is the "great" opera composer of the twentieth century. But the truly great opera composers of the past had risen, in one way or another, to the intellectual and human demands that their age made of them, to what was new and challenging in their times. Strauss declined this challenge. If he is the "great German composer" of his times, it is a weakness that we can find nothing of Germany in his work, except perhaps the tendency towards escapism, with a polarity of sentimentality on the one side and violence on the other, which would be typical in the 1930's of those who decided that they could make their peace with the yoke of fascism and at least "keep their minds free."

II

Gustav Mahler 1860-1911) possessed, in contrast to Strauss, a genuinely philosophical approach to music. This is seen in the deep seriousness of his works, consisting of colossal symphonies, some with vocal and choral movements, and of song cycles; in the integrity with which the formal structure mirrors his deepest emotional conflicts; in the absence of any Strauss-like showmanship; in the profound self-revelation they offer of a mind trying to come to grips with awesome problems of man and the universe. Yet even less than Strauss does he show a consciousness of the presence of a society about him, or of other people with problems that might concern him. His philosophy is one of unreality, the yearning for another world more real than the actual one. And thus it becomes only the mirror of his own unhappiness.

His art has no national breadth. And because it has no source in the outer world, its human imagery, or melodic fund, tends to be drawn from the past of German composed music, from Mozart, Beethoven, Schubert, Brahms and others, with these adopted melodies given a subjective turn, like the work of a gifted novelist whose characters and ideas seem largely taken over from past literature. The result can be a personally expressive music with a deep pathos, as we can hear for example in the first movement of his symphonic song cycle, *Das Lied von der Erde*, where the opening theme of Schumann's *Symphonic Etudes* becomes so poignant a clothing for the words *"Dunkel ist der Leben, ist der Tod"* ("Dark is life, dark is death.") But these works almost stifle for lack of fresh air. It is in such a context, making up part of the fund of past music on which he draws, that folk music enters, as in the "Hunter's Funeral March" and *ländler* of the First Symphony, the second movement of the *Second Symphony*, the last movement of the *Fourth Symphony*. These folk strains contribute no sense of the outer world, but only a childhood innocence, nostalgically recalled.

About the art of Arnold Schönberg (1874-1951), a school of music has grown which is resolutely opposed to anything that might resemble national expression. Schönberg combined the keenest of musical intelligences with the irrationality of one who regarded society as nothing but an enemy. His music has no reflection of the experiences that people take part in together. Its appeal is mainly to those who share his own loneliness. His atonality is no leap into a musical future, but the final and one-sided development of those elements in the music of Mozart, Beethoven, Schubert, Schumann, Brahms and Wagner with which those composers had expressed their moments of deepest inner unrest. Wide leaps from one note to another replace melodies drawn from the social heritage; chromaticism and perpetual key change are transformed into a system by which all sense of a "home" tonality, from which the music moves and to which it returns, is abandoned. Form collapses, in the sense of an organized structure reflecting a rationality or order that the composer finds in real life. For all the intricate designs of this music on paper, what the listener hears is only a succession of "moments," which are sometimes poignant outcries. With his "twelve-tone system" laying out a complete set of rules and principles for creating music on a purely atonal basis, Schonberg performed the colossal feat of offering to supplant single-handedly what it had taken a whole society over three centuries of its history to create. But what he actually did was to make his own unrest and alienation from his fellow men into a system for the entire art of music.

Atonal music and the "twelve tone system" have attracted composers of broader social mind than Schönberg. But what results is a complete detachment of the emotional world of their music from their outer-world interests. An example is Alban

Berg (1885-1935), a Schönberg pupil, whose opera *Wozzeck* (1917-21) is perhaps the great classic of atonal music. The drama from which Berg made his libretto had been written a century before by the short-lived, rebellious genius, Georg Buchner. It tells of a lowly, illiterate soldier who has taken a prostitute to wife. In the course of the drama he is sneered at, tricked and kicked about by his caste superiors. His wife betrays him to an arrogant drum-major. In a fit of insanity he kills his wife and drowns himself.

Popular elements enter Berg's score, like the folk song sung by a soldier in the second scene of the first act, the march music and military song in the following scene, the waltz music and popular ditty in the beer-garden scene of Act II, the children's game in the finale. But these are pulled apart harmonically as in a distorting mirror. At the same time they give the surrounding atonal fabric, by contrast, an added tone of fear and horror. In the score little thematic fragments are arranged in complicated fugue, sonata, canon and variation forms. But since the elements from which these forms are built are not in themselves significant statements or images—they are not even perceived as units by the ear—the forms make no impression as such. If the theme or motif does not embody the germ of a statement or thought, then the form built with such evanescent material cannot convey, as musical form must with its repetitions and variations, a train of thought.

With Anton von Webern (1883-1945), a pupil of Schönburg who carried his principles to a kind of logical extreme, the "theme" or building block becomes a single note, or two-note interval. Extravagant critiques have been written of such music, praising its "concentration" of form. But there is no virtue in "concentration" as such. A single note, or a two-note interval, or a chord, cannot play the role of a human image, or be an evocation of a situation of life. And so such music cannot create characterizations, or psychologies, distinct from one another. Similarly Berg's opera, like all music of this school when it evokes anything at all, portrays only the composer's inner world, his anguished impotence before a social life in which all that he sees are human being preying on one another, with humanism losing its social responsibility and therefore its dignity. Humanism dwindles down to the artist's awareness of solely his own existence.

One of the homes that atonal music has found is in music

for the cinema. The very fact that it gives the listening mind no independent formal tracks to follow, for its impact is that of a series of isolated "moments," makes it especially apt for this purpose; an expression of awesome suspense, fear, horror or mystery that will last for the exact few seconds demanded by the film footage. Schönberg's *Five Pieces for Orchestra,* which baffled its listeners in 1912, today is easy to listen to, sounding extraordinarily like film music. But this does not establish its greatness. As Tolstoi said in *What is Art?* one can get accustomed to almost anything. But in this work a phenomenal technical equipment is being used to say very little. Nor is there more social feeling in the turn to Jewish subjects of Schönberg's later years. Just as Schönberg always saw himself as the prophet of a new music, so in the opera *Moses and Aaron* (1931-51) he portrays Moses as the man who alone has the vision to understand the laws of God, and is surrounded by a bestial, cowardly and bloodthirsty mob. Most affecting in the music are the evocations of horror and the haunting outcries of loneliness.

Paul Hindemith (*b.* 1895) tried to give his romantic inwardness a strong, clear and firm objective structure, turning for his models to medieval polyphony and the art of the great baroque contrapuntalists. The structure "rings true," like the work of a dedicated craftsman. But his melodies are juiceless. They offer no openhearted, evocative song. When folk melodies occasionally are quoted in his work, as in the viola concerto *Der Schwanendreher,* they take on a typical Hindemith bleakness. The polytonality, or use of two keys at once, only serves to aggravate this emotional narrowness. With his masterly handling of counterpoint, he builds up a driving momentum and feeling of energy, and yet his music is predominantly elegaic in mood, occasionally leavened by an ironic wit. There is no emotional conflict or real drama in his symphonic works, and so there is sadness but no real tragedy. Whether he writes a "driving" work like the *Symphony in E flat* and *Concert Music for Brass and Strings,* a witty work like *The Four Temperaments,* or one in which the elegaic quality becomes most touching, as in the *Requiem, "For Those We Love,"* (a setting of Walt Whitman's "When Lilacs Last in the Dooryard Bloomed"), the spiritual message is the same; that of a face turned to the past.

The brief discussion given here to composers like Strauss, Mahler, Schönberg, Berg and Hindemith, is not meant to be commensurate with either their eminence or their musical powers.

It is due to the fact that they offer no illumination, except in a negative way, upon the problem being dealt with here, of music and nation. And while they have a flock of admirers and followers, it can be said that the future of their music is open to question. While their great musical gifts are unquestioned, their isolation in mind and heart from their people and nation has limited their development as human beings and as artists. It has narrowed their human sympathies, and left them with little of significance to say to the people whose world they share. Hegel touched on this attitude more than a hundred years ago, when he wrote of artists in whom "the thinker's courage has failed him to come to terms with the external world in question. . . . For such a man, the only relief available is a complete withdrawal into the secret world of the emotions, a prison-house of unreality he steps out never."

In an era when one of the most critical struggles in history was taking place between human progress and human destruction, they turned away, the result being cynicism (Strauss), and the yearning for another world than the real one (Mahler) with finally the acceptance of the fact of a dying world, Schönberg expressing his lonely horror, and Hindemith, in his medieval guild workshop, writing elegies. Many musicians and critics share such views, and to them, this is great art, while on the other hand the music of composers with humanist, social-minded feelings and deep national ties, like a Sibelius or Vaughan Williams, seems naive and backward.

Yet the world refuses to die. And as it slowly discovers a solution to its problems, it finds in the latter composers a precious quality which may make their work last longer than that of their more brilliantly equipped colleagues. It is the quality of heart; the warmth which comes from an attachment to others than themselves, so that even when sadness afflicts them, it is not their own despair but the troubles of a people and nation of which they are speaking. And this ability to get out of their own skin has also helped shape their work. More perhaps than any other composers, they have given new life in the twentieth century to the symphony, a form the basis of which lies in the breadth of life outside of him that the composer can capture.

III

Finland had traditionally been a battle ground and war prize between Sweden and Russia. In the nineteenth century, it had won part autonomy, as a Grand Duchy under the Russian Empire, with its own constitution. Life was hard, as in all countries where the great mass of people consists of peasantry, working on the land that others own. Sibelius' father, a doctor, had died while attending to the people during the typhus epidemic of 1867-68, aptly called "hunger typhus" because it was most virulent when crops failed. In the 1890's the Russian Imperial reins were tightened. This was answered by a clamor for Finnish independence. Some constitutional concessions were won during the Russian revolutionary outbreaks of 1905, but the grip of reaction was again soon tightened.

It was this struggle for Finnish cultural and political independence that fired the heart and mind of Jean Sibelius (1865-1957) as he came to maturity in the 1890's. A work as early as *En Saga* (1892, revised 1901) established him as basically an orchestral composer, addressing the nation from a public forum. It is somewhat more abundant in singing melody than his later works, but his originality of voice is already evident in the texture of the music. A succession of modal melodies is spun over a shimmering rhythmic-harmonic web, the *parlando*, declamatory melodic phrases being supported by rhythm-charged *ostinatos*. He has seized upon and made his own the double origin of folk music, in speech and human movement, and can create melodies of his own which sound completely folk.

The tone poem *Finlandia* (1899-1900) composed to fit the theme "Finland awakes" in a patriotic pageant, became an embodiment of national pride. Performances were for some years forbidden in Finland. It was more sweetly melodic than his later big orchestral works, but the melodies, with their "national anthem" character, had great distinction, and the fierce declamatory tone of its opening pages already presaged his later style.

The tone poems and symphonies that followed are a body of music unique in history. One can find a general background for them; for the tone poems, not so much the Liszt "philosophical" works as the patriotic works of Smetana's *My Homeland* cycle, and Dvorak's orchestral folk-tale works like *The Golden Spinning-wheel;* for the symphonies, not so much the German tradition as the Russian, of Tchaikovsky and Borodin. But never before had so great a body of symphonic works been so completely and unequivocally dedicated to national pride, national tradition and national freedom.

The subjects of many tone poems came from the *Kalevala,* an epic poem which had been put together as late as the nineteenth century from thousands of ballads, tales and saga-fragments that existed among the peasantry, preserved by them from tribal days. Likewise national in feeling are the tone poems that may be called "nature pictures," for in a land where the peasantry are engaged in a constant struggle with nature, the forces of which are felt with particular violence, nature legends have a special evocative power. In some, nature and myth merge with one another, as for example in *Tapiola,* an evocation of the "god of the forests."

The style of the tone poems is also the style of the symphonies. The *First Symphony* (1899) opens with a melodic recitative for clarinet, meditative and with a touch of pathos, over a roll of drums, and then the first theme proper comes, a fierce cry from the strings. Like this cry is the declamation with which *Tapiola* opens, in a tone of suppressed fury, although it was composed twenty-six years later. The difference between tone poem and symphony is that the symphonies are broader in the sweep of life they contain within a single work, and where the tone poems bring the past to bear upon the present, the symphonies are an immediate reaction to the state of the nation. Thus, while the early tone poems, such as *En Saga, The Swan of Tuonela* and the three *Lemminkäinen* legends, embodied a sense of the bardic past, reminding the people of their own independent language, their own culture, their ancient heroes, the *Second Symphony* (1901) came like a great wordless call for a free Finland.

This symphony indicates how completely Sibelius has been able to recast the classic symphonic framework into an embodiment of his own message, in which every phrase is "Sibelius" and Finland. He was an admirer and deep student of Beethoven. Characteristic of the symphonic form to him was "the profound logic that created an inner connection between all the motifs."[3] Where Beethoven's themes however are more sharply defined, those of Sibelius are more fragmentary and malleable. They have great individuality and expressive power at the same time. They proceed antiphonally, each appearing as an answer to the preceding one, and so an organic, binding tissue is created that infuses the entire work. So charged with power is the declamation he creates that it can stand alone, without lush harmonization. The first movement of the symphony exhibits this "bare" quality. There are no transitional or accompaniment passages. Every phrase from the very beginning, is an expressive motif, with a strong role to play. Two groups of such motifs are introduced, making up an "exposition," largely *parlando,* and even the theme heard near the beginning from oboe and clarinet, that sounds like a folk dance, is given a halting, *parlando* quality.

The symphony proceeds largely in terms of single declamatory lines or a two-voice polyphony. There is a "classic" development section, but wholly different in approach from either Beethoven's or romantic-style thematic development. Sibelius' motifs, charged with feeling, are put into ever-new shapes and combinations which become also a process of "giving birth to melody." Thus the first movement of the *Second Symphony* rises to a climax of tremendous antiphonal melodic declamation. There is no classical recapitulation, but instead a short, compressed recapitulation and coda. The form represents a more subjective approach to the symphony than the classic pattern, and the entire emotional process of this symphony is one of brooding, or "darkness," finally arriving at "light" and the outer world.

Sibelius is not the most prolific of songful melodists, but his lyrical lines nevertheless have great strength and distinction. The slow movement of the *Second Symphony* illustrates the process of the "birth of melody" from thematic fragments, the climax of the movement being the emergence of a poignant, funereal melody, like a requiem for the dead. The scherzo is not a folk dance but a typical example of the composer's rhythm-charged idiom, here also accompanied by fierce cries and ejaculations. The middle section however is a beautiful "Finlandia-type" song. The scherzo leads into the closing movement, a magnificent, grand, heroic processional reaching a stirring climax. It is an "outer world" statement, rousing the spirit like a banner waving.

What are the roots of this idiom? In 1892, after Sibelius had composed his choral-orchestral work, *Kullervo,* based on the *Kalevala* legends, he wrote, "The language of sound that I had employed in *Kullervo* was considered to give such thorough and true expression of Finnish scenery and the soul of the Finnish people that many were unable to explain it in any other way than that I had made direct use of folk melodies, especially of the accents of runic song, in my work. The genuinely Finnish tone of *Kullervo* could, however, not have been achieved in this way, for the simple reason that at the time the work was composed I was not acquainted with my supposed model. First I composed *Kullervo.* Then I went to Karelia to hear, for the first time in my life, the *Kalevala* runes from the lips of the people."[4] What this means, however, is only that Sibelius is not an "arranger" of folk material, but an original composer, handling the plastic material of folk song. He must have heard Finnish song in his youth. He may have gotten the feeling of a Scandinavian folkish lyricism from the Norwegian, Edvard Grieg (1843-1907), whose genius ran however to a more tender sweetness, in contrast to the starkness and strength of Sibelius. He may have learned something of the "folk touch" from the Russian composers, with their exploration of irregular scales. Finnish folk music is not a world apart. It is connected with German on the one hand, Slavic on the other. The English singer, Astra Desmond, writes, regarding Sibelius' songs, "In place of pure melody, Sibelius has evolved a kind of declamatory recitative (not in any way to be confused with what is known as *Sprechgesang*) which is singularly beautiful and quite peculiar to himself. As often in Sibelius' music, one feels he has tapped some primeval source of inspiration, so here one feels he has gone back to a rhapsodic style that ancient minstrels may have used."[5] Thus out of memories of the general style of Finnish folk music and an unerring feeling for the organic roots in declamation and rhythm of folk style itself, he was able to create an idiom which sounded to the Finnish people not in the least alien or strange; one that they accepted as their own.

A lighter, more lyrical period followed the *Second Symphony,* producing the *Violin Concerto* (1903-05), full of rousing folk-dance images that are nevertheless given a brooding, *parlando* character; *Pohjola's Daughter* (1906), which is like a blithe version of *En Saga;* and the *Third Symphony* (1907). Then the *Fourth Symphony* (1911) comes, speaking of a deep emotional crisis. Its slow movement, in which the "fragments" gradually build up to a melodic outcry of deep anguish, is the most heartbreaking section in his entire work. The last movement, with its vigorous rhythms tempered by discordant cries, is like an unsuccessful effort to regain hope. There may have been at the time a personal problem in the composer's mind. In 1908 he had undergone a throat operation, and for some years afterwards he had fears of cancer. But it is more likely that Sibelius, the patriot, is feeling the crisis of European society.

In 1911 Bartok produced one of his most lonely, despairing works, *Bluebeard's Castle.* Schönberg's *Pierrot Lunaire,* with its cries of fear, came in 1912. Stravinsky's *Rite of Spring,* a primitivistic "shock" piece flung in the face of civilization, came in 1913. The *Fourth Symphony* is Sibelius' own version of this desolation.

Then came the great war itself, which had been brewing, its tensions felt throughout Europe, for almost two decades. The Finns, like most of the small nations caught in the millstones of great-power conflicts, had no love for either side, but rather a hope for their own independence. And the Russian revolution of 1917 finally did bring Finland independence. The *Fifth Symphony,* first composed in 1915, revised in 1916 and rewritten in 1919, covers these years. It has something of the heroic-patriotic spirit of the *Second Symphony,* but without the clarity and forthright melodiousness of the earlier work. It inaugurates a "late style," in which there is a more complex, subtle harmonic texture, and a greater economy of themes, which are at the same time given a more intense development. The first movement begins with and expands upon a "horn call" motif, like a call to hope and action. There is a sadder answering motif, then a crescendo, and a wisp of what sounds like a peasant dance. The exposition is repeated in variant form, a declamatory development follows, and then the peasant-dance motif expands into a rousing scherzo-like section, the nearest to a "peasant picture" in all Sibelius. A dramatic apotheosis of the "horn call" motif ends the movement. The second movement is an enchanting set of variations on a rhythm-dominated melody. The concluding movement starts with a pulsating, rhythmic "perpetual motion," and then a powerful striding, bell-like theme appears, which grows to dominate the movement, like an unstoppable tread. It does not "sing," like the finale of the *Second Symphony,* but it is equally compelling. It could represent the march of Finnish independence.

Following this, major works are few. The *Sixth Symphony* (1923) is Sibelius at his most quiet and reserved. The *Seventh Symphony* (1924), in one movement, is a deeply touching work, one of the greatest examples of Sibelius' ability to spin a long, grand, continuously evolving melodic line. The line is tragic in feeling but without desolation, and is broken into by two interspersed folk-dance episodes. Commissioned from the United States was *Tapiola* (1925), with its declamatory motifs, *osti-*

natos and tread-like rhythm. It is the work of a consummate master in its immense structure built of the barest materials. Then, but for some short pieces, the last of which appear in 1929, there is silence. Sibelius was said to have been composing music, and there were rumors of a completed eighth symphony, but nothing came forth.

As to the reasons for this silence, we can only speculate. The Finnish declaration of independence came when Russia was being led by the Communists, who approved this independence. The Communist movement then grew in Finland, and a Finnish Workers Socialist government was proclaimed. Against it, Baron Carl Gustav Mannerheim, a Swedish Finn who had been a general in the Russian Tsarist army, an autocrat pro-German and royalist in mentality, raised an army of White Guards. With the aid of 12,000 troops from Germany, he overthrew the socialist government. Sibelius suffered discomforts from the Left, such as having his home searched for hidden arms. The White Guards, victorious with the help of the Germans, inaugurated however a frightful slaughter of the socialist sympathizers. David Hinshaw, a colleague and biographer of Herbert Hoover, and no friend of the Left, writes, "The White Guard, following victory, placed 80,000 Reds, men and women, in concentration camps of which an estimated 10,000 died of starvation."[6] The Encyclopedia Britannica states that the White Guards slaughtered "some 15,000 men, women and children."[7] And Hinshaw indicates the class forces attacking the socialist regime. "It was a contest of the old Finland's yeomen and pastors that was in part led by the Swedish-speaking educated classes against the new proletariat of the towns and the landless peasants."[8] The subsequent "independent" Finnish government, in which those still alive with socialist sympathies were removed from the voting rolls, invited a German prince to be its king, and Mannerheim at the same time sought to lead an army of intervention to overthrow the revolutionary regime in Russia. The collapse of the German Kaiser and his court saved Finland from the blessings of monarchy. A democratic, parliamentary constitution was established. Then 1929 saw the rise of the fascist Lapua movement, operating, as Hinshaw describes it, like a Ku Klux Klan, with beatings, kidnappings and murder of socialist-minded or liberal officials. He adds, "Some capitalist interests, high army officials and private banks, which had been supporting the Lapua movement, seemed unwilling for Finland to return to Parliamentary democracy."[9] In the 1930's, the country moved into the orbit of German financial political influence, and while Hitler was making his bellicose proclamations, Mannerheim again came to the fore, as head of the "Defense Council." The highly fortified Mannerheim Line was built a few miles from Leningrad. The Soviet Union took this line, in the war of 1939-40; then when Hitler attacked the Soviet Union, Finland became his ally. At the end of the war the Germans, before they were pushed out of Finland, devastated the north part of the country.

As to what Sibelius thought of these events that followed upon the emergence of an independent Finland, there is no indication. He never took part in politics. He certainly had no socialist sympathies, and was no friend of the Left. But it is hard to see him thinking of Mannerheim as a "national hero," or embracing Hitler as a friend of Finland. And it may be that his musical silence is due to the bewilderment he felt at what had happened to his country. In the 1890's, and early 1900's, the problem was a simple one. He was a Finnish patriot. Finland was not free. The nation was united about the demand for freedom. But after freedom came, there were complications; a land torn in two, bankers, landowners, middle class, fighting the proletariat and landless farm workers, the first murdering the second. All his life Sibelius had been attached to his nation heart and soul. This is what his music primarily expressed. And after the middle 1920's, it is possible that he no longer understood the nation, and no longer knew what to say to it.

IV

The English musical renaissance, of the end of the nineteenth and first half of the twentieth century, is one of the great events of contemporary music, the full importance of which has yet to be recognized on the world scene. It involved a galaxy of figures, not only composers but also critics and scholars, and drew as well upon the other arts. Among its roots, or the signs of its stirring, was the excitement generated by Dvorak's music in the 1880's, a proof of the power, freshness and "universality" of an art built on the base of folklore and national consciousness. Other signs were the challenging questions raised of English social and artistic life by John Ruskin and William Morris, and the sombre portrayals of the decline of the countryside, with the moral problems this brought up, in the novels and poems of Thomas Hardy.

Most important was the national self-criticism rising precisely when the Empire seemed at the height of its power, seen in the attacks upon the Boer War of 1899-1902, the sympathies felt for the Irish independence movement, the cultural impact of the rich Irish national poetry and drama, the Fabian Socialist movement and the growth of the English Labor Party. In challenge to the hardened arrogance of Tory and imperialist, such questions were raised as, what was the real England? What was happening to the English people? How did the poor live? What was the real English past, and English history? Among the figures of the renaissance were Cecil Sharp (1859-1924), with his historic researches in English folk music, that brought so fresh a knowledge as well of the ties between English and American folk music; the composer, scholar and critic, Sir Hubert Parry (1848-1918) who, as Vaughan Williams recounts, told him to "write choral music as befits an Englishman and a democrat;"[10] the editor Edmund H. Fellowes (1870-1951) who helped restore the knowledge of the great tradition of Elizabethan solo song and madrigal. Some of the outstanding composers were Sir Edward Elgar (1857-1934), Frederick Delius (1862-1924), and Gustav Holst (1874-1934), the latter two having an especially fine feeling for folk music.

The giant of this renaissance is Ralph Vaughan Williams (1872-1958), whose acceptance by his own land has been less than open-hearted. Certainly his long series of works did not fail to be respectfully greeted, and by the time of his death he was the recognized "dean" of English music. But it was a limited recognition. As Hubert Foss wrote, the "public is gradually discovering Vaughan Williams in his old age, having steadily neglected him during all the earlier years. But how often do we hear the Fourth Symphony, *Flos Campi,* the *Magnificat,* the Shelley songs? Is *Hugh the Drover* often played, or *Sir John in Love?*"[11] There has always been a greater excitement over more spectacular figures producing a shallower music. We can see this today in the acclaim, publicity and far more frequent performances given to Benjamin Britten (*b.* 1913), a brilliant and enormously masterful composer, who however seems to lack the challenge to national self-appraisal, and quality of heart, which give Vaughan Williams' works their depth.

Vaughan Williams' music, like that of other social-minded humanists, failed to conform to the surface intellectual trends. To the "modernists," he offered no glittering novelties of technique, no sensational proclamations of having "wiped out" the humanist past, no primitivisms, no "systems." He neither engendered nor allied himself to any "schools," with their implicit narrowness. And so, they arrogantly decided that he really did not belong to the twentieth century, of which they were the self-appointed spokesmen. A similar and silly judgment has frequently been passed on Sibelius, whom Vaughan Williams has always venerated. Thus Adolfo Salazar describes Sibelius as "still living in the nineteenth century."[12] But to the academicians, pretending to prize the humanist tradition, yet Tory-minded and cutting out its social and national heart, Vaughan Williams was equally disturbing. His music was too much of the twentieth century. It reminded its listeners of the common people, and of the disturbing, discomforting moral problems in English life. Tory minds will welcome a nationalistic music, of pomp and pride, but not a democratic national art. Vaughan Williams hinted, by his creative use of countryside music, that the genius of England lay among the common people. He ignored, in the English tradition, even the Handel grandeur with its impression of self-satisfied strength. He went for the tradition of his art to the great Elizabethan age, when in music, as in speech and poetry, the popular and the learned seemed to walk hand in hand.

The son of a clergyman, he had no radical political bent. But in the most natural, unobtrusive way, he thought of himself as one of the common people. Thus in the First World War, he enlisted as a common soldier, rejecting an officer's commission. His bent of mind may be seen in the poets he favors; not only Chaucer and Shakespeare, but Shelley, Blake, and from America, Walt Whitman. It may be seen also in such works as the *London Symphony,* which obviously paints a picture of the common people's London, and has in its closing movement a "march of the unemployed;"[13] the opera *Hugh the Drover,* dealing with a free-thinker among the ordinary people at the time of the Napoleonic wars, and with a boxing match as a central scene; the opera *Riders to the Sea,* using John Millington Synge's portrayal of the tragic life of the Irish fisher-folk; the opera *Pilgrim's Progress,* based on John Bunyan's great social-religious satire.

The characteristic Vaughan Williams idiom is a masterful absorption of the typical melodic turns of the older, modal English folk music, and of the sixteenth and seventeenth century English madrigal and song composers. He builds these into long-spun melodic lines, modally harmonized, and rarely emerging into clear-cut, rounded tunes. As themes in his symphonic works, they tend to have a romantic, subjective indefiniteness. How well he can use this idiom for a completely personal, true and modern expression may be seen in two comparatively early works; the song-cycle *On Wenlock Edge* (1909), to poems of Alfred Housman, which ranges from the blithe "Oh, when I was in love with you," to the poignant "Is my team plowing?" and the *Fantasia on a Theme of Thomas Tallis* (1910), for string orchestra.

The *Fantasia* opens with phrases from the Tallis melody, woven into a beautiful, free-flowing polyphony. Then when the main melody (originally a popular-style hymn by the Elizabethan master) appears, it seems to have been "born" out of the preceding music. It is changed into a continuously flowing, unrounded melodic line, supported by a polyphonic web spun of its fragmentary phrases. A "development section" follows, in which the theme is again broken into parts, with the music taking on a touch of drama, in antiphonal "statements and answers," while solo voices of the strings meditatively emerge from the full string body. The climax is a declamation by the full body of strings, after which there is a compressed recapitulation and coda. The music of the opening returns, but varied, and with touching, free cadenza-like figures from the solo string voices. In this work, the composer seems to have leaped back over the entire development of classical symphonic music, with its clear-cut themes and dramatic opposition of motifs—in fact he has mentioned his lack of feeling for the Beethoven style[14]—to the renaissance and early baroque. The texture of the music is that of the old English composers of fantasies for viols. But actually there are no old fantasies like it in mood, breadth or architecture. Despite its free-flowing polyphony and modal harmonies, its structure shows the touch of sonata-form, and the music has a twentieth century sensibility.

Like Sibelius, Vaughan Williams does not go through drastic changes of style. Yet at the same time, he rarely repeats himself. Each big work is markedly different from its predecessors, and full of surprises. The form described above, of the *Tallis Fantasy,* is a flexible one which the composer uses many times over, sometimes starting with a defined melody, and sometimes starting with litle melodic fragments which only at the end coalesce into a soaring, defined melody. The form takes on a shimmering rhapsodic character in *The Lark Ascending* (1914) for solo violin and orchestra, and a sensuous, oriental-sounding character in *Flos Campi* (1924), based on "The Song of Solomon," for viola, orchestra and wordless chorus. It is also a basic movement-form that appears in almost every one of his symphonies.

Such a "fantasia" movement for example is the second movement, "On a beach at night," of his *Sea Symphony* (1905-10). It offers a particularly beautiful example of a melody "being born" out of its germ phrases. The *Sea Symphony,* his first work in the form, links the classic tradition of the four-movement symphony with the great English popular choral tradition. Its feeling is deeply English, not only in its modal melodies but in its evocation of the sea, which fills a greater place in English life and thought than in that of perhaps any other nation. At the same time, using texts from Walt Whitman's "Song of the Exposition," "Sea Drift," and "Passage to India," it has a feeling of the brotherhood of humanity, calling to the sea, "Thou unitest nations," and singing "a chant for the sailors of all nations." The visionary indefiniteness of the closing measures carry out this mood, like a dream of the future, foreseeing, as Whitman does, "the lands to be welded together."

Wholly different in mood, moving from the sea to the great city of eight million inhabitants, is the *London Symphony* (1914, revised 1920). Yet the first movement is like the Vaughan Williams "fantasia" expanded to take on some of the lineaments of sonata form. The brooding slow introduction, with its upward motif, seems to engender other themes some of which are at the same time dramatic "opposites" to it; namely a chromatic descending motif, like a heartrending cry, and the jaunty rhythmic themes that follow. There is a meditative middle section, and a powerful, polyphonic recapitulation and coda, in which the outcry overwhelms the folksy humor of the more rhythm-dominated motifs. The slow movement is a beautiful "fantasia" again, on a melody of great tenderness, and as often in Vaughan Williams, with the solo strings touchingly used, like wordless human voices. The scherzo evokes a picture of festivities in the poor section of the city. The last movement begins with a sombre "hunger march;" then there is a harmonically distorted version of the scherzo dance music, and a slow epilogue, expanding on the brooding introduction to the symphony. It is in its way as bold a work as the "shockers" of the period, like *Rite of Spring;* a criticism of "official society," but bold in a humanist way, without primitivism, revealing the seamy side of civilized life.

A clue to Vaughan Williams' musical thinking may be found in the ballet or "masque for dancing," *Job* (1930), inspired by William Blake's illustration's for *The Book of Job.* In telling the biblical story of the forces of human love at war with the forces of evil, hypocrisy and Satan, he uses his folkish, tender and lyrical music to evoke the good forces, the "angels," while harsh and discordant versions of such themes accompany the forces of evil. The "devil's music" is not inhuman. It is a distortion of human feelings. It evokes the trouble, pain and anguish which life itself will bring to people. Applying this useful if oversimplified shorthand of "angel's music" and "devil's music" to the symphonies, the slow movement of the *Sea Symphony* is "angel's music." The discordant sections of the first and last movement of the *London Symphony* are "devil's music."

We can use this touchstone as well for the other big works. With the *Third Symphony,* the "Pastoral" (1922), we have "angel's music" from beginning to end. Having given us the sea and the city, the composer now turns to the countryside. It is in an unobtrusive way, a bold work. What other composer would write a symphony made up of four meditative slow movements? Yet they are sensitively varied. The first movement has a gentle rhythmic flow. It is in form a polyphonic "fantasia," beginning with a weaving *ostinato* figure, after which a lovely pentatonic melody occurs. The development is marked by a climactic, powerful crescendo. The second movement, by contrast, evokes almost a cessation of motion. It is built of haunting "bird call" motifs, like calls "from an unknown region," developing to a climax of a long-drawn, mystic trumpet call. In the third movement, a *scherzo-fantasia,* there is a greater feeling of human activity, with exuberant, yet inward-turning, folk dance motifs. The last movement brings everything together. It opens with an intensified version of the mystic trumpet call from the second movement, but now heard as a free-flowing melodic line for wordless soprano voice, over a soft roll of drums . In the middle section the folkish, pentatonic melody of the first movement reappears, but its development makes some passages sound like the trumpet call. There is a hint of turbulence, of unsatisfied human yearnings, with touching passages for the solo violin, and in the end these are quelled, as the mystic wordless soprano call is again heard.

The 1930's, the years of economic crisis, unemployment and the rise of fascism, brought forth the most concentrated example of "devil's music," the *Fourth Symphony, in F minor* (1935), a portrayal of tormented feelings. The style is basically the same as in the preceding works, polyphonic in texture and modal in melody, but the themes are fiercely declamatory, and the harmonies given to the melodic lines clash discordantly with one another. The first movement proceeds in this violent and searing mood until near the very end, when its second theme is transformed into tender and peaceful music. The second movement is lyrical and folkish in melody, a polyphonic fantasia, but with striking dissonances and a deep sadness. The highly contrapuntal third movement is a typical Vaughan Williams dance-scherzo, but rhythmically and harmonically distorted. The last movement is a continuation of the third, using some of the same material, proceeding through a fast, violent march or "quick-step," then through a slow, modal, more tender middle section, and ending again violently, with discordant fugal passages. If unrest dominates this work, it still does not overwhelm his warm-hearted lyricism.

A turning point in the esteem given to Vaughan Williams by the English public came with his music of the years of the Second World War. It is in his response to such terrible events that a great national artist proves his value. The response however was not on the journalistic level of battle or patriotic pieces. It may seem at first strange that the war period itself produced so grand and serene a work as the *Fifth Symphony, in D major* (1943), while the coming of peace was accompanied by the troubled *Sixth Symphony in E minor.* But 1943, when the conflict was at its height, called, in Foss's words, for "a recognizeable English voice of comfort and prophecy," and this is what the *Fifth Symphony* provided with its serenity and faith in humanity. The first movement, *Prelude,* is one of the finest symphonic examples of what has been called here the Vaughan Wililams "fantasia" form, with an opening like a mystic "call," a polyphonic texture, a somewhat turbulent middle section, and the climax in the recapitulation, as the melody which has been prepared for by the thematic fragments finally swells out. Then comes one of the finest of the composer's polyphonic and speech-inflected *scherzo* movements. The third movement, *Romanza,* is again in the "fantasia" form, but this time with a clearly defined, song-like melody entering near the beginning, and cadenza-like passages for woodwinds and solo violin adorning the middle and end. The last movement is a *passacaglia* on a theme which is an apotheosis of the first-movement melody, with great rhythmic vitality and sometimes a folk-dance character in the variations. The *passacaglia* dissolves into a tender epilogue, evoking the opening music of the symphony.

The *Sixth Symphony* is in contrast, largely "devil's music," up to its last movement; a troubled reckoning at the close of the war of how much it had cost in human tribulation and sacrifice. The first movement is in highly-curtailed sonata form, opening with a violent, declamatory theme which is expanded upon, and a second theme entering in contrast, deliberately awkward, jaunty, almost jazzy in its syncopation. In what could be a development section, the opening violent music returns, and then the second theme which, however, begins to show new, more gentle contours. Finally this theme "throws off its cloak" and emerges as a radiantly lovely melody in what may be called an "Elizabethan popular" vein. The slow movement is sombre, dramatic and troubled, with a main melody that although gentle, seems to be made out of the opening notes of the violent first-movement theme. The scherzo is jaunty but likewise troubled. It leads directly into the last movement, which is one of the most original, haunting, gentle and sad passages in all of the composer's work. It is written for strings, with soft interpolations by woodwinds, and muted brass, and preserves throughout its course a hushed quietness. The tenderly sad theme, continuously repeating itself in the flowing polyphonic texture, is a development of the main melody of the second movement. It is now less defined than previously, more a motif, less a melody, and it engenders little counter-melodies and meditative recitatives out of its phrases until the movement ends in what is almost a whisper.

The next two symphonies are more brilliant in virtuosity than the preceding works but less profound, indicating not a lessening of the composer's powers but perhaps the fact that no "big theme" had arisen to capture his symphonic imagination. The *Seventh Symphony*, "Sinfonia Antartica" (1952), embodied music that had originally been written in 1947 for a film, "Scott of the Antarctic." It uses a strange instrumentation to suggest the icy wastes, adding to the traditional orchestra wordless soprano solo and female chorus, wind machine, piano, celesta, glockenspiel, vibraphone, bells and blaring passages for organ. As always in Vaughan Williams, there is no attempt at pictorial music. It is a "nature piece" like the "Pastoral" symphony, and four of its five movements are slow. But this is no longer nature revealed as a friend of man, or "angel's music." The "devil" has touched this work. It depicts nature as a menace to be fought and conquered, and the work, with many haunting discordant passages, has the character of a requiem for the heroes who died. The *Eighth Symphony* (1955) is a curiously baffling work in its tight mixture of tenderness, exuberant humor, and unrest. Both are overshadowed by the affecting and deeply troubled *Ninth Symphony* (1957). The composer in his eighties was refusing to behave like the peaceful "dean," or "grand old man" of English music.

Vaughan Williams' style is a remarkable achievement. It goes back to the "Golden," pre-classical age of English music, but not in any sense of a flight to or search for refuge in the past. Rather he sees this past era of music as one left incomplete, with its vitality shown by its preservation among the folk, and so he can take up its threads, carrying them forward into the twentieth century. In using here such terms as "angel's music" and "devil's music" the intention has not been to force his music into narrow classifications, or to describe it as a kind of musical theology. The aim has been rather to make clear the two sides of his thought, each with its own characteristic musical expression, and the two at the same time constantly touching and affecting each other. Perhaps a better description would have been Blake's title, "Songs of Innocence and Experience." One side of his music is the pastoral strain, depicting the ideal closeness of people to nature, a music of peace, and tenderness, sometimes sprightly and joyful, sometimes touched by a mystical or elegaic quality. The other side of his music presents human misery, torment, questioning and protest, the one-sidedness forced upon human beings by modern industrial life, capitalism, machinery, "progress"; the human wreckage they create, the barriers they set up against the ability of people to live as rounded human beings. The problem raised is one that he cannot solve; two sides of life, both real, which he cannot bring together into one whole view. And so a visionary element enters his music, a feeling that somehow the questions he raises will be taken up by others. It is a glimpse of a future—how it will arrive, he does not know—in which people will live as brothers, in peace and close to nature.

His musical equipment is not the most spectacular in its ability to take up and solve formal problems. In fact other composers, both of his own land and elsewhere, surpass him in this respect. But it is something he has worked out himself, from the great tradition of music, and he can say of it as Verdi said, "My hand is strong enough to shape the sounds as I want them and to make the effect that I have in mind." It has furthermore enriched English music in a basic way, so that every composer who came after him has been affected by his presence. What makes his music loom so high is its profound clothing of a social thought best characterized by a passage from Blake:

Can I see another's woe
And not be in sorrow too?

V

Charles Ives (1874-1954), born in Danbury, Connecticut, son of a Civil War bandmaster, had like Vaughan Williams a profound democratic feeling and a love for popular music. Although he welcomed every type of popular song, from the Civil War patriotic songs, and band marches, to ragtime, closest to him were the hymn tunes. This tradition had taken on a unique place in American life, one that in turn reshaped the music itself. In New England, it had become through Sunday School and Protestant church services part of small-town democratic life. In the South, among the Negro people, it had taken on an even more creative life, for the church was one of the great centers of social and community life possessed by the Negro people.

It is through the creative use of hymn tunes that Ives became the first composer in big forms to create a musical language uniquely American, infusing it with his own warm humanity and dreamy yearning. We can feel this in the slow movement of his *Fourth Violin Sonata* (1914-15), or the last movement of the *Second Violin Sonata* (1903-10). A lusty and daring example is the song "General William Booth Enters Heaven" (1914), to the poem by Vachel Lindsay. The piano recreates the thumping sound of a Salvation Army band, while the vocal line imitates the shouts and trumpet fanfares of a Salvation Army revival meeting. The experiment, like so many in Ives, does not altogether come off; but near the end, as the hymn tune,

"Fountain," enters and takes command, the song attains a genuinely touching character.

What Ives tragically lacked is a professional mastery of musical art, enough to create a musical work that could stand up as an embodiment of his feelings, completely realizing them in musical form. There is not a single big-scale Ives work which can stand up this way. All have passages that however visionary and philosophical the intentions behind them, sound to the ear like a confused jumble of tones. Nor is the reason the somewhat desultory nature of his musical education, which comprised what he learned from his bandmaster father, his youthful experience as a church organist, his independent study of scores by the great composers, and some years at Yale with Horatio Parker. It was rather a detestation of the professional mastery of music, which was linked up in his mind with slickness and glibness, and with the corruption which came from the use of music as a business or profession.

To Ives, music was not a skill to be subject to marketplace bargaining, but a means for bringing forth what was most profound in the personality, a miracle through which human beings paralleled in their creativity an act of nature. And so it made sense for him to seek a livelihood elsewhere. He found it in the insurance business, which he entered because, as Henry and Sidney Cowell explain, he believed that "insurance companies were disinterested benefactors of the common man."[15] But he went further and had practically nothing to do with the professional music world at all, not even making efforts to have his works publicly performed. Nor did it bother him that some of his works were physically impossible to perform. He wrote in the "Postface" to his book of *114 Songs,* "Some of the songs in this book, particularly among the later ones, cannot be sung, and if they could perhaps might prefer, if they had a say, to remain as they are. . . . A song has a *few* rights the same as other ordinary citizens. If it feels like walking along the left side of the street—passing the door of physiology or sitting on the curb, why not let it? Should it not be free at times from the domination of the thorax, the diaphragm, the ear and other points of interest? . . . If it happens to feel like trying to fly where other human beings cannot fly—to sing what cannot be sung—to walk in a cave, on all fours—or to tighten up its girth in blind hope and faith, and try to scale mountains that are not—Who shall stop it?"[16]

Ives lived an isolated life. He was a social mind not at home in the society of his time. His America was a vision of a small-town democracy which had never been altogether true in the past, and was an anachronism in an age of big trusts, labor struggles and imperialist adventures in the Caribbean, the Pacific, and Latin America; an America without the antagonism of class struggle, without financiers or slums. Relics of this part real, part idealized democracy had been present in his Danbury childhood. It was bolstered in his mind by the influence of his father, who also passed down to him the moral fervor of the great debate which had taken place in the 1850's over the abolition of slavery. It was strengthened by his reading of Emerson, Whitman and Thoreau. He was bewildered by the new America he surveyed about him, with its great gap between what he saw as the innate kindliness and cooperativeness of the plain people and the ruthlessness of the "vested interests." He drew up a constitutional amendment which would make all major issues subject to approval by majority vote at elections. This project speaks for both his democratic thought and his lack of any comprehension of the forces at work about him, forces which such writers as Mark Twain, William Dean Howells, Hamlin Garland, Theodore Dreiser, Jack London, Lincoln Steffens and Upton Sinclair were beginning to analyze realistically, at the end of the nineteenth and in the first decades of the twentieth century.

His "anti-professionalism" in music was a way of objecting to the insidious commercialism of music as a profession. But just as he felt alien to the society of his time, so, raising objectives for his music that were fundamentally social, he set himself against the social character of the tools and language of music. He missed the fact that only by grasping the materials of music which are a common possession can the composer both speak his mind and move others. Thus, while he handled popular song warmly and affectionately, he also "developed" it in ways that the listener can find only incoherent, and he himself was not a prolific inventor of melodies.

If Ives had little contact with the present, he built up a remarkable vision of and insight into the democratic future. This was a future in which the one-sidedness of modern industrial life would be broken through, and every man would find in himself something of the artist. Here we have another reason for his anti-professionalism; namely a way of breaking ground for the future everyman-musician. "Every normal man—that is every uncivilized or civilized human being not of defective mentality, moral sense, etc., has, in some degree, creative insight (an unpopular statement) and an interest, desire and ability to express it (another unpopular statement). . . . If this is so, and if one of the greatest joys and deepest pleasures of men, is giving rein to it in some way, why should not everyone instead of a few, be encouraged, and feel justified in encouraging everyone including himself to make this a part of every one's life and his life—a value that will supplement the other values and help round out the substance of the soul?"[17]

Ives' music is full of baffling passages, progressions of dissonant chords and modulations that have no logic, and simultaneous melodic lines in such different keys and rhythms that they result only in a confused mass of discordant sound. Present day critics, like the Cowells, point out proudly that he, an "American" foreshadowed Debussy, Schönberg and Stravinsky. But there is no system to Ives' experimental use of harmony and rhythm, and the reasons he developed such practices were quite different from those behind European impressionism, atonality or polytonality.

One reason in Ives' mind was that these harshnesses meant "strength," as against a soft effeminacy of sweet, traditional, "soft" or "easy" sounds. He despised what he called "groove-colored premutations of tried out progressions in expediency," or ears "drugged with an overdose of habit-forming sounds." He carried this healthy anti-academicism, however, to the point of missing the real secret of the boldness of a Bach and Beethoven who, knowing the musical bonds between themselves and their listeners, could lay such powerful hands upon the latter. It is one thing to startle or shock an audience, and another to mystify it.

For another reason, Ives would point to the fact that in a town street, two rival bands would clash, performing in different key or pitch and different rhythms, or he would point to the noisy clamor of a Fourth of July celebration, and the hilarious "off-pitch" drunkenness of musicians at a barn dance. But simply to reproduce this confusion of sound was to substitute a meaningless naturalism for the human imagery through which music really depicts life. Some such confused-sounding movements, although with flashes of wit in all of them, are the cacophonous close of the *Second Symphony,* with "O Columbia, the Gem of the

Ocean" suddenly emerging out of the chaos, the "barn dance" movement of the *Second Violin Sonata,* and the "Arguments" movement of the *Second String Quartet.*

Most important of all, Ives saw in these outlandish harmonic patterns a principle of "freedom," which boiled down to the liberty to do anything he wanted, without regard for the fact that a socially inspired art must be so constituted as to be able to live a social life. He refused to allow his music to be interfered with by what he called "the artist's overanxiety about its effect on others." This "freedom" principle connected itself in his mind with the philosophy of transcendentalism, a heritage from Emerson, proclaiming the domination of the human spirit over matter. Thus many of Ives' "philosophical" movements start and end beautifully, with tender popular or hymn-tune melodies, and have a "transcendental" middle section, or "development," made up of this ineffectively discordant polyphony. An example is the second movement of the *Second Symphony.* There are a few examples in which this "philosophical" approach really jells, in a most original and haunting music. One is the short "tone poem," *The Unanswered Question,* in which trumpet and woodwinds carry on querulous and whimsical cries against a droning string background, a remarkable anticipation of Bartok's "night music" movements. Another is the inspired closing section of the last movement, "The Call of the Mountains," of the *Second String Quartet.*

Ives' genius and weaknesses are perhaps best summed up in the *Second Piano Sonata,* or "Concord" Sonata, composed in 1909-15. Its four movements are entitled "Emerson," "Hawthorne," "The Alcotts," and "Thoreau." It is wonderful to know that such a work exists. It is an act of homage to the four great, bold and critical minds, so different from one another, of New England in the mid-nineteenth century. Emerson had proclaimed, as in *The American Scholar,* the need to be a "whole man," a rounded thinker, against the stultifying one-sidedness of a society devoted to commodity manufacture, specialization, and the sale of skills on the market-place. Hawthorne, more of a mystic, had embarked on a searching moral evaluation of the Puritan tradition. Alcott was a ground-breaker in the field of public education, and a Utopian Socialist. Thoreau had proclaimed his defiance of the predatory Mexican War, of slave-holding, and of the laws by which John Brown was executed.

The thematic material Ives uses for his sonata consists mainly of hymn-tune melodies, and the opening four-note theme of the Beethoven *Fifth Symphony.* The sonata is a chain of meditations on this material, guided by the personality portrayed in each of the movements, and with the hymn tunes and the Beethoven theme in a remarkable way constantly dissolving into one another.

The most "philosophical" of the movements is "Emerson," and in spite of many touching moments, it does not "jell," or crystallize into an objective musical structure that can stand up. Ives not only indicates this himself, but makes a virtue of it, writing of this movement, "This is as far as I know the only piece which every time I play it or turn to it, seems unfinished. . . . Some of the four transcriptions as I play them today, especially in the first and third, are changed considerably from those in the photostat, and again I find that I do not feel like playing this music even now in the same way each time. Some of the passages now played have not been written out, and I do not know as I ever shall write them out as it may take away the daily pleasure of playing this music and seeing it grow and feeling that it is not finished and the hope that it never will be —I may always have the pleasure of not finishing it."[18]

"Hawthorne," a fantasy-scherzo, also does not altogether come off, although it has a captivating street-band episode and some haunting passages near the close in which the questioning, "philosophical" passages dissolve into one of Ives' beloved hymn tune or "organ-loft" images. "The Alcotts" is completely successful, although it is probably the kind of music which Ives himself would describe as "soft" or "easy"; a sweet stream of melody, marrying hymn tune and Beethoven, with a Scottish popular song entering in the middle section, and a splendid close in which both Beethoven and the hymn tune merge with the sound of bells. "Thoreau" is written throughout in Ives' vein of subjective, dreamy meditation, and in its latter part it jells into one of the most beautiful and original passages in all his music, the basic themes being woven into a subtly dissonant fabric which, as in Debussy's impressionism, takes on a haunting twilight atmosphere.

If Ives' work is looked at with a harsh objectivity, he must be considered a failure, in the sense that no major work is sufficiently realized, from beginning to end, to take a normal, active place in the country's musical life. Yet he must become especially precious to the American people. American composers, born after Ives, have written a vast amount of music with a professional finish and craftsmanlike polish which he did not possess. Much of it is enjoyable and some of it deeply moving. Whether or not it has a recognizeable "American" idiom, it represents part of what can be called the "American mind" of its time. But almost none of it has that feeling of necessity about it, of having penetrated deep into American life, of having tapped a current so real and fundamental that its expression in music can become an organic part of the social consciousness of the people. And it is the search for such a music that Ives represented in every work he conceived and every phrase he wrote down. He did not ask himself whether it was "proper" to raise in music such questions as the nature of American democracy, the relations between politicians and people, the New England intellectual and critical heritage, the Civil War, and the brotherhood of peoples. If music could not deal in some way with these matters, he would have no respect for it as an art. And so he represents a colossal challenge to the American composers who follow him, an "unfinished business" which somebody must take up.

VI

Another of the major twentieth century humanists has been associated with American life, Ernest Bloch (1888-1959). Born in Geneva, Switzerland, and associated with French musical life up to 1916, Bloch after 1920 took up permanent residence and citizenship in the United States. Central to his music is his Jewish consciousness, and he is the first composer of world stature to think in such terms.

The late nineteenth century had seen a rising cultural life among the impoverished and oppressed Yiddish-speaking communities of Eastern Europe, producing so great a writer as Sholom Aleichem, as well as fresh developments in folk music, and a popular musical art like the operettas of Abraham Goldfaden (1840-1908). Bloch's consciousness was different. His tradition was that of the assimilated Jew of Western Europe, embracing his country's heritage and culture, regarding it properly as his own, who finds, in the late nineteenth and twentieth centuries, anti-Semitism raising its head. It was apparent, from such phenomena as the government-sponsored Jew-baiting in Germany and the Dreyfus affair in France, that the "emancipation" of the Jews which accompanied the rise of capitalism and parliamentary democracy had the shakiest of foundations. The medieval spectre of the Jewish "usurer," enabling the Jews to be thrown as a sacrifice to the exploited and angry masses, was now being refurbished in the form of the spectre of the Jewish "banker" and the Jewish "alien." To an increasing number of Jewish people, living as an organic part of the nations in which they had long and deep roots, this brought a sharp awakening to their kinship to Jewish life of the past, and a search for what was continuous in the Jewish tradition.

Bloch's path was to play a serious and proud role in the cultural life of the land to which he belonged, to embrace its traditions since they were also his own, to master the most advanced tools of art, and to express within this what he saw as germane in the Jewish heritage. The result in his art is no brave affirmation, or vision of a glowing future. His Jewishness is backward-looking. At the same time his art asserts that since the Jewish traditon helped make the modern world, a consciousness of this tradition must be part of modern thought.

From Richard Strauss, one of his early admirations, Bloch took his critical approach to academic harmony. In Claude Debussy, he found the open door to the use of ancient, medieval and Eastern modes. He added a study of European medieval and renaissance polyphony, and of the forms of the classic giants such as Beethoven. Out of this Bloch created a style personal to him, modal in curve of melody and harmony, subjective in its "endless" line built of little, germinating and "open" phrases, with a rich harmonic texture sometimes expanding to a free, dissonant polyphony. It is a style much like that of Vaughan Williams, producing works that are sometimes startlingly similar in form and feeling.

We can see this if we compare the *Israel Symphony,* with its elegaic pastoral feeling, to Vaughan Williams' *Pastoral Symphony.* In addition, Bloch uses, as the English composer does, human voices, and string solos, as part of the orchestral texture. *Schelomo,* with its rhapsodic play of the solo 'cello against the orchestra, is a parallel to Vaughan Williams' *Flos Campi,* where the viola plays such a role, and both works evoke the Biblical image of Solomon. The *Second String Quartet,* with its tight thematic unity, and closing *passacaglia* compares to Vaughan Williams' *Fifth Symphony.*

The similarity is due less to direct influence than to a parallel sensibility. Different in Bloch's idiom is the specifically oriental feeling that his melodic lines take on, as in the slow movement of the *Second String Quartet,* and the occasional use of specifically Jewish motifs. These are sometimes evocations of Cantorial synagogue chants, and sometimes drawn from the Hassidic folk music which had appeared among the Jewish people of Eastern Europe in the early eighteenth century, particularly affecting folk music in its combination of poignance with joy and hope. The "purest" example of Bloch's use of Hassidic music, although a comparatively light work, is the set of three pieces for violin and piano, *Baal Shem* (1923).

The *Israel Symphony* (1912-16), the first large-scale work in which Bloch began to express his specific thinking about the Jewish heritage, has little if anything that is Jewish or Asian in melody. But it is an affecting work, which also establishes much of Bloch's basic approach to musical form. It is meditative, brooding, "inward" music, with a cyclic repetition of motifs, the fast sections made of the same proliferating melodic material as the slow, and the most moving sections, summarizing everything that went before, coming at the very close.

Schelomo (1915), however, is a profoundly Jewish work, and also a twentieth century world masterpiece. Its form, of a solo 'cello weaving a free-flowing, speech-accented melodic line, against the orchestra, is an imaginative expansion of the traditional sound of the Cantor and congregation in the Hebrew synagogue. The area of thought Bloch draws upon is partly the image of Solomon, evoking the glories of the ancient Hebrew kingdom, and partly the book of Ecclesiastes, with its deep sadness, not for self but for the tragedy of a people. There are at least four important melodic motifs in the opening section. They are not easy to grasp at first, for they seem to grow out of and subside into the surrounding musical texture, but each is a concentrated and affecting statement. They are not like the "first" and "second" subject-groups of the traditional classic symphony or sonata form. Rather they are like different voices in Bloch's mind, speaking to and answering one another. The work is not a "development" of these motifs but rather a free meditation, the music dwelling and expanding upon sometimes one, sometimes another, and reaching at the end a heartrending outcry. The genius of Bloch is in his plastic use of these motifs, so that they become the material of a heartfelt monologue, following every turn and nuance of his thought. And the very first of these motifs, sung at the outset by the solo 'cello, takes us into a distinctly Jewish area, that of the typical Hassidic prayer song. The others have a similar feeling. The middle section is a blaze of oriental color, with little interlocking, dancing rhythmic phrases, and the sound of pipes, of an Asian orchestra, while the oboe enters with an actual Hebrew melody that Bloch as a boy had heard his father sing.

Bloch never again wrote a major work so concentratedly Jewish. But the storm and passion opened up in *Schelomo* are continued in the *First String Quartet* (1916). He said it "was composed at a period of double crisis; the crisis of the world, at the outside, and the crisis of my own life, the expatriation from my native country, Switzerland. Thus it was a kind of synthesis of my vision of the world at that period."[19]

It is a high peak of his output; the nearest in his work to a classical breadth of architecture, with a rich, almost orchestral sound drawn from the four strings, and at the same time with some sections of violent, pounding rhythm and harsh dissonance linking it to the "shock" works which composers like Stravinsky and Bartok were writing in the period. Like them, Bloch felt the skepticism of "civilization" and "progress,"—the sense of a world gone back to primitive violence, that many sensitive minds shared on the eve of or upon the actual outbreak of world war. Notable is the sense of a single intense drama binding the four movements, enhanced rather than diminished by the variety of mood and melodic material.

The group of themes with which the first movement opens carry on the Jewish strains of *Schelomo*. There is a second group of themes, as in the classic sonata form, and a development of both first and second theme groups. But there is no classical recapitulation; only a short coda, in which the agitation subsides, making clear at the same time that there is "unfinished business." It is the classic form taking a romantic, "inward" turn. The entire texture of the movement is that of antiphonal voices, or statements and answers, declamatory, speech-accented, evoking memories of traditional ritual prayers. And if this may be called a reflection of the Jewish crisis, the second movement may be called a reaction to the world crisis, in its "shock" quality, produced by driving rhythmic *ostinatos,* deliberately harsh sounds with the bows striking near the bridge, and music in different keys and rhythms proceeding simultaneously. If there are similarities to Stravinsky's *Rite of Spring,* they are on the surface. The music is essentially different. There is no Stravinsky-like rhythmic mauling of body sensations, and no mechanization of melody. It remains lyrical and declamatory music, the *ostinatos* not imprisoning the melodic line but acting as an accompaniment and intensifying its outcry. The third movement may be called the "Swiss" section, winding Swiss folk motifs into a touching "pastorale." The last movement begins with a meditation on the three previous movements, indicating that it is a summation of the entire work. It engenders an intense drama, with passages that speak of the vigor and strength of real life. But there is no joyous triumph. The end of the work is a funereal lament. What this quartet discloses however is that if Bloch feels most deeply the tragic side of life, he does not succumb to it.

There is still intense "inner" drama, but less shock quality, with a move to a greater tranquility, in the impressive chamber works that follow; the *Suite for Viola and Piano* (1918-19); the *Sonata No. 1 for Violin and Piano* (1920), and the *Quintet for Piano and Strings* (1923-24). Greatest, and also the most Jewish, is probably the *Quintet.* The first movement is rhapsodical, its melodies slowly "born" out of the opening germ phrases, and the alternating slow and fast passages made of the same material. The slow movement is one of the most melodically beautiful in all Bloch, with a Jewish "lullaby" feeling, and this in spite of the fact that Bloch here uses quarter-tones. But as in the case of the "polytonality" of the *First Quartet,* Bloch is here not trying to invent new scales or harmonic systems. The quarter-tones serve to add a web of slightly indeterminate sound to the basic melody, an added tone of unrest, carrying the melody itself to the point where it seems to take on a momentary, evocative indefiniteness. The last movement starts with whirling oriental-style music, drawing at the same time upon Hassidic dance motifs. It is not a dance movement, however, but a propulsive rhythmic movement that is also fervently declamatory. It builds up a strong sense of real and vigorous life, but, as in the *Quartet,* ends with a sad lament.

There is a real serenity in the same period, and even joy. It is heard in the popular *Concerto Grosso* (1924-25), which uses Swiss themes, and the *Symphony "America"* (1926), which includes jazz motifs, and ends with an anthem offered by Bloch to his new homeland. Then the 1930's brought two major works on a Jewish theme, the *Avodath Hakodesh* or "Sacred Service" (1932-34), and *Voice in the Wilderness* (1936) for 'cello and orchestra. *Voice in the Wilderness* is poignant and affecting music, but does not cry out like *Schelomo.*

The *Sacred Service* is a big-scale work, a setting of texts largely from the Jewish Sabbath morning service. Perhaps what entered Bloch's mind while writing it was the rise of Hitlerism, with its militaristic war-mongering and frightful assault upon the Jews. But Bloch answers this crisis by reaffirming Jewishness as part of a general humanism. It is not noticeably Jewish in melodic material, but for some sections, such as the close of the first part or middle of the fifth part, in which Bloch draws directly and movingly upon traditional Jewish prayer motifs. Otherwise it is written in a close-knit style of modal polyphony. The text emphasizes Bloch's vision of the brotherhood of peoples. "O may all men recognize that they are brethren, so that one in spirit and one in fellowship, they may be forever united in thee." It ends with the traditional prayer for peace. And the combination of Jewish with non-Jewish melodic motifs reflects Bloch's thought of the place of the Jewish people in the modern world. He says of the text, "It symbolizes for me more than a 'Jewish Service,' for in its great simplicity and variety it embodies a philosophy acceptable to all men."[20]

The past weighs heavily on Bloch. This is seen in his elegaic sadness, and reflects itself as well in his form. His style resembles that of medieval and renaissance polyphony, but not because he makes a fetish out of recreating some period of the past. His subjectivity prevents him from carrying on the classic form which he admires so greatly, and his inwardness finds its clothing in these weaving, flowing "endless" polyphonic lines. It is a path others of our time have followed; a use of the armory of modern harmony and instrumental color to reconstruct on a new level of sensibility the earlier structural steps taken by the past of music. A unique achievement is his union of European and Asian traditions, with his Jewish consciousness as the impelling force. It reasserts the lesson of how organically tied are Europe and Asia. The lesson of course is there to be seen in the history of civilization, but it is still too often ignored.

Despising glibness or showmanship, Bloch also does not, as Hindemith sometimes does, seek objectivity through what is simply a finely worked, sound piece of structural craft. He involves the whole man in every work he writes, and whatever failures occur in his music are due to his inability to find a finished, realized form embodying what he is groping for. His subjectivity is never that of the "man alone." It is the unanswered question of the future of the Jewish people, and of a civilization inextricably bound up with their fate, that he feels so deeply. And because he speaks thus of those outside of him, his music is never lost or despairing.

A different side of Jewish musical life is seen in the work of an immigrant who came to the United States, Jacob Shaefer (1888-1936). There is a strange aspect to his career. The composer, in this country, of ten large-scale cantatas or oratorios, of about fifty songs, and of a number of Jewish folk song arrangements for chorus, performing them in packed auditoriums in New York and other cities to great applause, he nevertheless does not "exist" so far as histories of American music or lists of modern composers are concerned.

Just as Bloch represents the reaction of the "Western" Jewish people to the rise of anti-Semitism in the most "advanced" countries, so Shaefer speaks for the Jews whose origin was Eastern Europe. There anti-Semitism took the form of terrible pogroms, as well as the barbarism of ghetto restrictions. Hundreds of thousands joined the stream of immigrants to fill the needs of American industry, seeing the United States as the land of freedom; many of them people who had engaged in anti-Tsarist struggles in Russia and Poland until it was necessary for them to flee. In the United States, along with opportunities that did not exist in the semi-feudalism of Eastern Europe, they also found poverty, and a struggle between democracy and reaction. They built trade unions which are among the most honored in the history of the American labor movement. Among them had grown a rich Yiddish literature, of poetry, story and drama.

It was in this tradition that Shaefer worked. Born in the Polish Ukraine, trained in Hebrew Cantorial music, he arrived in the United States in 1910. He worked during the day and he studied music at night. His choral works were written to Yiddish texts, and drew upon the heritage of liturgical music, Hassidic song, and Eastern European Jewish folk song. With a remarkable vision, he built his own audiences and performing groups. He believed in the cultural creativity of ordinary people. Thus he trained great choruses of working men and women, as well as amateur instrumental groups, and it was they who performed the choral works he as well as others composed.

His work ranges from the folksiness of *A Bunt Mit A Statshke,* to the sombreness and liturgical quality of *Tvei Brider,* to a text by the great Yiddish writer, I. L. Peretz. If his work is not yet recognized as a part of American music, it is partly because of the insularity from which this American Yiddish culture suffered, not finding ways to build a bridge between itself and the main stream of American cultural life. A more important reason however is the "melting pot" theory which arose in American life along with the tide of immigration. "Melting pot" is an ambiguous term which could mean simply the forging of a nation through the collective contributions of people of many national origins. But as used between the 1890's and 1920's, paralleling an intensification of chauvinism and jingoism to the point of hysteria, it was undemocratic and reactionary. It reversed the truth that the United States had been the product of many peoples and many cultures, and was built by hard labor. It demanded that those coming to the country to labor and help build it must "melt away" that slag of their languages and cultural traditions, all of which had great potentialities for American life. It raised a stereotype of the "average American" as the white-collar businessman, generally Anglo-Saxon, while lumping together "labor" and "foreignness." It implied that trade unionism, a recognition of class differences in society, and socialism, for all their deep roots in American history, were things alien to America.

Shaefer could not accept the "melting pot" or "assimilation" in such terms. It meant not a flowering of old, rich cultural traditions under new conditions, but a sharp break, a wiping out of what had helped make him, a loss of identity. And so even as a musican he could not see himself as fitting into either the prevalent concert hall atmosphere or the popular music industry. And at the same time the path he carved out had much to give to his adopted country. Important, among other things, was his rejection of an over-specialized, one-sided musical life based on "active" composers and "passive" audiences. He made the audience itself active and musical, bringing about a close, reciprocal relationship between the composer and the people he served. In this respect, he put his finger on what will undoubtedly be one of the great developments of music in the future.

10. FOLK MUSIC IN THE REVOLT AGAINST ROMANTICISM

"Gauguin's present show is the admiration of all the men of letters. They are, it appears, completely enthusiastic. The collectors are baffled and perplexed. Various painters, I am told, all find this exotic art too reminiscent of the Kanakians. Only Degas admires, Monet and Renoir find this all simply bad. I saw Gauguin; he told me his theories about art and assured me that the young would find salvation by replenishing themselves at remote and savage sources. I told him that this art did not belong to him, that he was a civilized man and hence it was his function to show us harmonious things. We parted, each unconvinced. Gauguin is certainly not without talent, but how difficult it is for him to find his own way! He is always poaching on someone's ground; now he is pillaging the savages of Oceania."

—Letter of Camille Pissarro to his son Lucien, 1893.

I

French music of the late nineteenth century and first half of the twentieth century, for all its interesting creativity, suffers from the weakness of being a national movement which seeks a uniquely French aesthetic rather than a close bond to the life and mind of the French people. In its inception, its guiding spirit was less a discovery of France than an antipathy to Germany, born out of the defeat by the Germans in 1870. Upon the fall that year of the corrupt Second Empire of Louis Napoleon, the working people had spoken with an angry voice, forming the Paris Commune. But the Communards were massacred by a combination of French middle-class reaction and the invading German army, proving again how easily rabid nationalists of opposing camps can find common ground when faced by the propertyless demanding equal rights. The ensuing republic, with its drummed-up hysteria against the working class, had to look for help to its worst enemies, the royalists and monarchists.

In this bleak atmosphere, the tendency of composers was to confine their rebellion to the field of aesthetics, creating an "art for art's sake" anti-philistinism with a French label. Its twin enemies in musical style were academicism based on German classic models, and the heavy romantic, philosophically-bolstered and grandiose assault on the emotions represented by Wagner. And so a counter-style was erected, described in this way by one of its first architects, Claude Debussy (1862-1918): "Charming and tender delicacy . . . that clarity of expression, that terse and condensed form, which is the peculiar and significant quality of the French genius."[1] One would be hard put to fit such men as Rabelais, Chardin, Daumier, Courbet, Balzac, Hugo and Zola into so fragile a mold.

Debussy had little of a social mind. During the fierce struggle in defense of Dreyfus, which was actually the defense of the republic against its attempted overthrow by the upper Catholic Church hierarchy and the royalists, he scorned those who took up the cause of Dreyfus.[2] And a typical remark like the following is not the judgment of his fellow countrymen it pretends to be, so much as an attempt to bolster the refuge he sought from social movements. "We must . . . admit that art is of absolutely no use to the masses; it does not even express the mind of the *elite,* who are often more stupid than the masses."[3] At the time of the First World War, he affixed to the signature of his works, *"musician français,"* and as Leon Vallas writes, he "bore it as though it were a title of nobility."[4] But throughout his career there was the contradiction between his love for France and his failure to involve himself in its turbulent currents of life and ideas. And his art for all its inspired originality and the new area of psychological sensitivity it explored, remained an almost completely personal creation. On the heels of his own revolt, successive revolts arose against his own methods and style. Yet French music as a whole has yet to break with this mythical "national manner" of wit, whimsy and a fastidious approach to the drama of life, a "national style" taking the place of a national portrait.

Debussy embraced the philosophy of French symbolist poetry, which was in its own way as much a departure from reality as the Wagnerian fantasy. To it the images of the real world, the things of sight and sound, were only "symbols" for the seemingly inscrutable mysteries of life, insecure sensations in a surrounding chaos. Its consummate musical expression is the opera *Pelléas et Mélisande* (1892-1902) set to a drama of Maurice Maeterlinck. As in Wagner's *Tristan,* the setting is medieval, and no more than Wagner does Debussy try to create an actual society.

The Debussy-Maeterlinck music drama surrounds all its actions with an atmosphere of mystery and dream. There are a few hints of the life surrounding the castle in which the drama of frustrated love takes place, and these are symbolic; like the paupers who have been afflicted by famine, and come to die on the castle grounds, and the sheep being driven to slaughter. Wagner tried to give verisimilitude to his use of the Tristan legend with lengthy, detailed narratives of what had taken place before the action opened. In *Pelleas* nothing is explained. At the opening of the opera, Melisande is "lost." Where she came from, nobody ever knows. And they can never know, for in an irrational world, everybody is "lost."

Wagner made *Tristan* a symbolic presentation of his own nineteenth century philosophy of the hero's lordly right to love, and of love as the reality imposed against death. The action of *Pelleas* becomes symbolic of Debussy's view of his own world. Melisande is like a frail, pathetic elf, child-like, helpless yet destroying whomever she touches. The theme that runs through the opera is that of people surrounded by darkness, blind, searching for something they can never find. In the closing scene, Golaud cries, "I shall go to my grave as one that's blind." On a prosaic level, this is the cry of the husband who will never know whether his wife has been unfaithful, but on the symbolic level, it means that nobody can ever know anything.

The philosophy finds an apt musical clothing. The operatic writing represents the final stage in the romantic, flowing and "open" form, with no rounded songs or sections, no sharply contrasting parts. It is the dissolution of the classical balance between "outer" and "inner," with everything now "inner." The French language itself, in the speech-inflected lyrical fragments that make up the melodic lines, becomes a timbre, merging with the instruments in the magical flow of sound. There is an unbroken, homogeneous, flowing texture with only waves of rising or falling intensity depicting the growing passion between Pelleas and Melisande and the jealous violence of Golaud. The orchestra rather than the voices expands upon the deeper emotions, as in the radiant episode in the third act when Pelleas says, "It is noon, for I hear the bells ringing and see the children going to the shore to bathe in the sea," or the tragic outburst after the first scene of the fourth act when the old, blind King Arkel says, "If I were God, I would have pity for the hearts of men." The characters have no musical individuality. They are the various sides of Debussy's private fantasy, a subjective declaration of the impotence of people to defend themselves against the mysterious blows of life. This is the inevitable result of a quest for "freedom" carried on alone.

Debussy's "impressionism" is another name for this passivity of approach to life, with evocations of the movement of nature, the surge of waves, the patter of rain, the drift of clouds, the swirls and leaps of a fish in water becoming visceral sensations in his subjective fantasy. Renouncing the classical opposition of unrest and repose, dissonance and consonance, dramatic conflict and resolution, he builds his art in the realm of dissonance, revealing it as a "twilight" area with hitherto unsuspected beauties and refinements of mood. Through a sensitive spacing of notes and chords and a unity of harmony and timbre, as if the overtones of his instruments played a role in the harmonic thought, he creates a world of delicate sensibility and fine shades of unrest.

Adding to the passivity of feeling is the abandonment of rhythm as an evocation of outer movement. Instead, he writes for both voices and instruments a primarily *parlando-rubato* music, with little rhythm-charged passages emerging and subsiding, and rhythms used like melodic motifs. It is a rarefied form of the Wagnerian "stream of consciousness" music. Its magical harmonic-instrumental web, however, is interwoven with melodies suggested by the exotic scales of Asian music, like the music of Java that so interested Debussy when he heard it at the Paris Exposition Universelle in 1889. A powerful influence on it is Russian national music, and especially the folkish, speech-inflected melodic lines, modal and pentatonic scales, and irregular rhythms of Mussorgsky. Debussy made all this into a homogeneous style of his own, expressing his own unrest and distaste for what he felt were the vulgarities of civilization.

It is a strange contradiction that an art which owes so much to folk music should handle folk music itself like an exotic flower. Folk music appears in his work sometimes as a childhood memory, as in the piano piece *Jardins sous la pluie,* for example, or with a delicate humor, as in *Minstrels* and *Golliwog's Cakewalk,* where he uses American Negro rhythms that he might have heard in band cakewalks and in pieces like Louis Moreau Gottschalk's *The Banjo.* To enter his art such music must pay the price of giving up its robustness and evocation of popular life. This is true even of Spanish music, to which he felt particularly close. Sometimes Spanish music is subtly hinted at, as in the declamatory coda of the first movement of his *Violin Sonata.* But it lacks earthiness even when it fills an entire work, as in *Iberia* (1908). There Spanish melodic motifs and dance rhythms are woven into a meditative, *parlando* musical fabric, evoking the moods of a highly sensitive tourist rather than the feeling of the presence, except at a great distance, of the Spanish people. And yet the freshness and aptness of his harmony and timbres give the music a striking, pristine quality, showing a beautiful economy of means and the ability to preserve and finely polish the qualities of this music that made it so different from the traditional European musical currents. Also, there is a consummate integrity in his art. If he rejects much of life, he is deeply involved in what he does feel. His art has a tragic undercurrent, which gives it a depth not found in his more extrovert successors.

The music of Debussy's later contemporaries, like Erik Satie (1866-1925) and Maurice Ravel (1875-1937), and of the next generation, like Darius Milhaud (*b.* 1892), George Auric (*b.* 1899) and François Poulenc (*b.* 1899), seems at least to this writer to have less lasting power. Its scores are fascinating at first hearing. Yet they seem to have the insubstantiality of a fireworks display. Or else, seeking the light touch of popular urban "entertainment" music, what they achieve is the transitory quality of most of such music.

As against Debussy's "open," introspective and *parlando* approach, these composers tended to write a rhythm-dominated music, firmer in melodic contour, often controlled by dance rhythms. Despite the aspect this music took after the outbreak of the First World War of a "revolt against impressionism," it brought no appreciably greater breadth. Even in so fine a craftsman in well-wrought forms and so sensuous a melodist as Ravel, the premise on which "clarity" was achieved was the shutting away from music of most of the turbulence and drama of real life. The music of the "common people" was explored, including old French songs, American jazz, Spanish music, French music hall ditties, South American folk and popular music. But this was not a turn to the people themselves. It was rather an assumption of a sophisticated primitivism, a masquerade, a make-believe innocence and simplicity, a nose-thumbing at civilization. Out of it came a succession of witty and highly entertaining works.

And yet the brittleness of most of this music, in which the thinking about life dwindles to a matter of saying "no" to any serious problems, deprives it of lasting power.

A counterpart to Debussy's *Pelleas* is Ravel's little masterpiece of opera, *L'enfant et les Sortilèges* ("The Child and the Sorcerers") of 1924-25. Seemingly a children's opera, it is not for children at all but a pretense at looking on the world with a child's eyes, as if a profund truth could be captured by wiping out of mind the experience of the history of humanity. The music draws upon Chinese, jazz, old French folk and other exotic motifs. A filagree of coloratura notes wittily portrays a flickering fire. At one point the singers are told to miaow, in a hilarious duet for two cats. The score is gay and lovely, and better listening than others which pretend the "grand manner" but have nothing to say. And yet despite the lavish display of Ravel's artistry, the opera remains a pastime always on the verge of triviality.

The art of music takes its revenge for being treated so lightly. Its own history and development have set the standards to which a composer must rise if he is not to become a journalistic footnote. In the case of Satie, whose campaign against "seriousness" caused him to object even to Debussy's symbolism, most of his music, with the exception of two or three short piano pieces, has faded away. Milhaud, the master of the sophisticated "masquerade" using a succession of folk, popular and primitivist musical costumes, seems to have written very little which shows real substance, once the intriguing surface novelty has worn off. Poulenc, for most of his art, seems to be reliving the age of Louis XIV and Couperin, with an added hint of irony, and the music, but for some touching songs written during the Second World War, suffers from anemia. The most serious effort at imposing forms and substantial content has come from the Swiss-born Arthur Honegger (1892-1955). Yet in his works too, like the five symphonies and the vocal-orchestral works, *Le Roi David* (1921) and *Jeanne d'Arc au Bucher* (1938), there is a lack of distinctive melody, behind which lies an aloofness from the people and a bleakness of spirit.

II

In striking contrast to the French use of folk material is the Spanish art of Manuel de Falla (1876-1946). Falla was not a prolific composer and his life was a tragic one. In the Spain in which he was brought up, a rising national consciousness was managing to send forth healthy shoots, in music, literature and the graphic arts, despite the stultifying atmosphere of the most autocratic, medieval-minded court and church in Europe. There was a close connection to the intellectual life of France, as if France, in exchange for the robust Spanish folk material which its composers and writers found so attractive, were giving Spanish artists some freedom of action. Thus Picasso became the great Spanish painter in Paris, and Falla studied and developed his art in Paris for seven years, from 1907 to 1914. In 1931 at last, Spain became a republic. But this was overthrown in 1936-38 by the uprising of General Franco, supported directly by German and Italian fascist troops and indirectly by the Tory government of England, which had for a century looked on Spain as an economic province. Falla, although aloof from politics, was torn apart by these events. In 1938 Franco appointed him President of the Institute of Spain, but in 1939 he left for Argentina, where he died seven years later. His last decade was one of musical silence, except for a large vocal work, *L'Atlandida,* which had been started at about 1933, and was left unfinished at his death.

The folk music that Falla explored most richly was the *cante hondo,* or "Gypsy" music of Andalusia and South Spain, sometimes called *flamenco.* The roots of this music were not only Gypsy but Moorish and Arabic, and perhaps also included relics of the guitar, lute and vocal music of the sixteenth century, when in Spain, as in England, learned and popular music had moved hand in hand. Thus in other sections of Spain, like the "remote parts of Castile and the Asturias," J. B. Trend has heard "words and music of the old Spanish *romances* still being sung by washerwomen, and many other country people."[5]

The "Gypsy" music explored by Falla had become an integral part of the musical expression of the common folk. The term "Gypsy" itself in Spain was used generally to describe the poor, the "riff-raff" as the upper class saw the folk, the outlaws and rebels, particularly those with a swarthier skin. Although it produced its own rounded and distinctive melodies, *cante hondo* lived as an improvisational music, an intensified musical chant, capable of explosive protestations and heartrending cries, accompanied by chorus or punctuated by a cascade of guitar rhythms.

Its ties to a definite class are clearly shown in Falla's opera *La Vida Breve* (1904-05). The story is the familiar one in folk tale—because it is so familiar in life—of the daughter of poor folk who is loved and then heartlessly discarded by a young man of the gentry who marries in his own caste. Throughout the first scene, set in the home of the heroine, Salud, with a smithy in the back room, the *cante hondo* chant of the smithy workers is heard, with such words as "Others live in pleasure but we must sweat and labor." Some of the recitatives and arias are not greatly distinguished, for Falla has not fully sharpened his tools. But the first act *arioso* of Salud takes on an affecting *cante hondo* declamation. The words are in folk proverb style. "The life of the poor, who live in suffering, is always cut short." This gives its title to the opera; "The Short Life." In the second-act scene of the betrothal of the false lover Paco, to a woman of his caste, beautiful *cante hondo* music is heard, for solo voice and guitar, from the lips of a street singer called in to entertain the guests. This is followed by the famous Spanish dance often performed as a concert piece, and displaying the opposite side of Spanish folk music; brilliant rhythm-dominated and rounded *tempo-giusto* melody. Already in this opera Falla is, to use Bartok's phrase, "speaking folk music as if it were his mother tongue."

Falla never again attempted so direct a portrayal of the class antagonisms in Spanish society. He learned much technically from French music. His *Nights in the Gardens of Spain* (1909-15), consisting of three "nocturnes" for piano and orchestra, is impressionistic in style. J. B. Trend describes these nocturnes as "dream" pieces. Yet if we compare the work to Debussy's *Iberia* (1906-12), while the influence can be discerned of Debussy's refined subtlety of timbre and harmony, and Debussy's work is more brilliantly concise than Falla's, that of Falla has the more deeply Spanish folk quality. Unerring is his feeling for the ties of folk music to speech and movement. Thus the first movement, *At Generalife,* is a sensitive development of *parlando-rubato* motifs, while the second movement, *Distant Dance,* leans towards the *tempo-giusto*. The last, *In the Gardens of Sierra de Córdoba,* is wholly Andalusian, and interweaves song and dance strains. Miraculously the piano evokes the sound of a guitar or of a chanting voice. Likewise if we compare Falla's ballet *El Amor Brujo* (1915) to Ravel's *Rapsodie Espagnole* (1907), for all the effectiveness of Ravel's masterfully orchestrated and rhythm-charged dance movements, Falla's work, based on a Gypsy folk tale, speaks with a more authentic Spanish voice. Its melodies and rhythms, inflections and timbres, seem to tap new musical sources through which the people themselves speak.

III

The composer in this period who represents the most aloof, detached and mechanistic use of folk music is Igor Stravinsky (*b.* 1882). Born in Russia and a pupil of Rimsky-Korsakov, his brilliant early works were welcomed in France. Then when in 1917 revolution came, and in Gorky's words, "the frenzied people, moving like a grey avalanche, left the front and bent its course towards the villages, raising over the land its broad and angry 'mug',"[6] Stravinsky broke all ties with his homeland. Becoming first a leader in Parisian musical circles, since 1939 his main center has been the United States, where a throng of disciples and admirers has collected.

Stravinsky has been a dominating force in twentieth century music. He is supremely gifted in the handling of the sheerly physical elements of music, such as rhythm, timbre and dynamics, with harmony becoming an adjunct to rhythm and timbre. It is a one-sided equipment, but enough to enable him to become the groundbreaking, imperious figure in the assault against the humanist traditions of music. This "wiping out of mind" of the achievements of the past two centuries in capturing human psychology, conflict and drama, moved through three stages; primitivism, neo-classicism and theology.

His art brings to a head the contradiction between the two meanings of the word "feeling" in art. To put it in its most simple form, "feeling" in the arts can mean either to "touch the body" or to "touch the heart." The first refers to the sheer sense-effect of a work of art; its impact on eye and ear, and upon the body through kinesthetic reactions, like the "touch" sensations imparted by painting or the "movement" sensations imparted by rhythm. The second refers to the evocative impact of the human images in art, the memories they arouse of past experiences and their accompanying emotions, the kinship they awaken to other human beings, the relation they bear to conflicts in real life outside of the work of art.

This conflict between two aspects of "feeling" is found not only in twentieth century music but in literature and graphic art. The supremacy of the first aspect, the sheer impact of the materials of art, is upheld by T. S. Eliot in respect to poetry, and by the theorists of abstraction and non-objective art in respect to painting and sculpture. The truth is that these two aspects of "feeling" are inextricably bound together in every work of art. No vision in an artist's mind can become art until it finds an adequate sensuous form. Art must be built with all the intricate skills unique to it, and it must embody in its finished, objective shape all that the artist has discovered about the sensuous qualities of the materials with which he works. And so it is an easy but false argument to take the next step, and say that the sensuous clothing, the physical materials, the "touch," "ear" or "eye" appeal are all that are necessary, and make up the essence of art. Stravinsky went on to proclaim that music is "by its very nature, essentially powerless to express anything at all, whether a feeling, an attitude of mind, a psychological mood, a natural phenomenon, etc."[7] Yet as in the case of many twentieth century aesthetic pronouncements, this only attempts to make a "universal" law out of the composer's own narrow artistic pathway. Stravinsky's limitation is the inability to express in music any human relations to others in the same world as he, and this shows itself primarily in a catastrophic barrenness in respect to the creation of distinctive, evocative melodies.

This barrenness is apparent in Stravinsky's early "national" works, which also display, in their use of folk song, a lack of identification with the peasantry and common people who created this song. The fairy-tale ballet, *The Fire-Bird* (1910) goes beyond the music of Rimsky-Korsakov in rhythmic drive, orchestral brilliance and dissonance. But the sweet melodies in it are transplanted folk tunes, and there is no ability shown to shape new melodies out of them, or to develop them in depth. *Petrouchka* (1910-11) has an even greater abundance of adopted Russian folk melodies and motifs. In adition, there are other popular tunes like Joseph Lanner's Styrian dance, which Stravinsky would use again much later as the aria "Nonne monstrum rescituri" in the oratorio *Oedipus Rex*. His development of such melodies if it can be called that, is purely in terms of dynamics and timbre. They are not malleable material under his hands, which can be shaped into human portraits.

The scene of the ballet *Petrouchka* is a Carnival fair in St. Petersburg, at which a puppet show is displayed before the crowds. Petrouchka, the central puppet of the show, had been traditionally an old folk symbol, like his counterparts in other lands, Punch, Pulcinella, and Polichinelle. Ugly, the butt of jokes, he traditionally turned the tables on his enemies. In some versions he tricked courts, police, hangmen, and the Inquisition itself. He was indestructible. But in the scenario of Stravinsky's ballet, he is a pathetic character, a symbol for the artist impotently gibbering at his tormentors in a hostile society. The showman magically charms the puppets with his flute, so that they become alive. Petrouchka, grotesquely ugly, is seen making love to the beautiful ballerina. She however is enamored of the Moor, who throws Petrouchka out of the room. In the last scene the Moor pursues Petrouchka out in the midst of the crowd itself and kills him. The showman who represents the philistine merchant of art, explains to the horrified crowd that Petrouchka is only a wooden puppet, but at night, when the crowd has left, Petrouchka's ghost appears to the showman, jeering at him.

Thus the folk context is abandoned. The common people who make up the crowd are portrayed as mindless folk, almost puppets, while the puppet who miraculously comes alive becomes a medium for Stravinsky's own subjective fantasy. And this concept is carried out in the score. The folk themes are handled with a hard, brilliant objectivity, in driving *ostinatos,* like the Russian Dance in the second scene, and the score proceeds through contrasting rhythmic blocks, often clashing with one another. Interlaced are touching *parlando* and subjective passages, like wistful cries, as in the passage which follows the Russian Dance, in which the mechanical movements take on a breath of life and we hear Petrouchka's protestations of love.

Petrouchka remains one of the most masterful scores of the twentieth century, in the sheer sensuousness of its orchestral color, the dazzling brilliance of its everchanging rhythms, its dissonance, used with the same sensitivity as Debussy but more bitingly, and the almost magical combination of chords with instrumental overtones to create a constantly fresh sound. And it is at times not only brilliant but also touchingly expressive, affecting not only the "body" but the "heart." We can feel in it Stravinsky's inner loneliness. For the effect of the music is to show the living people as puppets, the puppet Petrouchka-Stravinsky as the living person, with a soul. The music embodies both the pathos which accompanies his rejection of the dramatic and boisterous main currents of life, and the wall he has built against the people around him. It belies his own later dicta about the inability of music to express psychological states. But to think of people as puppets serves to rationalize his aloofness from social life, and he would later even describe the ideal musical performer as a robot. "A man pulls a rope; but what happens at the other end is of no importance to him. He cannot make the bells ring more softly or more loudly. . . . The music is not in him; it lives in the bells. The man at the rope is the prototype of the ideal conductor."[8]

The Rite of Spring (1911-13) was written for Diaghilev's Russian Ballet and first produced in Paris, as had been *The Fire Bird* and *Petrouchka.* Its theme is the spring ritual of the primitive Slavonic tribes, with its worship of the earth and fertility dances, ending with the sacrifice of a virgin. It makes no effort of course to recreate the actual episode in human development represented by primitive life, with its first discoveries of nature and attempts to make nature serve human needs. Similarly the intricate rhythms have only a superficial relation to the rhythms of primitive or tribal music, with their organic ties to the complexities of tribal speech and dance. It is a fantasy-primitivism, a brutal image thrown into the face of civilization, frightening it, declaring that civilization is a myth and that the only reality is mysticism and violence.

In his rhythms and explosive dynamics, Stravinsky is no longer wittily teasing the listeners, as he had done in the abrupt rhythmic changes of *Petrouchka.* No element in music exerts a more strong and immediate physical impact than rhythm, and in the rhythms of this music Stravinsky can be said to have laid his fingers on the bodies of his listeners, tearing them apart. With a perverse genius, the rhythms are exploded out of their organic character as a representation of human movement; and out of their interplay of rise and fall, tension and rest. They become either a mechanistic, hammering beat, or a constant variation of pattern, so that a thundering impact will come where it is least expected and where it is calculated most to shock. Again he uses folk melodic motifs, but he attains the epitome of their mechanistic use, transforming them into pounding *ostinatos* which rob them of the lyrical feeling they have on the lips of the folk. As in *Petrouchka* there are subjective elements, such as the *Introduction* to Part I, where he uses *parlando* folk motifs, with layer rising upon layer of melody, and the impressionistic *Introduction* to Part II. But now the subjectivism is in sharper contrast to the violence of the dance episodes and is no longer felt in the entire score, as in *Petrouchka.*

The Wedding (1914-23), a ballet with solo voices and chorus, was intended by Stravinsky as an affectionately humorous picture of a Russian peasant wedding ritual. To the ear however it sounds as hard and mechanical, if not as violently brutal, as *The Rite of Spring.* The reason for this disparsity lies partly in

Stravinsky's kind of affection for the peasantry, which is like the regard one has for a domestic animal. The text is a mumbo-jumbo of the relics of primitive magical beliefs, tales and incantations that may be found in folklore, Stravinsky seeing in this folklore only the traces of the past, not the reflection of the present. He uses some actual folk or popular melodic motifs, but his treatment, instead of liberating them and expanding their emotion, imprisons them in a rigid pattern of hammering accents and *ostinatos.* The polyphony is machine-like, in contrast to folk polyphony, in which each singer has an awareness of what another singer is simultaneously doing. The imprisoned effect of the music is intensified by the hard, instrumental style of writing for voice, and by the instrumentation itself which is all percussive, including four pianos treated as percussion instruments. If we can learn to control or inhibit our visceral reactions, we can catch something of the comic feeling in the ballet, just as we can similarly catch something of Stravinsky's pathos of horror and loneliness in *The Rite of Spring.* But *The Wedding* portrays the peasantry as idiots—in kindly fashion, of course. What the city workers and peasantry of Russia were actually doing during the period the work was written—overthrowing the entire structure of Tsardom and aristocracy, and beating back a succession of armies of intervention—gives the work an irony which the composer did not intend.

The Soldier's Tale (1918), a mime-play with music, completes, with *The Wedding,* Stravinsky's first period; that in which he makes a prolific use of Russian folklore. The story comes from a group of folk tales, inspired by the oppressive recruitment of peasant youth for a twenty-five year term in the Tsar's army.[9] These tales told of the penniless, discharged soldier living through his courage, endurance, quick wit and resourcefulness. In some versions he even defeated death and the Devil. But as in *Petrouchka,* Stravinsky turns the folk-tale victory into defeat. The soldier, after some aimless adventures, is in the end captured and dragged away by the Devil. The main musical motif is a Gypsy theme that came to Stravinsky in a dream,[10] mechanistically transformed as customary in Stravinsky, and it is heard, in various versions, in the opening "Soldier's Violin" music, the "Royal March," 'Little Concert," "Tango," and final scene. There is a chorale made up of a discordant distortion of *Ein' feste Burg.* He also uses popular cabaret motifs. In addition to the tango, there are a waltz, and a passage in ragtime. The instrumentation, of violin, clarinet, bassoon, trumpet, trombone, doublebass and drums, is influenced by that of American small-band jazz. The combination of light-textured popular tone with machine-like *ostinatos* and dissonances, provides a sharper image of pathos within the jester's mask, than any previous or subsequent work. But it is bleak music, an ironic jest, like dancing on a grave.

In the works of the years that follow, Stravinsky's mastery of the machinery of musical sound is always in evidence. The Russian folk melody is easily cast off, since it never had a germinating relation to his musical thought. Two central themes that appear are classical legend, in the spirit that it had been revived by the seventeenth and eighteenth century courts, and religion. A major work in the first vein is *Oedipus Rex* 1926-27), an oratorio for soloists, chorus and orchestra, intended to be staged for actors wearing masks. A major work opening the second is the *Symphony of Psalms* (1930), for chorus and orchestra. His treatment of the Oedipus story is a masterly display of powerful "touch" or "body" sensations, substituted for a genuinely affecting human imagery or portraiture in music. It makes a tremendous aural impact, and is the kind of music which allows his disciples to write awe-inspiring program notes recounting its technical marvels. But the onlookers feel no kinship with any of the characters in the legend. The *Symphony of Psalms* has deeper subjective qualities, in passages such as the haunting, soft *ostinatos* near the end. But it is the kind of religious art that represents a purely personal incantation; the opposite for example to that of Bach, with its sweep of life and felt presence of a world of people, in joy, strife and suffering. It is religion built on despair, like T. S. Eliot's,

> *I said to my soul, be still, and let the dark come upon you*
> *Which shall be the darkness of God.*

In this period Stravinsky also begins to search about in the past of music both for actual scraps of melody which he can take over, or for melodic "formulas" with which he can concoct a succession of different styles. Bach, Donizetti, Tchaikovsky, Rossini, Pergolesi, Verdi are all drawn upon. In works where he takes actual tunes, like *Pulcinella* (1919) with its Pergolesi melodies, or *The Fairy Kiss* (1928) with melodies by Tchaikovsky, we can see sharply the qualities and limitations of his art. The tunes, in his new setting, are burnished, brilliant, and gleaming, as if cleansed of their harmonic "fat." And yet what has also been washed away is their human warmth. In works like *Oedipus Rex,* the *Violin Concerto, Orpheus, The Card Game, The Rake's Progress,* the borrowing is in terms of melodic scraps and formulas. Of this procedure Stravinsky writes, "As my temperament is not academic by nature, it is through the exercise of my intelligence and will-power that I am able to use the formulas of academicism. I do so just as deliberately as I might make use of folk music. These are the raw materials of my art."[11]

A complete change has taken place from the excitement of a Mussorgsky, Tchaikovsky, Smetana, or Dvorak in the presence of a living musical material, imbued with the presence of the people of their nation. The language of music now consists apparently of a number of formulas, of which one is as good as another. But of course, Stravinsky's creative process is not as mechanical as that, nor is it fully characterized by Constant Lambert's caustic remark about his "renowned impersonations of music." Behind the hard objective mask of Stravinsky's work lies a solitude as abysmal as that in Schönberg's cries of horror. It is the terrifying loneliness of one who has no feeling at all for the people of his nation, either old or adopted, or of the world; who is moved by no sympathies at all; who has carved out for himself a reasonable and even comfortable life as an artisan-musician, but dislikes the world he lives in and has no hope for any future. And so his refuge is art, which becomes a form of life of its own, with scraps from its past taking the place of the human imagery he cannot find in life itself.

IV

It is illuminating to compare the "primitivist" works of the 1910's and early 1920's, like Stravinsky's *Rite of Spring* and Milhaud's *L'Homme et Son Désir,* which attempts to evoke the Brazilian jungles, with the work of a composer who uses as his native language the kind of folk and popular material thus borrowed by the Europeans. Heitor Villa-Lobos (1887-1959) has neither Stravinsky's impressive composing equipment nor Milhaud's formal polish. Yet the best of his music—he is not always successful—has the warmth and sense of the presence of a cultured mind that is exactly the quality which the "primitivists" try to eradicate, with their mechanistic rhythms and deliberate "shock" sounds.

In his youth Villa-Lobos performed music in Brazilian movie theatres, and as he moved into public life he sought to break down the barrier between "popular" music and "art music." In 1932 he was appointed Director of Music Education in Rio de Janeiro, and he trained large choruses of school children in a repertory, as Nicolas Slonimsky writes, "ranging from Handel to popular songs and patriotic hymns."[12] It is the union of "art music" forms with popular strains that is his distinguishing characteristic as a composer, with the motifs of his music ranging from ancient Indian tribal music to melodies and rhythms like those heard in the city cafés; the "popular" Brazilan music heard throughout the Americas and Europe. He is probably the least subjective of all major living composers, and his enormous vitality is displayed in both the sheer quantity of his writing and its ebullient spirit.

Villa-Lobos has composed fine succinct works, like his song-group, *Serestas* and his set of piano pieces, *Cirandas,* both using folk material. But the torrent of music he pours out often takes the loosest of form, as in the *Chôros* and other works of the 1920's. "Chôros" means "street music," or an improvised "serenade," and the many works with this title differ widely in length and instrumentation. Thus *Chôros No. 1* is a little piece in popular dance style for solo guitar. *Chôros No. 7,* for solo violin, cello and five woodwinds, alternates melodious passages in popular Brazilian march and dance style with "primitive" cries, cadenza-like passages and declamations, lasting about nine minutes. *Chôros No. 6* is three times as long, and calls for a full symphony orchestra including native instruments. It is the loosest of rhapsodies, full of popular-style airs, sometimes accented by a dissonant counterpoint, and sounding like a musical counterpoint to a scenic train ride. Equally long and sprawling are *Rudepoema* (1921-26) for solo piano and *Momoprece* (1929) for piano and orchestra. The absence of any apparent organization in these works, apart from the loosely strung chain of musical ideas, is not due to any lack of formal knowledge on the part of the composer. Rather, taking up the kind of popular strains that any Brazilian would recognize as his own, he seems to delight in avoiding any structural sophistication which would alter their popular character.

The series of works begun in the 1930's, called *Bachianas Brasileiras,* are on the other hand outstanding for the comparatively disciplined structure. It is Bach, the composer of suites and *partitas* made up of preludes, toccatas, arias and dance-rhythm fugues, rather than the great contrapuntal architect, whom Villa-Lobos calls upon as god-father for these works. The range of instrumentation is as wide as in the *Chôros*. Thus *Bachianas Brasileiras No. 1,* one of the most beautiful, is for eight cellos. *No. 2,* with an engaging closing toccata called "The Little Train of the Capira," is for full orchestra. *No. 3* is for piano and orchestra. *No. 4* is for solo piano. *No. 5,* which in recorded form became a world-wide "hit," is for soprano voice and cellos. *No. 8,* with an especially rich and subtle contrapuntal texture, is for full orchestra.

The popular-style melodies which Villa-Lobos creates in these works are vigorous, bright and lovable, and they are joined to the "Bach" heritage with no hint of strain and affectation or of the forced marriage of "alien cultures." Equally "right" in context sound the occasional dissonances and more fragmentary, "primitive" Indian melodies. Such works put a finger on the basically popular character of much of Bach's writing, and the "naturalness" of his three-voice texture of bass, middle voice and *obligato* upper line. (In fact, the "New Orleans" style of American Negro jazz, based on marches and folk blues, moves in this kind of three-voice, polyphonic improvisation.) It is typical of what is happening in the modern world that as an answer to the "primitive" and "jungle" music produced in Europe, a music of such warmth, humanity, and insight into the past of European culture itself should come from a new nation like Brazil.

Nevertheless lack of formal discipline remains Villa-Lobos' great limitation. This does not mean academic discipline. The missing element is better called psychological discipline. His music does not coalesce into a genuine human portrait, seen in depth. We feel in it the presence of the Brazilan people, bringing together rich currents, ethnic and musical, of Africa, Europe and Brazilian Indian. We do not get much inkling from the music of how the people live, or of what they are thinking. But it is at the same time a new voice, and gives us an idea of the vast resources, human and musical, that are entering into the mainstream of world music as one country after another is throwing off its imposed poverty and backwardness, and developing an industry, learning and art.

V

The most striking achievements in developing strong and

expressive forms using both the starkness and humanity of folk material have come from Central Europe, in the work of men like Leos Janacek and Bela Bartok. If on the surface some of their work seems to parallel the "shock" works produced by a Stravinsky, the connection is accidental. For their music springs out of an attachment to and understanding of the peasantry, a profound national feeling, and a grasp of the creative, plastic qualities of folk music. It is not a lonely or self-centered art. It has the qualities missing in the "primitivist" music, including genuine tragic feeling, and an equally genuine joy in life. Its bleakness, harshness and deep subjectivity are a reflection of the tragic experiences of the nation itself. Yet it also expresses hope for the future.

Leos Janacek (1854-1928) was born in Moravia, a section of what is now Czechoslovakia, only thirteen years after Antonin Dvorak. Yet he found himself slowly, and his major works, including seven operas, two string quartets, the *Slavonic Mass* and a *Violin Sonata*, fall within the twentieth century. What also characterizes him as of a later generation is his abandonment of sunny optimism. His music reflects the conviction that the artist must come to grips with the harshest realities and represents the search for a different base for musical composition from that offered by the German romantic or classic tradition. We can sense this sharp break in the disturbed feelings expressed by Dvorak in 1886, when the then unknown Janacek had dedicated some compositions to him and sent them for his criticism. Telling of his genuine pride in the "precious gift" of such a dedication, Dvorak went on, "I must admit that in many places, especially in regard to your modulations, I was taken aback and unable to form an opinion. . . . But when I had played them through once, twice, three times, my ear gradually became accustomed and I said to myself: well, after all, it may be possible, but still we might argue about it. That is, however, unimportant. I think they are a real enrichment of our poor literature (poor in that kind of work). They are original, and what is more important, they breathe forth a truly Slavonic atmosphere . . . I congratulate you on your small but at the same time significant composition and hope that you will write more of the kind."[13]

Janacek had to struggle for acceptance of his bigger works, and today they are still insufficiently heard. His opera *Jenufa* (1894-1903) was not produced in Prague until 1916. It won great respect in Germany, and was performed by the Metropolitan Opera Company in New York in 1924-25. His last opera, *From the House of the Dead* (1928), based on Dostoievsky's novel, was performed in 1930 in Brno and in 1931 in Berlin, which before the coming of Hitler was an active center of interest in new music. Its sombre beauty came as a revelation at the Netherlands Festival of 1954. His music does not strive to be entertaining or intriguing to the ear, nor, on the other hand, does it shock or startle. It offers no new musical systems or construction devices that make for the founding of a school of composers or a body of disciples. Janacek's style is an attempt to create a kind of musical speech through which people will reveal their most heartfelt feelings, and what he discloses in it is a brooding, complex psychology. The style has a quality which it shares with that of Mussorgsky, of sounding as if it were creating the art of music over again from the beginning. There are roots in it of Moravian folk music, of which he made an intensive study, but there are few echoes in it of past composed music.

One of Janacek's innovations, begun near the end of the nineteenth century, was the intensive study of what he called "melodies of speech," putting into musical notation the inflections of characteristic speech phrases and even noting down bird calls and animal cries. "When anyone speaks to me, I listen more to the tonal modulations in his voice than to what he is actually saying. From this, I know at once what he is like, what he feels, whether he is lying, whether he is agitated or whether he is merely making conventional conversation. I can even feel, or rather hear, any hidden sorrow. Life is sound, the tonal modulations of the human speech. Every living creation is filled with the deepest truth. That, you see, has been one of the main needs of my life. I have been taking down speech melodies since the year '97. I have a vast collection of notebooks filled with them—you see, they are my window through which I look into the soul—but this is what I should like to emphasize: they are of the utmost importance to dramatic music."[14]

Like many innovations in modern music, this was really a conscious, special and thorough exploration of an aspect of the art that had been latent in it since its inception. The tie between music and speech intonations had been part of the craft, and in the back of the mind, so to speak, of every great opera and song composer. Nor had this tie ever been broken in instrumental music, as we can see in its recitatives, or its meditative and declamatory passages. To Janacek, as to Mussorgsky, it was "simple speech" rather than high-flown eloquence that he sought to set, and what he achieved was no mere adaptation of music to speech inflections, as in the customary recitative style. The clue to his "speech melodies" lay in the *parlando* aspect of folk music. His "speech" phrases, fragmentary as they may be, are genuinely melodic, and his style is made of an intense repetition of them, modulating at the same time, to create an organic musical texture, easily moving into actual folk-style music itself, as we can hear, for example, in *Jenufa* or the *First String Quartet.*

It is a music almost wholly *parlando* in style, always meditative and often infused with deep tragic feeling. Janacek's thought moves slowly, as if the composer were wrestling within himself for the hope he wishes to communicate. Often an entire work seems to be a transition from "darkness" to "light," with the "light" being evoked by the emergence of a more rounded contour of melody, sweeter and more sensuous, as in the closing part of the *Violin Sonata* and *Second String Quartet,* or the *Sanctus* of the *Slavonic Mass.* Indeed the all-over theme of both his first successful opera *Jenufa* (two operas preceded it, both still in manuscript) and his last opera, *From The House of the Dead,* is this movement from "darkness" to "light." *Jenufa* is set in a Moravian village, and its drama is of an unwed mother, betrayed by a dissolute lover, whose newly born child is killed by its frightened grandmother. But the heroine at the end finds a path to love and happiness. *From the House of the Dead* is an unsparing picture of the brutalities of life in the Siberian prison settlements written of by Dostoievesky, but it ends on a note of freedom and hope.

Janacek's is a different kind of national expression from that of Dvorak or Smetana. The people seem to be tearing at themselves, sometimes almost despairing, yet never losing their grip on life. Reflected in Janacek's sadness is the darkness brought upon the small nations of Europe as the great-power grip tightened near the close of the nineteenth century and in the twentieth, followed by the blood-bath of the first world war. The music has a subjective cast, but it is not the subjectivity of an artist removing himself from society, or looking only into his own mind and desires. The declamatory style does not make for strongly contrasting characterizations, or a varied sweep of life, but it becomes a musical language through which Janacek can raise his own powerful voice. He stands as an individual, crying out against what he finds false and oppressive in life. This impassioned declamation is apparent in not only the big works, but in short ones, like the two fragments of a piano sonata, entitled "Foreboding" and "Death," that he wrote in 1905, protesting the murder by German soldiers of Czech workmen on the occasion of a demonstration for a Czech University. The characterization of Janacek by the Czech conductor, Vaclav Talich, stands as well for the music. "Beautiful, hard, self-assertive, obstinate. A tough nut!"[15]

VI

Bela Bartok (1881-1945) is the most profound, contradictory and complex of the composers who based themselves on folk music. He created an art deeply subjective and often tragic, every fibre of which was connected to the great mass of common people of his nation, the peasantry. His father, a school teacher and gifted musician, died when Bartok was eight. After this, he writes, "my mother had to work as a school mistress and struggle hard for our daily bread."[16]

In 1905, along with the composer Zoltán Kodály, Bartok set out to study the fast disappearing Hungarian peasant music in the countryside. In 1911 he and Kodály formed a New Hungarian Musical Union. They received little help from the government. For the most part, Bartok carried on his folk music studies with whatever private resources he could scrape together. Hungary was a kingdom, presumably autonomous although ruled by the Austrian Emperor. The great Hungarian land magnates showed no interest in democracy or industrial progress, while the people lived in frightful misery. Bartok's researches, carried on with his attachment to the common people, were not of a kind to please the chauvinistic, race-minded Hungarian and Magyar nationalists. His discoveries were closer to a concept of the brotherhood of peoples, showing complex cross-currents of influence in folk music. He carried on studies of peasant music in other Balkan countries, North Africa and Turkey. In Turkey he could listen to a peasant singing an ancient chant, derived from the distant past of epic song and poetry, and write, "I could hardly believe my ears. Good Lord, this seemed to be the variation of an old Hungarian melody. I was overjoyed."[17]

Bartok's musical lifework may be compared to a great pyramid, the base of which is his monumental research in and collection of folk music, a task which he carried on with a devotion and scientific rigor probably unmatched in the history of music. It was not a matter merely of scholarly compilation of thousands of songs in notation and on phonograph records. With a creative composer's insight, he was able to provide a method of stylistic analysis, which could disclose the changes undergone by folk music and the layers upon layers of new growth. Above this in the pyramid are his volumes of settings, for chorus, solo voice, piano and other instruments, of folk songs, most of them Hungarian. These settings enter the realm of creative music, for although the melodies themselves are left scrupulously as Bartok found them, and he does not weaken them with academic harmonization, he invents counter-motifs in folk style that set off the melodies like jewels. Typical is the piano accompaniment, with its evocation of a harp, to "Black is the Earth" from *Eight Hungarian Folk Songs* (1907-17). The piano accompaniment to "In the Jailhouse," from *Twenty Hungarian Folk Songs* (1929), changing and developing in intensity from one stanza to the next, both takes the song as a whole into the realm of a little masterpiece of composition, and gives the listener a clue to the folk music connections of his percussive piano style, as heard for example in the slow movement of his *Piano Sonata.*

Then above these in the pyramid are the books of short creative compositions that use a great many actual folk melodies, like the *Piano Sonatina* (1915), *Forty-Four Duets for Two Violins* (Completed 1931), *Eighty-five Piano Pieces for Children* (1908-1945), and *Three Rondos on Folk Tunes* (1909). They are beautiful examples of simple polyphony, and of organized, rounded form, often possessing a sweet tunefulness absent from his bigger-scale compositions. Then, at the top of the pyramid, are his fully original large-scale works, which are comparatively few, compared to the life-work of other composers. Outside of his student efforts, they include six string quartets, three piano concertos, the *Violin Concerto,* the unfinished *Viola Concerto,* the *Piano Sonata,* the *Sonata for Two Pianos and Percussion,* the one-act opera *Bluebeard's Castle,* two ballets, the *Cantata Profana,* three works for small orchestra, and one work for full orchestra.

For these bigger and deeper compositions, Bartok drew upon the starker style of the older strata of Hungarian folk song. He did not quote actual songs. As he wrote, "What is the best way for a composer to reap the full benefits of his studies in peasant music? It is to assimilate the idiom of peasant music so completely that he is able to forget all about it and use it as his musical mother-tongue."[18] From this music he derived his subtle variants of *parlando-rubato* and *tempo-giusto* phrases, his use of pentatonic scales and of modes that broke with "the rigid use of the major and minor keys,"[19] as well as some of the percussive and dissonant patterns that seemed to him to accent the force of this style of folk melody.

With great excitement he discovered that Debussy and Stravinsky had moved along parallel paths, and saw this as a sign that the great sea of Asian, Russian and older European folk music was now relieving the comparative narrowness of the Western composed music tradition. "It seems therefore that, in our age, modern music has developed along similar lines in countries geographically far away from each other. It has become rejuvenated under the influence of a kind of peasant music that has remained untouched by the musical creations of the last centuries." There were differences he saw, however, among Debussy, Stravinsky and himself. Debussy's style, he said, was an "influence" of the folk. Stravinsky, in works like *The Rite of Spring*, was a supremely gifted "imitator" of folk music, in accord with his own aesthetic. Bartok for himself sought "neither peasant melodies nor imitations of peasant melodies" but a music thoroughly "pervaded by the atmosphere of peasant music."[20]

But this is only part of the story. For although we can trace the harsh and frequently forbidding passages of works like the *Second Violin Sonata* and the *Violin Concerto* to the patterns of peasant music, the result is not a music that the peasantry would consider in sound and spirit their own, as they would the folk-style works of Dvorak and Mussorgsky, or Bartok's shorter works like *For Children* and the *Violin Duets*. Bartok's bigger compositions express his own conflictful world; his reaction, sometimes violent, sometimes anguished, to the tragic situation of the Hungarian and Balkan peasantry, seemingly oppressed without hope of relief, trapped in great power politics, fated to be used as cannon fodder in great power wars.

So it is with the relation of his works to the classical tradition. Unlike Janacek, he uses with great inventiveness the symmetries and framework of this classic tradition, including sonata-form, the theme with variations, and the rondo. But his often unrelieved, dissonant harmony eliminates the kind of emotional drama and union of "inner" and "outer" worlds basic to the classical tradition. A musical analyst can make impressive diagrams of these symmetries and methods of organizing a unified work. But what the ear often hears is more like a succession of "moments," sometimes harsh and violent, sometimes improvisational and reflective, and at times suddenly flowering into melodic meditations of heartrending beauty, like the middle of the slow movement of the *First Violin Sonata* (1921) or the closing passages of the *Second Violin Sonata* (1922). Bartok could not find in his times the view of life that would enable him to really feel and recreate the classical form, although he seemed to be approaching this in the last years of his life. Yet his music, for all its frequent sadness, retains the peasant humor and tenacious grip on life.

Bartok's first published works, like the *Rhapsody for Piano and Orchestra, Op. 1* (1904) and the beautiful *First String Quartet, Op. 7* (1903), already show the leaning towards rather stark, "open" and *parlando* themes that lends his work its brooding, "inner" character. This sadness reaches a climax in the opera *Duke Bluebeard's Castle* (1911) and the *Second String Quartet, Op. 17* (1915-17).

The opera gives a new symbolic twist to the traditional story of Bluebeard. He is here not a wife-killer, but a tragically lost figure. As the curtain rises on the dark and gloomy castle, Bluebeard enters with his wife, Judith, who has run off with him despite the anger of her father and brothers. She wants to bring light into the castle darkness, and demands that Bluebeard give her the keys to the seven doors that she sees. Reluctantly he gives them to her, and one by one, she opens them. Each brings in light, but it is always blood-tinged. The first open door reveals his torture chamber. The second reveals his armory of blood-encrusted weapons. The third reveals his treasure of jewels, which also are blood-stained. The fourth opens on his flower garden, and the stems and earth of the plants are seen to be bloody. The fifth opens on the wide realms of his kingdom, over which the clouds cast a bloody shadow. The sixth reveals a lake of tears. Finally, against Bluebeard's pleading, Judith opens the seventh door, and his three former wives walk out slowly, dressed as queens. He kneels before them. And then, sadly, he places a crown on the head of Judith, who must now suffer the fate of the other three, and join them behind the seventh door. They represent the dawn, noon and evening of Bluebeard's life, and now Judith, the most beautiful of all, becomes the night. As the door closes behind her, Bluebeard cries, "And now it will be night forever," while the stage is enveloped in complete darkness.

The opera was composed at a time of premonitions of war, and in fact the prologue written for a later performance speaks of "wars raging in the world around us." It is one of Bartok's most despairing works, and its symbolism parallels what he saw as the state of the Hungarian peasantry at the time. The great mass lived in what may be called medieval backwardness and darkness. But how much better is progress, civilization, the "world outside," the world of light? It is a world of torture, of bloody wars, of treasures stained with the blood necessary to obtain them, of flower gardens or beauty stained with blood and of great realms won with bloodshed, of human misery and suffering. This is what "light" brings.

The music is moving and beautiful. It is composed throughout in *parlando,* speech-inflected vocal phrases, intensified by the orchestral fabric, and with a subtle interweaving of motifs which, as usual in Bartok, are unrounded, incompletely defined, and constantly evolving in line. They derive from Hungarian folk music, although the brooding "inward" quality which Bartok's harmony gives them takes them out of the realm of recognizeable folk-style music. Yet there are striking sections in which the music coalesces into what almost becomes a folk ballad, as in Judith's music when she enters the castle and cries, "How dark your castle is . . . poor, poor Bluebeard," or when the fifth door is opened on Bluebeard's realm, and his music takes on the tone of Hungarian patriotic or martial song. Also deeply affecting is the love music, occurring just before the seventh door is opened. Musically whatever difficulties the opera has for listeners rise out of its reserve and concentration. There is nothing to shock ears that had already absorbed the tone poems of Strauss.

A rather whimsical and even gay work appeared during the war years, the ballet *The Wooden Prince* (1914-16), employing little folk-style motifs that are woven into a flowing, impressionistic fabric. It creates a children's dream world where evil turns into good and love triumphs. But the *Second String Quartet* (1915-17), one of Bartok's indisputably great works, is searing in the intensity with which it expresses the anguish of the war years. While it does not sound like a folk-style work, its moods parallel those which the peasantry express in their misery; a deep sorrow counterposed to an outbreak of violence and anger.

Stylistically, it shows three varied structural and emotional uses of the *parlando-rubato* kind of melodic line. The opening slow movement, in sonata form, is dominated by its sorrowful first motif, which is somewhat bare when first heard but develops as an inner meditation, with powerful declamatory passages enriched by polyphony. It flowers at the end into a hauntingly sad folk-style melody. The second movement carries further a style that had been initiated in a short piano piece, *Allegro Barbaro* (1911); music of a harsh, discordantly harmonized rhythmic drive, reminiscent of the primitivism of Stravinsky's *The Rite of Spring.* But it is not as mechanistic as Stravinsky's music, nor do its rhythms seem to tear the body apart. They always preserve their organic tie to human movement. Past the middle of the movement, the rhythmic propulsion dissolves into slow declamatory strains. The last movement, the most tragic, is slow declamatory music rising to a climax of sad, powerful statements and answers, thoroughly inward-probing. In contrast to the first slow movement, it displays an almost complete cessation of rhythmic motion.

The culmination of this period in Bartok's mind and work is represented by the ballet or pantomine, *The Miraculous Mandarin* (1918-19). It tells a gruesome story of love and violence in a brothel setting. Its theme is that love is the one human element in a world of violence and depravity, and that even love is despairing. The music is the fullest expansion of the "Allegro Barbaro" style, fierce, harsh, dissonant and driving, the only partial relaxation being a satiric distortion of a popular-style waltz.

Then a new period begins. In the works that emerge in the 1920's and early 1930's, such as the two violin sonatas, the third, fourth and fifth string quartets, and the second piano concerto, the open expression of tragedy is abandoned. They are Bartok's most cryptic works, in the sense that he has now donned a jester's mask, with anguish shielded by an ironic wit. The musical elements he uses are the most primitive forms of Hungarian folk music; little *parlando,* pathetic phrases, developed in the manner of a meditative, improvising folk musician, and rhythmic *ostinatos* which have little dance quality but become also a kind of declamation. All this is intensified and punctuated by weird slides, "tone clusters," wheezing sounds made by the strings, and chords so dissonant that their impact is not a harmonic one, but only that of sheer percussive sound.

Typical is the *Third String Quartet* (1927), which is constructed like a grotesque version of a Liszt *Hungarian Rhapsody.*

The sad opening phrases, polyphonically developed, are punctuated by slides or *glissandos,* by *ponticello* sounds made with the bows playing near the bridge, and by harsh, dissonant answering chords. There are further touches of sad, painful melody, but they are always rudely broken off. The wild dance that follows is like folk music put through a prism of harmonic distortion, with a fugue texture. A haunting development of the slow opening motifs, with their cries of pain, follows, but it is again punctuated by slides and percussive sounds, and then the fast music returns. The music is bitter with a protective coating of ironic comedy, interspersed by poignant sighs; the expression of one to whom the world has fallen apart. The world seems to have no logic or rationality. It is not a world of misery, but one in which there are inexplicable tragedies, and also hope and joy. And the two are never able to come to a resolution.

Also in this period Bartok developed a new kind of slow movement, which would serve him for a number of major works to the very end of his career. It appears first in the movement called "The Night's Music" in his *Out of Doors* suite for piano (1926); a fanciful music of humming, buzzing and chirping sounds, through which little threads of touching, folk-style *parlando* melody are woven. It is seemingly light-spirited music, with an aura of insect and bird sounds that turn into capricious chuckles and sighs, and yet it is also a medium for Bartok's deepest pathos. Within this light whimsicality, the fine flower develops of Bartok's most subtle polyphony, with interweaving strands of melody, and each of these strands made up of fragments that are broken off and then taken up again. One of the more touching of such movements is the third (middle) movement of the *Fourth String Quartet* (1928). One of the most broad and grand is the slow movement of the *Second Piano Concerto,* opening and closing with a sad declamation between piano and orchestra, while the middle section is full of fanciful "night sounds."

In the *Fifth String Quartet* (1934), consisting of five movements, the three middle movements are all in the "night music" style, yet imaginatively varied. The second movement is a slow masterpiece of this fragmentary "night music" polyphony, its touching, sinuous melodic lines being begun, broken off, and resumed, while answering lines are reduced to little twangs, with sustained, droning chords beneath. In contrast to baroque and classical polyphony, which binds together in one emotion the various melodic voices, Bartok creates a kind of disassociation of his various lines, like different people musing, each oblivious of the other's presence, one emitting cries of pain while another is thinking of clouds, skies and eternity. The third movement is a fanciful erratically moving satire on sentimental dance motifs. The fourth movement begins and ends with little querulous plucked sounds and slides, and there is a frightening cry of sadness at its center.

With the explosions in Europe that followed the first world war, a short-lived Communist regime arose in Hungary. Among the forces that helped overthrow it were the denial of food and medicine by the relief commission headed by Herbert Hoover, and the invasion by a Rumanian army. A White Guard terror followed, under Admiral Nicholas Horthy, instituting a frightful slaughter of the left. The Hungarian republic that emerged was a virtual Horthy dictatorship, keeping the people in poverty and bolstering the power of the great landowners, who were anti-Semitic and opposed to any liberal ideas. Bartok seems to have had no political leanings, left or otherwise. But he found life and work in Hungary increasingly difficult, especially when, after the rise of Hitler, the Horthy regime took the country into the orbit of the Nazis, whom Bartok regarded as "bandits and assasins."[21] He travelled a good deal in the late 1930's, and from 1941 to his death made his home in the United States, living in poverty, although he did receive occasional commissions.

A change of style appears in the works of his last ten years, not so strikingly different that it can be called a new period, and yet perhaps foreshadowing one that could have come, had he not been cut off by death. The change is towards a greater softness and sweetness of melody, and a firmer architecture, with the form less fragmented to the ear. It is apparent in the *Music for Strings, Percussion and Celesta* (1936), which is masterful in its handling of a baroque structure. It starts with a slow fugue, beautiful and touching in melody. Then comes a light *scherzo,* followed by a lovely and touching "night music" movement. The conclusion is a fast folksy movement, in which the fugue theme is commented on again.

With the *Concerto for Orchestra* (1943), commissioned by Serge Koussevitsky and the Boston Symphony Orchestra, Bartok made a magnificent approach to the classic symphony. It starts with a painful, sad slow introduction, followed by a driving sonata-form movement, alternating a brusque declamatory theme with a tender folk-style melody. A hilarious scherzo follows, like a folk dance with witty overtones. Then a "night music" slow movement is heard, with an anguished cry at its center. Another scherzo follows, in which Bartok quotes the deliberately banal theme which Shostakovich had used to depict the Nazis in his *Leningrad Symphony,* and turns it into a sardonic polka. Is it another gibe at the Nazis? The closing movement is a dazzling piece of fugal hilarity, with a touching, declamatory end.

Bartok represents the end of a period, and at the same time helps lay the ground for a new development. He is the greatest of those in his generation who saw the peasantry as synonymous with the nation; a viewpoint no longer possible in the next generation. For the transformation of the countryside is a world-wide process. Whether under the conditions of capitalism or socialism, masses of peasants, farmers, farm workers and their children are entering city industrial life, and those that remain on the land are working under conditions of large-scale production that bring them close to the city working class. The cultural isolation of the countryside, which fostered the great oral tradition of folk music but the other side of which was poverty and illiteracy, is being broken down. Like the research of others in folk music, Bartok's devoted and intensive effort to record and preserve the old forms of folk music came at a time when this music was losing its currency as a living oral tradition. And the preservation of this music gives it renewed life on a different level, for it becomes part of the conscious national heritage, lending its vitality to new forms of musical creation.

As countries throw off their economic backwardness, a many-sided yet single cultural life begins to embrace the entire population. The implications of this change, in respect to national music, will be discussed in the next two chapters. One takes up the Soviet Union, where a bold program has been laid down to make the classical "art" heritage part of popular knowledge, and the goal has been raised of new composition in the line of this heritage, which will at the same time be a popular or "people's" music. The other takes up some aspects of the popular music produced in the United States, a production of extraordinary immensity, affecting the entire population, and with currents in it, notably that of jazz, of such vitality that they have become a world influence.

11. THE SOVIET UNION AND PROBLEMS OF A PEOPLE'S MUSIC

"Unless we clearly understand that only by an exact knowledge of the culture created by the whole development of mankind and that only by reshaping that culture can we build proletarian culture—unless we understand that we shall not be able to solve this problem. Proletarian culture is not something that has sprung nobody knows whence, it is not an invention of people who call themselves experts in proletarian culture. That is all nonsense. Proletarian culture must be the result of a natural development of the stores of knowledge which mankind has accumulated under the yoke of capitalist society, landlord society, bureaucratic society."

—V. I. LENIN, *The Tasks of the Youth Leagues* 1920).

I

In the Soviet Union, the direction taken by music is publicly argued and discussed as a force crucial to the economic, social and political life of the nation itself. Composers are expected to serve the people and help in the building of socialism. This was underlined by the criticisms levelled against composers in 1936 and in 1947-48, which most critics in the "West" looked upon as a means for driving music into the cause of propaganda at the expense of art. Yet the leading Soviet composers have not acted like frustrated creators. Prokofiev, having left the Soviet Union in 1918, returned in 1932, and from this time to his death in 1953 produced the greatest music of his career. Shostakovich, when he visited New York in 1949 to attend the Conference on Peace, did not speak like a man robbed of his freedom or crushed by dictation. He said, "We must join the beautiful and mighty voice of our art to the courageous voices of our people raised in the cause of peace and democracy. . . . May our struggle for peace, life and human dignity, our struggle against war, death and barbarism unite and strengthen our forces and serve the cause of the true rebirth and full flowering of the musical art of our time."[1]

To understand the mind of these Soviet composers, it is necessary to appreciate the fact that they love their country, respect its people, and believe in socialism. The contrast between Tsarist Russia and the present-day Soviet Union is a matter of history; on the one hand, a corrupt aristocracy, widespread poverty, disease, ignorance, misery, oppression of non-Russian nations, and on the other hand enormous productiveness, a torrent of books reaching the smallest towns, thousands of scientists graduating yearly from the schools, a multi-national culture, a vast popular audience for music and the arts. The composers admire deeply the comparative handful of brave people who challenged Tsarism in 1905, and were killed, jailed or exiled; the ragged troops, many of whom were workers with no military training, who beat back the armies of intervention in 1917-21, after socialism was proclaimed; the wisdom and fortitude that lay behind the transformation of the country, building heavy industry and sacrificing the immediate returns that labor could bring for the strength, security and basis for progress of the next generation; the widespread fortitude, self-sacrifice and heroism shown by the armed forces and the population as a whole in smashing the seemingly all-powerful invading German fascist army. They lament deeply the terrible losses and ordeals suffered during the war.

Socialism has furthermore brought forth a public unprecedented in the history of music. Every American musician who has given recitals in the Soviet Union has testified to the enormous, enthusiastic audiences, with high standards of taste, and made up not of a narrow band of "music lovers" or inveterate concert-goers but of average working people. The significance of this audience lies not only in its numbers. Far more important to the composer is the fact that he is considered by it a person of public stature whose talents are prized and considered essential to the well-being of the nation. His art is wanted and needed. Music has been freed from the need to act like a profitable business commodity, with the accompanying frightful competitiveness, jealousies and wasting of talent this forces not only upon composers but also on performers. To celebrate the people's accomplishments, to attempt to move closer to this public, to take on such themes as a call for world peace, is therefore not a task dictated "from above" but one corresponding to the composers' own desires.

Yet, as shown both by the critical discussions and the career of men like Prokofiev and Shostakovich, the path of Soviet music has not been a smooth one. A crucial esthetic question involved is the relation between partisanship and truth. To Marxist theory, there is no antagonism between the two. The working class, building socialism and eliminating all exploitation of one class by another, has no interest in anything but the truth, scientific and artistic. It does not fear change but welcomes it, for it has no stake in the "status quo." To it, ideas and institutions that no longer serve human needs and progress become irrational, for they are in conflict with the forward movement and realities disclosed by life itself. And so only those who stand with what is new, with what is being born, can see life steady and whole, and grasp truth in all of its ramifications. As against the theory that the world is running down, it sees enormous powers at hand for an unprecedented mastery and transformation of nature, creating new conditions for human growth. The understanding of the operation of society has also developed to the point where unemployment, poverty and war can be eliminated.

Through this vast collective effort, an equally vast liberation of the individual human spirit is made possible, no longer compressed and distorted by the demands of a cut-throat, competitive society but able to develop itself in a many-sided manner. Translated in terms of the arts, this means also that there is no essential antagonism between the artist's responsibility to the public and responsibility to his art, or between "outer" and "inner" truth. There need also be no antagonism between "creation" and "criticism." For criticism represents, in theory, the voice of the public made articulate and crystallized, summarizing its needs, its changed conditions of life, its new thought and psychology, and thus bringing the artist and public closer together. Yet in actual practice, most complicated problems arose.

II

Among the early works of Sergei Prokofiev (1891-1953), produced between 1910 and 1923, there are many that still adorn the concert world, like the *First Violin Concerto* (1916-17), *Scythian Suite* (1916), *Fugitive Visions* (1915-17), *Classical Symphony* (1917), *Third Piano Concerto* (1921), *Third, Fourth and Fifth Piano Sonatas* (1917-23), and the opera *The Love for Three Oranges* (1919). They show conflicting impulses in the composer. He turns more often than his experimental contemporaries, such as Debussy, Ravel, Stravinsky, and Milhaud, to the forms of concerto, symphony and piano sonata, at least preserving their skeleton outlines. And there is a genuine humanist quality in these works, apparent in their lovely and distinctive lyricism.

It is this fine melodic invention which differentiates him primarily from Stravinsky, apparent even in the Stravinsky-like *Scythian Suite.* Prokofiev's melodies are "Russian" in character, but without earthiness, seemingly drawn not from direct contact with folk and popular music as much as from a refined development of the past of Russian national music. Along with dreamy sadness, they sparkle with a genuine wit and joy in life. Nevertheless, Prokofiev is still the rebel against the past, the "nay sayer," the foe of whatever seems to have a touch of the academy. He lacks in these works the essential qualities of classic form; the contrapuntal texture with at least two interweaving voices, and the thematic development in terms of emotional drama and conflict. What passes for thematic development, as for example in the *Third Piano Concerto,* is a series of rhythmic transformations of his themes, using percussive effects and other novel timbres, and underlined by startling modulations and dissonances. He tends to write a "one-line" music.

Highlighting the weaknesses of this period is the opera, *The Love for Three Oranges.* The libretto, written by Prokofiev after an eighteenth century comedy by Carlo Gozzi, is a deliberately farcical travesty of fairy-tale melodrama. On stage there is also an audience, commenting upon and interfering with the spectacle before it. This audience is divided into "Lovers of Tragedy," "Lovers of Comedy," "Romanticists" and "Empty Heads" who like glamorous spectacles. Thus they make up "official society," the public before which the artist must cavort as an entertainer. And this becomes the main point of the opera; a satire aimed by the artist at his public. It is a typical form of twentieth century "revolt." The music makes no effort at human portraiture. Under a vocal line of constant recitative and declamation, without much melodic substance, there is a continuous orchestral commentary made of a chain of brilliant musical ideas, some of them hilarious. It is a finely written score, and yet one which indicates a constant strain on the part of the composer to keep its brittleness from showing.

The loosening of national ties, when the composer made Paris his headquarters from about 1924 to 1932, brought him almost to disaster. In some works, like the *Quintet for Winds and Strings* or the *Fifth Piano Concerto,* the hard metallic surface almost squeezed his melodic warmth out of existence. Other works had more sweetness. But his temperament did not lend itself to turning out a series of abstract musical constructions, or to finding ever new novelties to stimulate a jaded cosmopolitan audience. And for this reason his return to the Soviet Union, at the end of 1932, had the effect of a liberation. Noticeable is how eagerly he turned to forms that had an immediate social function; the *Lt. Kije* film music (1933-34), the perfect children's piece *Peter and the Wolf* (1936), the evening-long ballet *Romeo and Juliet* (1935), the great film score *Alexander Nevsky* (1938-39).

The new element is not that some of these are stage works, for he had written such in Paris. It is that they bring him now into a direct relation to a live national audience of which he feels himself to be a part. Its thoughts help shape his work, and he welcomes this because they are his own thoughts. Thus *Romeo and Juliet* reflects the love for Shakespeare in the Soviet Union, the constant performance of his plays, and the taste of an audience which would be disappointed if the composer did not do justice to the human elements of the drama. And he does this with a depth not felt in his music before. He suggests in a masterful way, through the music, the personality of Romeo, Mercutio, Tybalt, and the parents Capulet and Montague. At the same time he unifies the work musically by making it revolve about Juliet, and it becomes a moving, rhapsodic expression of young love. *Alexander Nevsky* draws upon a historical event, the Russian rebuff in the Middle Ages of an invading army of Teutonic knights, to express the patriotism of the Soviet people in answer to the mounting threat of Hitler's militarism.

III

Dmitri Shostakovich (*b.* 1906) was of a later generation. Where Prokofiev's "nay saying" had represented the unpolitical composer's resentment of all official society, the ebullient laughter of Shostakovich's early work represented a belief that this "sweeping away of the dead wood of the past" was connected to the building of a new society. His *First Symphony* (1924-25) established him as a composer of genius, not only in his homeland but in Vienna, Berlin and major American cities, though performances by conductors like Bruno Walter and Leopold Stokowski. And it owes its strength to the fact that its wit interlaced with lyrical tenderness, its brashness of sound, its gleaming orchestration splintered into fragments of solo outbursts, its all-over boisterousness, are combined with a solid organic structure, indicating a firm grasp of how a symphony had to be put together.

In the following decade, however, he had limited himself increasingly to the role of a jester, "standing the past on its head" with parodies of old melodic styles, as in the *Golden Age* ballet and the sprightly *Piano Concerto* of 1933. This jesting and parody style showed itself most fully in the opera *Lady Macbeth of Mtsensk* (1930-32). Its tragic story of lower middle class life in nineteenth century Russia was treated almost exclusively in a satiric vein, but for the touching chorus in the last act. The score is riotous in humor, as in the jazz music which accompanies the puppet-like gestures of the police, the dissonant fugue portraying the drunks at a wedding, and the love music parodying an air from *Rigoletto*. There is also a rather obvious piece of naturalistic illustration in the seduction scene, denoting another form of rebellion against what seemed to be outmoded, hypocritical prejudices.

In 1936 the Communist Party newspaper, *Pravda*, printed a scathing criticism of Shostakovich's opera. The article was entitled "A Muddle instead of Music," and said such things as this: "From the outset, the listeners were stunned by the deliberate and ugly flood of confusing sound. Shreds of melody and choking phrases of music were drowned out, burst forth to vanish again in a pandemonium of creaking, shrieking and crashes. . . . On the stage the singing was superseded by bawling. When the composer accidentally struck a simple, tuneful melody he seemed to shrink away from it as from a calamity and to hurl himself with renewed fury into a jungle of confusing sound, in places pure and simple unadulterated cacophony. . . . This is neither due to want of talent on the part of the composer nor to his inability to express simple and stirring sentiments. This was music deliberaely turned 'topsy-turvy.' "[2]

To understand this criticism and the remarkable leap in Soviet music it helped bring about, one must see that it was not what most critics in the West took it to be, simply an uncouth political interference with art, but part of a vital and far-reaching discussion of the direction of musical progress. The social base for this discussion lay in the industrial progress established by the two successful five-year plans, the turn of the tide on the countryside towards large-scale collective farming, the achievements in the conquest of illiteracy, and the growth of a great popular audience for the arts.

The move towards the creation of a nation-wide musical public, which at the same time was making the past of culture its own possession, enabled central problems of "socialist realism" to be raised as a practical task. One of these problems, in music, was the recapture of the past classic heritage, as against the "modernist" narrowness of forms and techniques. This implied not an imitation of the old eighteenth and nineteenth century composers, but the recovery of the great tools of musical composition which had enabled it to embrace every side of life, human feeling, and psychology. The other problem, closely connected, was that of arriving at a directness of musical expression which would provide a common ground between the composer and his listeners. This did not mean necessarily creating tunes "that a peasant could whistle," but the creation of melodies, or "human images," which drew upon or were linked to the common fund of music that was a social possession of the people. This is no more than the process basically followed by the great composers from Bach and Vivaldi to Mussorgsky, Verdi, Dvorak and Tchaikowsky. Only with these two conquests could the composer become, in a sense, the agent through which life itself could seem to have written his works, and musical forms be created that would be responsive to the storms and victories taking place in the real world, expressing the triumph of a new view of life and humanity.

The broadening of musical style is apparent in the works composed by Prokofiev upon his return to the Soviet Union, some of them written before the *Pravda* blast. Thus his typical "musical ironies" are heard in the satiric delineation of the feudal minded Montagues and Capulets in *Romeo and Juliet.* His grotesque, mechanistic, "hammer-blow" music with its acid dissonances appears as a perfect tonal clothing for the invading, burning, looting and terror-inspiring Teutonic knights in *Alexander Nevsky*. But these no longer become an "all-over style." They are a way of expressing one side of life and psychology, and alongside of them, in the same works, rises a contrasting human imagery, a richer stream of inspired lyricism than had ever been heard in his music before. And a crucial forward step in his art is the appearance of some genuine classic qualities, creating a rich emotional life through the symphonic development of themes. This is less apparent in the "pure" forms, like the *Second Violin Concerto,* than in what are seemingly "program" works. Thus in *Romeo and Juliet* the characterizations are built and the drama intensified through the variation of basic melodic themes, and the transformation of the love motifs in the closing tomb scene brings a new heroic and tragic grandeur to his art. The sturdy melodies of *Alexander Nevsky,* original yet in folk or popular style, act also like symphonic themes. The "battle on the ice" becomes a gigantic symphonic development section, using these themes that had appeared in the opening movements. In the aria, "On the Field of the Dead," a theme is developed that had been heard in the movement, "The Crusaders in Pskov." The last movement, "Alexander's Entry into Pskov," is like a recapitulation and coda, using previous motifs.

Another triumph was the *Fifth Symphony* (1937) of Shostakovich. In it he returned to the structural procedures of the *First Symphony,* but with a far greater richness of emotion, romantic "inwardness," and affecting drama. Typical of the new kind of big-scale, organic form he was able to create is the first movement. Its opening motifs all have a speech-inflected, "open" quality, as if by-products of the composer's meditation, and yet each plays a powerful structural role, so that the whole movement is a flowering of material announced in these first bars. The brusque motif heard at the very outset is of course central, and the entire movement seems to be aimed at its transformation into the radiantly hopeful form it takes in the recapitulation. The wisp of a motif that answers the first theme flowers into the great declamation pealed out by the orchestra at the climax of the development. The long-breathed, sighing melody that may be called the "second subject" is transformed into the menacing music, with its evocations of conflict, of the polyphonic development section. The second movement is a *scherzo* with a lovely dance-like lilt. The third movement is a beautiful "nocturne," evoking warm, yet disturbed feelings. Finally the last movement breaks out into daylight.

The entire symphony captured the moods of great numbers of people at the time, and not only in the Soviet Union; a troubled sadness, an ominous awareness of looming conflict, a determination to move ahead. Because of this breadth and "truth," it moves audiences over the world today, two decades after it was written.

Many notable works of Soviet music appeared after this

critical discussion. One is the Shostakovich *Quintet for Piano and Strings* (1940) with its beautiful balance between inner meditation and outer gaiety. Others are the ballet *Gayne* (1939) by Aram Khachaturian (*b.* 1904) with its captivating stream of fresh melody, and his concertos for piano (1937), violin (1940) and cello (1946). The latter especially explores Armenian folk music through the medium of the classic concerto form with a rousing vitality that makes it an adornment of world music. In the late 1930's and the 1940's the great galaxy of performing musicians began to take shape, like David Oistrakh, Lev Oborin, Emil Gilels and Sviatoslav Richter, whose masterful technique and interpretive insight into the entire world musical tradition, with none of the superficial glitter or temperamental caprices of the old school of virtuosi, indicated how high a level of musical life was being sponsored by the working people of the Soviet Union.

IV

In the 1940's this writer, finding the musical achievements of Shostakovich and Prokofiev so moving, believed the *Pravda* criticism of 1936 to be wholly salutary. If it appeared to be unnecessarily harsh and insensitive in its language, this seemed to be a surface mannerism, affected perhaps by the atmosphere of the times, the need in the Soviet Union to tighten its ranks in the face of the fascist threat from abroad. It was no secret that both Hitler and Mussolini had been strengthened and supported by powerful financial and industrial forces throughout the West, with hopes that Hitler would attack the Soviet Union. It was also apparent that the Soviet appeal for the containment of fascism, had it been taken up by other countries, would have saved the world from the horrible slaughter of the Second World War.

And yet it is now clear that the *Pravda* critique also set harmful tendencies in motion. However sound were the basic principles with which it started, it substituted harsh abuse for the critical duty to come to grips with the actual facts of the music. For the opera, far from being a "muddle" or an "ugly flood of confusing sound," was the work of a skilled, knowing craftsman who had said what he wanted to say very clearly. Far from "stunning" its audiences, the opera delighted many listeners with its wit and humor. The abusive terms carried a tone of castigation with an implied distrust of both artists and audiences. And in line with this spirit, the guilty opera was wthdrawn from circulation, as if its existence had a contaminating effect. The same attitude spread to the experimental music of the "West" which, instead of being examined in terms of its conflicting tendencies, similarly came to be abused as "decadence" and was rarely if ever heard. The result was a frigidity of critical atmosphere. There was a fallow field for bureaucratic criticism, using terms like "formalistic," "foreign to socialist man," and on the other hand "optimism" and "truth to life," without any searching examination of what "truth to life" actually involved in terms of musical expression and artistic integrity. Operas which took up a progressive historical subject, and set it to melodious recitatives, airs and choruses, could be hailed as in the "classic tradition," or as "Socialist realism," although the composers made no serious effort to cope with the complex problems of portraying human psychology through music in a way reflecting the times themselves. Some critics felt that it was better to say nothing than run the risk of being accused of mistakes. With the lessening of stimulating discussion, the composers of deepest integrity had to work out their problems mainly alone.

IV

The salutary effects of the re-examination of music were still apparent in the heights reached by Soviet music during the anti-fascist war. Certainly the Soviet music produced in wartime was unmatched by any elsewhere in the world, for the sensitivity with which it reacted to the issues involved in the struggle of humanity against barbarism, and the portrayal it gave of the ordeals. Nor could this have been done had not the criticisms of 1936 broken the manacles which in the name of "modernism" bound composers to the role of jesters or "nay-sayers." Prokofiev in 1940 had completed the lovely romantic-comic opera, *Betrothal in a Convent,* based on Sheridan's play *The Duenna.* During the war he also wrote the sweet, whimsical ballet *Cinderella,* and the polished, highly attractive *Second String Quartet* based on musical folk material of the North Caucasus. Wartime does not call for only desolate feelings. But he also took up the issues of the war in his opera, *War and Peace* (1941-42) based on Tolstoi's novel. And the face of the tragedy is also revealed in four works that were begun in 1939 and completed at various stages of the war, or immediately afterwards; the *Sixth Piano Sonata* (1939-40), *Seventh Piano Sonata* (1939-42), *Eighth Piano Sonata* (1939-44) and *Violin Sonata No. 1 in F minor* (1939-46). Then in

1944, when it was apparent that the tide of battle had turned against the fascists, he composed the *Fifth Symphony.* All these works are psychologically linked.

In the three piano sonatas, the handling of sonata form and piano timbre is much like that of his *Fifth Piano Sonata* which had been written more than fifteen years before. It is percussive music, weak in counterpoint. Now however there is a more intense, compelling drama, and a deep inward turn. These sonatas are like a private diary. The music is almost wholly speech-inflected, sometimes poignantly meditative, sometimes violently declamatory. Accenting the romantic inwardness, in the *Sixth* and *Eighth* sonatas, is the return of the first movement material in the last movement, not for any transformation or apotheosis but as a renewed, affecting retrospection on a tragic experience. In all three sonatas, and most of all in the *Eighth,* there are moments of incandescent emotion that places them among the greatest piano writing of the twentieth century.

The *Fifth Symphony* is like a move back to the outer world. The first movement does not have the dramatic clash and unity of "opposites" of the classic form. It is a meditation on two closely connected, long-drawn and speech-inflected melodies, reaching an exalted apotheosis in the closing measures. An exhilarating scherzo follows. There is a beautiful slow movement, with something of the mood of the tender love music in *Romeo and Juliet,* and last a driving *toccata* which has the feeling of a weight lifted off the mind. And perhaps the greatest of all these war works is the *F minor Violin Sonata.* It is truly a big work in the sweep of life it embraces. Its inspired melodies have a distinct Russian national character. The first movement, touching, slow and sadly thoughtful, is followed by a driving fast movement in which the percussive declamation gives the music (as in some parts of the piano sonatas) a touch of stridency. Then comes another "inner monologue," one of the most affecting pages in all Prokofiev's work. And the fiery last movement truly resolves everything that had gone before; a powerful statement of welcome to life but not without memories of tragedy.

The wartime works of Shostakovich, in comparison to Prokofiev's, reveal how different in style and temperament are the two composers, although they learn from each other's work. Prokofiev, the brilliant craftsman, prizes the clear. objective, succinct shaping of a work. He would never allow himself to write such sprawling works as the Shostakovich *Seventh, "Leningrad,"*

Symphony and *Eighth Symphony*. He is also more prolific in shapely, distinctive, singing melody. But Shostakovich has other powers which Prokofiev could never quite match; a mastery of a truly expressive, many-voiced polyphony, and with this the ability to create drama in depth through a cumulative thematic development. He comes closer than Prokofiev to the essential principles of classic architecture. His ideas are sometimes worked out slowly and painfully, making the music difficult to follow because of its excessive length. And yet, at the end, he will have probed into deeper conflicts.

Thus the *Leningrad Symphony* today seems too long. And yet, composed in 1941, mostly in Leningrad, at times with German shells raining on the city and the composer taking his turn on the rooftops to guard against incendiary bombs, it was something he had to write. It linked music with living history in a way that had never been done before, becoming a rallying cry in the concert halls of the anti-fascist world. It was no piece of musical journalism, but a genuine work of musical art, a deep reflection on war and peace, barbarism and humanity, and one has to accept its length because of the passages in which it coalesces into great and stirring music.

The first movement opens with a lyrical, tender portrayal of a land at peace. The long middle section, portraying the German *blitzkrieg* invasion, acts as a development section, for it is made of a grotesque transmutation of one of the peace themes. It is too drawn out and painful. But the close of the movement is again exaltedly hopeful and beautiful, despite the ominous reminder in its closing bars of the presence of war. The following scherzo is touching in its lyricism, and Russian in melody. Then comes a long, drawn out meditation, which moves slowly and yet powerfully towards the serene melody which takes shape at the close. The last movement is perhaps not altogether convincing, for it speaks of a victory which is still far in the future. Yet deeply affecting are its closing pages, with its apotheosis of the remarkable, complex theme with which the entire symphony had opened.

In two other wartime works, the composer's mastery of polyphony and thematic transformation enables him to write magnificent last movements that act as the capstone and climax of the entire work. One is the *Second Piano Sonata* (1943), in which he reveals the "inner life" of the war, in its worst moments, the tragic awareness of the frightful human destruction and yet the firm clinging to faith in the people's strength. The other is the *Trio for Violin, Cello and Piano* (1944), in which he touches on Jewish themes, for tragic expression. In both works the composer seems to lay himself completely bare.

The first movement of the *Second Piano Sonata* is inconclusive, putting into contrast a tremulous opening theme and march-like second theme without arriving at any emotional resolution. The second movement is a speech-inflected, questioning meditation so austere that the composer seems withdrawn from his listeners. Then comes the powerful last movement; a set of variations on a theme which has two parts, one a four-note questioning phrase derived from the second movement, and the other a tender Russian folk-style melody, that is close kin to the march theme of the first movement. These two disparate parts of the theme create at the outset a feeling of unrest and potential dissonance. The variations that follow develop both of these sides of the theme. At first the folk-style melody is adorned with tender ornamentation and a beautiful, expressive counterpoint, touched by pathos. Then abrupt rhythmic changes, percussive patterns and dissonant harmonies take over, the music seeming to explode into fragments, with a long, almost unbearable communication of pain and unrest. A climax is reached of sad, declamatory descending chords, and then a grand and noble "funeral march" variation provides the resolution, followed by a hauntingly beautiful lament. Finally the folk melody reappears, now without the questioning surrounding phrases, and breathing a quiet hope.

In the *Trio* likewise the great last movement ties together the threads laid down in the preceding movements. It is wild, richly polyphonic, tragic music opening with Jewish Hasidic dance themes which are put in conflict with a sad, descending, chromatic phrase. The conflict continues for almost the entire movement, down to its closing, requiem-like phrases. Here again the meaning of the music is not hard to decipher. It is first of all the struggle of life against death. The *Trio* was written in memory of a friend of the composer, the Jewish musicologist Ivan Sollertinsky, who had died in 1944. But it is also not far-fetched to say that the significance of the music extends beyond the death of a single figure. It evokes the struggle for life of the masses of Jewish people against the massacres instigated and carried out by German fascism.

V

In 1947-48 new and harsh criticisms were levelled at leading

Soviet composers, the main documents being a speech by A.A. Zhdanov delivered at a conference of musicians in 1947 and a statement on music by the Central Committee of the Communist Party in 1948. As in the case of the 1936 critical discussions, there were solid insights. Salutary was the urging of composers to get closer to the people, whose self-sacrificing heroism in the war was a matter of history. Another stage in socialist realism was reflected in the suggestion that music could break out of the narrow confines of the concert hall, so that composers would write for the thousands of amateur choral and instrumental groups, and take up the task of creating songs for the people. There is a vision here of the breakdown of the barrier between "art music" and "popular music," bringing into modern life, but on a broader arena, the tradition whereby a Handel, Mozart, Schubert, Dvorak, Grieg and Verdi had given the people wonderful popular songs along with their more ambitious symphonic or operatic works. There is again the urge to restore a classic breadth to music that would at the same time be an inspiring force in building socialism.

And yet, absent from the criticisms is the recognition of the fact that the war had caused deep wounds, physical and psychological, which the rise of the "cold war" had intensified, and which could not be cured by ignoring them. Art had to recognize them, in order to be true to life. Added was a menacing tone. Based on the belief that the very victories of socialism made the class struggle grow sharper, it implied that artists who failed to follow the preferred procedures were more than simply weak, slow or mistaken; they were allied to the "class enemy."

There is the tone of command. "The Soviet people expect their composers to produce music of high ideological and technical standards in all genres—opera, symphony, choral music, popular song and dance music." [3] It is as if the failure to produce great symphonies, songs and operas were due only to wilful perversity on the composers' part. Again there are abusive epithets. The same Central Committee statement accuses the Soviet composers of "renunciation of melody" and "confused, neuropathological combinations that turn music into cacophony, into a chaotic conglomeration of sounds." [4] All their achievements, including the remarkable works of the late 1930's and the war years, are scornfully demolished. For, referring to the criticisms of 1936, the statement says, "Notwithstanding these warnings . . . no change has been effected in the realm of Soviet music." [5] How could it be that the great strides of socialist society failed to produce a socialist realist art? The answer is found in the influence of the "class enemy." "Survivals of bourgeois ideology have not yet been overcome among part of the Soviet composers, and these survivals are being nurtured by the influence of present-day decadent West European and American music." [6]

Following these criticisms, the outstanding composers continued to produce works of great beauty. The reason is that the criticisms were impelled by a thought with which they found common ground. This was the need to close the ranks, and to assert the unbroken vigor of Soviet society, in the face of brandished atom bombs and the menace of another war; a war which many influential figures in the West were openly speaking of as a main order of immediate business. During the anti-fascist war itself certain figures had been speaking freely of their hopes that Germany and the Soviet Union would "bleed each other to death." In the postwar years, Germany had become the most favored nation for American loans, investment, and economic rebuilding, while every effort seemed to be made to block the recovery of the Soviet Union, which had suffered such terrible losses in bearing the brunt of the fascist attack. Yet, even more than in 1936, the criticisms short-circuited the process of attaining the very musical goal they upheld. They tended to work against the faithful reflection of life, and the recapture of the "classic" heritage, which they seemed to advocate.

"Classic" does not simply refer to a successful style of the great past. It is art which, while probing the world of individual psychology and conflict, relates it to the outer world of human and social activity. Thus "inner" and "outer," depth of feeling and clarity of thought, go together. For this reason, every composer of the past who made a "classic" contribution to the heritage, also made a contribution to the further penetration of human psychology in music. And for the same reason, a "classic" and realistic art of the present, although it must be "educated" by the great achievements of the past, cannot create in the past style.

With each crisis and forward step in society, human psychology has changed and deepened. This is certainly seen in our own age. Just as every forward step in society has appeared as a countermovement to a frightful and devastating attack upon human life, so in our own times, the great hopes and sense of world brotherhood rise in combat against a terrible despair, horror and pull to the past such as no past age has ever seen. The issues at stake in the world today, permanent peace and progress against the most horrible of wars, are reflected in deeper inner conflicts than ever before. And the classic art of our age must do full justice to the profound psychology of our age. Thus it is perfectly understandable that a socialist society will have no use for an art expressing only horror at a "dying world," or the loneliness of an artist with no feelings for his fellow human beings. Yet some subjectivity is inevitable in a society which has undergone such struggles. Zhdanov asks, "Is music to become a soliloquy on the part of the composer? If so, why force it on the people?" [7] But a soliloquy may be a necessary stage through which a composer must pass to arrive at a classic or realistic art, and the soliloquy itself may touch on questions alive in the minds of others.

A mistake of the criticisms, as this writer sees it, was to make subjective feelings, a sense of deep sorrow and struggle against death, synonymous with "bourgeois decadence." Such feelings are not "bourgeois." The Soviet people had suffered. The greatness of the wartime works, and of some postwar works as well, by composers like Prokofiev and Shostakovich, is that they probed to the bottom the anguish of such losses. Perhaps in some works the sense of tragic loss outweighed the expression of optimism. Probably no work attained a classic roundness of view. But if classic art, with its realistic and whole view of life, is essentially optimistic, its optimism is mature. It can come only from a conquest of tragedy, not an avoidance of it.

Both Zhdanov's speech and the Central Committee statement show awareness of a central weakness in Soviet musical life, the bleak critical atmosphere. There is no creative discussion. "When there is no creative discussion, no criticism and self-criticism, there can be no progress either," [8] Zhdanov says. But critics must analyze correctly the "classical heritage," not merely praise it. They must, in appraising contemporary works, weigh them against what is actually in the mind and thought of the people, not merely uphold an abstract "optimism." They must appreciate the complex problems raised in creative work that is "true to life." They must master the complex trends and conflicts in world music about them. For "bourgeois" music is not an undifferentiated mass of decadence. There are profound national expressions, deep humanist trends, and among them, valuable discoveries. Even in the music of composers who are fearful, lonely, self-centered, horrified by life, there are expressions of personal suffering. Such works must be characterized in terms of their limited view of life and people; not exalted, as happens often in the West, as the "music of the future," or as an expression of "modern man." But on the other hand there is no value in such jeering epithets as Zhdanov employs, like "they make one think of a dentist's drill," or "a musical murder van," [9] or an implication that their creators are insane.

And so the critical statements fail to recognize the fact that the low level of Soviet music criticism is due to the harsh, dogmatic, commanding line already laid down in 1936, and intensified in 1947-48. They make the situation worse, by implying a kind of self-sufficiency in Russian culture, past and present, raising a danger of cultural narrowness. There follows upon this an insidious trend towards Russian nationalism. This is never openly stated, for in theory, the Soviet Union is opposed to any form of national chauvinism, and was the first country to make racism a punishable crime. Yet anti-Semitism, kindled by the fascist invading forces, was allowed to show its head for a short while. The Central Committee's statement on music, when dealing with Muradeli's opera *The Great Friendship,* attacked certain people of the North Caucasus, in line not with history but with a prejudice held by Stalin, as exposed in the 1957 congress of Soviet composers.[10] The Central Committee speaks of Russian classical opera as "the best in the world;" [11] a wholly unnecessary and unsupportable statement, and harmful, for with all respect to the achievements of Russian opera, there are some necessary lessons in operatic form that are better learned elsewhere.

Among Prokofiev's fine postwar works was the cantata *On Guard for Peace.* It is a subjective work, not making a completely convincing, architectural whole. But it has many inspired passages; the opening reminiscence of the tragedy of war, the images of people rebuilding the land and of children singing, the beautiful lullaby of a mother whose song shows that she is troubled by past evils and present dangers, the touching image of a child dropping off to sleep. And especially captivating in Prokofiev's last works is the tenderness he feels for youth, which serves as well to unlock his happy stream of melody. This is heard in the ballet, *The Stone Flower,* and the suite, *Winter Holiday.* And it attains a most beautiful expression in the *Seventh Symphony,* composed shortly before his death. This is not a dramatic or heroic symphony. In fact much in it comes close to his ballet style. But it is a perfectly molded, lovely work, full of dreamy pathos and rollicking high spirits.

The works of Shostakovich that follow the criticisms show him not composing any "ultra-simple" music as some Western critics predicted, or secretly carping at "authority," as others guessed would happen. He takes from them what seems to him to be true and useful, is always the patriot, deeply attached to the land and people, and always the humanist. His breadth is greater, his technique surer.

The *Song of the Forests* (1949) is one of the most transparent of his big works. On the surface, it is a cycle of songs for tenor, bass and chorus, on the theme of the transformation of nature under men's hands. Yet in the varied character of the songs, we get a little panorama of Russian life; the children, the 'teen-age youth, the older people with sad memories of the past, the sweetness of love and spring. And masterly is the subtle binding and unifying connection from one song to another, the opening theme of the work appearing in ever new transformations, up to the big climactic double fugue.

If this work does not touch on the tragic side of life, we can find it in the beautifully written *Fourth String Quartet,* of the same year, which opens in a delicate and whimsical vein, but closes with a heartrending conflict like that which ends the wartime *Trio.* Along with these came a wholly different kind of work, the *Eleven Jewish Songs* (1948), which are wholly original "art" songs, beautifully singable, using motifs of Jewish folk music and based on the texts of familiar Jewish folk songs. Also close together came the three *Ballet Suites,* of 1950, with their irrepressible high spirits, and the *24 Preludes and Fugues,* of about 1951, which are a remarkable set of studies in expressive polyphony, sometimes gay, like Nos. 3, 7 and 8, and sometimes poignantly moving, like Nos. 16, 22 and 24. They also show him breaking new ground for Russian music.

Then came, in 1954, two deeply tragic works. The *Tenth Symphony* is laid out on the general lines of the *Fifth* and *Seventh.* The first movement, with its brooding opening, is in sonata form, but deeply subjective, with a tragic conflict at its core. The third movement has a bitter irony, using dance rhythms. The last movement is not happy, but fiercely declamatory. The *Fifth String Quartet,* which immediately preceded the symphony, is more dissonant in its opening movement, and more poignantly beautiful in its slow movement. Their composition came at a time when war tensions were at their height, and is not far-fetched to see a connection between this and the sombre mood of these works.

Folk music does not play a central role in the art of Shostakovich, and he is not a prolific melodist, athough he has written some solid popular songs. The national character of his art lies in the way in which, through his big works, he has made himself a sensitive barometer of the feelings of the people. No other Soviet composer has touched so deeply as he on the tragic side of life, and at the same time he has written popular works of a merry, frolicsome and boisterous, open-hearted humor.

He is a profound student of his art, and outstanding in his style is the rich, always expressive polyphony, and his ability to build a large-scale structure out of the plastic manipulation of germinal motifs, carrying a rich psychological burden. The indefinite, evolving character of his themes and his transformation of them, so that a beautiful, haunting melodic line will come at the climax of a long, troubled meditative development, points up an affinity to the romantic rather than classic symphonic tradition. Or, in other words, he is also a subjective child of the upheavals of our time. But his art never surrenders to subjectivism, and there is always a struggle within it. There is little or no academicism in his art. He uses both traditional harmonies and the dissonant clash of different keys as he needs them, to express the feelings that move him. Wholly a product of the Soviet Union, the great appeal of his work in other lands, much different in economy and social life, indicates that the "socialist realism" which he strives to attain involves no cryptic aesthetic private to socialism. However strange or foreign the term may appear elsewhere, the music itself speaks of experiences shared in common everywhere.

On May 28, 1958, the Central Committee of the Communist Party of the Soviet Union issued a brief statement in which it spoke of the criticisms of 1948 as containing "some groundless and undeservedly harsh appraisals of the work of a number of talented Soviet composers." It also reasserted "the principle of strengthening the bond between art and the life of the people." [12] By the very nature of Soviet musical life, this will be the prelude to a widespread discussion among composers, critics and the public as to the achievements and mistakes of the past and the new paths that can be opened up.

To many in the West, all this is a strange procedure, and even a statement like "strengthening the bond between art and the life of the people" will seem to some to be an infringement on the freedom of the composer. And yet the history not only of the arts but of all society asserts the truth that the arts are both an individual and social product, and that since human lives depend on one another, the freedom of the individual, which the arts express so powerfully, is a collective task which people must accomplish together and in cooperation. In the Soviet Union this relationship between art and social life, between the individual and society, is placed on a conscious level as something that can be worked out, not left to chance and accident. To thus combine theory and practise brings up the danger of dogmatism, of a hard-and-fast theory that, losing touch with the realities of both art and social life, acts to hamper the free response to reality that is the lifeblood of great art. That such a danger is real may be seen in the mistakes that occurred and that are now recognized.

And yet certain truths are uncontrovertible. One is that part of the basic procedure of the Soviet Union is the ability to correct itself. Another is that the general path of Soviet music has been a correct one in terms of the needs of both artists and the mass of people, for it has produced results of the most fruitful kind. Soviet music is thriving in terms of its vast and still growing popular audiences, its growing galaxy of superbly talented performers, its musical education, and its creative composition. If terms like "socialism" or "socialist realism" are strange and alien to many people elsewhere, the music produced in the name of such terms is not strange or alien. Its speaks to people everywhere powerfully and affectingly, as an echo of the humanity they feel in themselves.

By the same token, such a term as "socialist realism" may be recast in a way that indicates the relevance of what it stands for to those whose basic belief, whatever their politics, is in the kinship of people and the progress of humanity. It calls for the recapture of the great musical tools of the musical past, enabling forms to be built that are capable of reflecting the many sides of life. It asks for the development among artists of a social mind, responsive to the problems of the people about them, especially those most exploited, and doing the productive labor of society. It calls for artists to be thinkers, enlightened by what history, science and the struggles for progress in society have made it possible for men to know. It seeks an outlook based on a conscious grasp of the unity of "inner" and "outer" worlds, of human psychology and social reality. It calls for a partisan faith in the future of humanity, and opposition to ideologies, dogmas and prejudices that drag humanity backward, that proclaim the alienation of people from one another, or the impotence of society to master such problems as starvation, poverty, racism and war. It seeks to build an active audience, with a two-way, reciprocal relationship between it and the creative artist. It builds towards a cultural life in which there will be no artificial barrier between "fine art" and "popular art," one in which the needs of people for song and dance can be supplied by the most equipped composers, who also may write complex, big-scale works; one in which both simple and complex works will be created with integrity; one in which the mass of people will know the historic achievements of musical art, and will be active participants in musical life.

Socialist realism is not a special technique, a new invention, a narrow style or musical cult. The music produced under its name stands or falls in the same way that all music stands or falls, and has done so in history. That is by its ability to move people, to make them conscious of their kinship to others, to help them to understand the problems with which life confronts them as it confronts all others in the same world, and to give them the strength to overcome the obstacles in the path of their common progress and growth.

12. JAZZ AS FOLK AND ART MUSIC

"The most magnificent drama in the last thousand years of human history is the transportation of ten million human beings out of the dark beauty of their mother continent into the new-found Eldorado of the West. They descended into Hell; and in the third century they arose from the dead, in the finest effort to achieve democracy for the working millions which this world had ever seen. It was a tragedy that beggared the Greek; it was an upheaval of humanity like the Reformation and the French Revolution. Yet we are blind and led by the blind. . . . One reads the truer deeper facts of Reconstruction with a great despair. It is at once so simple and human, and yet so futile. There is no villain, no idiot, no saint. There are just men; men who crave ease and power, men who know want and hunger, men who have crawled. They all dream and strive with ecstasy of fear and strain of effort, balked of hope and hate. Yet the rich world is wide enough for all, wants all, needs all. So slight a gesture, a word, might set the strife in order, not with full content, but with growing dawn of fulfillment. Instead roars the crash of hell; and after its whirlwind a teacher sits in academic halls, learned in the tradition of its elms and its elders. He looks into the upturned face of youth and in him youth sees the gowned shape of wisdom and hears the voice of God. Cynically he sneers at 'chinks' and 'niggers.' He says that the nation 'has changed its views in regard to the political relation of races and has at last virtually accepted the ideas of the South upon that subject' . . . Immediately in Africa, a black back runs red with blood of the lash; in India, a brown girl is raped; in China, a coolie starves; in Alabama, seven darkies are more than lynched; while in London, the white limbs of a prostitute are hung with jewels and silk. Flames of jealous murder sweep the earth, while brains of little children smear the hills.

—W.E. BURGHARDT DU BOIS, *Black Reconstruction* (1935)

I

The most widespread American influence on twentieth century world music is that of jazz. A creation of the American Negro people, it has become an American national art, with Negro and white performing in friendly collaboration. And it has been both studied and enthusiastically performed in countries like England, France, Italy, Sweden, Germany, Australia and Japan.

Jazz may be described as a music of African tribal roots which has gone through a rapid "hot-house" development in a country the most advanced in the world in industrial production and one that has made the commercial production of popular music into a major industry. Jazz has grown as an organic part of this music-manufacturing industry, constantly feeding ideas into it, and yet at the same time has been in constant opposition to its standardized procedures. It exhibits the perfect taste of a people often with little or no professional musical education, when they create music as a communal emotional expression, for at its best it has a plastic economy and purity in the handling of melody, rhythm and tone color foreign to commercial popular music and comparable to art music.

Its history reveals many lessons which throw new light upon all music; the absorption by folk music of material from the most varied sources, including art music, and their transformation into a new homogeneous art; the rise in folk music of a natural, improvised polyphony; the influence of the human voice upon instrumental style inspiring the development of fresh, expressive instrumental timbres. Its secret of growth is based on a principle actually very old in music and rooted in folk art, but appearing strikingly fresh and vital in twentieth century America and Europe; improvisation, not simply as a display of individual technique, but as a collective and social act, and as a form of immediate communication between performer and listener. For this reason, while an integral part of American commercial popular music, jazz has played the role within this music of a rebel, raising a banner of freedom. To musicians employed in the business of manufactured popular musical entertainment, with its dehumanized division of labor and apportionment of specialized tasks, it has opened up a creative path, restoring the unity of musical inventor and performer, like a humanization of music making.

The first forms of jazz were the ragtime and blues heard among the Negro people in the 1890's and the first decade of the twentieth century. This music differed from the anonymous, group music of slavery in that it was a solo music, reflecting the hard-won ability of Negro people, after the end of slavery, to move from place to place and to assert their individuality as entertainers. Some of these musicians, coming from the most poverty-stricken and depressed areas of life in the Southern states, became legendary figures in the Negro communities.

Ragtime was the more "educated" music. Its creators were pianists, many of whom had gotten some rudimentary musical instruction. A factor in its rise was the fact that in this period cheap upright and player pianos could be found almost anywhere they went. Ragtime embraced a wide area of music, from popular airs of the period, Spanish tangos, and quadrilles, to operatic airs such as were commonly found in easy instruction books for the piano. Thus one of these inspired ragtime pianist-composers, Ferdinand "Jelly-Roll" Morton, in his recordings made with Alan Lomax for the Library of Congress in 1938, has shown how in the early years of the century a French gavotte and the *"Miserere"* from Verdi's *Il Trovatore* were transmuted into ragtime pieces. The first prolific ragtime composer, Scott Joplin, had ambitions to write operas dealing with Negro life, aimed at "educating" his people, and had he been able to break out of the trap which kept such musicians from mastering the heritage or from being taken seriously as musicians, he might have become a truly notable figure.

Ragtime pieces were generally in two-part form, the second part contrasting to the first like the "trio" of a Sousa march, and this form moved into the "verse" and "chorus" of the typical 32-bar jazz popular song. Its special characteristic was its complex, continuous opposition of two rhythms. The bass line, for example, will accent each second beat of a four-beat measure, while the melody line will accent every third beat, thus creating a syncopated alternation of accents on strong and weak beats. This constant "catching up" of the rhythm could have been heard in some of the more joyous or "jubilee" spirituals, like "On My Journey to Mount Zion," or "I Want to Be Ready, Walking into Jerusalem Just Like John." It could have been heard in the slave dance known as the "cakewalk," and in minstrel music. In other words, it was a renewed flowering of a musical style that had been preserved by the Negro people, perhaps from Africa. But within every such flowering, enabling old materials to be transmuted into something new, lay a new content. And the special expressive content of ragtime was its wit; a kind of ironic, playful musical laughter, full of rhythmic stops and starts, of shocks and surprises.

A tradition of such satire, masked by buffoonery, had existed in the cakewalk. Thus an old Negro entertainer, Shephard N. Edmonds, as quoted by Rudi Blesh and Harriet Janis, describes the cakewalk: "The slaves, both young and old, would dress up in hand-me-down finery to do a high-kicking, prancing walk-around. They did a take-off on the high manners of the white folks in the 'big house,' but their masters, who gathered round to watch the fun, missed the point." [1] The wit of ragtime, like all folk wit, is a semi-secret language, understood only by those possessing the key. The key is the ability to grasp what is unsaid, through what is said. This rests on a familiarity with the aspect of life, or music, which is being thrown into high relief by being thus artfully distorted or stood on its head.

Because of the kind of hard-boiled defiance and independence latent in ragtime, it was often heard—and this would also be true of the blues and jazz—in places that put no premium on respectability; saloons and houses of prostitution. Then after being derided, it was suddenly "discovered" by the commercial music industry, hard-pressed for new ideas. Fortunes were made by white imitators and followers, on musical ideas learned from Negro musicians. And the music was often at the same time misunderstood and vulgarized, its surface characteristics heavily stressed while the subtle humor slipped through the imitator's fingers. This process would be repeated throughout the entire history of jazz.

II

The origin of the blues is still cloudy. A great number of very different folk and popular songs are known as "blues," like "Careless Love," "St. James Infirmary," "It Takes a Worried Man to Sing a Worried Song," "When the Sun Goes Down," and "How Long, How Long," the only connection among them being a balladeer sadness. But within this general body of song there is a unique form that is more specifically the "blues;" a Negro creation. It is not a fixed song so much as song material, malleable, and capable of infinite variations and melodic sprouts, which remain at the same time unmistakeably "blues." It speaks of an African current flowering into a new form of folk art, indigenous to the American land. Suggesting African roots is the irregular scale, which may embrace from three to seven notes. In its simplest form, it is anchored about a tonic note, a "dominant" five tones higher, and an intermediate note dangling between the major and a minor third. Thus it falls outside the major-minor pattern, and in the seven-note form, this character is emphasized by flatting the seventh note. The melody is highly speech-inflected or *parlando-rubato,* with the singer often making a strong expressive use of the "blue note" flattened third and seventh, along with slurs from one note to another, to emphasize certain climactic words.

Yet—and this is a basic difference from African music—the blues are an architecturally rounded song form, for all their looseness. The song unit consists of three "statements," each within four bars of music. The first is built of descending, lamenting phrases; the second repeats the first, but with greater tension; the third is a rounding out. This reflects as well the "dialectic" of the word stanza, which consists of three lines, the first challenging or arousing the interest of the listener, the second line repeating the first, and the third rounding out the thought.

Other African seeds flowered in the blues texture. One is African polyphony, which the blues developed in a manner that can be compared to the "trio-sonata" texture of baroque music. There is a melody line, that of the singer, which continues for two and a half bars, and then an "obligato," antiphonal line, or answer, rises from the accompanying instrument, such as guitar or piano, to fill out the four bar statement. And third is the bass line, which provides the underlying 4/4 rhythm and also the "blues chords." There is no such free three-part polyphony in other American folk song. Also unique is the interplay of rhythms, the *parlando-rubato* melody contrasting to, subtly anticipating or lagging behind, the basic beat.

An integral part of the blues is the special wit and humor, rising out of the contrast between statement and answer, between the unflagging beat and the speech-inflected freedom of melodic accents. The difference in this respect between blues and ragtime is that in ragtime the wit is uppermost, providing the sparkling surface; in the blues, it is the lamenting song that takes over, while the wit becomes a constant brake or check on the outpouring of feeling. It is as if the expression of misery had always to be wrapped up in a note of irony or defiant refusal to succumb. As Willis L. James' powerful Negro work song says, "Don't pity me down!"

How and when did this blues form arise? It is not found in African music. It is not heard in other music of the Americas created or deeply influenced by Negro people, such as that of

Cuba, Haiti or Brazil. It is not heard among the spirituals, although some spirituals suggest the blues, like the descending, sad phrases of "Sometimes I feel like a motherless child, a long way from home," or the three line stanzas, with the second lines repeating the first, of "He Never Said a Mumberlin' Word," the great "Crucifixion" spiritual which Roland Hayes points out as definitely African in origin.[2] Field calls, "shouts" and "hollers" are suggested as an origin of the blues with their descending phrases and slurred notes, but they also are not exactly the blues. However the fact that blues singers are called frequently "blues shouters," and many blues are called "moans," indicates what the music itself confirms; the close connection of the blues to a cry of the human voice.

In music and words the blues reflect the conditions arising in the last decades of the nineteenth century, when after the terrible onslaught against the Negro people which followed their achievement of freedom from slavery, many became homeless wanderers. Thus E. Franklin Frazier writes, "Among the million Negroes who deserted the rural communities of the South, there were thousands of men and women who cut themselves loose from family and friends and sought work and adventure as solitary wanderers from place to place. Some of the men had their first glimpse of the world beyond the plantation or farm when they worked in sawmills, turpentine camps, or on the roads."[3] The music, of self accompanied solo song, is that of a wanderer. The words tell of events that happened in one place or another, and a frequent theme is that of the railroad, symbolic of travel and swiftness of movement. A blues line like "Well, I'm going to buy me a little railroad of my own" expresses, as Russell Ames points out,[4] the resentment of discrimination on the railroads.

W. C. Handy, in his autobiography, *Father of the Blues,* describes the brutality with which these wanderers were treated in St. Louis. "I slept on a vacant lot at twelfth and Morgan streets, a lot I shared with a hundred of others in similar circumstances. I slept on the cobblestones of the levee of the Mississippi. My companions were perhaps a thousand men of both races . . . . Two popular songs grew out of the brutality of the police in those days, *Brady He's Dead and Gone* and *Looking for the Bully*. Policemen carried nightsticks about a yard long. They had a way of hurling these at the feet of fleeing vagrants in such a way as to trip up the fugitives. One frequently heard of legs broken in this way."[5]

Handy was the first to write down and publish blues songs, in 1909, but as he recounts, the form itself of the blues existed long before. He was himself a somewhat educated musician, with an upbringing close to the middle class, and the music known to the most exploited, vagrant and laboring Negroes came to him as a strange surprise. "A lean, loose-jointed Negro had commenced plunking a guitar beside me while I slept . . . . The singer repeated the line three times, accompanying himself on the guitar with the weirdest music I had ever heard.[6] . . . The primitive Southern Negro as he sang was sure to bear down on the third and seventh tones of the scale, slurring between major and minor. Whether it was in the cotton fields of the Delta or on the levee up St. Louis way it was always the same . . . I had never heard this slur used by a more sophisticated Negro, or by any white man." [7]

It is not sufficient to say that the blues simply "arose" among the Negro people. What stamps a work as "folk" is that it expresses the communal mind and becomes part of communal life, not that it is collectively created, and in folk art there have always been inspired individual creators, whose work came to be absorbed in the common heritage. The likelihood is that the unique, rounded and yet germinating form of the twelve-bar blues was created out of familiar material by such a genius, and was then taken up by one singer after another, the others finding in its very malleability an apt form for anything they wanted to say in words and music.

As for the period, it would seem to be the beginning of the 1890's. Among Negro folksingers, the earliest blues is reputed to be a song called "Joe Turner Blues," and the singer "Big Bill" Broonzy recounts the legend about "Joe Turner;" that he was a mysterious figure who during the great catastrophes of 1891-92, would bring help to poor people, Negro and white. Such catastrophes, like river floods, high winds and tidal waves, always wreaked their greatest devastation on the Negro and poor white population, who lived in flimsy shacks near the waterfront on in the lowlands. At the same time "relief" and assistance customarily went first to the houses of the wealthy. The blues could have risen at a time of such devastation. And certainly there are many such flood stories among the blues, one of the most beautiful being Bessie Smith's "Blackwater Blues."

Among the blues composers and singers were Negro women. Women have always played a strong, leading role in Negro life.

Under slavery, with families broken up, the fathers traded away. children often knew only one parent, the mother. Two of the great heroes both in the Underground Railroad escapes and in the fight for the right to vote after the Civil War, were Harriet Tubman and Sojourner Truth. In the renewed oppressiveness of the late nineteenth century, a double burden fell on the women, often deserted by men who were themselves desperate, and this shattered love relation is expressed in countless blues, from the woman's viewpoint. Her indignation is often fierce. Frazier quotes a Negro woman, "I tried nineteen years to make a husband out of him but he was the most no 'count man God ever made. Since I seen I could make no husband out of him I left him." With little change, this could become the words of a blues.

Typical is Bessie Smith's "Lost Your Head Blues." It starts, "I was with you, baby, when you didn't have a dime." Then it tells bitterly the man's changed attitude when he had some money, and goes on to a declaration of independence. "I'm gonna leave, baby, ain't gonna say goodby, but I'll write you and tell you the reason why." Following is a lament over the price of independence, a "moan." "Days are lonesome, nights are so long, I'm a good gal but I've just been treated wrong." This of course comes from the 1920's, when the blues, having inspired the development of jazz and in turn influenced by jazz, became in the hands of great popular artists like Bessie Smith something approaching a fine art form. Thus "Lost Your Head Blues" has not merely rounded stanzas but a cumulative development, reaching a climax in the cry of the woman against double oppression.

III

Jazz proper rose in New Orleans in the early years of the twentieth century. To the Negro people at the time, there was a sharp demarcation between "gospel songs," which were sung in churches; "blues," which were a profane or secular music, of the countryside and labor camps; "ragtime," which was a virtuoso piano music heard in cities like Sedalia, Memphis and St. Louis, often in red-light districts; and "jazz," which was a "Creole," or New Orleans music. Each had its own style.

The word "Creole" spoke not only of Creole folk songs but of the French influences in New Orleans, including French folk songs, reels, gavottes and quadrilles which were played by Negro musicans at balls for the white "masters," and also the opera house for which New Orleans had been musically renowned. There were also street parades, and the Negro fraternal lodges had their own bands. It was from band music that jazz took its basic instrumentation, of clarinet, trumpet, trombone, and tuba, only the latter being later replaced by a plucked string bass.

Much early jazz was a march music, which at the same time could be turned into dance music, like the "one-step." It embraced the popular marches known from Civil War times, and the inspired marches of John Philip Sousa (1854-1932). Sousa, son of a Portuguese father and Bavarian mother, had been a variety hall musician before he became the leader of the United States Marine Band. He knew and respected Negro music, and in turn influenced it. The Sousa strain can be heard for example, in one of the classics of early jazz, the new Orleans marching tune "High Society."

Yet what made jazz unique was that even when it most closely resembled the march, it combined with this the characteristics of both ragtime and blues. From ragtime came the dazzling free rhythmic solos of the "melody" instruments against the underlying beat, giving the whole performance a feeling of exuberance and individual life contrasting to the mechanical pattern of the military march. Thus ragtime pieces became marches, and marches became "rags." These ragtime solos could also embody blues phrases and "blue notes". The blues also became transformed from a vocal to an instrumental music, using the band instrumentation but with a free, interweaving three-voice polyphony or antiphonal "statement and answer," the instruments such as clarinet, trumpet and trombone taking on deeply expressive vocal inflections. Slow blues played as dances were "slow drags;" fast blues were "stomps." The blues could infiltrate music of the most varied origins such as the march, Creole songs, Spanish dances, popular ballads, with a variation on the melody taking on typical blues phrases, rhythms, and slurred "blue notes." Typical of blues style was the "break;" a sudden, expressive rhythmic gap, with a blues phrase rising in answer, and the "riff," or blues phrase repeated in *ostinato* style, with melodic solos above. The blues became the expressive heart of the jazz improvisation, preserved as an unbroken thread throughout all the subsequent changes of jazz band form and instrumentation. As to the folk blues singer, so on a higher level to the instrumentalists in collective improvisation, the blues provided the infinitely flexible material through which the soloist could speak his heart.

Shortly before the first world war, small band jazz, known as "Dixieland," using a New Orleans band instrumentation with added piano, providing a music of marches, one-steps, ragtime songs with blues phrases and intonations, began to be heard about the country. It was at this time that the first "shock" works were being heard in European music, like Stravinsky's *Rite of Spring.* But it was in the postwar, "jazz age" 1920's that jazz captured the major part of American popular music, with much of it in the process, becoming commercially hardened and vulgarized.

A complex period was opened up by the first world war. There was a vast increase in production and profit-making, born out of the war industry. The United States had changed from a debtor to a creditor country, and instead of being a field for foreign investment was seeking investment abroad. To the great mass of citizens, there was the uneasy feeling that the country was now a world power, and its diplomacy was at variance with its proud democratic heritage. The masters of wealth did not have any greater ease of mind. The appearance of socialism in Russia, beating back all attempts of the great powers to strangle it, was a spectre arousing hysteria. The 1920's opened with the Palmer raids, jailing and deporting hundreds of people on the basis of the principle that disloyalty to the interests of trusts, banks and monopolies was disloyalty to America. Open violence was used against the workers seeking to bring trade unions into the great mushrooming industries like meat-packing, auto, oil, steel and rubber. A tidal wave of jingoism arose, aimed at the immigrant families who made up the great mass of the working people in the factories, and at the Negro people. The Ku Klux Klan, discovering mysterious sources of funds, anti-Negro, anti-labor, anti-Semitic and anti-Catholic, became a power North as well as South. Large-scale hypocrisy entered American life as never before with the constitutional amendment prohibiting alcoholic liquor. It made millions of citizens into law-breakers, and fostered gangsterism as a grotesque underworld form of large-scale financial enterprise, corrupting political parties, police and courts.

The music produced in this era reflected the unease of mind of the people. A band of young American composers found the "liberation" they had been seeking in the bleak, sardonic primitivism and motor energy of *avant-garde* European music, producing music equally percussive, dissonant, hiding its lonely nostalgia under a hard-boiled surface, like Aaron Copland's *Piano Varia-*

tions. And the same moods, without the same craftsmanship, were found in the popular commercial jazz, with its blatant instrumentation and pounding rhythm, lacking in the warmth, wit, sensitivity and folk spirit of the music as the Negro people had produced it. The hard-boiled surface of the Negro jazz style was copied, without its inner pathos. And it was this side of jazz that was taken up by European composers, as another primitivism, part of their bleak, ironic portrayal of an inhuman civilization. It was used thus by Shostakovich in his *Lady Macbeth of Mtsensk,* Gliere in *The Red Poppy,* Stravinsky in *L'Histoire du Soldat,* Milhaud in *Le Creation du Monde,* Weill in *The Threepenny Opera,* Krenek in *Johnny spielt auf.*

Yet some work of quality appeared amidst the flood produced by the popular music industry. Its wild growth reflected the prosperity of the 1920's. No other country was able to make so prolific a use of the new inventions such as radio and the pronograph, exploiting the vast market of people hungry for musical entertainment. Nor could the industry rest on its old stock in trade of sentimental ballads, European style waltzes and operettas, like those of Victor Herbert, or Irish, Negro and Italian dialect songs. Both its growth, and the interest in new rhythms like the tango or fox-trot, made the search for fresh talent imperative, and amidst the host of commercial hack workers composers genuinely gifted in melody were discovered like W. C. Handy, Irving Berlin, Hoagy Carmichael, George Gershwin, Vincent Youmans, Jerome Kern, Thomas "Fats" Waller, Richard Rodgers and Cole Porter. The victory of the new music over the old was seen in the ingratiating scores that appeared for the Broadway musical comedies; Vincent Youmans' *No, No Nanette* (1924) with songs like "I Want to be Happy" and "Tea for Two;" Richard Rodgers' *A Connecticut Yankee* (1927) with "Thou Swell" and "My Heart Stood Still"; Jerome Kern's *Show Boat* (1927) with "Old Man River," "Why do I Love you?" and "Can't Help Lovin' that Man"; George Gershwin's *Girl Crazy* (1930) with "Embraceable You" and "I've Got Rhythm."

Music like this represents the song-producing industry, or "tin pan alley" of the 1920's, at its best. There is something sad as well as captivating about both these songs and the shows from which they come. The texts are the most prosaic doggerel and mindless dramas ever set to music, reflecting the perpetual terror of the commercial producer at the thought of ever taking an honest, open look at real life, even through the spectacles of comedy.

Show Boat was a slight exception in its feeling, if a sentimental one, for the American scene, and its sympathetic, if patronizing portrayal of a Negro. The part was made famous first by Jules Bledsoe and then by Paul Robeson. The music lives in its sweetness of melody, but this lacking any inspiration towards musical adventure from the text, falls into a conventional mold. Meaningless are the harmony and instrumentation. The older literature of operetta, had suffered, like the Broadway musical show of the 1920's, from a lack of real musical character-creation, being content to offer a string of tunes. But compared to these Broadway shows of the 1920's, the works of Johann Strauss, Milloecker, Offenbach, Gilbert and Sullivan, Victor Herbert, are masterpieces of musical craftsmanship. Tin-pan-alley music at its best is a broken and half-realized art.

Of all the popular song and musical show composers who appeared in this period, George Gershwin (1898-1937) had the most fresh and distinctive style, with least of the "old world" about it. It took its substance from Negro ragtime and blues, but transformed this into something unique to Gershwin. His rhythms, lilting and syncopated, were sophisticated and "hothouse" in comparison to the open air feeling of marching jazz, but were witty and captivating. His melodies lacked the heartbreak and lurking, sardonic laughter of the blues, but were nevertheless wry, jaunty, tender and sweet. And it was he who with many song hits behind him, took the step into serious musical composition, producing such works as *The Rhapsody in Blue* (1924), *Piano Concerto in F* (1925), and *An American in Paris* (1928). They have a solid place in American musical history. For all their structural crudities, they live, sing and hold together. They indicate that the material of American popular music, including jazz, can be used successfully for greater musical and artistic ends. Their themes are typical of the best Gershwin songs, and he has transmuted them into genuinely symphonic material. These works confirm the truth that for a writer of good symphonic music, it is a great help to be able to write a good song.

The 1920's also saw a lusty growth of creative jazz, almost unnoticed by and independent of tin-pan-alley, and mirroring the changed conditions among the Negro people. The demand for labor by the mushrooming war industries had served to break down some jim-crow restrictions, and more than a half-million Negroes left the South for cities like Chicago, New York, Detroit and Philadelphia. There were racism and segregation to be faced, taking violent form as in the race riots whipped up by real-estate interests in Chicago. Yet in Chicago the Negro communities played a militant role in union organization. A Negro, Oscar De Priest, was elected to Congress.

Musicians had moved North as well, and the jazz that developed in cities like Chicago was a flowering of seeds born in the South; an amalgamation of New Orleans marches and ragtime pieces, with that fluid, poignant, sardonic blues improvisation at their heart, and worked up through performance after performance into instrumental pieces, sensitive in instrumentation, many-voiced in texture. It is a remarkable music, with the odor of folk earth on it, but advanced beyond any folk music and moving to the level of a small-form art music in its knowing, skillful and collective working out. It is a music, born of folk art, but growing under twentieth century conditions, its roots in the South, but its finished form reflecting the greater freedom and independence of both the musicians in the Northern cities, and the Negro communities for whom they played. And the phonograph record industry played an unintentional role in helping this music grow, for it discovered a flourishing market among the Negro communities for the recordings of artists like Bessie Smith, Joe "King" Oliver, Louis Armstrong, Ferdinand Morton, and the groups about them. However weird and even barbarous the industry thought this music to be, referring to the recordings as "race records," it was willing to exploit this profitable market, especially as since the musicians were Negro, most of them could be paid very little.

One of the reasons for the perfection of style of this music, in contrast to the commercial jazz, was that to the white performers, music was simply a way of making a living; to the Negro, it was a form of national group expression, its common language of the blues permitting both a collective improvisation and a direct communication to the listeners. Yet, despite the barriers of racism and segregation, which not only poured scorn on this "race" music but also forbade white musicians to play alongside of Negro, an increasing number of young white musicians, like Leon "Bix" Biederbecke, Jack Teagarden and Benny Goodman began to study and play in this style, valuing its freedom of expression, and its breakdown of the barrier between performer and creator.

IV

In 1927, Nicola Sacco and Bartolemeo Vanzetti were executed by the State of Massachusetts allegedly for robbery and murder, although the evidence showed they were obviously innocent. Their real offense was that they were, to use the refined words of the trial judge, "those anarchistic bastards." Their execution disclosed again a basic truth of American life; The existence, side by side with the great tradition of pride in and defense of democracy, of a tradition of brutal, selfish, wealth-inspired anti-labor violence proclaiming itself as "Americanism." The movement in defense of Sacco and Vanzetti enlisted some of the finest minds in American life, and indicated that even in the midst of the "jazz age," the democratic battle was gathering intensity. Then in 1929 the stock market collapse brought an abrupt end to the "jazz age" itself. In the five years following, the face of United States political and cultural life was transformed. The struggles of the unemployed for relief and jobs, the unstoppable movement of the workers in the great monopolized industries for the right to form unions, the angry defense by the farmers of their land against the mortgage-holding banks, brought deep democratic currents to the surface. These linked up with the world-wide horror of working people and all democratic people against fascism. With people of every national background, including Negro and white, discovering that they had common problems and needed one another, with gigantic battles of ideas breaking through in the political arena itself, a host of myths and stereotypes began to melt away. The history of the country was re-examined, and temporarily forgotten truths of its democratic heritage restored.

One product of the "proletarian thirties" was the first systematic collection and study of American folk music, aided by the operations of the work relief projects in the arts and by the Library of Congress. Another was the heavy blow given to cultural racism. Demolished was the racist approach to Negro music which described creative jazz as "jungle sounds" while ignoring its sensitivity, wit and pathos, and which ignored the earthy realism of the blues to transform them into an erotic performance for white slumming audiences. The folk roots of jazz and the blues were recognized. Jazz itself reached a new height of controlled and polished form, with Negro musicians in the leadership, such as the splendid bands grouped about Edward Kennedy "Duke" Ellington and William "Count" Basie.

Two trends arose, mutually influencing each other; that of a large-band music, and that of a "chamber music" of from three to seven players. Both of them explored the inexhaustible ore of the blues and also improvisationally reshaped popular tin-pan-alley songs in terms of the blues style and idiom, creating a finely organized music in which melody, harmony and instrumental timbre made one integral texture. Different from the instrumentation of the "New Orleans-Chicago" jazz of the twenties was the expanded role of the saxophone, both as a solo instrument and as a choir, in interplay against the brass choirs, and the elaboration of the "rhythm section," of piano, bass, guitar and drums, playing a sensitive harmonic and melodic as well as percussive role. The developed jazz band was an instrumental body of extraordinary sensitivity.

Also discovered in this decade were the riches of blues piano improvisation, by self-taught folk composers like Jimmy Yancey, Meade Lux Lewis and Pete Johnson. The best of the music thus produced, like the best of the rags, marches, blues compositions and "stomps" of the 1920's, although not written down, existing only on records, collectively makes up one of the most unique and vital bodies of music yet produced in the United States. As before, the new ideas, largely coming from Negro musicians, were adopted by the commercial music industry, stereotyped and vulgarized. Large and small band music, partly composed, partly improvised, was commercially known as "swing." Blues piano music was known as "boogie-woogie." But there grew as well an open recognition by white musicians of their debt to the Negro. Benny Goodman's band, which won enormous popularity, gave composer credit (something new for tin-pan-alley) to the Negro classic arrangements of blues, rags and stomps that he included in his repertory. Goodman and Artie Shaw broke a long-standing, unwritten racist law by including Negro musicians side by side with white in their bands, although this aroused fury in many parts of the country, and the racist practises they fought are still today far from eliminated from the music industry.

The democratic currents which showed themselves in the jazz of the 'thirties were also felt by the Broadway musical theatre. *Of Thee I Sing,* with music by George Gershwin and text by George S. Kaufman, Morris Ryskind and Ira Gershwin, was the most brilliant and intelligent satire yet to emerge from the New York musical stage.

Gershwin's *Porgy and Bess* was a further step towards an opera touching with some seriousness on the life of the Negro people. It did little justice to its subject, substituting for invidious stereotypes the patronizing ones common to white people who declare themselves "friends of the Negro" but show a total ignorance of their real life and mind. The story is melodramatic and the characterizations are childish. The inanities, for example, of the mock-spiritual, "It Ain't Necessarily So," are a sharp contrast to the dignity and poetic imagination of the great treatments of Biblical legend in the spirituals created by the Negro people themselves. Missing from the music-drama was the central factor of Negro life in the United States; the struggle for liberation, and the character of the oppression the people suffered. The situation could probably not have been much remedied at the time by having a Negro write the text. Negro people in popular cultural life still worked in an atmosphere of constant defensiveness, always aware of the manifold forms of prejudice and misunderstanding, using wit and even a mask of buffoonery as a protection, unwilling to speak openly. And to this day, there is no area of the American theatre, musical or otherwise, in which the Negro people can develop an art wholly shaped to their own satisfaction, without the hampering censorship brought by the presence of white agents, producers, managers, collaborators, critics and audiences. Yet *Porgy and Bess* showed the strength that could come from a move in the direction of the actualities of American life. And it was adorned by the Gershwin stream of melody, which consciously tapped Negro sources.

In 1936 came Marc Blitzstein's *The Cradle Will Rock,* in which a well-equipped composer used the idiom of jazz and popular ballad in the deliberately sardonic style of Kurt Weill's *The Threepenny Opera.* Its text, attacking the labor-baiting, strike-breaking and fascist-minded forces in American life, was too strong for acceptance by either the Federal theatre project, for which it had been written, or the Broadway commercial stage. But it was a popular-sponsored success.

Thus, just as "new" had supplanted "old" in the 1920's, with the jazz strains replacing the European-style operetta, so in the 1930's and early 1940's "new" again supplanted "old." The musical show in which an inane plot served as a vehicle for comedians, tap dancers, singers of "hit" tunes and a display of chorus girl pulchritude, was replaced by a more realistic approach to life and to musical form. The triumph of the new may be seen in the character of the shows that continued to win favor such as *Oklahoma, Carousel* and *South Pacific* by Rogers and Hammerstein, Cole Porter's *Kiss Me Kate,* and Kurt Weill's *Street Scene.*

Among "art composers" most dedicated to the purity and integrity of their style, a desire appeared to be "understood" and to find some contact with an audience by drawing upon folk music and finding themes in the American scene. Four composers may be cited as typical; William Grant Still (*b.* 1895), Virgil Thomson (*b.* 1896), Roy Harris (*b.* 1898) and Aaron Copland (*b.* 1900). No monumental achievements appeared; a sign not of the futility of the approach, but of the immensity of the problem. There was little searching critical discussion in musical circles of the way in which music achieves true national expression, or of the use of folk material other than the superficial process of quoting actual folk tunes.

In the *Afro-American Symphony* and the opera, *The Troubled Island,* Willian Grant Still tackled projects directly in the great tradition of a Dvorak and Mussorgsky. But while he produced works using Negro folk material with great dignity, warmth and beauty, lacking in them was the richness of texture and psychological depth necessary for greatness. Not enough of the knowledge contained in the heritage of past music was brought to bear upon the problems of the present. Thomson, in the cinema score, *The Plough that Broke the Plains* and the operas, *Four Saints in Three Acts* and *The Mother of Us All,* tended to use folk music in light, almost playful style, reminiscent of Poulenc and Milhaud in France. It is an art circumscribed by an abhorrence of the classic tradition, seeing it as too "pompous," and an equal abhorrence of the romantic tradition, as too self-revelatory. Its emotional life is limited to whimsicality, light tenderness and wit. Yet what it does display, if not depth, is the genuine love of the composer for his material.

Harris, in works like the *Third Symphony* and *Folk Song Symphony,* moved to the other extreme of a deep subjectivity, saturating himself in folk song but letting its melodic contours and sense of the outer world be drowned in a diffuse modal harmony and a brooding inner life. Nor does his polyphonic texture add real strength, for it has no links with the outer world of human movement and social activity. The moving yet unrealized quality of his work is a tragedy, for more than most American composers, he feels folk music as a creative and germinating material.

Copland's music remained restricted to a narrow emotional life, which had little room for the great drama taking place in American life outside of him. He moved between a nostalgic sadness and an outburst of hard motor energy and excitement. He fashioned a perfect musical style for this emotional life, one that was lean, economical and with his distinctive signature. Never is there a platitude in his work. Every sound is used lovingly. But the works in which folk themes entered, like *Appalachian Spring, Billy the Kid, Rodeo* and *A Lincoln Portrait,* failed to break this restrictive emotional framework. The folk tunes he used were beautiful. But they were handled with a Stravinskian aloofness, given a polished and clean-cut setting, expertly varied, and yet never used as a malleable material for human portraiture.

Yet, in this period of the 1930's and early 1940's, American music came closer to providing a richly democratic, if still incomplete, national expression. This achievement was the collective contribution of the best of jazz, of the best of the popular musical plays, of the folk-inspired "art" music, and of the rediscovery of the treasures of American folk music.

V

The "Cold War" of the late 1940's and 1950's with its brandishing of hydrogen bombs, its McCarthyite witch-hunts, its steps so inimical to the interests of the American people as the rebuilding of the great German trusts, cartels and armament industry which had brought Hitler's fascism into being, the support of Latin American dictators like Jiménez in Venezuela and of fascist governments like that of Franco in Spain, has had a chilling effect on trends towards a democratic national expression. Many composers have withdrawn into a shell.

And yet, there is a groundswell in the direction of a musical art in which the American people can recognize their own presence, and it shows itself in a move towards the breakdown of the barrier between "art" and "popular" music. Other than in jazz, the greatest activity in this direction has been in music for the theatre. The following works of recent years can be cited, none of them achieving the stature of a great American opera, but together adding up to an impressive movement. One is

Marc Blitzstein's *Regina,* with its fine social-critical drama, adapted from Lillian Hellman's *The Little Foxes,* and its frequently affecting musical setting, despite its lack of deep musical characterization. Another is Earl Robinson's *Sandhog,* with a libretto by Waldo Salt, embracing a warm approach to the working people of the land, and possessing genuinely lovely melody. There are Douglas Moore's *The Ballad of Baby Doe,* with a libretto by John LaTouche, and Carlisle Floyd's *Susannah,* which turn to the American scene and make an engaging use of folk strains. Notable is Robert Kurka's *The Good Soldier Schweik,* with a libretto based by Lewis Allen on Jaroslav Hasek's great novel. It is distinguished by its bold anti-war satire and its brilliantly witty score, with fine lyrical touches. There is Gian-Carlo Menotti's *Maria Golovin,* with its seriousness of plot and fine craftsmanship in setting text and stage action to music. A product of the Broadway theatre is Leonard Bernstein's *West Side Story,* composed to a book by Arthur Laurents, with its plea to end racism, and its strong, effective score, if somewhat too driving, hard and primitivist in its handling of jazz and popular musical motifs.

A potent influence upon American musical life has been the movement rising among all the world's peoples for a permanent end to war, which shows itself also in a deep interest by each nation in the life of others, and in an exchange of culture to an extent greater than ever before. And the United States music which still most fascinates other countries is that of jazz.

In jazz, there have been fresh developments since the end of the Second World War, with again Negro musicians leading the way, like John "Dizzy" Gillespie, Thelonious Monk, Charlie Parker, Errol Garner, Charles Mingus, and John Lewis and his Modern Jazz Quartet. It has moved to a knowing exploration of harmony, rapid modulation through the circle of keys, dissonance, the interplay of two keys at once, and the utmost refinement of timbres. With Gillespie, it expresses a derisive wit aimed at the platitudes of commercial popular music, and there is a similar, if more impish, commentary in Thelonious Monk. Parker, drawing upon the blues for a touching, speech-inflected music, expressed a lonely and sometimes anguished emotional life. With Mingus there is also an explosion of lonely, bitter feelings. Garner combines an airy wit with a sweet lyricism.

With the Modern Jazz Quartet, the collective improvisation of jazz approaches a refinement of sound, mood and texture like that of impressionist composition. About them there have risen a flock of lesser talents, including also empty virtuosi, imitators and commercial vulgarizers. As always in jazz, only a comparative few have something to say of value. But a notable aspect of this "progressive" or "modern" jazz is that it has won a devoted popular audience, eagerly following its trials and errors, unintimidated by its experimental laboratory; a quite different situation from the classical concert hall, where the announcement of a "new" American work is likely to drive an audience away with its prospect of mystification or boredom.

Modern jazz, to its creators, represents the final, conclusive answer to the charge that jazz is an amateur, unlettered music and the product of inspired ignorance. But the freedom it proclaims is only that of the musician asserting his own integrity in the face of a musical world, still run by the market place and inimical to human values. It is also weak in form. Those who speak learnedly of the "form" achieved by modern jazz are making the same mistake as that of theoreticians of "art" music. They substitute a refinement of techniques and of textures, a succession of "moments," for genuinely strong art form, with its cumulative, developmental emotional experiences and sweep of life. And it is hardly possible for the jazz creators to take up such broader problems because of the conditions under which jazz operates, with talents bartered and sold like commodities, with unending threat of unemployment, and with a constant pressure for "novelties" to keep a musician's name before the public whether or not he has evolved some fresh musical ideas. There is no leisure but that brought by the lack of a job, no arena or forum in which a musician thinking seriously about life can work out the tools to create new forms of breadth and significance. There is no opportunity to range over the real heritage of music. Even the most inspired jazz musicians have little chance for growth.

The career of a jazz musician tends to follow an almost ironclad pattern. He feels that he has something vital of his own to say. He develops a style, a "musical speech," in which he says it. He has a struggle for recognition. He is recognized, and perhaps even lionized, with articles written about him, and he may discover his name mentioned in books. Disciples and imitators appear. Then a few years pass, new names push his to the background, and although the books on jazz may describe him as a "genius," he has all he can do to keep his head above water.

For the truth is that although talent is an individual gift, the conditions for growth are laid down by society.

Jazz has its limitations even as a "national expression" of the American Negro people, as seen by the fact that they have developed other powerful forms of musical expression. There is the living stream of music heard in the Negro churches, the "gospel" singing of women like Mahalia Jackson, Rosetta Tharpe and Marie Knight, the striving of composers like William Grant Still or Ulysses Kay to master the "learned" heritage of music, the communication of the human core of the tradition of song which a Roland Hayes, Marian Anderson and Paul Robeson bring to the concert hall.

Jazz is a special product of the American Negro people within the artistic shambles of the commercial music industry, and in a society in which they are denied basic freedoms. It embodies a defiance of surrounding hostile and oppressive forces, with its growth, forms and textures shaped by a pathos and bitterness wrapped in a protective clothing of wit. If it has found so wide an acceptance among other peoples, who also collaborate in its creation, this is because they also feel the need for the freedom implied in its defiant expression. It is not a "music of the future" which will supplant the traditional musical heritage, as some of its historians claim. It is a valid, moving expression of its times. Its importance, aside from the body of genuine music it has by now already provided, is that is says something central to American life that no other American music, "art" or "popular," has said. It is that the strength of American music lies in its ability to speak for human freedom, that the demand of the Negro people for freedom strikes a response in the heart of other peoples, and that so long as the Negro people are not free, socially, politically and culturally, no American people are free socially, politically and culturally. If the American people have not yet in sufficient numbers demanded the eradication of racism from American life, the influence of jazz has nevertheless been to make a host of people conscious of the corrosion in social and cultural life brought by this undemocracy and inhumanity.

To this jazz adds the reiteration of other truths about music. One is that music is a democratic art, not an art of an "elite," and that there are vast creative powers latent among the masses of people. Another is that music can flower in the most miraculous way from a handful of folk motifs, granted that the musician himself has something real and heartfelt to say in response to life. The growth of jazz, with its flock of performers and its audiences, also indicates the deep hunger for music on the part of the American people. This hunger is revealed as well in the vast sales of "classical" music through longplaying records, and the number of young people who take up "art" music despite the forbidding conditions of making a living through their musical talent. All these trends point to the coming breakdown of the artificial barrier between "popular" and "art" music.

What kind of music will we have when racism will be considered an incomprehensible relic of barbarous times? When the great heritage of centuries of musical art, along with the treasures of folk music, become a widespread popular possession? When music, like all the arts, will be considered a necessity of life, part of the development of the "whole man," without regard to its need to show a market-place profit or to be an exclusively professional career? When an all-over concept of music of integrity, serving a mutitude of uses from dance and song to an expression of the deepest psychological portraiture and most sweeping drama, will replace the meaningless compartmentalization into "folk," "art," "popular," and "classical?"

Jazz will be part of it, as will symphonies, chamber music, tragic music drama, musical comedy, and popular song, all of them linked to one another in an honest portrayal of American life. It is in the direction of such a music that the United States will make its great world contribution, granted the elimination of racism, the ability to turn the immense productive forces of our land to the ending of starvation and poverty, the ability to turn the achievements of science from weapons of destruction to tools for the conquest of nature, and the opportunity of all peoples to progress peacefully with each helping the other. These are not dreams. They are today's unfinished business. They are the set of keys that will unlock the full creative resources of the nation.

AFTERWORD: THE INTEGRATION AND INFLUENCE OF POPULAR SONG

The Wretchedness of Satan's wrath
Will come to seize you at last
'Cause even he frowns upon the
Deeds you are doing
And you know deep in your heart
You've no covenant with God
'Cause He would never countenance
People abusing
You know apartheid's wrong (Qha), wrong (Qha)
Like Slavery was wrong (Qha), wrong (Qha)
Like the holocaust was wrong (Qha), wrong (Qha)
Apartheid is wrong (Qha), wrong (Qha), wrong
It's wrong (Qha), wrong (Qha), wrong (Qha),
wrong (Qha), wrong (Qha), wrong (Qha),
wrong (Qha), wrong (Qha)

—Stevie Wonder, from *Its Wrong (Apartheid)* (1985) *

I

In 1960, Sydney Finkelstein identified an honest portrayal of American life as the bright future for an American music of integrity. Sadly, what he identified as unfinished business still remains an open agenda for the United States. Political leadership since 1960 has pursued weapons of greater destruction, leading to the current proposals which call for powerful laser systems in space, in the controversial Strategic Defense Initiative. Although society has benefited greatly from many of the technological advances of the past three decades, society has also suffered from the increasingly transient living patterns and from the threat of destruction that has hung over its collective head since the advent of the nuclear age.

Although racism remains endemic in American society, the progress towards racial equality of the 1960's and 1970's has provided noticeable gains for many Americans of color. Outrageous poverty still exists, particularly affecting minority groups and women in this country, and racism remains the official policy of the government of South Africa; however, the 1988 presidential campaign saw the first widely received candidacy by a black candidate. The campaign of Jesse Jackson provided Michael Dukakis with stiff competition for the Democratic presidential nomination.

Finkelstein did not predict the rise of the feminist movement and the ensuing implications for American society. As women achieve equal status, the musical representation of their role has been affected. American Country-Western music, derived in part from the English folk song tradition, has provided a view of the changing role of women. With increasing sophistication, Country-Western music has documented new attitudes towards women.[1] Originally the docile object of affection, women have recently been referred to as members of the work force, as the strong partner in relationships, and as the equal of men at home and in the workplace.

Women also have achieved a position of power behind the scenes in the recording and entertainment industry. Women like Dolly Parton, Tammy Wynette, and Loretta Lynn developed their careers from small regional followings to major entertainment businesses, with control over their own resources and choices.

Also, Finkelstein could not have foreseen the societal upheaval resulting from the assassinations of John F. Kennedy, his brother Robert, and that of Martin Luther King, Jr. He could not have imagined the national soul searching evoked by the American involvement in the Vietnam War and the loss of integrity following Richard Nixon's resignation from the presidency.

Nonetheless, Sidney Finkelstein's paradigm of the relationship of music to social and historical currents applies to the past thirty years. The social upheaval, the soul searching, and the loss of faith in political authority inform recent popular music. Although Finkelstein probably overestimated the importance of jazz to the American mainstream, he was accurate in that a popular musical expression would best reflect societal patterns. The 1960s and 1970s produced a series of poet-musicians, playing folk idioms, including Bob Dylan, Leonard Cohen, Judy Collins and Joan Baez. Their works evoked the soul and conscience of the nation on issues from peace to equal rights. But clearly the most popular genre of the past thirty years has been Rock and Roll.

II

Early Rock and Roll addressed the emerging economic vitality of American youth. The market for 45 rpm records was astounding to the staid recording industry of Tin Pan Alley. Quickly, the youth market matured, calling forth the rise of the long playing record, cassette tape recording, and eventually the compact disc and digital audio tape.

As the youth market for Rock and Roll matured, the music also grew beyond "spoon, moon, and June." Cogent lyrics addressed the issues of the Rock decades and the musicians and composers of the era provided a voice for the issues.[2]

The Beatles, and after their breakup the individual members of the band, provided a dominant voice of social commentary. Their music reflected youth's concern with sexual awareness, drugs, and political maturation. John Lennon provided a focal point in a movement towards peace with songs like "Give Peace a Chance," "Imagine," and in much of his work with Yoko Ono.[3] Lennon later paid for his notoriety with his life in a bizarre shooting, in which a young man tried to claim notoriety through assassination.

As Rock and Roll entered the 1970s, a new generation of musical groups grew from the earlier bands. The leading lights of three 1960s groups, David Crosby, Steven Stills, and Graham Nash (later with Neil Young), combined to form a supergroup known by their last names. The level of their playing and singing was noticeably better than many previous groups, and their commitment to a vision of peace was strong.

A good example of this commitment was Neil Young's response to the shooting of demonstrating students by the National Guard at the Kent State University campus on May 4, 1970.

Tin Soldiers and Nixon coming
We're finally on our own
This summer we'll hear the drumming
Four dead in Ohio

Neil Young, from *Ohio* (1970)

Crosby, Stills, and Nash made their initial widespread impact on the music scene at the Woodstock Music and Art Fair. In 1969, from August 14–17, the Rock community demonstrated its numbers with a four day festival of "Music, Peace, and Love" at a farm outside the small town of Woodstock in rural upstate New York. Although somewhat marred by bad weather and inadequate organization, the Woodstock festival drew nearly 500,000 people and the interaction of a large group of people responding to a call for "Music, Peace, and Love" was the inspiration for several other large scale festivals.

Into the 1980s, the model of the music festival continued to reflect societal change. From September 4–6, 1982, the U.S. Festival concert took place in San Bernardino, California. Organized by Stephan Wozniak, the co-founder of Apple Computers, the U.S. festival provided a significant symbol of the integration of musical genre and technological advance.

The 200,000 people in attendance at the three-day festival were treated to state of the art audio and video techniques. The sound system for the musical groups was the finest yet used at such an event, producing over 400,000 watts of power for the six satellite speaker setups. Along with the first-rate sound, several large television screens were placed throughout the natural amphitheater to accommodate all viewers.

Describing the experience as a "great time" and "a nice quiet concert,"[4] the concert-goers did not seem to mind the indirect nature of the musical experience. Live acts were alternated with taped performances and computer generated video images. The technological link was accepted as a valid means of communication and did not hinder the sense of community likened to the Woodstock Fair.

The interchangeability of broadcast and live music is perhaps the most drastic change to occur in musical perception. Over forty years ago, Theodor Adorno criticized the electronic reproduction of classical music over the radio. He claimed that radio degraded the classics to a mere entertainment, by its standardization and the loss of listener control.[5]

New technology has created a situation where live music is now the great exception to the average listener. The population is surrounded by recorded and broadcast music. Live performances are still valued, yet serious as well as popular artists have created careers from the recording studio rather than the concert stage. The Beatles stopped live performances in 1966, still to create some of their greatest works, including *Sergeant Pepper's Lonely Hearts Club Band,* released June 2, 1967. Glenn Gould performed solely in the recording studio for most of his career. The great diversity of recorded material far outreaches concert or radio availability. For most listeners, the convenience of musical choice has come to outweigh the live performance.

III

The 1980s have seen some of the unification of musical style that Finkelstein predicted. Popular folk, Rock, and Jazz elements have enriched concert music, and the line of demarcation between popular and serious music is not always clear. The increasingly diverse ethnic and social backgrounds of the American population and the tremendous gains in national and international communication have allowed many diverse musical worlds to coexist.

Any of the major recording chain retail outlets can supply a wide array of music, far beyond the imagination of anyone even thirty years ago. The gamut of music history is readily available, and music from all parts of the earth.

The easily attainable and readily disposable nature of so many ideas overwhelms a fledgling composer. With such a selection of styles upon which to draw, the composer must constantly review and renew his or her principles of form. The West German, Karlheinz Stockhausen, has provided an astonishing array of new structures and sound sources, combining traditional and non-traditional materials. Stockhausen has been a model for the American composer, typically producing a new style each year.[6]

Interestingly, the drive for new sound technics, and the accompanying rationale for the selection, has often widened the gap between the composer and audience. Milton Babbitt suggested that the gap was irrelevant in his provocative essay "Who Cares If You Listen."[7] Babbitt well represents the rational model of the modern academic composer. His attitude prevails in many of the universities that sponsor the serious composers of the late twentieth century, and perversely, the economic or popular success of a composer can lead to ostracism by his or her peers.

This abstract, isolated process of composition, often with little intent of communication, has produced many intellectual challenges for music theorists, but no coherent style has emerged to interest a large public. A concert of new work is considered a success if a small auditorium is half filled with the composers' friends and relatives. Compared to the half million attendees at the Woodstock Music and Art Fair, the modern academic concert world is a miserable failure.

Yet, the small world of academic composition reflects the gains of women. This is the first generation of composers not assumed to be male. The number of significant concert commissions are limited, and still disproportionately to men; nonetheless, groups of women musicians and composers are finding an audience for their work.

Some composers have reacted to the rational model of composition with styles of great simplicity. In 1970, George Crumb emphasized vocalism and color in his *Ancient Voices of Children* on texts by Garcia Lorca.[8] Well received by his audience, Crumb is virtually ignored in the scholarly literature. The attraction of this vocal work is in part due to Lorca's poetry, which especially evokes human, emotional response, rather than rational analysis.

Perhaps the greatest simplicity is found in the works of the minimalist composers, Terry Riley, Steve Reich, and Philip Glass. The minimalist movement is predominantly American, starting in the 1960s and reaching its greatest audience in the late 1970s and early 1980s. Minimalist music is characterized by simplicity of materials and often high degrees of repetition. By simplifying thematic and source material to bare four or five note motives, the composers were striving for increased perception.

The repetitive musical materials combined well with other media, particularly theater. Steve Reich has achieved popular success with *Einstein on the Beach* (1975) and other large theater works, including *Satyagraha* (1980) and *Akhnaten* (1984).[9] His combination of simple diatonic materials, high dynamic levels, and electronic instruments has provided a cross-over audience from Rock enthusiasts; yet, like George Crumb, Reich and the other minimalists are mostly ignored by the scholarly world.[10]

It is not hard to understand the widespread appeal of a musical style that eschews rationalization and complexity, in favor of direct unencumbered expression. The music of direct expression should be more readily accepted by audiences barraged by technological complexity and nightly recitations by the electronic press on a world seemingly out of control. A music of simplicity would naturally draw a warmer response than a rational music in the modern world of harsh complexities.

IV

The future of American music still promises to be a future of integrity. The widespread increasing sophistication of musical reproduction continues to support the huge market for popular music and the social influence of the leading popular figures will have access to an ever expanding audience.

Popular musical idioms will probably continue to exert strong influence on the world of serious academic composition. Although the diversity of musical taste will continue to allow the variety of rational styles in limited concert settings, this diversity should allow the more popular academic styles room to develop in the university setting, too.

The future popularity of Rock and Roll seems secure, and the social consciousness of the leading performers continues to address important issues in society. Predictions of future musical trends are best left to others; however, it seems likely that moves toward nuclear disarmament and human rights would occupy the thoughts of socially conscious musicians. Stevie Wonder has been a leader in the campaign against apartheid in South Africa, and 1988 will see performance tours by Bruce Springsteen and Sting in support of human rights.

The electronic nature of the transmission of music will continue to effect the musical experience. The traditional gap between performer and audience in the concert hall takes on a new meaning in a society where an overwhelming majority of the music is transmitted electronically. It is a matter of concern that the passive concert hall audience has been replaced by a passive television, radio, and recording audience.[11] Yet, the response to broadcast concerts about human rights, aid to the homeless, and aid to American farmers has been positive, and society seems willing to forego the direct concert hall experience.

The implications of this trend indicate that the truly popular music, meaning the music appealing to the largest audience, will have an increasingly powerful effect on the musical world. As long as the popular artists continue to be socially responsible, their influence will lead towards that music of integrity described by Finkelstein. The increased use of electronically produced and manipulated sound sources seems likely in a passive musical society accustomed to large scale electronic transmission of sound, although the minimalist movement to simplicity described above supports the use of simple electronic sources.

Therefore, the current task before musicians is the integration of simple means in an increasingly complex world of electronic transmission. The influence of the popular musician over the academic composer should continue to grow and the isolated world of academic music will respond to the social agenda of the popular culture. The total integration of popular and serious music seems unlikely in the near future; however, a combined interest in the issues of peace, equal and human rights, and nuclear disarmament should bring the various worlds of music closer together.

REFERENCE NOTES

[1]For insight into the Country-Western scene, see Charles Hamm "Diamonds in the Rough—Hillbilly and Country-Western Music" in *Music in the New World,* Norton, N.Y., 1983, pp. 460–497.

[2]For an interesting summary of the Rock era until 1980, see Hamm, *work cited.,* pp. 618–654.

[3]Much information about Lennon's work has been collected by Albert Goldman in *The Lives of John Lennon,* William Morrow, N.Y., 1988.

[4]*The New York Times,* September 6, 1982, p. 11, col. 3.

[5]T.W. Adorno, "A Social Critique of Radio Music," *Kenyon Review,* vii, 1945, pp. 208–217.

[6]The best study of Stockhausen's music is Roger Maconie's *Works of Karlheinz Stockhausen,* London, 1976.

[7]*High Fidelity* VIII/2, Feb. 1958, pp. 39 ff.

[8]For an insightful analysis of these songs see Glenn Watkins, *Soundings: Music in the Twentieth Century,* Schirmer, N.Y., 1988, pp. 613–618.

[9]*Ibid.,* pp. 572–580.

[10]Reich does attract more attention than the other composers, see K. Robert Schwarz, "Steve Reich: Music As a Gradual Process," *Perspectives of New Music,* xix, 1980–1981, pp. 373–392; xx, 1981–1982, pp. 225–286 and Keith Potter, "The Recent Phases of Steve Reich,: *Contact,* xxix, Spring, 1985, pp. 28–34.

[11]Music of the avante garde, sometimes referred to as experimental music, has been most concerned with the passive audience. For a discussion of the aesthetics of experimental music, see Christopher Ballantine, "An Aesthetic of Experimental Music" in *Music and Its Social Meanings,* Gordon and Breach Publishers, N.Y., 1984, pp. 107–133.

REFERENCE NOTES

INTRODUCTION

[1] Quoted in Gilbert Chase, *America's Music,* McGraw-Hill, N. Y., 1955, p. 392.
[2] Alfred Einstein, *A Short History of Music,* Vintage Books, N. Y., 1954, p. 191.
[3] Ralph Vaughan Williams, *National Music,* Oxford Univ. Press, N.Y., 1935, pp. 85-86.
[4] Alfred Einstein, *The Italian Madrigal,* Princeton Univ. Press, Princeton, 1949, Vol. I, p. 22.
[5] Vaughan Williams, *work cited,* p. 124.

CHAPTER 1

[1] Cecil J. Sharp, *English Folk Song,* Simpkins, London, 1907, pp. 31-34.
[2] Bela Bartok, *Hungarian Folk Music,* (transl., M.L. Calvocoressi), Oxford Univ. Press, London, 1931, p. 3.
[3] George Pullem Jackson, *White Spirituals in the Southern Uplands,* Univ. of North Carolina Press, Chapel Hill, 1933, pp. 242-73.
[4] *Sioux and Navajo Folk Music,* Ethnic Folkways Library, long-playing record P. 401, Recorded by William Rhodes.
[5] Franz Boas, *Primitive Art,* Oslo, 1927, p. 319.
[6] Herbert Aptheker, *"The Negro Woman," Masses and Mainstream,* N. Y. Feb. 1949, pp. 10-11.
[7] Curt Sachs, *Our Musical Heritage,* Prentice-Hall, N. Y., 1948, p. 22.
[8] Bartok *work cited,* p. 1.
[9] Sharp, *work cited,* p. 15.
[10] A.L. Lloyd, *The Singing Englishman,* Workers Music Association, London, no date, p. 19.
[11] Ralph Vaughan Williams, *National Music,* Oxford Univ. Press, London, 1935, p. 60.
[12] Bartok, work cited, pp. 2-3.
[13] Y.M. Sokolov, *Russian Folklore,* (transl. by C. R. Smith), Macmillan, N. Y., 1950, p. 17.
[14] Bartok, *work cited,* p. 52.
[15] *Ibid.,* p. 2.
[16] Sachs, *work cited,* p. 184.
[17] Einstein, *A Short History of Music,* p. 80.
[18] Sachs, *work cited,* p. 83.
[19] Paul Henry Lang, *Music in Western Civilization,* Norton, N. Y., 1941 pp. 270-71.
[20] Manfred F. Bukofzer, *Sumer is Icumen In: A Revision,* Univ. of California Press, Berkeley, 1944, p. 104.
[21] Hugo Leichtentritt, *Music, History and Ideas,* Harvard Univ. Press, Cambridge, 1947, p. 96.
[22] Gustave Reese, *Music in the Renaissance,* Norton, N. Y., 1954, p. 833.

CHAPTER 2

[1] Manfred F. Bukofzer, *Music in the Baroque Era,* Norton, N. Y., 1947, p. 135.

[2] Romain Rolland, "Lully," in *Romain Rolland's Essays on Music,* Allen, Towne & Heath, N. Y., 1948, p. 48.

[3] Leo Schrade, *Monteverdi,* Norton, N. Y., 1950, p. 266.

[4] *Ibid.,* pp. 180-81.

[5] Ralph Kirkpatrick, *Domenico Scarlatti,* Princeton Univ. Press, Princeton, 1953, p. 167 (The quotation is from Dr. Burney).

[6] Hans T. David and Arthur Mendel, Ed., *The Bach Reader,* Norton, N. Y., 1945, p. 50.

[7] *Ibid.,* p. 52.

[8] *Ibid.,* p. 75.

[9] *Ibid.,* p. 279.

[10] *Ibid.,* p. 262.

[11] *Ibid.,* p. 301.

[12] G.G. Coulton, *Medieval Panorama,* Macmillan, N. Y., 1947, pp. 681-94.

[13] Philipp Spitta, *Johann Sebastian Bach* (transl. Bell and Fuller- Maitland), Dover, N. Y., 1951, Vol. II, p. 525.

[14] *Ibid.,* Vol. III, p. 106.

CHAPTER 3

[1] Romain Rolland, "Origins of Eighteenth Century Classic Style," in *Rolland's Essays on Music,* p. 68.

[2] Karl Geiringer, *Haydn,* Norton, N. Y., 1946, p. 53.

[3] *Ibid.,* pp. 78-79.

[4] *Ibid.* p. 86.

[5] Edward Holmes, *The Life of Mozart,* (first published 1845), Everyman's Library, London, p. 58 (no date).

[6] *Ibid.,* p. 95.

[7] *Ibid.,* p. 77.

[8] Emily Anderson, Ed. and Transl., *The Letters of Mozart and His Family,* Macmillan, London, 1938, Vol. I, p. 137.

[9] Holmes, *work cited* p. 259.

[10] Geiringer, *work cited,* p. 66.

[11] Holmes, *work cited,* p. 235.

[12] Quoted by H.C. Robbins Landon, annotations for *Haydn: The Creation,* Haydn Society records, HSLP 2027.

[13] Alfred Einstein, *Mozart,* Oxford University Press, N. Y., 1945, p. 183

[14] H.C. Robbins Landon, *The Symphonies of Joseph Haydn,* Macmillan, N. Y., 1956, pp. 566-69.

[15] Geiringer, *work cited,* p. 319.

[16] Robbins Landon, same as 12.

[17] Anderson, *work cited,* Vol. III, p. 1250.

[18] *Ibid.,* Vol. III, p. 1327.

[19] Einstein, *work cited,* p. 458.

[20] Anderson, *work cited,* p. 1332.

[2] Hermann Ullrich, *The Magic Flute: History, Symbolism, Significance,* Musical Quarterly, Vol. I, No. 2 Middlebury, Vt., pp. 105-6.

[22] A.C. Kalischer, Ed. *Beethoven's Letters,* transl. J. C. Shedlock, J.M. Dent & Co., London, 1909, Vol. I, p. 110.

[23] *Beethoven's Letters,* transl. Lady Wallace, Hurd and Houghton, N. Y., 1867, Vol. I, p. 36.

CHAPTER 4

[1] Kalischer, *Beethoven's Letters,* Vol. I, p. 30.

[2] Paul Bekker, *Beethoven,* J.M. Dent, London, 1925, p. 23.

[3] *Beethoven's Letters,* transl. by Lady Wallace, pp. 43-34 (Letter also in Kalisher, p. 56.)

[4] Marion M. Scott, *Beethoven,* J.M. Dent, London, 1951, p. 53.

[5] Anton Schindler, *The life of Beethoven,* Ed. Moscheles, reprinted by Oliver Ditson from the London Edition of 1841, Boston, no date, p. 134.

[6] *Ibid.*

[7] *Ibid.,* p. 135.

[8] Scott, *work cited,* p. 161.

[9] Kalischer, *work cited,* p. 110.

[10] *Ibid.,* p. 103.

[11] *Ibid.,* p. 100.

[12] *Ibid.,* p. 189.

[13] *Ibid.,* p. 259.

[14] *Ibid.,* pp. 261-62.

[15] *Ibid.,* p. 179.

[16] *Ibid.*

[17] *Ibid.,* p. 360.

[18] *Ibid.,* p. 188.

[19] *Ibid.,* p. 377.

[20] Schindler, *work cited,* p. 51.

[21] Kalischer, *work cited,* p. 353.

[22] Kalischer, *work cited,* Vol. II, pp. 335-36.

[23] *Ibid.,* p. 168.

[24] *Ibid.,* p. 345.

CHAPTER 5

[1] Heinrich Heine, "The Romantic School in Germany," in *Prose Writings of Heinrich Heine,* Ed. Havelock Ellis, Walter Scott, London, No Date, p. 90.

[2] Otto Erich Deutsch, *The Schubert Reader,* Norton, N. Y., 1947, pp. 128-29.

[3] *Ibid.,* p. 435.

[4] *Ibid.,* pp. 711-12.

[5] *Ibid.,* p. 717.

[6] *Ibid.,* pp. 727-28.

[7] *Ibid.*, p. 738.
[8] Franz Liszt, *Dir Zegeuner und ihre Musik in Ungarn,* 1861.
[9] Herbert Weinstock, *Chopin,* Knopf, N. Y., 1949.
[10] Henryk Opienski, Collection, *Chopin's Letters,* Transl. E. L. Voynich, Knopf, N. Y., 1931, p. 166.
[11] *Ibid.*, p. 254.
[12] *Ibid.*, p. 163.
[13] *Ibid.*, p. 168.
[14] *Ibid.*, pp. 357-58.
[15] *Ibid.*, p. 254.
[16] *Ibid.*, p. 136.
[17] *Ibid.*, p. 349.
[18] *Ibid.*, p. 397.
[19] Franz Liszt, *Life of Chopin,* transl. from French by M.W. Cook, Oliver Ditson, Boston, No date, p. 25.
[20] V.I. Belinsky, "A View On Russian Literature in 1846," in *Selected Philosophical Works,* Foreign Languages Publishing House, Moscow, 1948, pp. 355-57.
[21] Hugo Leichtentritt, *Music, History and Ideas,* Harvard Univ. Press, Cambridge, 1947, p. 23.

CHAPTER 6

[1] Hector Berlioz, *Memoirs,* Knopf, N. Y., 1932, p. 69.
[2] *Ibid.*, p. 17.
[3] *Ibid.*, p. 32.
[4] Jacques Barzun, *Berlioz and the Romantic Century,* Little, Brown, Boston, 1950, Vol. I, p. 351.
[5] *Ibid.*, p. 353.
[6] Ernest Newman, *Stories of the Great Operas,* Garden City, N. Y., 1930, Vol. I, p. 287.
[7] Ernest Newman, *The Life of Richard Wagner,* Knopf, N. Y., Vol, III, 1941, p. 400.
[8] *Ibid.*, p. 510.
[9] *Ibid.*, Vol. I, 1933, pp. 171-72.
[10] *Ibid.*, Vol. III, p. 259.
[11] *Ibid.*, p. 462.
[12] *Ibid.*, Vol. IV, 1946, pp. 94-99.
[13] *Ibid.*, p. 272 footnote, p. 277.
[14] Philip Radcliffe, *Mendelssohn,* J.M. Dent, London, 1954, p. 115.
[15] James G. Huneker, *Franz Liszt,* Scribners, N. Y., 1911, pp. 142-44.

CHAPTER 7

[1] Franz Werfel and Paul Stefan, Ed. *Verdi: The Man in his Letters,* Fischer, N. Y., 1942, p. 261.
[2] *Ibid.*, p. 138.
[3] *Ibid.*, p. 142.

[4] *Ibid.*, p. 217.
[5] *Ibid.*, p. 227.
[6] *Ibid.*, pp. 196-97.
[7] *Ibid.*, p. 352.
[8] *Ibid.*, p. 361.
[9] Dyneley Hussey, *Verdi,* Pellegrini and Cudahy, N. Y., 1949, p. 171.
[10] Francis Toye, *Giuseppe Verdi: His Life and Work,* Knopf, N. Y., p. 115.
[11] Werfel and Stefan, *work cited.*, p. 360.
[12] Frantisek Bartos, *Bedrich Smetana: Letters and Reminiscences,*. Artia, Prague, 1955, pp. 110-11.
[13] *Ibid.*, p. 82-83.
[14] *Ibid.*, p. 67.
[15] *Ibid.*, p. 114.
[16] *Ibid.*, p. 70.
[17] Modeste Tchaikovsky, *The Life and Letters of Peter Ilich Tchaikovsky,* Ed. Rosa Newmarch, John Lane, N. Y., p. 248.
[18] V.I. Lenin, *Articles on Tolstoi,* Foreign Languages Publishing House, Moscow, 1951, p. 10.
[19] N.A. Dobrolyubov, *Selected Philosophical Essays,* Foreign Languages Publishing House, Moscow, 1948, pp. 420-37.
[20] Nikolay Rimsky-Korsakov, *My Musical Life,* Knopf, N.Y., 1923, p. 39.
[21] Modeste Tchaikovsky, *work cited,* p. 647.
[22] *Ibid.*, pp. 251-53.
[23] Jan Leyda and Sergei Bertensson, Ed., *The Mussorgsky Reader,* Norton, N.Y., 1947, pp. 111-13.
[24] George Thomson, *Studies in Ancient Greek Society; The Prehistoric Agean,* International Publishers, N.Y., 1949, p. 437.
[25] M.D. Calvocoressi, *Mussorgsky,* Dutton, N.Y., 1946, p. 18.
[26] Leyda and Bertensson, *work cited,* p. 112.
[27] Calvocoressi, *work cited,* p. 112.
[28] Rimsky-Korsakov, *work cited,* p. 125.
[29] Leyda and Bertensson, *work cited,* p. 227.
[30] *Ibid.*, p. 327.
[31] *Ibid.*, pp. 243-246.
[32] *Ibid.*, p. 250.
[33] The score of the complete *Khovanshchina,* including the parts excised by Rimsky-Korsakov, may be found in the edition of Paul Lamm, 1931. For those who wish to study it in recordings, the "complete" opera, London XLLA (four records) suffers from the above mentioned cuts. The missing scenes will be found in *Great Scenes from Khovanshchina,* Vanguard VRS-6022 (1 record).
[34] Leyda and Bertensson, *work cited,* p. 402.

CHAPTER 8

[1] Walter Niemann, *Brahms,* Tudor, N. Y., 1937, p. 163.
[2] Peter Latham, *Brahms,* Pellagrini and Cudahy, N. Y., 1949, p. 49.
[3] *Ibid.*, p. 59.
[4] Quoted in Werner Wolff, *Anton Bruckner,* Dutton, N. Y., 1942, p. 17.

[5] Quoted in Latham, *work cited*, p. 86.

[6] Otokar Sourek, *Antonin Dvorak; Letters and Reminiscences* Artia, Prague, 1954, p. 193.

[7] Latham. *work cited.*, p. 88.

[8] *Ibid.*, p. 100.

[9] A Finnish version of the ballad Brahms used may be heard on a Folkways long playing record, P-505, Music of the World's Peoples Vol. 2.

[10] Nieman, *work cited*, p. 269.

[11] Sourek, *work cited.*, pp. 222-23.

[12] *Ibid.*, p. 92.

[13] *Ibid.*, p. 98.

[14] Rayford W. Logan, *The Negro in American Life and Thought: The Nadir 1877-91*, Dial, N. Y., 1954, p. 268.

[15] *Ibid.*, p. 161.

[16] Paul Stefan, *Anton Dvorak*, Greystone, N. Y., 1941, p. 199.

[17] Sourek, *work cited*, p. 152.

[18] *Ibid.*, p. 158.

[19] *Ibid.*, p. 166.

[20] V. Fischl, Ed. *Antonin Dvorak, His Achievement*, Lindsay Drummond, London, 1943, pp. 52-53.

[21] Alec Robertson, *Dvorak*, J.M. Dent, London, 1947, p. 170.

[22] Sourek, *work cited*, p. 158.

[23] Modeste Tchaikovsky, *The Life and Letters of Peter Ilich Tchaikovsky*, Ed. Rosa Newmarch, John Lane, N. Y., 1906, pp. 570-71.

[24] *Ibid.*, p. 197.

[25] Edwin Evans, *Tchaikovsky*. Pellegrini and Cudahy, N. Y., 1949, p. 95.

[26] Tchaikovsky, *work cited*, p. 238.

[27] *Ibid.*, p. 229.

[28] *Ibid.*, p. 249.

[29] *Ibid.*, p. 259.

[30] *Ibid.*, pp. 255-57.

[31] Evans, *work cited*, p. 122.

[32] Tchaikovsky, *work cited*, p. 357 .

[33] Gerald E.H. Abraham, *Borodin: The Composer and His Music*, Reeves, London, no date, p. 34.

[34] Leyda and Bertensson, *The Musorgsky Reader*, p. 328.

[35] Nikolay Rimsky-Korsakov, *My Musical Life*, Tudor, N. Y., 1936, pp. 129-30.

[36] *Ibid.*, p. 141.

[37] *Ibid.*, p. 128.

CHAPTER 9

[1] Mosco Carner, *The Waltz*, Max Parrish, London, 1948, pp. 56, 57.

[2] G.W.F. Hegel, *The Philosophy of Fine Art*, G. Bell, London, 1930, Vol. I, pp. 327-28.

[3] Karl Ekman, *Jean Sibelius*, Knopf, N. Y., 1938, p. 191.

[4] *Ibid.*, p. 116.

[5] Gerald Abraham, Ed., *The Music of Sibelius*, Norton, N. Y., 1947, p. 109.

[6] David Hinshaw, *Heroic Finland,* Putnam, N. Y., 1952, p. 41.
[7] Encyclopoedia Brittanica, 14th Edition, 1949, article on Finland.
[8] Hinshaw, *work cited,* p. 40.
[9] *Ibid.*, p. 57.
[10] Hubert Foss, *Ralph Vaughan Williams,* Oxford Univ. Press, N. Y., 1950, p. 24.
[11] *Ibid.*, pp. 39, 40.
[12] Adolfo Salazar, *Music in Our Time,* Norton, N. Y., 1946, p. 85.
[13] The description, "hunger march" and "march of the unemployed" is presented in the account of the London Symphony by the conductor, Albert Coates, who was close to the composer.
[14] Foss, *work cited.*, p. 22.
[15] *Ibid.*, p. 144.
[16] Henry and Sidney Cowell, *Charles Ives and His Music,* Oxford Univ. Press, N. Y., 1955, p. 38.
[17] Charles Ives, *Postface to "114 Songs,"* reprinted with Charles Ives, "24 Songs," Overtone Records, New Haven, No. 7.
[18] *Ibid.*, Following quotations are from the same source.
[19] Cowell, *work cited,* p. 13.
[20] Ernest Bloch, Notes to *First String Quartet,* Columbia Masterworks, Set M-392.
[21] Ernest Bloch, Notes to *Sacred Service,* London Records, LLP 123.

CHAPTER 10

[1] Claude Debussy, *Monsieur Croche: The Dilettante Hater,* transl, B.N. Langdon Davies, Lear, N. Y., 1948, pp. 99-100.
[2] Edward Lockspeiser, *Debussy,* Dent, London, 1936, p. 69.
[3] Debussy, *work cited,* p. 186.
[4] Léon Vallas, *Claude Debussy,* Oxford Univ. Press, N. Y., 1933, p. 1.
[5] J.B. Trend, *Manuel de Falla and Spanish Music,* Knopf, N. Y., 1934, p. 11.
[6] Maxim Gorky, *Culture and the People,* International Publishers, N. Y., 1939, p. 34.
[7] Eric W. White, *Stravinsky: A Critical Survey,* Philosophical Library, N. Y., 1948, p. 117.
[8] *Ibid.*, p. 90.
[9] Y.M. Sokolov, *Russian Folklore,* Macmillan, N. Y., 1950, p. 490.
[10] White, *work cited,* p. 80.
[11] *Ibid.*, p. 159.
[12] Nicholas Slonimsky, *Music of Latin America,* Crowell, N. Y., 1945, p. 143.
[13] Bohumir Stedron, *Laos Janacek: Letters and Reminiscences,* Artia, Prague, 1955, p. 73.
[14] *Ibid.*, p. 90.
[15] *Ibid.*, p. 204.
[16] Bela Bartok, "Autobiographical Note," Tempo, No. 13, London, 1949, p. 3.
[17] Bela Bartok, "On Collecting Folk Songs in Turkey," Tempo, No. 13, 1949, p. 16.

[18] Bela Bartok, "The Influence of Peasant Music on Modern Music," Tempo, No. 14, Winter, 1949-50, London, p. 19.

[19] Bartok, "Autobiographical Note," p. 5.

[20] Bartok, "The Influence of Peasant Music on Modern Music," p. 22.

[21] Halsey Stevens, *The Life and Music of Bela Bartok,* Oxford Univ. Press, N. Y., 1953, p. 84.

CHAPTER 11

[1] Daniel S. Gilmor, Ed. *Speaking of Peace,* Edited Report of the Cultural and Scientific Conference for World Peace, N. Y., March 25-27, National Council of the Arts, Sciences and Professions, 1949, p. 126.

[2] Quoted in Ivan Martynov, *Dmitri Shostakovich,* Philosophical Library, N. Y., 1949, p. 49.

[3] Decisions of the Central Committee, C.P.S.U.(B), *On Literature and Art,* (1946-48), Foreign Language Publishing House, Moscow, 1951, p. 37.

[4] *Ibid.,* p. 33.

[5] *Ibid.,* pp. 32, 33.

[6] *Ibid.,* p. 36.

[7] Andrei A Zhdanov, *Essays on Literature, Philosophy and Music,* International Publishers, N. Y., 1950, p. 93.

[8] *Ibid.,* p. 78.

[9] *Ibid.,* p. 90.

[10] *Soviet Studies,* Oxford, Vol. IX, No. 1, July 1957, pp. 108-16 (Summary of March 1957 Congress of Soviet Composers, by Basil Blackwell).

[11] Decisions of Central Committee, (cited above), p. 32.

[12] Reprinted as Supplement to *Soviet Literature,* No. 6, Moscow, 1958.

CHAPTER 12

[1] Harriet Janis and Rudi Blesh, *They All Played Ragtime,* Knopf, N. Y., 1950, p. 96.

[2] Roland Hayes, *My Songs,* Little, Brown, Boston, 1948, p. 121.

[3] E. Franklin Frazier, *The Negro Family in the United States,* Dryden Press, N. Y., 1951, p. 210.

[4] Russell Ames, *The Story of American Folk Song,* Grosset & Dunlap, N. Y., 1955, p. 254.

[5] W.H. Handy, *Father of the Blues,* Macmillan, N. Y., 1947, pp. 27-28.

[6] *Ibid.,* pp. 74-76.

[6] *Ibid.,* p. 120.

[8] *Big Bill Broonzy—His Story* (Interview with Studs Turkel) Recorded, Chicago, 1956; Folkways Record 3586, N. Y.

INDEX